MODERN HISTORIES OF CRIME AND PUNISHMENT

For Clan + Paul,

Xmas 07

Some more light reading from Bristol, with a little help from my friends.

Martin

Critical Perspectives on Crime and Law

Edited by Markus D. Dubber

EDITED BY MARKUS D. DUBBER
AND LINDSAY FARMER

Modern Histories of Crime and Punishment

STANFORD UNIVERSITY PRESS

STANFORD, CALIFORNIA 2007

Stanford University Press
Stanford, California

©2007 by the Board of Trustees of the Leland Stanford Junior University. All rights reserved.

No part of this book may be reproduced or transmitted in any form or by any means, electronic or mechanical, including photocopying and recording, or in any information storage or retrieval system without the prior written permission of Stanford University Press.

Printed in the United States of America on acid-free, archival-quality paper

Library of Congress Cataloging-in-Publication Data

Modern histories of crime and punishment / edited by Markus D. Dubber and Lindsay Farmer.
    p. cm.—(Critical perspectives on crime and law)
  Includes index.
  ISBN 978-0-8047-5411-8 (cloth : alk. paper)—
  ISBN 978-0-8047-5412-5 (pbk. : alk. paper)
  1. Criminal justice, Administration of—Great Britain—History. 2. Criminal justice, Administration of—India—History. 3. Criminal justice, Administration of—History. 4. Criminal liability—History. 5. Crime—History. 6. Punishment—History. 7. Criminal law—History. I. Dubber, Markus Dirk. II. Farmer, Lindsay, 1963–

KD7876.M63 2007
345.009—dc22   2007014963

Typeset by Newgen in 10/14 Janson

Für C.Th.D., *For S.A.,*
mit historischem Bezug *of course*
M.D.D. *L.F.*

Contents

	Contributors	ix
	Acknowledgments	xi
	Introduction Regarding Criminal Law Historically *Markus D. Dubber and Lindsay Farmer*	1
1.	Character, Capacity, Outcome: Toward a Framework for Assessing the Shifting Pattern of Criminal Responsibility in Modern English Law *Nicola Lacey*	14
2.	Criminal Responsibility and the Proof of Guilt *Lindsay Farmer*	42
3.	"An Inducement to Morbid Minds": Politics and Madness in the Victorian Courtroom *Joel Peter Eigen*	66
4.	The Meaning of Killing *Guyora Binder*	88
5.	"An Extraordinarily Beautiful Document": Jefferson's "Bill for Proportioning Crimes and Punishments" and the Challenge of Republican Punishment *Markus D. Dubber*	115
6.	The Myth of Private Prosecution in England, 1750–1850 *Bruce P. Smith*	151

7. Hans Litten and the Politics of Criminal Law
   in the Weimar Republic 175
   Benjamin Carter Hett

8. Civilizing Darwin: Holmes on Criminal Law 198
   Gerald Leonard

9. Bodies, Words, Identities: The Moving Targets
   of the Criminal Law 224
   Mariana Valverde

10. Criminal Law at a Fault Line of Imperial Authority:
    Interracial Homicide Trials in British India 252
    Martin Wiener

11. Crime and Punishment on the Tea Plantations
    of Colonial India 272
    Elizabeth Kolsky

12. "Enfeebling the Arm of Justice": Perjury and
    Prevarication in British India 299
    Wendie Ellen Schneider

    Index 329

Contributors

Guyora Binder is University at Buffalo Distinguished Professor of Law, SUNY Buffalo.

Markus D. Dubber is professor of law and director of the Buffalo Criminal Law Center, SUNY Buffalo.

Joel Peter Eigen is Charles A. Dana Professor of Sociology, Franklin and Marshall College.

Lindsay Farmer is professor of law, University of Glasgow.

Benjamin Carter Hett is assistant professor of history, Hunter College, CUNY.

Elizabeth Kolsky is assistant professor of history, Villanova University.

Nicola Lacey is professor of criminal law and legal theory, London School of Economics and Political Science.

Gerald Leonard is professor of law, Boston University.

Wendie Ellen Schneider is associate professor of law, University of Iowa.

Bruce P. Smith is professor of law and codirector of the Legal History Program, University of Illinois.

Mariana Valverde is professor, Centre of Criminology, University of Toronto.

Martin Wiener is Mary Gibbs Jones Professor of History, Rice University.

Acknowledgments

Early versions of the chapters in this book were first mooted at a workshop in June 2005 at SUNY Buffalo Law School, which was co-hosted by the Baldy Center for Law and Social Policy and the Buffalo Criminal Law Center and supported by a generous workshop grant from the Baldy Center. Ellen Kausner and Joe Schneider helped make the workshop a success; Lynn Mather and Nils Olsen helped make it possible. Sara Faherty prepared the manuscript for submission with great editorial patience. Last, but not least, Sophie Dubber often asked the right question at the right time. We thank them all.

Markus D. Dubber
Lindsay Farmer

MODERN HISTORIES OF CRIME AND PUNISHMENT

INTRODUCTION

Regarding Criminal Law Historically

MARKUS D. DUBBER AND LINDSAY FARMER

1. New Trends in the History of the Criminal Law

Around thirty years ago the history of crime and punishment was transformed by the publication of two books. While markedly different in their style and ambitions, the books had an immediate and continuing impact through their combination of fresh theoretical perspectives and compelling historical narrative. Both exerted a significant influence in areas that go far beyond their subject matter, but both were especially important to the study of the criminal law.

The first of these books was *Albion's Fatal Tree*,[1] which grew out of the work of the Centre for the Study of Social History at the University of Warwick under the direction of E. P. Thompson. This was a series of studies of eighteenth-century English law and society that demonstrated the centrality of the criminal law, and in particular the Bloody Code, as an instrument of government at both the local and national level. Particularly influential was Douglas Hay's essay "Property, Authority and the Criminal Law," which looked at the use of the criminal law to protect the property interests of the aristocracy and small gentry. Hay argued that a combination of terror and mercy was used by the landowning classes to reinforce the authority and legitimacy of the law and to extract deference from the unpropertied classes. This theme was developed in the other essays, which showed how the criminal law served particular class interests and reinforced a particular ideological vision of social order. And notwithstanding E. P. Thompson's famous remarks about the double-edged quality of the rule of law, the essays demonstrated how the criminal law was central to the preservation and control of property rights in eighteenth-century England.[2] This approach was immensely influential because it placed the question of whose interests the law served at the center of inquiry, and it showed how the criminal law was central to the exercise of political and social power. This led to an explosion of studies in the history of criminal justice and policing in eighteenth- and early nineteenth-century England that addressed the questions of the relationships between criminal law, social class, and state power.[3]

The influence of Michel Foucault's *Discipline and Punish* has arguably been even more pervasive.[4] As a study of the birth of the prison and the transformation of the criminal law in early nineteenth-century France, the book has been heavily criticized by historians who point to a cavalier attitude toward the sources and a tendency to read too much significance into texts by minor authors. However, the true importance of the book lies in the theoretical questions that it opens up about the relation between law, power, and knowledge in modern society. While it is notoriously difficult to summarize Foucault's complex argument, the central question of the book concerns the techniques through which power is exercised in modern society. Challenging those perspectives that take the state and law as central to the understanding of the operation of power, Foucault argues that the exercise of power in modern society is characterized by a combination of disciplinary techniques and what he terms *biopower*.[5] While the former operates on individuals located in institutions such as prisons, factories, schools, and hospitals by surveillance and control with the constant aim of the more efficient distribution and use of power, the latter is concerned with the management of populations through the science of statistics and techniques of political economy. The prison was seen as central in the network of institutions through which social control was exercised in modern society, offering the means by which individuals could be disciplined and the population of actual and potential delinquents could be supervised. The criminal law was a tool through which the "economy of illegalities" could be regulated. It defined norms of behavior and degrees of deviation, making possible the operation of the new forms of discipline and legitimating the power to punish.[6] Foucault's work, then, demanded recognition of how the control of delinquency through the criminal law was continuous with operations of power in other institutions of modern society.

Both books taught criminal lawyers that the history of their discipline could not be understood as the unfolding of reason through the development of doctrine, as a simple progression from a barbaric and irrational past toward a humane and enlightened present[7]—or, for that matter, as a simple regression in the opposite direction. The criminal law was a means by and through which class power was exercised or legitimated or was to be understood as one technique among others through which modern forms of criminality were constructed and social control was exercised. These approaches to the history of the criminal law raised a range of novel questions for criminal law scholarship. Whose interests did the criminal law, or particular criminal laws, serve?

What ideological functions were performed by general theories of criminal responsibility? How central was the criminal law to certain modes of governance in modern society? And how is the power of the criminal law exercised in different social and geographical contexts? The attempts to answer these questions have stimulated a huge amount of new scholarship in the history of criminal law and punishment.

If initially the focus of criminal justice history was the social context of crime and law enforcement, this has now broadened to include the concepts and categories of the criminal law itself. And, from being a matter that was of interest only to historians, work is now emerging from a range of different intellectual and disciplinary traditions. Social historians of crime have looked at the changing contours of criminal liability to show how certain categories that have been taken as given by criminal lawyers, such as homicide or assault, have been constructed and how changing patterns of enforcement have shaped the social meaning of these crimes.[8] They have looked at defenses such as insanity to trace the relationship between legal and medical understandings of mental abnormality and the way that these have shaped our understanding of criminal responsibility.[9] And some recent important work has begun—investigating the history of criminal procedure and evidence in the context of the criminal trial—to enhance our understanding of how crimes were prosecuted.[10] From within cultural studies there have come a number of readings of particular trials or historical episodes that have thrown light on the social and cultural assumptions that ground ideas and concepts. This scholarship has looked, for example, at the relationship between the form of the novel and the development of the penitentiary idea or at the development of ideas of interiority in literature and modern concepts of subjective legal responsibility.[11] Postcolonial theory has examined the place of the criminal law in the imperial project and has shown how legal concepts or practices of enforcement were developed in the imperial context.[12] It has used this to show how apparently universal concepts of liability could be shot through with assumptions about race and how the rule of law could play a central role in the sustaining of practices of oppression and control. And criminal lawyers themselves have begun to take a closer interest in the historical development of concepts of criminal liability as a way of challenging certain taken-for-granted assumptions about responsibility.[13]

This work has been important to challenging and transforming both the method and content of criminal law scholarship; the chapters in this book represent all of these strands in recent criminal law historiography while moving beyond them to raise new questions and open up fresh perspectives on the discipline of criminal law.

2. Gaining Perspectives on the Criminal Law

The chapters in this book can be read in many ways. As readers bring their own perspectives and interests to bear on them, any number of connections across problems, theories, doctrines, countries, and systems may emerge before their eyes. Here we will highlight some of the strands that we see running through the various chapters.

One of the central goals of this book is to capture the variety of contemporary scholarship in the history of criminal law. Indeed, it is notable that while exciting work is being done in various disciplines, including work described as being interdisciplinary in nature, it is not always the case that there is engagement or debate among these bodies of work—or indeed with the discipline of criminal law. The aim then is both to reflect the plurality of approaches in this area and to illustrate how drawing on these different perspectives can stimulate new and critical perspectives on the modern criminal law.

This approach raises the methodological question of what is to be gained from disciplinary pluralism. This matters both as a problem of research method—how a historian or literary theorist or sociologist, for example, might be able to incorporate the insights or methods of other disciplines in their own research—and as an issue of how the insights that are gained might be brought to bear on the analysis of the criminal law. The first of these, while important, requires no further discussion at this point, as the chapters themselves provide an excellent illustration of some of the diverse ways academics working in different disciplines have addressed this problem. The second requires further discussion, however, for lawyers are notoriously disinterested in history. Even in common law systems, which rely on precedent, lawyers will approach the interpretation of historical texts in terms of how they might be used as resources for the resolution of contemporary problems, rather than worrying about any sensitivity to historical meaning or context. Law, it might be suggested, is impervious to the criticisms of historians.

One response to this kind of concern might be that disciplinary pluralism is a proper end in itself, because it shows us how certain concepts are contingent rather than given and are socially constructed rather than representing a natural state of affairs.[14] This is undoubtedly important in challenging the taken-for-granted assumptions of a discipline such as law where there is a long-standing tendency to equate its understanding of human nature or social order with the way the world must be. But this is hardly a complete response, for it does little to show how these categories or concepts have been constructed or how they shape, or are shaped by, the role of law in the production of social order.[15] It is, in other words, necessary to go further. We can point here to a number of further tasks for the critical historical analysis of law. First, it is necessary to trace the genealogy of particular concepts or crimes to analyze how their significance might shift over time and how the development of a particular offense is shaped by changes in enforcement, prosecution, or punishment.[16] Offenses must be understood in terms of their place within a body of criminal law, whose internal order or rationality is itself shifting over time. These conceptions of law or social order are then linked to broader social or cultural understandings of wrongdoing, responsibility, or the self. And, finally, it is necessary to examine the role that law plays in the legitimation of forms of governmental practice—and the uses to which history is put in the legitimation of the criminal law. This is all the more pressing because criminal law—particularly in the common law world—has relied so heavily on history and tradition for legitimation in place of a more sustained effort at a principled normative justification of state punishment in light of an understanding of the purposes and institutions of the modern democratic state.[17]

The critical, as opposed to the legitimating, potential of criminal law historiography has yet to be fully realized.[18] The same is true, if to a slightly lesser extent, of comparative studies of criminal law. Gaining spatial, or jurisdictional, distance helps to highlight the critical purchase of temporal distance.[19] The chapters in this book explore histories of criminal law without regard to traditional domestic or systemic boundaries. Issues in Canadian, English, German, Indian, and U.S. criminal law are explored, with criminal law norms drawn from precedent, statutes, codes, and jury verdicts in common law and civil law countries. While none of the chapters is explicitly comparative, collectively they add up to a stimulating study in comparative criminal law history.[20]

However, even here the aim goes beyond that of using the comparative method as a means of demonstrating the plurality or contingency of different understandings of criminal law. Systems of criminal law do not develop in isolation from each other but are embedded in power relations between different states or between states and their colonies,[21] and as a consequence it is necessary both to trace the movement of different concepts between systems as part of a project of colonial or imperial governance and to acknowledge that the same law might have a different meaning or significance applied in a colonial context. Several chapters in this book expose the need to investigate more carefully this, often neglected, aspect of the history of criminal law. Postcolonial theory can thus help us gain a fresh, and more nuanced, understanding of the sociopolitical context of the operation and enforcement of the criminal law. The role of criminal law and other state-sanctioned violence in colonial governance, moreover, reveals fruitful, if disturbing, continuities with criminal law in postcolonial settings and, more generally, in governance under conditions of war or emergency.

The lessons of postcolonial theory or a comparative historical methodology go beyond the obvious context of, say, the imperial governance of British India and might usefully be applied to a study of the relations between the criminal law in England and the United States.[22] There is a tendency in criminal law scholarship to refer to something called "Anglo-American" criminal law. Though a convenient shorthand, this term may be taken to suggest an identity between the laws of England and the United States on the basis of their common law roots and a certain affinity between the concepts of criminal liability. However, the precise nature of this affinity is rarely subject to analysis, and subsequent divergences in the uses of criminal law as a tool of certain governmental practices are ignored. What, it must be asked, is the function of the continuing deference among American criminal lawyers to both the English roots of the law and to the kind of theorizing that has grown up under its head? Why, given that American criminal law has existed as a distinct, and distinctive, system since at least the late eighteenth century, is there still felt to be a need to refer to cases and academic writings from the "motherland"? This may be thought to imply the universality of these concepts of fault and liability—one that is hardly borne out in practice. Several of the contributors address the question of how the universality was constructed—in India and in the United States, as well as in Canada—and how this project was linked to certain practices of enforcement and the need to legitimate government. The essays show how the criminal law cannot simply be understood as a collection of concepts relating to fault but must be understood within the context of a framework of political institutions and practices of enforcement.

More fundamentally, several chapters in this book explore the oddly understudied question of modernity in criminal law. Criminal law, while remaining deeply rooted in its antiquated taxonomy of *mens rea* and *actus reus*—malice aforethought and malignant heart—wantonness, willfulness, and the depraved mind, is revealed both to resist and to reflect modernity in its substantive conceptions of crime and responsibility and in its procedural mechanisms and modes of disposition. Where the language of fault often suggests continuities that reflect the unchanging character of human nature or wrongdoing, this frequently masks quite substantial transformations in legal practice. It is now accepted that there were radical transformations in policing and punishment in the early part of the nineteenth century as the development of the modern state brought about huge transformations in criminal justice.[23] However, there is far less understanding of how these changes were both enabled and in turn transformed by the substantive criminal law. A key argument here is that of differentiation. Several contributors point to how the development of modern concepts of subjective criminal liability was accompanied and underpinned by the development of the police power, of summary jurisdiction, or, in the colonial context, of special jurisdictions and powers that enabled the state to enforce the criminal law in different ways in different contexts.[24] The modern conception of the responsible legal subject is shown to have played a crucial role in legitimating the operation of state power; unraveling and interrogating that conception thus should help us better understand the place of criminal law in modern society.

Finally, and most straightforwardly, the chapters in the book can be read as providing illuminating historical context to some of the familiar core questions of criminal law doctrine that structure not only criminal law scholarship but also criminal law teaching—from the general part of criminal law (e.g., rationales for punishment, involuntariness, *mens rea*, culpability, responsibility, self-defense, insanity, diminished capacity) to its special part (e.g., homicide, theft, possession, homosexual offenses, perjury). As a result, they can be regarded as a set of supplementary readings for courses and seminars on criminal law.

3. Chapter Overview

While there are many crosscutting themes in the chapters in the book and there is a risk that imposing artificial groupings might obscure some of these, we see the chapters as falling into three main groups: the history and theory of criminal responsibility and agency, general theories of crime and punishment, and the comparative history of criminal law.

The first group (Lacey, Farmer, Eigen, Binder) examines the nature of responsibility in law and in other disciplines, such as medicine, that interacted with law in the setting of the criminal trial. These chapters show how the modern legal conception of responsibility and agency developed in particular legal settings, drawing on broader cultural conceptions of agency while in conflict with other important disciplinary understandings of the person.

Lacey argues that the attribution of criminal responsibility historically has balanced principles of character and capacity, rather than privileging one to the exclusion of the other as is often silently presupposed in debates among criminal law theorists. Moreover, she urges that the precise application of the ideas about the nature of criminal responsibility, whether they focus on character or capacity, must be understood within the broader context in which the criminal law is used to produce social order. The histories of crime and punishment, in other words, are always also histories of state power, just as criminal law is but one, albeit a particularly intrusive, form of state action.

Farmer cautions that students of the attribution of responsibility must look more closely at the history of the central institutional locus of that attribution, the criminal trial. The history of the subjective element of criminality is also the history of epistemological difficulties raised by inquiries into mental states. Farmer thus illustrates how the development of concepts in substantive criminal law is linked to changes in the procedure, the law of evidence, and the prosecution of crime.

Drawing on extensive research into the role of medical testimony in nineteenth-century English insanity trials, Eigen examines the instability of the traditional legal conception of agency in the face of the development of new medical knowledges of the person. Historically, criminal law has spent considerably more energy on exploring the myriad ways an accused may be said to lack the capacity to commit crimes than on setting out just what it means to possess the requisite capacity. Eigen's essay is of surprising, or perhaps telling, contemporary significance, particularly in the United States where the law of insanity bears an uncanny resemblance to nineteenth-century English law, as was recently confirmed by the U.S. Supreme Court in an opinion that might be mistaken for a treatise on nineteenth-century English insanity law.[25] The tension within concepts of agency and its absence that Eigen exposes continues unresolved to this day.

Finally, in an important rereading of the development of the law of homicide, Binder challenges the commonly held modern view that different forms of homicide can be distinguished only on the basis of the mental state of the accused. A central argument of his paper is that this emphasis on mental states has closed off our understanding of how early homicide law was based on a fundamentally different understanding of culpability. He shows how developments in the doctrine of *mens rea* in the late eighteenth and early nineteenth centuries paralleled reformulations of the *actus reus* of the crime. He thus demonstrates how ideas of agency and responsibility—that is, of subjective aspects of criminal liability more broadly—cannot be read in isolation from conceptions of action or the definitions of particular crimes—that is, objective prerequisites.

The second group (Dubber, Smith, Hett, Leonard, Valverde) shifts the focus of historical analysis from the conditions of individual criminality to the construction of crime and its punishment, either in general or in relation to particular crimes and thus to the nature of criminal law as a state enterprise.

Drawing on his recent work on the police power,[26] Dubber traces the failure to distinguish between the police power (which is committed to order) and law (which requires a commitment to respect for the citizen as an autonomous subject) to the writings of Thomas Jefferson on this subject. He argues that modern American criminal law can usefully be viewed as a system that derives from the state's long-standing power to police, which in turn is rooted in the householder's discretionary power to discipline members of his household. He suggests that this is an important context for understanding the punitiveness of modern American criminal law and, further, that a consequence of the blurring of these two categories is that the question of the legitimation of punishment of the autonomous citizens of a republic remains unseen and unaddressed.

Something of this autonomy-based conception of criminal law might be thought to have survived in English law, which for a long time conceived of crime as an interpersonal conflict between the offender and his victim. This quaint conception fits uneasily with modern procedural mechanisms for processing crime that pit the state (or the people) against the defendant. This tension has certainly escaped many historians of English criminal law who have assumed that the prosecution of crime was, until recently, largely conducted by private individuals. Smith directly challenges this assumption in a revealing study of the widespread prosecution in early nineteenth-century London of metal theft and unlawful possession in police offices by police officers before police magistrates and without identifiable victims. His work thus suggests that, even as the modern conception of the responsible subject was emerging in criminal law doctrine, it was accompanied by sweeping changes in the definition, enforcement, and prosecution of crime.[27] Like Dubber's, his work suggests that our understanding of the modern criminal law must account for these practices, as well as the prosecution of higher crimes, and that they provide an important context for understanding changes in the attribution of responsibility in the modern law.

In an illuminating study of political trials in Weimar Germany, Hett illustrates the interplay between political uses of the criminal law, on the one hand, and the use of the criminal law to depoliticize political conflicts, on the other. In Hett's telling, the activist lawyer Hans Litten emerges as a figure who insists on the rule of law as an essential guarantor of stability in the sphere of crime and punishment and seeks to destabilize the existing political regime through that very insistence. Litten is seen as both resisting the transformation of criminal law into a tool of oppression by a police state and recognizing—and exploiting—the necessarily political nature of criminal law.

Both as a judge and as a jurist, Oliver Wendell Holmes was keenly aware of the need to approach the task of producing and adapting ostensibly objective legal norms within the context of the political might of the state (though he would not have put it in quite this way). Leonard offers an original reassessment of Holmes's views on criminal law which, until this point, have escaped systematic attention, in startling contrast to his views on virtually every other subject. Holmes set out not only to turn (consequentialist) punishment theory into (substantive) criminal law doctrine, but also—and just as unusually—to locate the criminal law within legal science as a whole, thus addressing important—and historically little considered—questions regarding the relationship between criminal law and, most notably, the law of torts. Leonard shows how Holmes's remarks on criminal law both have been misread by many modern commentators and marked an important point of departure for the development of modern American criminal law.

Finally, in this section, Valverde examines the construction of homosexual offenses within the history of English, U.S., and Canadian criminal law. By documenting the various efforts at criminalizing homosexual behavior and thereby normalizing the "abnormal," she shows how a conception of the crime as one "against nature" continues to wield significant power even within a modern law that claims to respect sexual autonomy under the rule of law.

The chapters featured in the third section (Wiener, Kolsky, Schneider) can be seen as offering a commentary on, and a critique of, the chapters in the previous two sections while extending the history of criminal law beyond its conventional field of inquiry. They illuminate the conventional historiography of crime and punishment by removing it from—and thereby exposing the implicit limits of—its familiar geographic and social setting and thus exemplify the considerable, and as yet largely untapped, critical potential of comparative analysis in general and comparative history in particular in the field of criminal law.

All three chapters examine the operation of the penal process in the British Empire, and specifically British India. All three are more than rich exercises in colonial history; they invite an exploration of the interdependence of the parallel histories of criminal law in India and criminal law in England and, more broadly, of the significance of colonial criminal law for a more nuanced understanding of modern criminal law as a whole.

On the basis of a close study of two interracial killings and their procedural aftermath, Wiener looks at the significance of rule-of-law precepts in the face of racial discrimination and class prejudices. Wiener finds a penal process that neither perfectly manifests the abstract equality associated with the rule of law nor simply brings to bear the colonial state's superior power. Instead, what emerges is a system of criminal law at odds with itself, unable to conform to either model—liberal objectivity or despotic oppression, law or police.

Focusing on similar criminal cases, Kolsky examines the efforts of Indian nationalists to bring European subjects in India within the criminal jurisdiction of local courts. She thereby reveals the dialectic between subject and object in imperialist governance that is often obscured by an exclusive focus on the practices and proclamations (and even qualms) of the governors rather than the governed. Her chapter thus reminds us that the history of modern criminal law is not only one of the unremitting assertion of state punitive power but also of individual and communal resistance to it.

Schneider zeroes in not on specific cases but on a specific crime. She investigates the development and adaptation of the law of perjury in India as the colonial power struggled to transform racial prejudices regarding the exceptional mendacity of local-process participants into abstract legal norms while enlisting local custom to maximize the deterrent effect of penalties threatened and inflicted. The conception of the addressees of these norms and threats as not only "other" but also inferior informed the choice of penal control methods, presumably rendering a strict adherence to rule-of-law norms less attractive than the seemingly more straightforward use of more blunt instruments of behavior modification, a phenomenon that is quite familiar from the history of modern criminal law in general.

4. Looking Back to Look Ahead

Unlike *Albion's Fatal Tree* and *Discipline and Punish*, this book is not driven by a single vision of the right way to do criminal law history. Rather than claiming to be an illustration of proper criminal law historiography, it is a showcase of various disciplinary, methodological, and theoretical approaches that, taken together, promise to make a contribution to our understanding of the history of criminal law. If we have a broader aim, it is that of raising awareness of the work that is being done by historians, lawyers, theorists, and sociologists on the history of the criminal law and of the resources that these offer for the critical analysis of the modern criminal law. The historical analysis of crime and punishment is not a freestanding inquiry into a distinct institution or body of legal doctrine, but in the end amounts to a daunting, yet exhilarating, venture into the webs of governance and control that constitute social and political life.

Notes

1. Douglas Hay et al., *Albion's Fatal Tree: Crime and Society in Eighteenth-Century England* (London: Allen Lane, 1975); arising out of the same project and having a

comparable influence was E. P. Thompson, *Whigs and Hunters: The Origin of the Black Act* (London: Allen Lane, 1975).

2. Thompson, *Whigs and Hunters*, pp. 258–269.

3. See, e.g., J. M. Beattie, *Crime and the Courts in England, 1660–1800* (Princeton, N.J.: Princeton Univ. Press, 1986); Peter King, *Crime, Justice, and Discretion in England, 1740–1820* (Oxford: Oxford Univ. Press, 2000). Much of the work is reviewed in Joanna Innes and John Styles, "The Crime Wave: Recent Writing on Crime and Criminal Justice in Eighteenth Century England," *Journal of British Studies* 25 (1986): 380–435.

4. Michel Foucault, *Discipline and Punish: The Birth of the Prison* (New York: Pantheon, 1977). The argument was further developed in *The History of Sexuality*, vol. 1, *The Will to Knowledge* (New York: Pantheon, 1978).

5. See Michel Foucault, "Governmentality," in *Essential Works*, vol. 3, *Power*, James D. Faubion and Paul Rabinow, eds. (New York: New Press, 2000), pp. 201–222, at p. 219.

6. See ibid., pp. 298–306.

7. A charge famously made about Sir Leon Radzinowicz's celebrated *A History of English Criminal Law and Its Administration from 1750*, 5 vols. (London: Stevens, 1948–1986). For a more recent account of English law stressing doctrinal development see K. J. M. Smith, *Lawyers, Legislators and Theorists: Developments in English Criminal Jurisprudence, 1800–1957* (Oxford: Oxford Univ. Press, 1998).

8. See, e.g., Martin J. Wiener, *Men of Blood: Violence, Manliness, and Criminal Justice in Victorian England* (New York: Cambridge Univ. Press, 2004); Shani D'Cruze, *Crimes of Outrage: Sex, Violence and Victorian Working Women* (DeKalb: Northern Illinois Univ. Press, 1998). See also King, *Crime Justice, and Discretion in England*; Beattie, *Crime and the Courts in England*.

9. See esp. Joel Eigen, *Witnessing Insanity: Madness and Mad-Doctors in the English Court* (New Haven, Conn.: Yale Univ. Press, 1995), and *Unconscious Crime: Mental Absence and Criminal Responsibility in Victorian London* (Baltimore, Md.: Johns Hopkins Univ. Press, 2003).

10. See John H. Langbein, *The Origins of Adversary Criminal Trial* (Oxford: Oxford Univ. Press, 2003); David J. A. Cairns, *Advocacy and the Making of the Adversarial Criminal Trial* (Oxford: Clarendon Press, 1998); Allyson N. May, *The Bar and the Old Bailey, 1750–1850* (Chapel Hill: Univ. of North Carolina Press, 2003).

11. See John B. Bender, *Imagining the Penitentiary: Fiction and the Architecture of Mind in Eighteenth-Century England* (Chicago: Univ. of Chicago Press, 1987); Lisa Rodensky, *The Crime in Mind: Criminal Responsibility and the Victorian Novel* (New York: Oxford Univ. Press, 2003).

12. See "Forum, Colonial Order, British Law: The Empire and India," *Law and History Review* 23 (2005): 589–706; Radhika Singha, *A Despotism of Law: Crime and Justice in Early Colonial India* (Oxford: Oxford Univ. Press, 2000).

13. For a review, see Nicola Lacey, "In Search of the Responsible Subject: History, Philosophy and Criminal Law Theory," *Modern Law Review* 64 (2001): 350–371. See also Alan Norrie, *Crime, Reason and History: A Critical Introduction to the Criminal Law*, 2d ed. (Cambridge: Cambridge Univ. Press, 2001).

14. This is the kind of approach taken by critical legal studies. See, e.g., Robert W. Gordon, "Critical Legal Histories," *Stanford Law Review* 36 (1984): 57–125.

15. For an examination and critique of the idea of social construction, see Ian Hacking, *The Social Construction of What?* (Cambridge, Mass.: Harvard Univ. Press, 1999).

16. See, for example, the chapters by Binder and Valverde in this volume.

17. For a sustained examination of the uses of a conception of tradition in the legitimation of Scots criminal law, see Lindsay Farmer, *Criminal Law, Tradition and Legal Order: Crime and the "Genius" of Scots Law, 1747 to the Present* (Cambridge: Cambridge Univ. Press, 1997).

18. On criminal law history as critique, see Markus Dirk Dubber, "Historical Analysis of Law," *Law and History Review* 16 (1998): 159–162.

19. On comparative criminal law as critique, see Markus Dirk Dubber, "Comparative Criminal Law," in *Oxford Handbook of Comparative Law*, Mathias Reimann and Reinhard Zimmermann, eds. (New York: Oxford Univ. Press, 2006), pp. 1287–1325.

20. For a recent promising example of comparative criminal historiography, see James Q. Whitman, *Harsh Justice: Criminal Punishment and the Widening Divide between America and Europe* (New York: Oxford Univ. Press, 2003).

21. See the chapters in this volume by Wiener, Kolsky, and Schneider for different interpretations of criminal law as part of a project of imperial governance in India.

22. The chapters in this volume by Leonard and Dubber make a start at subjecting this relationship to critical analysis.

23. See, e.g., Foucault, "Governmentality." On policing see Mark Neocleous, *The Fabrication of Social Order: A Critical Theory of Police Power* (London: Pluto Press, 2000) and Markus D. Dubber and Mariana Valverde, *The New Police Science: The Police Power in Domestic and International Governance* (Stanford, Calif.: Stanford Univ. Press, 2006). On punishment see Michael Ignatieff, *A Just Measure of Pain: The Penitentiary in the Industrial Revolution, 1750–1850* (London: Macmillan, 1978); David J. Rothman, *Conscience and Convenience: The Asylum and Its Alternatives in Progressive America* (Boston: Little, Brown, 1980).

24. See, e.g., the chapters in this volume by Smith, Dubber, Kolsky, and Lacey.

25. See *Clark v. Arizona*, 126 S. Ct. 2709 (2006).

26. See Markus Dirk Dubber, *The Police Power: Patriarchy and the Foundations of American Government* (New York: Columbia Univ. Press, 2005).

27. See also Bruce P. Smith, "The Presumption of Guilt and the English Law of Theft, 1750–1850," *Law and History Review* 23 (2005): 133–171.

ONE

Character, Capacity, Outcome

Toward a Framework for Assessing the Shifting Pattern of Criminal Responsibility in Modern English Law

NICOLA LACEY

At the start of the twenty-first century, it is little exaggeration to say that responsibility stands as the central question of normative criminal law theory.[1] The state's obligation to prove not only that a defendant has committed criminal conduct but that he or she is responsible in the sense of being fairly held accountable for doing so is seen as the key to justifying the imposition of liability and punishment. Appellate cases in most legal systems of the common law world are as often concerned with the interpretation of the conduct element of criminal offenses as with the responsibility condition or the defenses. However, a brief survey of not only legal texts and theoretical monographs but also draft codes such as the U.S. Model Penal Code testifies to the contemporary preoccupation with questions about the "fault element," that is, the conditions under which it is appropriate to hold an individual responsible for his or her actions. These responsibility conditions form the backbone of what is often called "the general part" or "general principles" of criminal law: they are seen as forming the indispensable framework for a proper grasp both of the structure of criminal law doctrine and of the justification of criminal law and punishment in a modern democratic society.

These responsibility conditions are widely seen as being grounded in broader conditions of human capacity: people are responsible for what they do intentionally, knowingly, recklessly, or negligently because such action—unlike inadvertent conduct—engages their powers of understanding and self-control.[2] This vision of responsibility as grounded in capacity is in turn embedded in notions of human agency, which underpin the great Enlightenment philosophies so widely diffused in European culture during the eighteenth century. The capacity theory of criminal responsibility is not, however, the only way of looking at the normative basis for the responsibility conditions. Particularly in recent criminal law theory there has been a revival of interest in the idea that criminal responsibility is and should be founded not primarily on capacity but rather on an evaluative assessment of the moral character displayed in putatively criminal conduct.[3] Here, too, ideas of agency are central but are understood in a significantly different way. These two ways of conceptualizing criminal responsibility sit alongside a third idea, less widely supported in the normative literature, that locates responsibility in the relationship between an agent and the harms or other outcomes that she causes. The philosophical and doctrinal literature on these different ideas of responsibility is as extensive as it is rich. Yet there has been relatively little research on how and when these ideas found their way into the doctrines of the common law. How has English criminal law's conception of responsibility changed since the middle of the eighteenth century and the diffusion of modern, Enlightenment ideas of the moral importance of human agency? And what is the relationship between these changes in legal framework and broader social, political, and economic changes? The project of mapping the emergence of various principles of responsibility, assessing their relative influence, and explaining their place in sustaining the stability and power of criminal justice as a form of social governance remains to be accomplished.

In what follows, I aim to make a preliminary contribution to that overall explanatory project. My substantive aim is to elaborate a conceptual framework for further analyzing the relevant legal developments, setting out a number of (perhaps competing, perhaps coexisting) principles on which the attribution of responsibility has been, or might be, based: two principles founded in the notion of human capacity, two founded in ideas of character, and one founded in the agent's relationship to outcomes that she brings about. I shall argue that this conceptual mapping can provide some important tools for the broader sociotheoretic project. For the shifting balance between these different ways of conceiving and attributing responsibility, and in particular their distribution among the various stages of criminal justice decision making, can furnish important clues to the changing role of criminal justice in the array of modes of social governance over the last 250 years. I want to suggest that this sort of interpretive analysis may shed light not merely on criminal law as an institution in its own right but also as an index of broad social changes.

I also aim to make some contribution to our understanding of how different disciplinary methods may combine, and in particular of how the resources of philosophy, history, and the social sciences contribute to our understanding of criminal justice. Most research in the field works within one of three disciplinary frameworks: doctrinal legal scholarship, analytic philosophy, or the social sciences.[4] My suggestion is that none of these approaches is in itself adequate for providing the broad theoretical understanding that is needed here.

There remains, therefore, an important task of integrating their insights so as to produce a multidisciplinary study that explores the relationship between the legal basis of criminal liability and the broader ideas of responsibility influenced by socioeconomic and political changes and by the rapid expansion of the social and natural sciences over the relevant period. Methodologically, therefore, I want to argue for a move away from a conception of criminal law theory, as founded primarily in analytic philosophy and the systematic analysis of legal doctrine, toward the kind of Nietzschean "genealogical" approaches explored in Bernard Williams's later work[5] and in Foucauldian "histories of the present" of criminal justice.[6] My aim is to historicize the structure as well as the content of criminal law within a broad sociotheoretic framework, drawing links between the conceptual structure of criminal law doctrine and the substantive social functions that criminal law and punishment have been expected to perform at different points in history, and thus to construct a dialogue between criminal law theory of a doctrinal and philosophical temper and sociohistorical studies of criminal justice.

In pursuing this overall project, I suggest that we may usefully set out from a relatively simple set of hypotheses that provide a framework for our investigation and a means of exploring the linkages between particular conceptions of responsibility and the substantive role of criminal law in modern social governance. Ideas of individual responsibility for crime develop, I suggest, as responses to structural problems of coordination and legitimation faced by systems of criminal law. The content and emphasis of these problems can be expected to change according to the environment in which the system operates: important factors include the distribution of political interests and economic power, the prevailing cultural and intellectual environment, the organization and relative status of relevant professional groups, the array and vigor of alternative means of social ordering, and the prevailing balance between criminal law's quasi-moral aspects and its regulatory, instrumental aspects. Within this basic framework, which I shall set out in more detail later, we may approach criminal responsibility as a practice of attribution specific to criminal law yet connected with prevailing intellectual ideas, including philosophical theories about the nature of human beings. The practical orientation of responsibility in criminal law, decisively shaped by the institutional context of the criminal process, suggests, however, that we should leave ourselves open to the possibility that the relationship between moral-philosophical and legal conceptions of responsibility is more oblique than is generally assumed in criminal law theory. Moreover, it makes it possible that multiple and philosophically variegated conceptions of responsibility are operating within criminal law practices of attribution without any necessary illogicality or incoherence.

In tracing the development of ideas of criminal responsibility in Britain over the last 250 years, I would argue that four principal variables call for examination: the individual's relationship with the state; beliefs about whether the individual's interior and mental world is susceptible to empirical or legal investigation; the (expanding) social functions of criminal law and their implications for the structure of the criminal process and for ideas of judgment and responsibility; and the emergence of a scientific view of criminal behavior as determined by social environment or nature. The substantive hypothesis that I want to explore is that, from the late eighteenth century to the mid-twentieth century, criminal law's doctrinal conception of responsibility was moving from one overtly founded in ideas of disposition and character toward a bifurcated approach that has two key dimensions. The first is a "capacity" or "opportunity" conception, which grounds criminal responsibility in certain cognitive and volitional states. The second is a notion of responsibility grounded in the outcome that an agent produces, where the relationship between agent and outcome is sometimes (though not invariably) mediated by a conception of the agent's distinctive social role. The relationship between these two dimensions is complex, notwithstanding the resonance between the opportunity version of capacity-responsibility and the role-based version of outcome-responsibility. It is noteworthy, however, that in terms of ideological salience (as opposed to practical significance), the capacity principle has dominated over the outcome principle in criminal law theory. I want to argue that this capacity principle takes hold in criminal law significantly later, and for somewhat different reasons, than has generally been argued, its increasing salience being intimately linked with the gradual (incomplete) move from a criminal process based on local and lay knowledge to one based on centralized and systematized procedures and definitions, administered by professionals. Furthermore, I suggest that this historical analysis can shed light on the reasons why contemporary English criminal law's realization of capacity-responsibility takes two different forms: "objective" and "subjective." While objective responsibility conditions such as negligence reflect criminal law's status as both a system of quasi-moral judgment and a regulatory system, subjective conditions such as intention reflect a factual, psychological conception of the conditions of responsibility, distancing the criminal law's overtly evaluative role in a way that may be attractive under conditions of moral pluralism. I will also make some suggestions about not only the relationship between the capacity and outcome principles but also the reasons why the capacity theory continues to be imperfectly observed in contemporary English criminal law. Here I will consider how character-based responsibility-attribution has survived in the criminal process, albeit often unacknowledged or displaced to the prosecution and sentencing stages. In this context, recent developments such as the creation of a sex offender register, the expanded admissibility of character evidence, and mandatory sentencing laws provide an interesting object of interpretation.

1. Excursus on Method: Responsibility in Philosophical Criminal Law Theory versus Histories and Sociologies of Responsibility

Most of the large literature on criminal responsibility falls into one of three categories. First, there are treatises focused on the conceptual analysis of responsibility: for instance, Hart's *Punishment and Responsibility* (1968), Moore's *Placing Blame* (1998), Horder's *Excusing Crime* (2004), and Tadros's *Criminal Responsibility* (2005).[7] Second, there are treatises focused specifically on the historical development of legal doctrines of criminal responsibility: for instance, Fletcher's *Rethinking Criminal Law* (1978) and Smith's *Lawyers, Legislators and Theorists* (1998).[8] These two genres of work evince only a limited interest in the relationship between legal and broad social, political, and institutional changes. Third, there are social histories of criminal justice and procedure such as Garland's *Punishment and Modern Society* (1990), Wiener's *Reconstructing the Criminal* (1991), Langbein's *The Origins of Adversary Criminal Trial* (2003), Damaška's *Evidence Law Adrift* (1997), King's *Crime, Justice, and Discretion in England, 1740–1820* (2000), and Whitman's *Harsh Justice* (2003).[9] These, conversely, are relatively little concerned with the specificities of legal-doctrinal conceptions of responsibility. Only a small literature brings, as I suggest we need to do, these bodies of scholarship into dialogue with one another.[10] The consequence is that our contemporary debate about responsibility as the key legitimating device of the criminal law is dominated by the first two groups: legal and moral philosophers and scholars of criminal law doctrine. To get a sense of the strengths—and weaknesses—of this analytic tradition, it is therefore worth reviewing some of the more influential contemporary theories of criminal responsibility. Because of his influence—and since I have spent the last few years studying his work—I shall use H. L. A. Hart's theory as a suitable exemplar.

It is hardly an exaggeration to say that Hart's theory of responsibility as grounded in a set of cognitive and volitional capacities, along with its associated theory of the *mens rea* principle in criminal law, a theory of excuses and a justification of punishment, forms the starting point or a principal object of criticism for virtually all subsequent work in the field. Responsibility in Hart's sense guarantees the justice of criminal punishment by confining that punishment to those who had a fair opportunity to conform their behavior to the precepts of criminal law. His theory of punishment, with its theoretically disaggregated general justifying aim and principles of distribution, cannot provide any effective normative guidance on when, if ever (as Hart contemplated), the "compromise" of prima facie unjust "strict" liability based on pure outcome-responsibility (as opposed to a role-based version of outcome-responsibility reconcilable with the fair-opportunity principle) would be justified by compensating utilitarian aims.[11] But within the confines of the presumption of a requirement of *mens rea*, his account of responsibility provides both a remarkably accurate fit with late twentieth-century criminal law doctrine in both Britain and the United States and a persuasive rationalization of the contribution of proof of responsibility to the legitimacy of criminal conviction and sanction.[12]

Yet in relation to his theory of criminal responsibility, Hart's theoretical project encounters some methodological complications that relate to an ambivalence about the extent to which his account should be grounded in an understanding of the wider practice within which appeals to responsibility are embedded. Unlike his earlier work with Tony Honoré on causation,[13] the work on responsibility draws only sparingly on actual legal materials. But the message is nonetheless clearly that the account of capacity-based responsibility is the best account of responsibility to be drawn from criminal law. Yet Hart is not much interested in the institutional features of criminal law that underpin the emergence of this notion of responsibility: once elicited, "responsibility" is invested implicitly with a sort of objective or even metaphysical status at odds with his professedly linguistic and socially grounded method. Moreover, outcome-based strict liability, where outside the role-based bounds of the fair-opportunity conception, floats in a different system, and one that Hart makes no real attempt to integrate within his overall justificatory account. It is worth noting that this inclination to marginalize or dismiss the incontrovertible empirical phenomenon of outcome-based strict liability is a pervasive characteristic of normative criminal law theories. Of course, this can be justified in frankly normative terms: one can argue, as Tadros has recently done, that widespread strict liability such as that of the so-called regulatory offenses simply cannot be rationalized within a morally adequate theory of criminal responsibility and should be excluded on that basis.[14] But such a strategy calls into question the status of the account as a theory *of* criminal responsibility, understood as a concept, which has a real—and changing—social existence. What, in other words, are the criteria of accountability to actual practices of criminal responsibility that have to be recognized by the criminal law theorist?

To see the intimate links between the development of legal concepts and their institutional basis, we have only to engage in some fairly basic historical or comparative research. To take a historical example, the modern, agency-based notion of capacity-responsibility that Hart articulates finds strong voice in various forms within Enlightenment political and moral philosophy from the late seventeenth century onward. Yet it finds almost no expression in even the most systematic accounts available of the common law until very much later.[15] In Blackstone's *Commentaries*,[16] for example, there is virtually no "general part" of criminal law elaborating principles of responsibility. Rather, ideas of fault or mechanisms of exculpation are considered interstitially in the context of particular offenses, and the organizing principle is not the general part as we understand it today but the nature of the various public wrongs taken to constitute crime.[17] Yet more significantly, even in J. F. Stephen's draft code produced in the late nineteenth century,[18] the articulation of general conditions of liability, including principles of responsibility and excusing conditions, is vestigial: indeed, notwithstanding the massive social, political, and legal changes of the intervening century, the structure and balance of Stephen's treatise are remarkably similar to Blackstone's. It is therefore the more striking that, seventy years later, Glanville Williams was able to produce a treatise of several hundred pages on "the general part" of criminal law.[19] By this time, the idea that the key to understanding criminal law lay in a grasp of the general conditions of liability had assumed such centrality that Williams never felt the need to write the planned sequel on criminal law's "special part," that is, its offenses. The principle of responsibility as Hart understood it, which might have been thought to be central to criminal law doctrine at least since the Enlightenment and which did form a key part of the modern codes of the continent of Europe from the late eighteenth century on, therefore took well over a century to find its way into English criminal law doctrine. Writing in an era of confidence in the illuminating power of linguistic philosophy, however, Hart, like Williams, was uninterested in the historical specificity of the conception he articulated.

The explanation for the relatively late development of general principles of responsibility in the common law, as I have argued in detail elsewhere,[20] has two dimensions. The argument proceeds from the hypothesis, sketched earlier, that the principle of responsibility plays two key roles in the current system of criminal law. First, it legitimates the state's imposition of criminalizing power, in the context of liberal expectations about individual freedom and the proper limits of state power. As English society moved slowly away from its status-based structure toward a vision of persons as presumptively equal members of the polity, the state needed a new form of license to punish: as the problem of justification became more acute, the conditions of responsibility helped to legitimate the state's power to punish by ensuring its consistency with and respect for individual autonomy. Second, once the precise conditions of responsibility come to be delineated in legal doctrines, they serve as a coordinating device, at the level of both knowledge and values. They enable and constrain the forms of knowledge or evidence that may be produced in the courtroom, and they help to map the relationship between legal and other forms of social knowledge such as that deriving from the medical sciences.[21] And they coordinate this practical, knowledge-gathering enterprise with the values key to the process of legitimation, thus fostering the practical imperative of finality in dispute resolution.[22]

How does this help to explain the late emergence of doctrines of capacity responsibility in English criminal law? Looking first at the legitimating role of criminal responsibility, the argument is that the liberal, democratic, and humanist sentiments that necessitate an appeal to individual responsibility to legitimate criminal law were relatively weak in Britain at the end of the eighteenth century, except in relation to very serious crimes such as murder. In this context, as John Langbein has argued, the criminal justice system operated with something closer to a presumption of guilt than a presumption of innocence.[23] To put it differently, the functional notion of responsibility in criminal law practice was closer to a notion of responsibility for character[24]—with character evidence dominating both trial and pretrial processes, those with bad reputations were much more likely to be prosecuted and almost certain to be convicted—than to a notion of responsibility as founded in an investigation of capacity in the sense of fair opportunity to conform to the law on this occasion. Indeed, as Dubber has argued, the idea of malice, which is often thought of as the precursor to modern, psychological forms of *mens rea*, may have found its roots as much in the idea of meanness of status as legitimating degrading punishments as in a notion of substantive evil or wickedness.[25] The law reform debates that produced the various Criminal Law Commissioners' Reports during the first part of the nineteenth century strongly reflect the legitimating appeal of modern ideas of capacity-responsibility among the elite,[26] but the remarkable fact is that criminal law itself managed perfectly well without articulating it. This is not, of course, to say that the notion of capacity responsibility or indeed, as Joel Eigen argues,[27] of the moral significance of purposeful as opposed to inadvertent behavior was irrelevant to the practice of criminal law. For example, though there was no legal definition of insanity until the middle of the nineteenth century, juries were clearly acquitting or, from 1800, awarding a special verdict to defendants who appeared insane, on the basis of their incapacity. But—and here is the problem for Hart's method—it cannot thereby be claimed that there is a fully formed concept of responsibility at work in criminal *law* understood in doctrinal terms. A legal doctrine of responsibility developed only gradually, spurred by a perceived legitimation deficit that became increasingly acute as, among other things, democratic sentiments and practices spread and formal inequalities of social status diminished.

Of equal relevance to the sociotheoretic dimension of criminal law theory is the coordination aspect of the principle of responsibility in criminal law. Just as the early nineteenth-century English common law had no pressing legitimation need for an across-the-board requirement of proof of *mens rea*, neither did it have an institutional structure that could have managed such proof. The idea of human capacity as the proper and feasible object of proof in a courtroom, though it came more quickly in civil than in criminal law, depended on a complex infrastructure that was still in its infancy and one that, as Lindsay Farmer has shown, displays the intimate links between substantive and procedural law.[28] At a minimum, this included a systematic law of evidence; regular representation by lawyers capable of presenting and developing doctrinal arguments; law reporting allowing emerging doctrines to be communicated across courts; and a system of appeals allowing the interpretation of emerging doctrines to be challenged, tested, and clarified.[29] Of these minimal institutional conditions, only the second was in place by 1850 (a general right to legal representation having been introduced in 1836), with law reporting developing interstitially, the law of criminal evidence developing gradually throughout the century up to the Criminal Evidence Act of 1898, and a system of criminal appeals not in place until 1907. Furthermore, these developments in legal institutions were themselves embedded in, and premised on, a cluster of broader social, economic, and political developments. Principal among these were industrialization and urbanization, which both prompted a decline in the reliability of local and informal structures of control and information-gathering and gave a new impetus to the state's interest in crime control; changes in political and cultural sentiments that underpinned increasing revulsion against the arbitrary and bloody features of the ancien regime in criminal justice; and the increasing centralization and administrative competence and ambition of the state.

These among many other factors fundamentally changed the nature of criminal law, at once underlining the need for a clearly articulated notion of individual responsibility while pushing the borders of criminal liability out into new areas in which the costs of proof of responsibility were seen as disproportionate to the multiplying regulatory functions that criminal law was being asked to perform. From the mid-nineteenth century on, English criminal law, unlike the criminal law of many of its European neighbors, had two very different aspects, often in tension with one another. First, it continued to be regarded as a quasi-moral system, embodying widely shared social norms thought to be of key importance; second, it came to be used by government, and to some extent seen by citizens, as a relatively neutral, instrumental tool of social regulation.[30] The quasi-moral dimension of criminal law came increasingly to be seen in terms of a principle of capacity- or opportunity-based responsibility, while the regulatory dimensions are more easily rationalized in terms of a (less often articulated) version of outcome-based responsibility.[31] Of course, the use of criminal law for regulatory purposes was not a nineteenth-century invention. As Dubber has argued, criminal laws such as vagrancy laws had been used for centuries as a mechanism of "the police power": power oriented to governing a population conceived as a set of objects or resources to be managed rather than as a group of self-governing agents subject to the rule of law.[32] But with the slow emergence of a more democratic political system, the legitimacy of the police power became more problematic—a tension exacerbated by the acceleration of the state's regulatory deployment of the criminal law to govern the newly emerging industrial and urban life. (This is a tension that, as Dubber also argues, persists to this day and is reflected not only in most criminal law theorists' embarrassment as to how to theorize the regulatory offenses but also in the vacuum in constitutional or human rights–based assessment of the police power, as most recently and vividly reflected in antiterrorism measures.) One of my key arguments is that the shifting balance between these quasi-moral and the regulatory aspects of criminal law must be central to any interpretation of doctrines of criminal responsibility.

Someone anxious to defend a primarily philosophical approach to theorizing criminal responsibility such as Hart's will retort that none of this in any way threatens either the normative credentials of his account or its applicability to late twentieth-century English criminal law. The first point may be conceded, though it strikes me as obvious that the normative recommendations of particular principles such as responsibility are to some degree founded in social facts—facts about not only human beings but also about the shape of the social world—and vary in their relative strength along with those founding conditions. This is a point to which I shall return later. But even a full concession does not rescue Hart's account from the need to attend to the broader social and institutional context that shapes the significance of doctrines of responsibility in criminal law. For his account purports not merely to be normative but also to have explanatory power. Historical, comparative, or sociolegal understandings of the role of responsibility in criminal law that affect our interpretation of the shape and relative importance of the concept in criminal law are therefore factors that his account cannot ignore. I should emphasize that this is not necessarily to deny, as Victor Tadros has suggested some of my own work does,[33] that there is no general "core" to the idea of responsibility, a core related to the idea of human agency and accountability for conduct that acts as a constant thread amid shifting theories of responsibility over time and space. It is, however, to argue that this core is a relatively thin one, and that the inflection that it is given by varying social and institutional conditions and practical imperatives is so decisive that no theorist of criminal responsibility can afford to ignore it. Only if we attend to this socioinstitutional basis and its inflection on criminal law's conceptual framework can we understand, explain, and even predict how legal decision makers such as judges interpret and apply the concept. As Hart's enterprise implicitly concedes, one does not have to be a legal realist or to deny the distinctively normative, action-guiding quality of law to take the view that legal theory has this sort of explanatory aspect.

The argument for a more socially grounded jurisprudential analysis of responsibility can be related back to Hart's general jurisprudence and in particular to his relatively parsimonious conception of law as a system of more or less formally articulated rules.[34] As has been famously discussed in relation to Hart's theory of adjudication, Hart showed little interest in the operation of the discretion that he saw as characterizing "hard cases."[35] A fortiori, the operation of the range of discretionary powers that shape factors such as which cases come to court and how they are prosecuted stood well beyond his delineated terrain. Yet there are powerful reasons for thinking that we can understand the full significance of legal concepts such as responsibility only if we take the trouble to inform ourselves about precisely these surrounding forms of power and decision making, which contribute significantly to the balance that criminal law strikes at any particular time between its competing quasi-moral and regulatory aspects. I shall try to illustrate this point with two examples before proceeding to elaborate a more diverse set of responsibility principles that might help us to map, and begin to make sense of, the overall jigsaw puzzle of responsibilization in the criminal process.

First, within the terrain of criminal law in which a relatively robust responsibility or *mens rea* requirement exists—the law of murder or theft, for example—not only other features of legal doctrine (notably the scope of defenses) but also the (typically rather limited) time frame in which an offense is situated and the shape of the rules of evidence in constraining the kinds of information that may be presented to the court may compromise the investigation of individual responsibility in a full sense. To take a recently much debated example, the tendency to frame prosecutions in relation to single incidents marginalizes the relevance of the experience of background factors such as long-term domestic abuse to the volitional dimension of responsibility, hence leading to a finding that victims of such abuse are fully responsible for an ultimate attack on their abuser.[36] In several jurisdictions, this situation has recently been reversed.[37] I do not want to take a position here on the merits of this change in the law of provocation and self-defense, or on the very limited extent to which criminal defenses incorporate factors in a defendant's background that might be thought to compromise their cognitive or volitional capacities or block inferences of vicious character (let alone features of environment, such as radical social inequality, which might be relevant to the fairness of differently situated individuals' opportunities to conform their behavior to the law). I merely wish to point out that the legal realization of responsibility depends not merely on the articulation of a liability rule but on a cluster of other assumptions and discretionary powers that we need to understand if we want to have a full view of the meaning and significance of responsibility in criminal law.

The second, converse example has to do with strict liability offenses. These, of course, are the most controversial aspects of criminal law from the point of view of Hart's normative theory of capacity-based responsibility. Yet, intriguingly, a welter of empirical evidence suggests that the actual prosecution of these offenses is overwhelmingly focused on people whom the prosecuting authority view as responsible in something like the capacity sense.[38] Even if the normative notion of outcome-responsibility is rejected, this does not necessarily weaken the case for a capacity-responsibility requirement in the law itself: the prosecutorial discretion that strict liability offenses expand may be subject to various forms of abuse. But, as legal theorists, we should be interested in how broad social attitudes and power relations conduce to or against the realization of idea(l)s of responsibility in the enforcement as much as the letter of criminal law. This militates in favor of a broader view of law than that adopted in Hart's descriptive jurisprudence and in favor of a generalization of the sort of attention devoted to issues of trial, prosecution, and sentence[39] that is so often absent from philosophical analysis.

These arguments about the relevance to jurisprudence of the social bases for legal ideas such as responsibility have, finally, decisive implications for the normative aspect of special jurisprudence. For if conceptual ideas have institutional and other conditions of existence—if, for example, a notion of capacity-responsibility, or indeed of character-responsibility, can be realized in criminal law only on the basis of certain institutional developments and in the context of a cluster of social and cultural conditions—this has clear implications for the pursuit of the normative project. To the extent that the ambition of special jurisprudence is to affirm, and not merely to delineate, certain key legal concepts, we must surely be interested in the conditions that facilitate—or hamper—their institutional realization. Yet Hart's theory, in common with most philosophically motivated projects of special jurisprudence, rests at the abstract level of institutional structures and pays little attention to what Lewis Kornhauser has called "realized institutions" inhabited by particular individuals and none whatsoever to "functioning institutions" situated and operating in a specified social and physical environment.[40] To the extent that such "functioning institutions" are a necessary condition for the realization of our concepts, this is a deficit in his—and any other structurally and methodologically similar—theory.

2. *Mapping Principles of Responsibility-Attribution Across the Space of Criminalization*

In this section, I want to begin to take the argument forward by sketching a more disaggregated conceptual map for the purposes of analyzing the historical development of ideas of criminal responsibility. This part of the chapter is premised on several conclusions from the analysis provided so far. First, I assume that a full assessment of operational principles of responsibility must take into account the total spread of criminal justice practices—legislation, policing, prosecution, plea-bargaining, judicial, and jury decision making—on questions of both liability and sentence, while attending to the specificities or responsibility-attribution at each stage. These overall processes may usefully be conceptualized as the (more or less integrated) practice of "criminalization." Second, I assume that the realization of moral or philosophical ideas of responsibility has institutional conditions of existence and that our analysis of criminal responsibility must, accordingly, be historically and system specific. Third, I assume that ideas of responsibility play certain structural roles in legitimating and coordinating practices of criminalization. And, fourth, I assume that it is possible, even likely, that multiple ideas of responsibility may be operating in practices of criminalization at any one time. It will therefore be useful to develop a differentiated scheme of possible attribution principles for interpretive purposes. The division of attribution principles into three family groupings—capacity, character, and outcome principles—is familiar in criminal law theory.[41] I shall suggest, however, that it is useful to make a further subdivision between these overall principles, generating a more sensitive analytic scheme.

A. "CAPACITY" PRINCIPLES: CHOICE AND OPPORTUNITY

As I have already argued, the dominant way of thinking about responsibility in contemporary British and U.S. criminal law doctrine turns on the notion of human (or, more rarely, corporate) capacity. On this view, the foundation of not only a person's status as a responsible agent answerable to the normative demands of the criminal law[42] but also of an attribution of responsibility for specific actions lies in human capacities of cognition (knowledge of circumstances, assessment of consequences) and volition (powers of self-control). The crucial factor is how these human capacities—human agency—are engaged in advertent conduct: to put it crudely, responsible conduct is conduct that the agent chooses. This notion of capacity-based responsibility naturally issues from a focus on so-called subjective principles of *mens rea*—intention, recklessness, or foresight of relevant consequences, knowledge, and so on—forms of *mens rea* that essentially consist in subjective mental states on the part of the defendant. Prime examples in English case law would include *R. v. Morgan* ([1976] *AC* 182, now reversed by the Sexual Offences Act of 2003) and *B. v. D.P.P.* ([1998] 4 *All E.R.* 265). Many commentators have noted the increasing emphasis on this form of subjectivism, though there is considerable disagreement about the degree of its realization and the timing of and reasons for its ascendancy. On Smith's view,[43] it is a by-product of utilitarianism, which implies not merely the impropriety but the ineffectiveness of attaching culpability to inadvertent conduct. It has also been argued to be associated with the increasingly psychological view of human agency attendant on scientific developments during the course of the nineteenth century.[44] In other accounts, both Alan Norrie and I have argued that its progress may be explained partly in terms of its ability to provide a legitimating principle that is relatively independent of any evaluation of the relevant conduct.[45] The proof of intention or subjective recklessness being a question of fact, the emphasis is simply on proof of the requisite mental state; a feature that may be useful in a system that criminalizes a huge range of conduct, much of it beyond the terrain of "real" or "quasi-moral" crime and in which moral pluralism or value conflict risks tensions that a factual view of *mens rea* may help to keep out of the courtroom.

Whatever the merits of these competing or complementary accounts of the rise of choice-based principles of responsibility, it is clear that, both conceptually and practically, they are not the only show in town when it comes to capacity principles of attribution. For the basic moral intuition underlying the capacity view can be interpreted in another way, with decisive implications for the shape of criminal law. If the basic moral intuition is that it is legitimate to hold people criminally responsible only for things that they had the capacity to avoid doing, we can realize this intuition in one of two ways. We can do so through proof of subjective choice in the sense of intention, awareness, or knowledge, or we can ask—as Hart did—whether the defendant had a fair opportunity to conform his or her behavior to the criminal law standard. This second approach has the implication that not only subjective mental states but also "objective" standards like negligence, practical indifference, or the imposition of reasonableness constraints in the specification of defenses may be accommodated. It also, therefore, offers an account more likely to be able to rationalize the actual shape of systems of criminal law. From the point of view of the argument that Norrie and I have advanced, this is, however, at the cost of revealing that a criminal trial is, inevitably, in the business of making a potentially controversial normative evaluation of the defendant's conduct. The question to be proven is no longer the relatively neutral, factual, and dualistic, Did D cause P's death? If so, did D do so with intent to cause death or grievous bodily harm? Or, Did D have sexual intercourse with P? If so, did D do so intentionally and aware that P was not consenting? It is, rather, Did D do these things in circumstances in which we would say that D had had a fair opportunity to avoid them? The answer to this question may, of course, be provided by proof of intent or subjective recklessness. But it might also be answered in terms of D's indifference or omission to advert to a risk that would have been obvious to a reasonable person, or to which it would be reasonable for us to expect D to advert, such that we would be inclined to say that D had a fair opportunity to avoid homicide or rape. So long as we are confident that D has the capacities of a reasonable person, this fair-opportunity view is perfectly consistent with the moral intuition underlying the capacity principle of criminal responsibility. A further perceived advantage of the opportunity version of capacity-responsibility is that it is less obviously susceptible than the choice version to the truth of determinism, in that the evaluation can be relative to socially pervasive reactive attitudes.[46] The issue, in other words, is not what we "could" have helped, whether we "could" have chosen otherwise, but what prevailing social norms judge us to have had a fair opportunity to help or choose.

B. "CHARACTER" PRINCIPLES: OVERALL CHARACTER; EXPRESSED DISPOSITION TOWARD THE RELEVANT CRIMINAL LAW NORMS

The idea that an attribution of criminal responsibility is in some sense an evaluation of character has been advanced in radically different guises by Michael Bayles (in Humean form and in relation to criminal responsibility in general), by John Gardner (in Aristotelian form and in relation to defenses, conceptualized as mechanisms ensuring that we are not held responsible for things that are out of character),[47] in my own early work, and most recently by Victor Tadros.[48] In its most radical form, it is thought by capacity theorists to be morally unacceptable to the extent that, unless we are held to have capacity for our characters, character-responsibility implies holding us accountable for things that we could not, or had no fair opportunity to, avoid; it has also been argued that it is premised on an inappropriately ambitious vision of the moral role of criminal law.[49] Since my purpose in this chapter is interpretive rather than normative, I shall set these objections aside for the moment. It is worth noting, however, that it is also possible for character and capacity notions to be combined, as Martin Wiener has persuasively argued they were in the early Victorian criminal justice project,[50] which aspired not merely to hold people responsible for conduct disclosing bad character but also to use the penal process to reshape character, in part precisely by engaging the capacity-based agency of subjects.

The more radical of the two character principles that I want to distinguish may be labeled the "overall-character principle," which holds that the attribution of criminal responsibility is founded in a judgment that the defendant's conduct is evidence of a wrongful, bad, disapproved character trait: disregard of human life, indifference to sexual integrity, lack of respect for property rights, and so on. The criminal law, on this view, seeks to convict, label, and stigmatize those of bad character or disposition: the principle of responsibility-attribution is merely a function of the overall meaning and purpose of criminal law in its quasi-moral mode, and the criminal conduct is at root a symptom of the underlying rationale for conviction and punishment, namely, bad or antisocial character. A crucial question therefore arises as to the scope of the conduct that is regarded as evidence relevant to this judgment of criminal character. Systems adhering to an overall-character principle would be those in which broad character evidence is admissible: not merely previous convictions of offenses with similar facts but criminal record in general and perhaps even general evidence about lifestyle, employment history, and so on. (In case this sounds far-fetched, it is perhaps worth remembering that systems of this kind are not unknown in the contemporary world.) In its more cautious form, however, character-responsibility restricts itself to an evaluation of the specific conduct that forms the basis for the present allegation. The relevant question becomes not, Is D's conduct evidence of criminal character? but rather Does D's conduct in causing P's death or having sexual intercourse with P express a settled disposition of hostility or indifference to the relevant norm of criminal law or at least acceptance of such a disposition? or, in Tadros's terms, Does D's conduct qua moral agent display the sort of vice that calls for criminal law's communicative role of expressing moral indignation to be invoked?[51] This formulation opens up an obvious path to the elaboration of defenses such as duress, provocation, self-defense, or—possibly—mental incapacity. It also preserves the specific allegation of criminal conduct as central to the rationale for conviction and punishment and is founded on a particular understanding of D's status as a moral agent: a reasoning being responsible for his or her beliefs, desires, emotions, and values. While taking a more cautious view of relevant evidence, it would also naturally locate an attribution of responsibility within a broader time frame than that implied by the capacity principles.

C. OUTCOME-RESPONSIBILITY

It has also been argued—notably by Tony Honoré [52]—that being the cause of a particular outcome may under certain circumstances ground an attribution of criminal responsibility. Honoré's argument for "outcome responsibility" is based on the idea that we are truly responsible for the outcomes of our actions, even when they are accidental, in the sense that we could not have done otherwise than we did. Honoré's argument is that the results of our actions become a part of our sense of identity, of who we are: even though we are related to unintended outcomes differently than to intended results, they nonetheless engage our agency in some morally relevant way. For example, if a person accidentally injures another person while driving, most of us would find it morally repellent if the person simply shrugged their shoulders and said, "Oh well, it was really nothing to do with me; it was just an accident." Cases of absolute liability in criminal law are cases of pure outcome-responsibility: instances of strict liability subject to defenses, and in particular to a due diligence defense, might be regarded as hybrids of outcome and capacity-based responsibility of the fair-opportunity kind, the latter based on a special genre of responsibility related to socially approved yet risk-generating roles such as driving or engaging in various commercial or productive processes.

3. Applying the Scheme to Practices of Criminalization

Having sketched this more differentiated approach to analyzing principles of responsibility-attribution, I will now try to illustrate how this might be applied across the different stages of the criminal process, so as to generate a more nuanced interpretation of how responsibilization operates in criminal justice practice.

A. *MENS REA* AND DEFENSES

The main debates about criminal responsibility have been focused on the stage of criminal law doctrine and its application in the courts, notably in terms of the *mens rea* principle and the elaboration of the defenses. The assumption of most criminal law theorists is that criminal law is, or at least should be, based on one coherent principle of responsibility; the majority of contemporary British and U.S. criminal law theorists see this as being one of the two capacity principles sketched previously, albeit that both character theories and theories seeking to integrate character and capacity have recently attracted significant interest.[53] But at an interpretive level, it is relatively easy to demonstrate that English and U.S. criminal law move between the two capacity principles and moreover apply in some areas principles of liability that resonate with aspects of the outcome and character principles. Let us focus on the capacity principles first. The existence of offenses such as manslaughter, which can be committed through negligence—a form of objective *mens rea*—as well as the reasonableness threshold applied to elements of most of the defenses, affords substantial evidence of the operation of the opportunity principle. Does this mean that the fair-opportunity theory is a better account of English criminal law than the choice theory? I would argue that it does not. To establish this argument, we would have to be sure that the offenses to which entirely subjective principles of *mens rea* apply—murder, for example—count as instances in which the "choice" guaranteed by proof of intention or subjective recklessness *amounts in itself* to proof that the defendant had a fair opportunity to act otherwise than he or she did. This, however, can be disputed. For the limited scope of the defenses, as well as the restricted time frame in terms of which the defendant's choice is set, prevents the court from making the sort of overall assessment of the fairness of the defendant's opportunity that is invited by the application of an open-ended "reasonableness" test. In subjective *mens rea* cases, the law is interested, in other words, not so much in the fairness or otherwise of the circumstances in which the defendant made his or her choice but rather in the choice itself. Of course, the defenses do some moral fine-tuning here. But it remains the case that application of a subjective *mens rea* test does not itself invite an assessment of fair opportunity. Hence it may be argued that criminal law is pluralistic even across capacity principles. Furthermore, the existence of many offenses of strict liability to which no due diligence offense applies shows that contemporary English criminal law also espouses principles of outcome-responsibility to a significant degree. The applicability of the general defenses to most of these offenses means, however, that it is outcome-responsibility of the hybrid kind: if not guaranteeing fair opportunity, the law is at least ruling out liability in certain particularly egregious instances of lack of fair opportunity.

Can it be argued that any aspects of criminal law's liability standards lend themselves to interpretation as based on character rather than on capacity or outcome principles? I would argue that there are indeed significant traces at least of the more cautious version of the character approach in contemporary English criminal law. My reason for arguing this lies both in substantive law and in the law of evidence. Tadros's recent monograph makes a powerful case that only a version of what I have called the "cautious" character theory can capture the essentially evaluative and communicative nature of criminal condemnation. Tadros argues that both *mens rea* requirements and many defenses represent the criminal law's attempt to restrict responsibility-attribution to those who, qua agents, have displayed a morally vicious character through the relevant conduct.[54] Indeed, he argues that the operation of the prevailing, open-ended reasonableness tests may under certain circumstances invite inappropriately broad character inferences, punishing for vices such as ignorance rather than restricting criminal punishment to appropriate moral terrain such as willful blindness, indifference, and so on. (This is a symptom, perhaps, of the curious vacuum in contemporary criminal law in relation to a substantive theory of criminalization, itself a product of the factual-scientific orientation of the subjectivist capacity theory and of a certain discomfort with the morally controversial nature of criminal judgment.[55])

I would argue that the large number of evidential presumptions operating in English criminal law, as well as a smaller number of conclusive, legal presumptions, operating against defendants, give further reason for thinking that character principles operate at the level of formal conviction. Presumptions may or may not leave room for a capacity interpretation. If someone is, for example, conclusively presumed to have raped a person whom he has defrauded as to the nature and quality of the act of sexual intercourse, the law might be interpreted as saying that this person's conduct has conclusively expressed an indifference to the law's antirape norm, or it could be argued that the basis for the attribution of responsibility for rape lies in the choice to defraud or the fair opportunity not to have defrauded. But the evidential presumption that someone who has sex with a person who is very inebriated or unconscious does so without either consent or a reasonable belief in consent seems to put the capacity aspect of responsibility onto the back foot: this behavior is assumed to express indifference to the antirape norm *unless* the defendant can produce evidence rebutting the inference. It may be argued, of course, that such presumptions—like the many presumptions operating in the area of drug offenses—are designed to overcome the problems of proving the advertent forms of responsibility associated with the choice version of the capacity principle crafted in dualist terms. But the selection of the specific circumstances around which the presumptions operate is informed by judgments about behavior that may be assumed to express antisocial or criminal practical attitudes or character. Once again, therefore, we seem to be confronted with a hybrid rather than a pure approach to responsibility in criminal law doctrine. This conclusion is strengthened by the fact that English law has recently changed in such a way as markedly to expand the forms of character evidence admissible in criminal trials. This broadened admissibility of character evidence[56] will inevitably shape the practices of attributing criminal responsibility in the trial process, changing the structure of knowledge-coordination at the trial by providing material from which judge and jury may form evaluative, character-based assumptions that will supplement legal capacity-based tests wherever—as is usually the case—they are sufficiently open-ended to admit of character-based inferences.

B. PRETRIAL PRACTICES: POLICING AND PROSECUTION

When we broaden our focus from the moment of attributing formal responsibility in criminal law doctrine toward the earlier and later moments in the practice of criminalization, the evidence of multiple principles of responsibility increases markedly, and includes, unfortunately in my view, marks not only of the cautious but also of the overall-character approach. Take, for example, the plentiful evidence from many jurisdictions of differential policing and prosecution practices structured around the social axes of race, ethnicity, class, and gender. The process of selecting the pool of people to whom formal attributions of criminal responsibility will be applied is inevitably affected not only by police and prosecution judgments about choice or fair opportunity but by assumptions about character or disposition—themselves, unfortunately, sometimes based on inaccurate and prejudiced stereotypes about the kinds of people likely to be involved in criminal conduct. The extent and nature of such character-based judgments is, of course, a matter for empirical investigation; but such evidence as we have, particularly about police attitudes, suggests that they are pervasive.[57] Historians of English criminal justice have noted that the locally based practices of filtering cases for prosecution up to the reforms of the early nineteenth century were heavily structured by local knowledge of character and reputation: local justices of the peace and grand juries were decisively influenced by such information, while character evidence was hugely important to the conduct of criminal trials.[58] In relation to a world in which manifest rather than subjective criminality was the order of the day,[59] it comes naturally to make the link between these pretrial and evidential practices and the overall shape of the principles of responsibility being applied to criminal defendants. Practices of policing and prosecution in colonial societies provide yet more vivid instances of decision making shaped decisively by generalized assessments of character, generally structured on racial lines.[60] Today, particularly in Britain and the United States, where criminal justice scholarship is marked by a curious and in my view unproductive division of labor among criminologists, criminal lawyers, and students of the criminal process and punishment, criminal law scholars have trained their focus on the substance of criminal law (supplemented to some extent by the law of evidence), diverting attention from the consequences of pretrial practices to the patterns of responsibilization *as realized in criminalization practices as a whole.* Among other things, this has led to an underdeveloped legal debate about the consequences of even formal pretrial developments, which are based on or invite character-based responsibility attributions—some of them distinctly of the overall rather than the cautious variety. Perhaps the most obvious example here would be the creation in both the United Kingdom and the United States of sex offender or pedophile registers, which in effect mark out a certain group of people as presumptively criminal in character.[61] Another would be various antiterrorism laws on both sides of the Atlantic, which use nationality or citizenship as rules of thumb for potential terrorist criminality.[62] A further instance is the diffusion of preventive detention for those suspected of involvement in terrorism—the links here with crude assumptions about character all too evident in the U.S. vice-president Dick Cheney's recent comment, "The important thing here to understand is that the people that are at Guantánamo are bad people."[63] In England, there is also the amazing survival of the (female-) gender-specific status "common prostitute."[64] Beyond this, the rapid advance of genetic technology opens up the real possibility of a pretrial criminal process significantly shaped by genetically based assumptions as to character in the sense of likelihood of engaging in criminal conduct. In the face of this genetic revolution, the principles of responsibility so central to criminal law doctrine may quickly become marginal unless vigorously defended in the context of an understanding of the potential relevance of DNA evidence to traditional practices of legal responsibility-attribution.

C. POSTCONVICTION PRACTICES: SENTENCING AND PUNISHMENT

In England and Wales, the moment of conviction has long heralded a significant dilution in the defendant's process rights, not least in relation to constraints on the sort of evidence taken as admissible and relevant to decisions about sentence and execution of sentence. Whether in the guise of pleas in mitigation, presentence reports, psychiatric reports, reports by probation officers or prison staff, a welter of information about the convicted person's character becomes central to the decision-making process. This stretches well beyond past criminal record, encompassing judgments or information about lifestyle, attitudes, and compliance with probation or prison discipline. At a formal level, in significant developments in both the United Kingdom and the United States, legislation and policy structuring sentencing has in recent years added impetus to character-based attributions: three-strikes laws, other mandatory sentences for certain kinds of offenses, and dangerous-offender policies of one kind or another all provide examples. As Pillsbury has argued, these arrangements amount not only to punishment for bad character but also define that character in inflexible terms at the legislative level, thus removing the possibility of an individualized judgment that is arguably central to the very idea of treating defendants as agents.[65] Again, this of course does not show that character-based principles shape the attribution of formal criminal responsibility. But it does show that even to the extent that formal criminal responsibility is based on a precondition of choice or fair opportunity, the full implications of that formal responsibility will be decisively shaped by character-based judgments that modify the practical realization of criminal responsibility in the sentencing and penal processes.

Conclusion

This chapter having been largely a conceptual mapping exercise, its conclusion is more by way of an agenda for future research than a concrete set of findings. I hope at least to have established two things. First, a more differentiated conceptual scheme for identifying principles of responsibility can be of use in arriving at a more sophisticated interpretive analysis of both criminal law doctrine and the other rules and practices that surround the criminal law in the pre- and posttrial processes. Philosophical analysis here operates as an indispensable tool in the broader interpretive project of tracing practices of responsibilization in the criminal process. Second, there is strong reason to believe that, even within criminal law doctrine, criminalization is operating with multiple conceptions of responsibility rather than one unitary approach.

The purpose of this exercise has not been merely descriptive. Rather, the object of the analytic framework is to provide a more sophisticated interpretation of the shifting balance of principles of responsibility-attribution in criminalization over time, both within criminal law itself and across the practices of criminalization. On my initial interpretation, the history of post-eighteenth-century English criminal justice is characterized by a gradual development and strengthening of capacity-based principles within the criminal law, necessitated by the imperatives of legitimation and fostered by the increased capacity of the trial system to handle evidence about choice or opportunity combined with its diminished capacity to draw on local knowledge about character or reputation. The legitimation imperatives militated to displace character-based judgments to the pre- and posttrial processes, where they were less visible, more targeted to populations unlikely to excite political sympathy, or both, and to the hiving off of outcome-based principles of attribution to a special, ill-defined category of quasi crime dignified as regulatory offenses: a powerful descendant, as Dubber has argued, of the inherently vague police power, as yet uncontained within any satisfactory modern democratic or constitutional theory.[66] The initial interpretation, which I have advanced in this chapter, is doubtless in need of refinement. But to the extent that this is persuasive, what does the resurgence of overtly character-based practices tell us about the place of criminalization among modes of social governance or about the overall trajectory of our societies? Is this one more manifestation of law-and-order politics, of Garland's "culture of control" or Young's "exclusive society"?[67] Or is it better understood as a renewal of confidence in the law's authority to make quasi-moral, evaluative judgments, combined with a refreshing willingness to be up front about these rather than disguising them beneath purportedly factual findings of intention or knowledge?[68] Is it, conversely, a product of diminished confidence in the ability of courts to manage capacity-based judgments? Or is it rather a precursor of a new form of status society emerging with the genetic revolution or within political economies such as the United States and the United Kingdom that are characterized by disparities of wealth so large that they amount to a status distinction? Are we seeing a reversal of the slow trend toward capacity-responsibility in English criminal law from the early nineteenth to the mid-twentieth centuries, and, if so, why? Though the main focus of my future research on this topic will be historical, I see its purpose as highly relevant to these issues of contemporary interpretation. Indeed, I think that any intelligent analysis of today's criminal process needs to be grounded in an account of its history and path to its present position.

Notes

1. This chapter takes up and elaborates one aspect of the framework of a long-term project on the development of ideas about criminal responsibility in the modern English common law. The full project is set out in more detail in my "In Search of the Responsible Subject: History, Philosophy and Criminal Law Theory," *Modern Law Review* 64 (2001): 350–371 and "Responsibility and Modernity in Criminal Law," *Journal of Political Philosophy* 9 (2001): 249–277.

2. For the classic statement of this position, see H. L. A. Hart, *Punishment and Responsibility* (Oxford: Clarendon Press, 1968).

3. See most recently Victor Tadros, *Criminal Responsibility* (Oxford: Clarendon Press, 2005).

4. While most of the relevant social science research is sociological, psychology, political science, and economics have also made significant contributions.

5. *Truth and Truthfulness* (New Haven, Conn.: Princeton Univ. Press, 2002).

6. Michel Foucault, *Discipline and Punish: The Birth of the Prison*, A. Sheridan, trans. (Harmondsworth, UK: Penguin, 1977); David Garland, *The Culture of Control* (Oxford: Oxford Univ. Press, 2001).

7. Michael S. Moore, *Placing Blame* (Oxford: Clarendon Press, 1998); Jeremy Horder, *Excusing Crime* (Oxford: Oxford Univ. Press, 2004).

8. George Fletcher, *Rethinking Criminal Law* (Boston: Little, Brown, 1978); K. J. M. Smith, *Lawyers, Legislators and Theorists* (Oxford: Clarendon Press, 1998).

9. David Garland, *Punishment and Modern Society* (Oxford: Oxford Univ. Press, 1990); Martin Wiener, *Reconstructing the Criminal* (Cambridge: Cambridge Univ. Press, 1991); John H. Langbein, *The Origins of Adversary Criminal Trial* (Oxford: Oxford Univ. Press, 2003); Mirjan R. Damaška, *Evidence Law Adrift* (New Haven, Conn.: Yale Univ. Press, 1997); Peter King, *Crime, Justice, and Discretion in England, 1740–1820* (Oxford: Oxford Univ. Press, 2000); James Q. Whitman, *Harsh Justice* (Oxford: Oxford Univ. Press, 2003).

10. Exceptions include Lindsay Farmer's *Criminal Law, Tradition and Legal Order: Crime and the "Genius" of Scots Law, 1747 to the Present* (Cambridge: Cambridge Univ. Press, 1996); Alan W. Norrie's *Crime, Reason and History* (London: Weidenfeld & Nicolson, 1993) and *Punishment, Responsibility and Justice* (Oxford: Clarendon Press, 2000); R. Antony Duff, Lindsay Farmer, Sandra Marshall, and Victor Tadros's project on the criminal trial, *The Trial on Trial*, vol. 1, *Truth and Due Process* (Oxford: Hart Publishing, 2004) and *The Trial on Trial*, vol. 2, *Judgment and Calling to Account* (Oxford: Hart Publishing, 2005). See also Markus Dirk Dubber, *The Police Power: Patriarchy and the Foundations of American Government* (New York: Columbia Univ. Press, 2005).

11. See Hart's *Punishment and Responsibility*, chap. 1. For further discussion, see Nicola Lacey, *State Punishment* (London: Routledge, 1988), pp. 46–56.

12. This is not to say that Hart's argument has gone unchallenged: see, for example, Tadros, *Criminal Responsibility*, pp. 54–70.

13. *Causation in the Law*, 2d ed. (Oxford: Oxford Univ. Press, 1959).

14. *Criminal Responsibility*, pp. 16–17, 73–74.

15. For a more detailed discussion, see my "In Search of the Responsible Subject," *Modern Law Review* 64 (2001): 350–371 and "Responsibility and Modernity in Criminal Law," *Journal of Political Philosophy* 9 (2001): 249–277.

16. William Blackstone, *Commentaries on the Laws of England* (Chicago: Univ. of Chicago Press, 1979) (originally published from 1765 to 1769).

17. See Guyora Binder's chapter in this collection and, further on Blackstone and *mens rea*, Binder, "The Rhetoric of Motive and Intent," *Buffalo Criminal Law Review* 4 (2002): 15–27.

18. *A History of the Criminal Law of England* (London: Macmillan, 1883).

19. Glanville Williams, *Criminal Law: The General Part*, 2d ed. (London: Stevens & Sons, 1961). I am grateful to Tony Smith for alerting me to the fact that Williams originally planned a four-volume work, with additional volumes on offenses against property, persons, and the state. The success of the one volume as an independent work is, however, highly significant.

20. See note 1.

21. I do not mean to imply here that the relationship is all in one direction: clearly, emerging social knowledges such as medicine may themselves have effects on ideas of responsibility, as Eigen's contribution to this volume demonstrates.

22. See John D. Jackson, "Managing Uncertainty and Finality: The Function of the Trial in Legal Inquiry," in *The Trial on Trial*, vol. 1, *Truth and Due Process*, Duff et al., eds., pp. 121–145.

23. John H. Langbein, "Shaping the Eighteenth Century Criminal Trial: A View from the Ryder Sources," *University of Chicago Law Review* 50 (1983): 1–36. See also Bruce P. Smith, "The Presumption of Guilt and the English Law of Theft, 1750–1850," *Law and History Review* 23 (2005): 133–171.

24. See further the chapters by Binder and Schneider in this volume.

25. See further Binder's chapter in this volume and Dubber's *Police Power*, pp. 38, 181 and chap. 7.

26. See Smith, *Lawyers, Legislators and Theorists*.

27. In his contribution to this volume.

28. See Farmer's contribution to this volume.

29. For an excellent historical analysis, see John D. Jackson, "Managing Uncertainty and Finality."

30. Think, for example, of the role of English criminal law in regulating public health or safety both directly and indirectly by acting as a backup to licensing.

31. My historical interpretation in terms of character, capacity, and outcome models overlaps with Fletcher's influential characterization of the patterns of manifest, subjective, and harm- or risk-based criminality in *Rethinking Criminal Law* (Oxford: Oxford Univ. Press, 1978), but mine attempts to locate them within a broader sociotheoretic frame.

32. Dubber, *Police Power*.

33. Tadros, *Criminal Responsibility*, pp. 3–8.

34. This is a conception that is also put in doubt by recent analyses of the rhetorical structure of criminal trials and in particular of the influence of cultural frames in the jury's reading of evidential narratives; see, for example, Robert P. Burns, "The Distinctiveness of Trial Narrative," in *The Trial on Trial*, vol. 1, Duff et al., eds., pp. 157–177. As Burns argues, this implies that the normatively and functionally most appealing trial structure is itself socially contingent.

35. Ronald Dworkin, "Hard Cases," *Harvard Law Review* 88 (1975): 1057. See, generally, Dworkin's *Taking Rights Seriously* (London: Duckworth, 1977).

36. Donald Nicolson and Rohit Sanghvi, "Battered Women and Provocation," *Criminal Law Review* 1973:728; John Gardner and Timothy Macklem, "Compassion without Respect? Nine Fallacies in R. v. Smith," *Criminal Law Review* 2001:623; Victoria F. Nourse, "Passion's Progress: Modern Law Reform and the Provocation Defense," *Yale Law Journal* 106 (1997): 1331.

37. See, for example, in relation to England and Wales, *R.v. Smith* (2000) 4 *All E.R.* 289.

38. W. G. Carson, "White-collar Crime and the Enforcement of Factory Legislation,"

British Journal of Criminology 10 (1970): 383; Keith Hawkins, *Environment and Enforcement* (Oxford: Clarendon Press, 1983); Nicola Lacey, Celia Wells, and Oliver Quick, *Reconstructing Criminal Law*, 3d ed. (Cambridge: Cambridge Univ. Press, 2003), chaps. 1 and 5.

39. There are, of course, exceptions to this rule: see, for example, R. A. Duff, *Trials and Punishments* (Cambridge: Cambridge Univ. Press, 1988) and *Punishment, Communication and Community* (Oxford: Oxford Univ. Press, 2001).

40. Lewis Kornhauser, "Governance Structures, Legal Systems, and the Concept of Law," *Chicago-Kent Law Review* 79 (2004): 355, 362–364.

41. See, for example, Tadros, *Criminal Responsibility*; Jeremy Horder, "Criminal Culpability: The Possibility of a General Theory," *Law and Philosophy* 12 (1993): 193.

42. I am in agreement with writers like Duff, Horder, and Tadros that there is a distinction to be drawn between attributions of responsibility in specific cases and a broader judgment that a subject lacks in general the capacities that underpin responsibility. These latter subjects are properly regarded as exempt from criminal responsibility, and this is the most natural way to understand "defenses" such as insanity or infancy. Space, however, precludes me from pursuing this issue in more detail. See Duff, *Trials and Punishments*; Tadros, *Criminal Responsibility*, chap. 5; Jeremy Horder, "Determinism, Liberalism and Criminal Law," *Current Legal Problems* 49 (1996): 159; and Nicola Lacey, "Partial Defences to Homicide," in *Rethinking English Homicide Law*, Andrew Ashworth and Barry Mitchell, eds. (Oxford: Clarendon Press, 2000).

43. *Lawyers, Legislators and Theorists*.

44. Cf. Roger Smith, *Trial by Medicine* (Edinburgh: Edinburgh Univ. Press, 1981); Joel Peter Eigen, "Lesion of the Will: Medical Resolve and Criminal Responsibility in Victorian Insanity Trials," *Law and Society Review* 33 (1999) 425.

45. Alan W. Norrie's *Crime, Reason and History*, 2d ed. (Cambridge: Cambridge Univ. Press, 2006); Nicola Lacey, "In Search of the Responsible Subject: History, Philosophy and Criminal Law Theory," *Modern Law Review* 64 (2001): 350–371.

46. See P. F. Strawson, "Freedom and Resentment," in *Free Will*, Gary Watson, ed. (Oxford: Oxford Univ. Press, 1982).

47. See Michael Bayles, "Character, Purpose and Criminal Responsibility," *Law and Philosophy* 1 (1982): 5 (drawing on Hume's philosophy); John Gardner, "The Gist of Excuses," *Buffalo Criminal Law Review* 1 (1998): 575. See also Dan M. Kahan and Martha C. Nussbaum, "Two Conceptions of Emotion in Criminal Law," *Columbia Law Review* 96 (1996): 269; Nicola Lacey, "Partial Defenses to Homicide," in *Rethinking English Homicide Law*, Andrew Ashworth and Barry Mitchell, eds. (Oxford: Clarendon Press, 2000). See also essays by Kyron Huigens ("Homicide in Aretaic Terms"), Kenneth W. Simons ("Does Punishment for 'Culpable Indifference' Simply Punish for Bad Character?"), and Victoria F. Nourse ("Hearts and Minds") in a special issue, *The New Culpability: Motive, Character and Emotion in Criminal Law*, Guyora Binder, ed., *Buffalo Criminal Law Review* 6 (2002): 97, 219, 361. See also Kyron Huigens, "Virtue and Inculpation," *Harvard Law Review* 108 (1995): 1423; Alan C. Michaels, "Acceptance: The Missing Mental State," *Southern California Law Review* 71 (1998): 953. On character and responsibility more generally, see Ferdinand Schoeman, ed., *Responsibility, Character and*

the Emotions (Cambridge: Cambridge Univ. Press, 1987); Moira Gatens and Genevieve Lloyd, *Collective Imaginings* (London: Routledge, 1999), chaps. 3 and 6 (on Spinoza and responsibility); Peter Arenella, "Character, Choice and Moral Agency: The Relevance of Character to Our Moral Culpability Judgments," *Social Philosophy and Policy* 7 (1990): 59; Bernard Williams, "Persons, Character and Morality," in *Moral Luck*, Bernard Williams, ed. (Cambridge: Cambridge Univ. Press, 1981), p. 1. For criticism of the normative recommendations of various character theories see R. A. Duff, "Choice, Character and Criminal Liability," *Law and Philosophy* 12 (1993): 345; R. A. Duff, "Virtue, Vice and Criminal Liability: Do We Want an Aristotelian Criminal Law?" *Buffalo Criminal Law Review* 6 (2002): 147.

48. *State Punishment* (London: Routledge, 1988).

49. See Duff, "Choice, Character and Criminal Liability" and "Virtue, Vice and Criminal Liability."

50. Martin J. Wiener, *Reconstructing the Criminal: Culture, Law, and Policy in England, 1830–1914* (Cambridge: Cambridge Univ. Press, 1990). Victor Tadros also sees a place for capacity principles within his primarily character-based theory. *Criminal Responsibility*, in particular chaps. 2, 5, 12. In his view, however, the moral force of the capacity principle is itself parasitic on the more basic sense in which criminal law expresses a judgment of the character displayed in an agent's conduct. Nonetheless, I think it could be argued that a vision of humans as, under normal conditions of agency, in some sense capacity-responsible for their beliefs, desires, and dispositions does underlie Tadros's account.

51. For Tadros, actions that are out of character may nevertheless be objects of responsibility, on the basis that D showed a culpable failure to resist, hence accepting, a vicious disposition.

52. "Responsibility and Luck: The Moral Basis of Strict Liability," *Law Quarterly Review* 104 (1988): 530 (reprinted in *Responsibility and Fault* [Oxford: Hart Publishing, 1999], p. 14).

53. See references at note 47.

54. *Criminal Responsibility*, pp. 23–43. An agent acts, on Tadros's view, qua agent, when he or she is motivated by reasons that cohere with his or her more general set of values and dispositions.

55. *Criminal Responsibility*, chap. 13. On the lack of any convincing account of where we draw the boundary between criminal and noncriminal conduct, see Leo Katz, "Villainy and Felony: A Problem Concerning Criminalization," *Buffalo Criminal Law Review* 6 (2002): 451.

56. Criminal Justice Act of 2003, § 98-101.

57. For a summary of the evidence in the United Kingdom, see Coretta Phillips and Ben Bowling, "Racism, Ethnicity, Crime and Criminal Justice" in *The Oxford Handbook of Criminology*, Mike Maguire, Rod Morgan, and Robert Reiner, eds., 3d ed. (Oxford: Oxford Univ. Press, 2002), p. 579.

58. See Lacey, "Responsibility and Modernity in Criminal Law," p. 258n; for an important corrective to the view that these practices were not state-directed, see the chapter by Smith in this volume.

59. Fletcher, *Rethinking Criminal Law*. See also the chapter by Binder in this volume, and, on the related concept of *manifest madness*, the chapter by Eigen in this volume.

60. See the chapters by Kolsky, Schneider, and Wiener in this volume.

61. See, for example, Sex Offenders Act of 1997, Sexual Offenses Act of 2003.

62. See, for example, Terrorism Act of 2000.

63. As quoted in the *New York Times*, June 13, 2005, p. A14.

64. See Nicola Lacey, Celia Wells, and Oliver Quick, *Reconstructing Criminal Law*, 3d ed. (Cambridge: Cambridge Univ. Press, 2003), chap. 5.3.b.

65. Samuel H. Pillsbury, "A Problem in Emotive Due Process: California's Three Strikes Law," *Buffalo Criminal Law Review* 6 (2002): 483.

66. In part 3 of *Police Power*, Dubber moves toward the development of a theory of "substantive due process" that might have the capacity to confine and rationalize the police power within a framework appropriate to a modern constitutional democracy.

67. David Garland, *The Culture of Control* (Oxford: Oxford Univ. Press, 2001); Jock Young, *The Exclusive Society* (London: Sage, 1999).

68. For a persuasive analysis of the dangers of disguising the inevitably evaluative dimension of responsibility attributions, see Victoria F. Nourse, "Hearts and Minds: Understanding the New Culpability," *Buffalo Criminal Law Review* 6 (2002): 361–388.

TWO

Criminal Responsibility and the Proof of Guilt

LINDSAY FARMER

1. Introduction

Now it is obvious that it is impossible really to know for certain what was passing in the mind of the accused person; it can only be surmised by a process of inference from what is known of his conduct. Of course in early times the difficulty felt in ascertaining the mind of man and the rule that a prisoner could not himself give evidence tended to produce the practice of imputing *mens rea* from certain given sets of circumstances. In more modern days the difficulty has not been regarded as insuperable.

—J. W. C. TURNER

J. W. C. Turner made this characteristically modern statement about the mental element in criminal law in an influential essay first published in 1936. That the basis for his argument was somewhat controversial need not concern us here,[1] for what is important about the essay is the articulation of a standard of subjective proof in relation to a recognizably modern tripartite division of criminal fault (intention, recklessness, and negligence), together with the confidence of his claim that earlier difficulties in establishing the content of the accused's mind have been surpassed. Of course, he concedes, while this knowledge is, in truth, unattainable, the modern law has nonetheless developed techniques for knowing the unknowable and escaping the clumsy and moralistic practices of the early common law. Where, in early times, the law was forced to rely on presumptions that created fixed inferences about the mental state of the accused, it was no longer necessary to presume that a man intends the natural consequences of his actions, a form of constructive *mens rea* that Turner criticized. Instead, it was the task—albeit a difficult one—of the jury to interpret all the evidence, including the testimony of the accused where this was available, and thus to "come to a decision as to what must have been in the mind of the man himself."[2]

Such statements about the form and the proof of the mental element in crime are now commonplace, and judges are accustomed to charging juries in these terms. However, this familiarity can lead us to overlook the distinctively modern characteristics of this formulation. While the task of the jury was (and is) a difficult one, what is more important here is the claim about the knowability of the mind of the accused and the question of the type of evidence that can establish this. Much recent scholarship has focused on the subjective form of this kind of *mens rea* and the emergence of a new kind of legal subject, and it is worth identifying the significant features of the mental element in the modern criminal law. First of all, it is differentiated. Where the earlier common law determined criminal liability on the basis of the undifferentiated concept of malice,[3] subjective *mens rea* is broken down into the three forms of intention, recklessness, and negligence, which are to be distinguished on the basis of an assessment of the relation between the possible consequences and the attitude of the accused toward these consequences. Thus, for Turner, intention denoted not only foresight of possible consequences but also that these consequences were desired; recklessness was foresight of, or indifference or inadvertence to, possible consequences, with no desire to bring them about; and negligence, which Turner did not regard as criminal, was the pursuit of a course of conduct without awareness of the possible consequences.[4] Second, by distinguishing between different attitudes of mind, such as desire and motive, awareness or indifference, Turner sought to provide an objective means for the assessment of the subjective state of mind, as the different elements could be broken down and assessed. Third, this modern test aimed to abandon the moral language of fault in the common law (malice, wickedness, gross culpability, etc.) and to replace it with a descriptive, psychologized concept of fault. It was believed that the existence of states of mind was a matter of fact and was thus as susceptible to legal proof as any other matter of fact.[5] More generally, this understanding of mental states sought to abstract from ideas of character or situation, as these had been important to earlier conceptions of *mens rea*.[6] Finally, it has been argued that this new conception of the legal subject was a response to changing social and economic conditions and the development of a new kind of governmental project, one that privileged the self-governing autonomous subject.[7]

Now it is without question that Turner's argument was programmatic rather than being an accurate description of practice. Older, character-based conceptions of *mens rea* survived in the English criminal law at least into the 1960s as the judiciary was reluctant to adopt the new tests on a wholesale basis, and it is arguable that these tests were never fully adopted outside the law of homicide.[8] Notwithstanding this, Turner's argument raises the important, and somewhat neglected, question of how the state of mind of the accused person was to be proved in court. He himself says little about this question, beyond outlining the legal test: it must be inferred from the conduct of the accused, the accused's testimony, and knowledge of the circumstances. And it is this question of the proof of guilt, rather than the intellectual history of the ideas of fault, that is my focus in this chapter, for I want to situate the development of these doctrinal rules within the broader context of the changing criminal trial. It is a precondition of any particular form of liability that there be certain practices of evidence and proof. What, however, allows Turner to assert with such confidence that particular states of mind can be distinguished and proved in a court of law? What sort of evidence could count as proof of a particular state of mind? What kind of transformation of legal procedures occurred to make it possible that the state of a person's mind at the time of the commission of certain acts was something that was capable of being proved in court? What, in other words, are the legal and cultural practices that made possible the emergence of certain forms of liability, and what can knowledge of these practices contribute to a critical analysis of modern conceptions of subjective responsibility? In other words, we should not only be concerned with the new subject of the criminal law but also with the way that subjectivity is reconstructed in the trial.

In this chapter I propose to look at changes in form of the criminal trial and in the law of evidence that, I shall argue, made possible the development of a modern legal subjectivity. However, I shall also use this analysis to explore and challenge some of the assumptions that are often made about subjective criminal responsibility, particularly in relation to the principle of autonomy. It is, as I suggested in the preceding, often argued that this modern conception of responsibility recognizes the individual as an autonomous, self-governing subject, such that the imposition of punishment can be legitimate only under circumstances where this autonomy is fully recognized by the law.[9] It is further argued that the modern trial protects the individual against the state through the recognition of autonomy in criminal procedure: the requirements of "fair trial" or "due process of law," embodied in principles such as the presumption of innocence or the requirement of proof beyond reasonable doubt.[10] I shall argue that the development of criminal procedure in this formative period for the adversarial trial was usually motivated by a desire to facilitate prosecution rather than by respect for autonomy and, moreover, that the version of subjectivity that emerges from this process should qualify many of the assumptions that are often made about the respect for autonomy in the modern criminal law.

It should be clear that this is not an account of the development of either the criminal law or criminal procedure in general but of the development of a particular and highly influential conception of responsibility in relation to a particular type of trial—usually, though not exclusively, trials for murder. It is, nonetheless, indisputable that this kind of trial and this version of responsibility have a symbolic importance that far exceeds their practical significance.[11] There is a risk, of course, that focusing on these narrow concerns may lead to a reproduction of the narrow focus of much contemporary criminal law theory, which, while claiming to look at general concepts of liability, usually looks at those that apply only to a small number of serious crimes against the person and which rarely takes account of the institutional context. However, I would argue that what is crucial here is the focus on a broader procedural, institutional, and cultural context than the philosophical approach to questions of criminal responsibility normally allows and the different perspective that this opens on the development of criminal liability and the meaning of the adversarial trial.

The chapter is in two sections. The first looks at changes in the form of the criminal trial, particularly the development of what I call the "reconstructive" trial in the second half of the nineteenth century, which, I shall argue, replaced the scaffold as the "public climax of state justice and its imaginatively defining scene."[12] The second looks at the role of various evidential and legal presumptions in the proof of *mens rea*, the different forms of evidence that were placed before the court, and how these were to be interpreted.

2. The Reconstructive Trial in the Late Nineteenth Century

The story of the decline of public punishment, focused on the birth of the prison, is well known, but it has not always paid sufficient attention to the impact of these reforms on the criminal trial.[13] The transformation in crime and punishment was driven in large part by the desire to make punishment more certain and effective, but it was also concerned with the symbols of legal authority and the legitimacy of criminal justice. Critics of the Bloody Code were concerned not only that the use of capital punishment was ineffective in deterring crime but also that the public display of authority in the spectacle of the scaffold was too easily subverted, as the condemned refused to display the appropriate degree of contrition and the behavior of crowds became increasingly difficult to manage. The reformers argued that the criminal justice system resembled a lottery in which few offenders were detected, fewer still convicted, and capital punishment was inflicted on those unfortunates who did not have the social resources to make a successful plea for mercy.[14] And in the early part of the nineteenth century, the Bloody Code was repealed to be replaced by new institutions of policing and punishment, principally the penitentiary but also the use of transportation, which offered the possibility of more certain detection and the more measured infliction of punishment. As a consequence, punishment became a secret process, hidden behind the walls of the prison, operating on the soul or mind rather than the body of the condemned person.

Yet the decline of the scaffold as the symbol of criminal justice and the move to secret punishments did not mean the decline of symbolism altogether, but rather it meant that different institutions acquired a symbolic importance and that the legitimacy of the system came to rest on different symbols of justice. McGowen has argued that the reform of the Bloody Code led to the creation of a new image of criminal justice, as reformers sought to secure wider public support for the legal system.[15] The authority of the criminal law was no longer to be based on the personal authority of the judge and the widespread use of the pardon. Justice was instead to operate through the impersonal application of predetermined (and less severe) laws, introducing distance, uniformity, and impartiality in place of the interplay of severity and mercy. The trial was central to this image as a means of displaying the legitimate consequences of a criminal act, the representation of punishment as an idea.[16] There was a double principle of publicity at work, with the publicity of the penal norm linked to a new form of procedural publicity in the trial. With the decline in the public display of punishment, the spectacle of justice thus shifted from the scene of punishment to that of judgment.[17] The trial was a means of staging questions of individual guilt and innocence, crime, and punishment—although ironically its symbolic role was to increase in inverse proportion to its practical importance to the criminal justice system.

If this shift points toward the importance of the image or ideology of criminal justice, how ritual and symbols play an important role in the creation and operation of social institutions, it leaves open the important question of how the adversarial trial was "staged" and how (if at all) this changed over the course of the nineteenth century. An understanding of the "staging" of the trial is necessary to seeing how the different elements of the trial could combine and contribute to the overall image of justice. This is not to suggest that there was a conscious attempt to make the courtroom theatrical or to increase the drama of the trial. Historians of the English adversarial process have drawn attention to the muted nature of the nineteenth-century trial—the fact that there seemed to have been a deliberate eschewing of publicity, that flamboyant or overdramatic advocacy was frowned on, and that the courtroom was organized so as to minimize dramatic potential.[18] However, this should not lead us to think that trials were not still in an important sense staged. Trials are never exclusively about the identification and punishment of wrongdoers; they are always also about the relation between the legal and social order. In the procedures and rules for the determination of truth, in the standing of the various actors, in the kinds of questions that can be determined, and in its relation to the broader criminal justice system, the trial is always something more than a simple legal procedure for the determination of guilt and innocence. The trial is a communicative process, which might either conflict with or reinforce the image of a universal and impartial legal order.[19] It is a form of public ritual of shaming or degradation.[20] It is also an imaginative space in which complex stories are told and new forms of responsibility contested.[21] The question of staging, then, is concerned with the trial as a legal and social event and the way that this changes over time: the way that reality is reconstructed and represented in the courtroom;[22] the relationship between substance and procedure; the relationship between written and unwritten laws;[23] the distribution of roles, burdens, presumptions; and even the way that the courtroom is spatially organized so as to represent the authority of the law.[24] Thus, even in the absence of conscious attempts to "stage" or dramatize the law, it is nonetheless the case that the criminal trial is ordered so as to present the accused, the judge, the law in such a way as to perform certain social functions. My aim in this chapter is to show how developments in the trial in the second half of the nineteenth century worked to throw a new focus on the state of mind of the accused, but one that must qualify any simple account of the increasing individualism of the criminal law.

Recent work on the history of the adversarial trial has focused on reforms in criminal procedure and evidence in the period up to the passing of the Prisoner's Counsel Act of 1836.[25] Langbein, in particular, has argued that this act is significant, giving legal recognition to changes in the practice of trials that had taken place over the course of the eighteenth century and marking the formal point of transition between the early modern "altercation trial" and the "testing the prosecution" trial that characterizes the modern adversarial system. The altercation trial was rapid, required the accused to speak, and largely focused on the question of the amount of punishment the accused was to receive. The reformed trial, by contrast, was slower, structured by exclusionary rules of evidence, a contest between lawyers before a silent accused, and increasingly concerned with determining the question of guilt or innocence.[26] However, I want to challenge Langbein's argument in two important respects.

First, while the passing of the 1836 act was undoubtedly important in establishing certain procedural safeguards and establishing the trial as an adversarial contest between prosecution and defense cases, this merely established a structural framework within which the trial was to develop. Indeed, the trial at the end of the century looked very different, both as a consequence of changes in the detection and prosecution of crime and as a result of piecemeal reforms of procedure, evidence, and substantive law. The early nineteenth-century reforms opened up a space in which questions of guilt, intention, and evidence could be explored more fully than hitherto.[27] Second, while Langbein's analysis of the 1836 act reinforces McGowen's argument about the image of justice being based on impartiality and the legalization of the trial, it says little about the staging of the trial. It is not enough to know that the prosecution case is being tested; it is also important to understand how that case is put together: who speaks, what kind of evidence is led, and what the prosecution is trying to prove. Indeed, I have preferred the term the *reconstructive* trial to that used by Langbein precisely because I wish to draw attention to how the trial in this period is given over to the reconstruction of past events to make the court witness to the truth of the events and so prove the guilt of the accused person.[28] Of course, the trial has always been reconstructive—concerned with the proof of past facts—to some extent, but the way it has done so has changed substantially over time. In the late nineteenth century the issue of *what* was being reconstructed and *how* it was being reconstructed has changed quite significantly. These developments can be illustrated by examining the trial of Dr. Crippen.

The trial of Dr. Hawley Harvey Crippen for the murder of his wife by poisoning took place in 1910.[29] As a murder case it was unusual because of the absence of clear evidence linking the alleged victim and the human remains found in the cellar of Crippen's house. Crippen also achieved notoriety for his transatlantic flight from justice with his mistress, who was disguised as a man, and their eventual detection through the use of wireless telegraphy and apprehension before disembarking their ship. Much of the infamy surrounding Crippen is based on his supposed callousness. Not only did he poison his wife and bury her dismembered body in the cellar of their house but he also invited his mistress to come and live in the same house, and she was seen in public wearing the wife's jewels. Even when found guilty he showed neither remorse nor emotion. It is also iconic of that peculiarly English crime of passion—celebrated by Orwell—the suburban poisoning, with Crippen's mild, clerkish exterior masking a cruel and passionate nature.[30] However, although the trial attracted a great deal of public attention, it was not particularly remarkable by the standards of its day. Certain features, however, show how the trial had changed since the early nineteenth century.

First, the trial was long, taking place over five days. Long trials were not unknown before 1900 (and Crippen's trial was not typical of all trials), but until the latter part of the century trials would rarely last longer than a day, or two days at the most. This was in part for the reason that once sworn, a jury in a case of felony was prohibited from separating until a verdict had been delivered, which led to the unpopular and expensive practice of detaining juries. In practice, judges would sit late to finish a case, with the result that the defense case was often heard late in the day when jury members were tired and their concentration poor.[31] The case of Mary Blandy, for example, who was tried at the Oxford Assizes in 1752 for the poisoning of her father, began at 8 a.m. and finished at 9 p.m. on the same day, the jury deliberating for only five minutes. In addition, although in the late nineteenth century the length of trials was continuing to grow, the overall number of trials was decreasing, as a consequence of the rise of plea-bargaining and the growth of summary jurisdiction, and it was these trials for serious crimes that attracted the greatest amount of public attention.[32]

One of the principal reasons why trials were getting longer was because of the greater number of witnesses being produced. Here, the prosecution case was based on the evidence of thirty-two witnesses and took the best part of three days to present. The defense case was somewhat shorter, consisting of only five witnesses, but their testimony still took over a day and a half to present. The prosecution witnesses included relations, friends, and acquaintances who gave evidence as to Crippen's speech and behavior following the disappearance and supposed death of his wife and also to their surprise at seeing Ethel le Neve wearing her jewelry. There were pieces of short testimony from witnesses, including police constables, surgeons, and even undertakers giving details about the discovery, removal, and storage of the human remains from the cellar, necessary to link the corpus delicti to the evidence presented in court.[33] However, what was significant was not only the number of witnesses but also the identity of certain key witnesses. The authority of the professional detective and scientific expert was central to the interpretation of the evidence of the crime. Much of the prosecution case was based on the evidence of the investigating detective, Inspector Dew, and of five expert medical witnesses who testified as to the identity of the remains found beneath the cellar floor and the likely cause of death—poisoning by "hyoscin." The defense in turn brought in three experts in an attempt to refute the prosecution case on these points. Finally, a key moment in the trial was when Crippen gave evidence under oath on his own behalf, a significant change in criminal procedure that was permitted only following the Criminal Evidence Act of 1898.[34]

The number and identity of prosecution witnesses shows how the prosecution aimed to reconstruct the crime through the process of detection.[35] The order witnesses were called followed a strict chronology: from the point his wife went missing; to the involvement of the police in the search for the missing woman; to the discovery, removal, and analysis of human remains from the cellar of Crippen's house. The presentation of witnesses suggests suspicion hardening into a sense of certainty of wrongdoing, only finally suggesting premeditation with evidence of Crippen's purchase of poison. The increased number of witnesses reflects the involvement of a professional police force in the process of investigation, as they were better able to take statements and keep records of those who were spoken to in the course of the investigation.[36] The police were not only increasingly involved in collecting evidence but also themselves testifying—the evidence of Chief Inspector Dew being of particular importance in securing the conviction. The professional detective testified about the process of investigation, what he had heard and seen for himself. His evidence helped to organize the testimony of the initial witnesses, confirming their suspicions by taking the investigation over as a police matter. He also demonstrated the superior skills of the professional investigator, being alert to inconsistencies in statements or to the presence of clues of wrongdoing.[37] Thus, the case being tested was not only a legal one but was backed by the authority and power of the police, such that by the time Crippen came to testify on his own behalf, his testimony was not so much a presentation of an opposing account of the events—as it would have been in an altercation trial—but something to be inserted into the account that had already been organized by the police and prosecution.

Another significant feature of the case was the lengthy presentation of technical forensic evidence as part of the case for both prosecution and defense.[38] Medical witnesses were not unknown in earlier trials but doctors rarely had specialized knowledge of forensic medicine, and there was no systematic procedure for the investigation of suspicious deaths.[39] In the notorious case of Captain Donnellan, for example, tried in 1781 for the murder by poison of his brother-in-law, the body of the victim had been buried for a week before being disinterred for a postmortem.[40] This rather haphazard system was reformed in 1836 with the passing of an act permitting coroners to order medical examinations in the case of suspicious deaths and providing for the payment for postmortem examinations and medical witnesses at Coroner's Inquests.[41] Although this system was not immediately effective, the act laid the basis for the more systematic investigation of suspicious deaths, increasing the likelihood that deaths by poisoning would be detected. At the same time, the science of forensic medicine was developing and a body of Crown forensic experts emerged, the most notable of whom was Sir Bernard Spilsbury, who testified for the prosecution in the Crippen case and who would play a key role in the detection and prosecution of crime. This body of men attained a level of celebrity through their involvement, usually for the Crown, in most of the notable criminal trials of the late nineteenth century.[42] The authority of these "medical detectives," resting on a combination of scientific expertise and a carefully cultivated reputation for aloofness and impartiality, was put to the service of the prosecution. As Jones has written,

> Whereas the police did practical work at the level of investigating and detecting crime, forensic experts also did symbolic work, creating the impression that, once the power of the scientific vision had been harnessed to law, not even the cleverest of villains would escape conviction.[43]

The increasing use of expert witnesses, and their appearance for both prosecution and defense, had also led to changes in the rules governing this evidence, in particular with respect to the hardening of the distinction between fact and opinion. In the eighteenth-century poisoning cases of Blandy and Donnellan previously mentioned, it is notable that the medical witnesses were asked to express their opinions about the likely causes of death.[44] Indeed, in the Donnellan case, the reluctance of the defense expert, Dr. John Hunter, to comment on whether a potion drunk by the victim was a likely cause of death was widely regarded as having had an unfavorable impact on the defense case.[45] In the case of Blandy, the leading expert, Dr. Addington, was asked to give his opinion on whether the accused was truly distressed about the state of her father, and by implication by her guilt—suggesting that at this time the testimony of such experts was valued as much for its moral as scientific authority.[46] By the late nineteenth century the situation was very different, as experts were confined to speaking only on the facts and not to expressing opinions about the ultimate issue in the case.[47] The appearance of conflicting expert evidence, however, was regarded as something that had to be tested by the adversarial process of the law, under cross-examination. In the Crippen case the credibility of one of the defense experts was lost when he broke down under cross-examination and admitted that he had made an error as to the part of the body a certain piece of skin had come from. The second defense expert—the author of a standard textbook on poisons—had lamely to suggest that he had changed his opinion in the past weeks about the toxic effect of a certain drug.[48]

Notwithstanding the increasing importance of the police and forensic experts, it was the lawyers who played the most important role in the trial. First counsel and then the judge would organize the evidence and present theories of the case in their opening and closing addresses and through the cross-examination of witnesses. I shall say more about this later, so at this point I want principally to note how some barristers achieved a public profile, even a kind of celebrity, for their skills in breaking down witnesses under rigorous cross-examination or for performances convincing reluctant juries to either convict or acquit.⁴⁹ Indeed, many popular accounts of trials from this period present cases as conflicts whose outcome might be determined by the choice of counsel, or the identity of the judge, or by the outcome of the clash between counsel and the accused. In this sense the trial was literally staged for the jury—and, by extension, for the external audience of newspaper readers. Their role was not only to look for clues but also, in an important sense, to judge the performance of the actors in the trial.⁵⁰ The trial might have exalted individuality over the display of state authority in the public execution, but in the staging of the reconstructive trial it was the personalities of the lawyers, detectives, and scientific experts that came to dominate.

3. Evidence and Its Interpretation

Turner pointed out that the modern mental element in crime displaced legal presumptions in favor of the use of evidence—and particularly circumstantial evidence—and in this section I want to look at the relation between legal presumptions, evidence, and proof in the context of the reconstructive trial. I shall briefly summarize some changes in evidence law before going on to look at the central question of how evidence was to be interpreted or evaluated in the courtroom. The bulk of scholarship on the history of the laws of evidence has focused on exclusionary rules, looking either at how they developed in the course of the eighteenth century—whether as a result of the desire to protect the jury or owing to the "lawyerization" of the trial—or at the subsequent relaxation of some of these rules in the course of the nineteenth century.⁵¹ While this scholarship has told us a lot about the increasing professionalization of the bar and its control of trial procedure, it has had less to say about how this affected the substantive law or conceptions of responsibility. It is also the case that the legal developments go well beyond a simple concern with exclusionary rules, and changes in the law of evidence drew on and reflected broader debates in late Victorian culture about the nature of testimony and proof.⁵²

I want to note three particular developments that are central to an understanding of the late nineteenth-century trial. First, while the eighteenth century had seen a rise in the use of circumstantial evidence, nineteenth-century law reflected a growing concern about the nature of the inferences that could be drawn from evidence of facts.⁵³ A number of treatises published over the course of the century questioned the view that circumstances could not lie, pointing out that the proof of an event depended less on the number of witnesses than on the quality of the evidence and the nature of the inference that could be properly drawn.⁵⁴ They argued that proof was a matter of probability, and that the proof of crime required the jury to judge the credibility of witnesses, together with the "number, independence, weight and consistency of those elementary circumstances."[55] The proliferation in the amount of evidence due to changes in policing and the organization of the prosecution made these problems of inference and probability more acute, and this was an issue that was addressed in various ways by counsel and the judge. Second, along with the greater use of medical testimony about mental states where the nonresponsibility of the accused through some form of mental estrangement was in issue, the new discipline of criminal psychology began to address more general questions of the relation between states of mind and actions.[56] The growing awareness of the complexity, and often opacity, of motives and desires threw new emphasis on the skill of examining and interpreting suspects and witnesses. Texts such as Gross's popular manual on criminal psychology, translated into English in 1911, explicitly tutored legal professionals on such topics as how to interpret mental states from the outward appearances of witnesses and suspects.[57] Third, many customary rules and practices that had been within the discretion of the trial judge began to be formalized, as they were argued by lawyers and discussed by treatise writers looking for some underlying rationale to the hodgepodge of evidentiary rules.[58] Underlying these changes was a fundamental shift in the basis of the law from rules based on the competency of witnesses to those concerned with the reliability and credibility of evidence in the trial.[59] One of the key functions of the trial thus became that of judging the quality of the evidence.

These developments are reflected in the passing of the Criminal Evidence Act of 1898, which permitted the accused to give evidence on oath, and in its impact on the trial. This is of further interest because it has been suggested that the reform was consistent with the developing emphasis on individual responsibility in nineteenth-century political and legal thought: the responsible individual should not be denied the opportunity to participate in his or her own trial.[60] The principal concern in the debates leading to the act was not the credibility of the accused person. Persons with an interest in the outcome of civil proceedings had been allowed to testify following the passing of the Evidence Act of 1843, and the Criminal Law Amendment Act of 1885 made persons charged with certain indictable offenses competent witnesses on their own behalf.[61] There was thus a growing confidence that courts would be able to identify false or misleading evidence, even when given under oath.[62] The most important question driving the demand for reform was a mounting concern over the silence of the accused in criminal trials following the reforms of 1836 and 1848. The passing of the act, as Bentley has noted, was to change irrevocably the shape of the trial.[63] One consequence was to facilitate the task of securing a conviction on the basis of circumstantial evidence. If the prosecution presented a strong case, then

> it is in practice necessary for the prisoner to go into the box and endeavour to give an innocent explanation of the facts proved against him, an endeavour which, experience shows, frequently strengthens the case of the prosecution to an extent which makes conviction a certainty.[64]

This thus placed a greater emphasis on accused persons and the question of whether they would give evidence on their own behalf, making them the focus of the trial—but not necessarily in a way that enhanced their autonomy.

The impact of these changes can be seen in relation to the general issue of how evidence should be evaluated, and, specifically, how evidence of mental state should be evaluated.[65] If the general problem of circumstantial evidence is that of making the facts speak for themselves, we have noted that the growth in the availability of facts meant that this was increasingly less likely to happen, and that the jury required guidance on the evaluation of evidence. This in turn meant that the importance of counsel and judge, as interpreters of the evidence, increased greatly—a state of affairs acknowledged by Sir Richard Muir in his opening speech to the jury.[66] An important issue, however, was that of how counsel and judge should interpret this evidence to represent the interior thoughts of the accused. For counsel, this was done in opening and closing speeches to the jury, and much of the debate around the Prisoner's Counsel Act of 1836 concerned the question of who should have the final word and how counsel should speak.[67] After 1841 the practice of allowing the judge to summarize the evidence and address the jury had become firmly established, though there was some debate over the extent to which the judge should express his opinion about the facts in the case.[68] Lord Chief Justice Alverstone was careful to state his neutrality, that he had no wish to express an opinion, and that if he appeared to do so he was merely indicating a possible view of the facts.[69]

In murder cases generally, an inference of malice aforethought might be drawn from the use of a weapon in an assault, the type of attack, or even the nature of the wound.[70] This intersected with the felony-murder rule of substantive law, which by the turn of the century required that the initial felony be of such a type as to be likely to cause death.[71] There were, however, specific problems in relation to poisoning—including knowledge of poisons and of the consequence of application, as well as the fact that poisoning cases turned on proof of who had administered the poison—which meant that these kinds of inferences could not readily be drawn. In view of these difficulties, we find that the question of motive becomes a key issue in the representation of Crippen's mental state. Thus, Crippen's counsel placed great stress on the apparent absence of motive, whether financial or emotional, arguing that this made the prosecution account of Crippen's actions inexplicable.[72] By contrast, the prosecution relied on Crippen's motive of wanting to be with his mistress, variously described as lust for a woman and lust for money, as a way of telling a coherent story about the disappearance of his wife and his subsequent flight—simultaneously asserting dismissively that an adequate motive was rarely shown for murder.[73] This is significant given the standard efforts in definitions of intent to distinguish strongly between intent and motive. In general, as Turner argues, the latter is irrelevant; the focus of the criminal law is more narrowly on the question of whether the action was freely chosen.[74] In practice, this distinction was almost always transgressed, as lawyers relied on questions of motive in the construction of narratives that sought to make sense of the actions of the accused person.

A second important factor was the use of evidence of character, and it is important to note that, even well into the twentieth century, proxies such as evidence of character could stand in place of evidence of a particular mental state—perhaps not surprisingly, given the legal development of tests such as provocation around the idea of building "good character."[75] This was particularly the case in so-called secret crimes, such as rape or sodomy—and murder by poisoning—where there were no witnesses to the commission of the crime.[76] Evidence of good character could establish the standing or respectability of the accuser or victim, and by inference their mental state or predisposition to commit certain acts, and was permitted if it was relevant to the nature of the offense charged and related to the period of the offense.[77] Restrictions on evidence of bad character were stricter. The prosecution could not present evidence to the court either of general bad character or of prior convictions, unless rebutting evidence of character as part of the defense case or under the "similar fact" exception.[78] These prohibitions were further tightened with the passing of the 1898 act, which restricted cross-examination of the accused as to character and previous convictions unless they had put the character of the prosecutor or prosecution witnesses at issue.

Given that the restrictions on character evidence had been getting stricter throughout the century, it is perhaps surprising to find evidence of character playing such an important role in the Crippen case. Much of the defense cross-examination of prosecution witnesses was aimed at showing Crippen's good character. A medical colleague, Dr. Burroughs, was asked whether he would describe Crippen as kind-hearted and well-mannered, willing to render any little service to his wife.[79] A friend of his wife, Clara Martinetti, was asked whether she thought him a kind-hearted man, and his mistress's landlady, Emily Jackson, was prompted to state that she thought him one of the nicest men she had ever met. The defense never missed an opportunity to ask witnesses to comment on their favorable impression of him and placed a great deal of stress on his good character and reputation.[80] The prosecution case, by contrast, aimed to demonstrate his essential duplicity—shown in his extramarital affair, his admitted lies about the disappearance of his wife, and his calmness in continuing to go about his everyday business.[81] Just as importantly, his coolness under the pressure of sustained questioning was presented as confirmation of his character and his capacity to perform the monstrous deeds of killing and dismemberment that were alleged by the Crown.[82] Lord Chief Justice Alverstone also referred to the need to examine the character of the accused in his charge to the jury, immediately going on to point out that the jury could not rely on the mere statement of Crippen as "[h]e has on his own confession lied for his own purpose, and was prepared to lie, if necessary, for the purpose of his own advantage."[83] Although he qualified this by stating that the general question of bad character was irrelevant to guilt of the specific crime charged, his suggestion that it was relevant to an inference that Crippen had lied about the disappearance of his wife shows how character could be used as evidence of intent.

The final issue in the evaluation of evidence that I want to consider is that of how the demeanor of witnesses, and in particular the accused, could be judged, for we find both counsel and the judge directing the jury to base their judgment on an assessment of the self-presentation of the accused person. Oldham has noted that little attention was given to the question of how evidence should be evaluated in the eighteenth century, with attention being drawn only to the question of the problematic relationship between courtroom manner and veracity in the early nineteenth century.[84] Where veracity had been linked to the swearing of the oath, and the accused disqualified from testifying on oath because of the temptation to perjury, it came to be accepted that the court had to make its own judgment on the truthfulness of testimony and the weight it should be given. One way of measuring this was through circumstantial evidence, and Welsh has noted how one of the perceived advantages of circumstantial evidence over direct testimony was that it could catch the lie through weaving a more complete and intricate picture of events.[85] However, we also find more attention being given to the question of how guilt or unreliability would manifest itself in the person of the witness or accused—an issue that, as we have noted, became particularly acute following the passing of the 1898 act. Even a confession or statement on oath was not necessarily clear or unambiguous evidence of intent.[86] Cross-examination could play an important role in the uncovering of the false or unreliable witness, but equally important was the judging of the demeanor of the accused.

The centerpiece of the Crippen trial was the lengthy cross-examination of the accused, which took up most of the fourth day of the trial. This was remarkable less for any particular admissions or moments of drama than the way the sustained and intensive examination contributed to the prosecution's case as to the essential duplicity of Crippen. Long passages of the questioning focused on the lies that Crippen had told, the pretenses he made, and the subterfuges that he had employed.[87] Sir Richard Muir, in the closing speech for the prosecution, called the jury's attention to the evidence of his lack of emotion at key stages in the commission and concealment of the alleged crime and under cross-examination.[88] He went on to say that although some men had "marvelous control" over their inner feelings, his calmness was not evidence that he could not have committed the crime. The jury was to consider whether he was the type of man who could conceal and control his true thoughts and motives. The judge in his charge to the jury took up the theme, placing great stress on the lies told by Crippen both in and out of the witness box and the importance of relying on what they had seen and heard in the courtroom.[89]

While the admonition to rely on the evidence presented in court is formulaic, and no doubt of great importance in an age where there were few restrictions on pretrial publicity, it is also an instruction to jury members to rely on everything that was seen and heard in the courtroom in making their judgment. In this we see that the words and actions of the accused person are scrutinized increasingly closely, to reveal the hidden meaning—that which cannot be concealed because it is beyond conscious control and is given away by the small gesture or the unconscious.[90] In other words, the jury should look for clues, going beyond the formal posture or the overt statements of the individual, in the accused's demeanor to see what lies behind or what the person is seeking to conceal.[91] In an important sense, then, behavior at the trial could become evidence of the capacity to commit the crime.

4. The Proof of Guilt

The end of the nineteenth century can be described as the age of the trial. Criminal trials played as melodramas in which gruesome crimes were reenacted for the benefit of an eagerly attentive public. Lawyers and forensic experts became minor celebrities, their appearances in court eagerly anticipated. Those accused of crimes were subjected to unprecedented levels of scrutiny, their performance in court seen as holding the key to an understanding of their actions, with every member of the public acting as prospective jury member or amateur sleuth. The trial itself was seen as offering a window on society, enacting not only the punishment of individual wrongdoers but also representing the effectiveness of the system in detecting and punishing crime in general. And we have seen how changes in the detection and investigation of crime, in criminal procedure, and in the law of evidence combined to stage the trial in this way. However, in concluding, I want to offer two suggestions as to how this account of the development of the reconstructive trial complicates, or even undercuts, the conventional view of the rise of the responsible, autonomous subject of criminal law.

The criminal trial at the turn of the twentieth century displayed individualism rather than autonomy. It is clear that, as we have seen, the adversarial trial changed in significant ways in the course of the nineteenth century. One of the important outcomes of this process was the development of a space and language to talk about intention and responsibility—at least in relation to certain crimes—and that this tightened the definition of crimes such as murder.[92] Turner could readily assert the knowability of the mind of the accused, but it is far from clear that this recognition of the subjectivity of the accused was accompanied by a recognition of procedural autonomy. Far from acknowledging the autonomy of the accused, the procedural developments that we have examined increasingly handed power to counsel and the judge. Initially silenced by the formation of the adversarial trial in 1836, the accused became the subject of the trial only at the cost of a loss of autonomy. This is nowhere clearer than in the discussion of mental states, where loss of control of the process of interpretation meant that control of issues of intent and motive were taken away from them. The responsible legal subject is constructed through and by the means of these legal procedures.

This also has important consequences for how we think about the process of judgment. It is frequently argued that the modern jury operates on the basis of empathy, placing themselves in the position of the accused person to judge whether a reaction was reasonable or consequences foreseeable.[93] However, what I have argued here would suggest that this kind of identification relies as much on distrust and that this distrust is institutionalized in certain features of the adversarial trial. Circumstantial evidence is preferred to direct testimony; cross-examination is designed to reveal the unreliable witness; and the jury is encouraged to look beyond the surface of appearances, to see what the accused person cannot conceal. The modern trial, arguably, institutionalizes a "hermeneutics of suspicion,"[94] and, if this is so, it must challenge the idea that the function of the jury is based on empathy, or perhaps more precisely that empathy is not only about identification that can exist only on the basis of an assumed likeness.

Notes

Epigraph. "The Mental Element in Crimes at Common Law," in *The Modern Approach to Criminal Law*, Leon Radzinowicz and J. W. C. Turner, eds. (London: Macmillan, 1945), p. 199 (originally published in 1936, *Cambridge Law Journal* 6:31).

1. Because it overplayed the centrality of subjective tests of *mens rea* in a gloss on the history of English criminal law. For criticism, see Jeremy Horder, "Two Histories and Four Hidden Principles of *Mens Rea*," *Law Quarterly Review* 113 (1997): 95–119; K. J. M. Smith, *Lawyers, Legislators and Theorists: Developments in English Criminal Jurisprudence, 1800–1957* (Oxford: Clarendon Press, 1998), pp. 297–304.

2. Turner, "Mental Element," p. 200.

3. On malice, see James Fitzjames Stephen, *A General View of the Criminal Law of England*, 2d ed. (London: Macmillan, 1890), chap. 5; Courtney Stanhope Kenny, *Outlines of Criminal Law* (Cambridge: Cambridge Univ. Press, 1904), chap. 3.

4. Turner, "Mental Element," pp. 206–211. More recent analysis of these concepts may differ in details, but the structure is essentially the same. See, e.g., R. A. Duff, *Intention, Agency and Criminal Liability* (Oxford: Blackwell, 1990); Victor Tadros, *Criminal Responsibility* (Oxford: Oxford Univ. Press, 2005).

5. See Nicola Lacey, "Responsibility and Modernity in Criminal Law," *Journal of Political Philosophy* 9 (2001): 249–276 at 268–269. It is significant that in another essay in the same volume Turner argues that criminal law must be seen as a branch of criminal science. See Leon Radzinowicz and J. W. C. Turner, "The Meaning and Scope of Criminal Science" in *Modern Approach to Criminal Law*, p. 25.

6. See Lacey, "Responsibility," pp. 256–261; Horder, "Two Histories" On character and crime in nineteenth-century thought, see Martin Wiener, *Reconstructing the Criminal* (Cambridge: Cambridge Univ. Press, 1990).

7. See Nicola Lacey, "In Search of the Responsible Subject: History, Philosophy and Criminal Law Theory," *Modern Law Review* 64 (2001): 350.

8. Smith sees 1957 as the key date, with the passing of the Homicide Act and following the 1953 publication of Glanville Williams's *Criminal Law: The General Part* (London: Stevens & Sons, 1953). K. J. M. Smith, *Lawyers, Legislators and Theorists: Developments in English Criminal Jurisprudence, 1800–1957* (Oxford: Clarendon Press, 1998). It is arguable that the Criminal Justice Act of 1967 was more significant.

9. See, e.g., R. A. Duff, *Trials and Punishment* (Cambridge: Cambridge Univ. Press, 1985); Markus D. Dubber, *Victims in the War on Crime* (New York: New York Univ. Press, 2002).

10. For an interesting theoretical discussion of the "fair trial" in historical perspective, see Mireille Hildebrandt, "Trial and 'Fair Trial': From Peer to Subject to Citizen," in *The Trial on Trial*, vol. 2, *Judgment and Calling to Account*, R. A. Duff et al., eds. (Oxford: Hart Publishing, 2006, pp. 15–36).

11. See Lindsay Farmer, *Criminal Law, Tradition and Legal Order: Crime and the Genius of Scots Law, 1747 to the Present* (Cambridge: Cambridge Univ. Press, 1997), chap. 5, on homicide and the criminal law.

12. Jonathan H. Grossman, *The Art of Alibi: English Law Courts and the Novel* (Baltimore: Johns Hopkins Univ. Press, 2002), p. 7; Franco Moretti, *Signs Taken for Wonders: Essay in the Sociology of Literary Forms* (London: Verso, 1983), p. 138.

13. Michel Foucault, *Discipline and Punish: The Birth of the Prison*, part 1 (London: Penguin, 1977); V. A. C. Gatrell, *The Hanging Tree: Execution and the English People, 1776–1868* (Oxford: Oxford Univ. Press, 1994); J. M. Beattie, *Crime and the Courts, 1660–1800* (Princeton, N.J.: Princeton Univ. Press, 1986).

14. On the image of the lottery and the reform movement, see David J. A. Cairns, *Advocacy and the Making of the Adversarial Criminal Trial, 1800–1865* (Oxford: Oxford Univ. Press, 1998).

15. Randall McGowen, "The Image of Justice and Reform of the Criminal Law in Early Nineteenth-Century England," *Buffalo Law Review* 32 (1983): 89–125.

16. See also Katherine Fischer Taylor, *In the Theater of Criminal Justice* (Princeton, N.J.: Princeton Univ. Press, 1993), p. 22. In nineteenth-century France there was a rebuilding of courthouses, principally the Palais de Justice in Paris, to present the trial as spectacle or theatre, "reviving iconicity when its traditional subject, the ruler, had been displaced by a diffuse new subject, the public" (p. xxi).

17. Foucault, *Discipline and Punish*, p. 9. He goes on to argue that the criminal trial develops a new focus on the accused person, looking behind their acts to the pathologies of their character. While this might be true of French criminal procedure, it is clearly not the case in the English adversarial trial, where a consequence of the reform of the criminal law was the silencing of the accused. See my later discussion. For an account that develops Foucault's argument in relation to French criminal procedure, see Taylor, *In the Theater of Criminal Justice*, "Introduction."

18. See Taylor, ibid., p. 13, also comparing it to a Protestant meeting house and noting that the English courts limited public access and interest through the charging of an admission fee.

19. See, e.g., R. A. Duff, *Trials and Punishments*, chap. 4. Cf. Doreen J. McBarnet, *Conviction: Law, the State and the Construction of Justice* (London: Macmillan, 1981), on the ideology of triviality. See also McGowen, "Image of Justice and Reform."

20. See David Garland, *Punishment and Modern Society: A Study in Social Theory* (Chicago: Univ. of Chicago Press, 1990), pp. 70ff.; H. Garfinkel, "Conditions of Successful Degradation Ceremonies," *American Journal of Sociology* 61 (1956): 420–424. This raises two further important points. First, that in the modern system different courts have different rituals and thus a different relation to the overall system (see, e.g., Pat Carlen, *Magistrates' Justice* [London: M. Robertson, 1976]). Second, that there is an important question of how the ritual is structured. It is not enough merely to invoke the social importance of ritual.

21. Grossman, *Art of Alibi*; Lisa Rodensky, *The Crime in Mind: Criminal Responsibility and the Victorian Novel* (Oxford: Oxford Univ. Press, 2003); John B. Bender, *Imagining the Penitentiary: Fiction and the Architecture of Mind in Eighteenth-Century England* (Chicago: Univ. of Chicago Press, 1987).

22. For contemporary analyses along these lines see, e.g., W. Lance Bennet and

Martha Feldman, *Reconstructing Reality in the Courtroom. Justice and Judgment in American Culture* (New Brunswick, N.J.: Rutgers Univ. Press, 1981); Bernard Jackson, *Law, Fact and Narrative Coherence* (Liverpool: Deborah Charles Publications, 1988).

23. See Carolyn Conley, *The Unwritten Law: Criminal Justice in Victorian Kent* (Oxford: Oxford Univ. Press, 1991); Martha Merril Umphrey, "The Dialogics of Legal Meaning: Spectacular Trials, the Unwritten Law, and Narratives of Criminal Responsibility," *Law and Society Review* 33 (1999): 393; Martin Wiener, "Judges v. Jurors: Courtroom Tensions in Murder Trials and the Law of Criminal Responsibility in Nineteenth Century England," *Law and History Review* 17 (1999): 393.

24. See Clare Graham, *Ordering Law: The Architectural and Social History of the English Law Court to 1914* (Aldershot: Ashgate, 2003); Taylor, *In the Theater of Criminal Justice*.

25. See John Langbein, *The Origins of the Adversary Criminal Trial* (Oxford: Oxford Univ. Press, 2003); Allyson N. May, *The Bar and the Old Bailey, 1750–1850* (Chapel Hill: Univ. of North Carolina Press, 2003); Cairns, *Advocacy*.

26. Langbein, *Origins of the Adversary Criminal Trial*.

27. Eigen argues that a latent effect of the reforms of the penal code in the 1830s was the creation of such a space. See Joel Peter Eigen, *Unconscious Crime: Mental Absence and Criminal Responsibility in Victorian London* (Baltimore: Johns Hopkins Univ. Press, 2003), pp. 158–160.

28. On the reconstructive trial generally, see Michel Foucault, "Truth and Juridical Forms," *Essential Works*, vol. 3., *Power*, James Faubion, ed. (New York: New Press, 2000).

29. F. Young, ed., *Trial of Hawley Harvey Crippen* (Edinburgh: William Hodge, 1919).

30. George Orwell, "The Decline of the English Murder," *The Decline of the English Murder and other Essays* (Harmondsworth, UK: Penguin, 1965).

31. D. J. Bentley, *English Criminal Justice in the Nineteenth Century* (London: Hambledon, 1998), pp. 63–64, 275–277. Once enclosed, a jury was prohibited fire, food, or drink, a rule that was not abolished until the Juries Act of 1870.

32. See R. M. Jackson, "The Incidence of Jury Trial during the Past Century," *Modern Law Review* 1 (1937): 132. On the rise of plea bargaining, see George Fisher, *Plea Bargaining's Triumph: A History of Plea Bargaining in America* (Stanford, Calif.: Stanford Univ. Press, 2003); Michael McConville and Chester Mirsky, *Jury Trials and Plea Bargaining: A True History* (Oxford: Hart Publishing, 2005).

33. It was, of course, increasingly necessary to prove that the tested samples were those that had been removed from the crime scene.

34. On the movement for reform, see D. Bentley, *English Criminal Justice in the Nineteenth Century* (London: Hambledon, 1998), chaps. 15–18.

35. Though this might be a tactical decision and change with the type of case. However, even if most murder cases would begin with the body and evidence of the cause of death before connecting the accused with the death and showing evidence of intent, this still mirrors the detective process.

36. And the prosecuting counsel was instructed by the director of Public Prosecutions, a post created by the Prosecution of Offences Act of 1879.

37. Chief Inspector Dew searched the house and noticed the presence of loose bricks in the cellar floor, *Trial*, pp. 40 and xxxi. On police and detection see Claire Valier, "True Crime Stories: Scientific Methods of Criminal Investigation, Criminology and Historiography," *British Journal of Criminology* 38 (1998): 88–105.

38. On the rise of expert testimony generally, see Stephan Landsmann, "One Hundred Years of Rectitude: Medical Witnesses at the Old Bailey, 1717–1817," *Law and History Review* 16 (1998): 445–94; Carol Jones, *Expert Witnesses: Science, Medicine and the Practice of Law* (Oxford: Clarendon, 1994); Mark Essig, "Poison Murder and Expert Testimony: Doubting the Physician in Late Nineteenth-Century America," *Yale Journal of Law and the Humanities* 14 (2002) 177–210.

39. See J. D. Havard, *The Detection of Secret Homicide* (London: Macmillan, 1960), chaps. 1–4; Ian A. Burney, *Bodies of Evidence. Medicine and the Politics of the English Inquest, 1830–1926* (Baltimore: Johns Hopkins Univ. Press, 2000).

40. This took place only because of the pressures of relatives of the accused who wished to dispel suspicion, and it was only subsequently followed by a Coroner's Inquest. The accused made several attempts to prevent or delay the post-mortem. See J. F. Stephen, *A History of the Criminal Law of England*, vol. 3 (London: Macmillan, 1883), pp. 371–388.

41. 6 & 7 Wm. IV c. 89 s. 1. An act requiring the registration of births and deaths was passed in the same year, showing the public health concerns that motivated both pieces of legislation.

42. See Jones, *Expert Witnesses*, chap. 5.

43. Ibid., p. 88. On Spilsbury, see Douglas Browne and E. V. Tullett, *Bernard Spilsbury: His Life and Cases* (London: Harrap, 1951).

44. Stephen, *History*, vol. 3, pp. 381–387; *Trial of Mary Blandy* (Edinburgh: W. Hodge, 1914), pp. 80–88, 101–104.

45. Stephen, *History*, vol. 3, 385–386; Havard, *Detection*, p. 8; [S. M. Phillipps], *The Theory of Presumptive Proof; or, An inquiry into the nature of circumstantial evidence including an examination of the evidence on the trial of Captain Donnellan* (London: W. Clarke, 1815).

46. *Trial of Mary Blandy*, p. 103.

47. *R. v. Wright* (1821) Russ & Ry. 456; 168 E.R. 895.

48. *Trial*, p. 143.

49. The most famous was probably Edward Marshall Hall, but other celebrated criminal counsel included Richard Muir (counsel in this case), Edward Carson, and F. E. Smith.

50. See Lindsay Farmer, "Notable Trials and the Criminal Law," in *Droit et Société*, Philippe Chassaigne and Jean-Philippe Genet, eds. (Paris: Presses de la Sorbonne, 2003), p. 149–170.

51. For recent surveys, see T. P. Gallanis, "The Rise of Modern Evidence Law," *Iowa Law Review* 84 (1999): 499–560; Langbein, *Origins of the Adversary Criminal Trial*, chap. 4; C. J. W. Allen, *The Law of Evidence in Victorian England* (Cambridge: Cambridge Univ. Press, 1997).

52. To date these debates have been of greater interest to literary and cultural historians than lawyers. See Alexander Welsh, *Strong Representations: Narrative and Circum-*

stantial Evidence in England (Baltimore: Johns Hopkins Univ. Press, 1992); Jan-Melissa Schramm, *Testimony and Advocacy in Victorian Law, Literature and Theology* (Cambridge: Cambridge Univ. Press, 2000).

53. Barbara J. Shapiro, *"Beyond Reasonable Doubt" and "Probable Cause": Historical Perspectives on the Anglo-American Law of Evidence* (Berkeley: Univ. of California Press, 1991), chap. 4, documents the acceptance of circumstantial evidence, which could not lie, in preference to the potentially false testimony of a single witness. Welsh, *Strong Representations*, p. 30, suggests that in the eighteenth century circumstantial evidence was a "prosecutorial property" because it allowed prosecutors to evade earlier restrictions on forms of proof for serious crimes.

54. See Phillipps, *Theory of Presumptive Proof*; William Wills, *An Essay on the Rationale of Circumstantial Evidence, Illustrated by Numerous Cases* (London: Longman, 1838); W. M. Best, *A Treatise on Presumptions of Law and Fact with the Theory and Rules of Presumptive or Circumstantial Proof in Criminal Cases* (London: S. Sweet, 1844). There are also treatments of the issue in standard works such as Thomas Starkie, *A Practical Treatise of the Law of Evidence and Digest of Proofs in Civil and Criminal Proceedings* (London: J & WT Clarke, 1824).

55. Best, *Treatise*, p. 248. That this was a matter of membership of a moral community also led to the conclusion that Englishmen abroad, and specifically in India, should not be tried by those who could not understand his habits of mind or mode of conduct.

56. See esp., Joel Peter Eigen, "Sense and Sensibility: Fateful Splitting in the Victorian Insanity Trial," in R. A. Melikan, ed., *The Trial in History*, vol. 2, *Domestic and International Tribunals, 1700–2000* (Manchester, UK: Manchester Univ. Press, 2003).

57. Hans Gross, *Criminal Psychology: A Manual for Judges, Practitioners and Students* (Boston: Little, Brown, 1911), esp. part 1, title A, topic 3. See also Hugo Münsterberg, *On the Witness Stand: Essays on Psychology and Crime* (New York: Doubleday, Page, 1909). George Frederick Arnold, in *Psychology Applied to Legal Evidence and other Constructions of Law*, 2d ed. (Calcutta: Thacker, Spink, 1913), notes difficulties of applying English law and presumptions to India due to differences of race.

58. See, e.g., the law on the admissibility of dying declarations, discussed in Bentley, *English Criminal Justice*, pp. 214–219. On the earlier justifications for the exception see Malcolm Gaskill, *Crime and Mentalities in Early Modern England* (Cambridge: Cambridge Univ. Press, 2000), chaps. 6 and 7.

59. E.g., Langbein, *Origins*, p. 236, argues that the basis of the hearsay rule shifts from a concern with the best evidence to being a means of controlling the fact-adducing process at trial. See also Gallanis, "Rise of Modern Evidence Law," pp. 536–537. This is also connected with the declining importance of the oath and the use of perjury prosecutions. See the chapter by Schneider in this volume.

60. Allen, *Law of Evidence*, chap. 5, esp. at p. 184. For a contrary view see S. E. Farrar, "Myths and Legends: An Examination of the Historical Role of the Accused in Traditional Legal Scholarship; a Look at the Nineteenth Century," *Oxford Journal of Legal Studies* 21 (2001): 331–353.

61. 6 & 7 Vict. c. 85. See also Cairns, *Advocacy*, pp. 77–82. The 1885 act was aimed principally at preventing blackmail in prosecutions for sodomy.

62. For a discussion of the various ways the accused might put his or her side of the story prior to 1898, see Bentley, *English Criminal Justice*, chap. 15.

63. Bentley, *English Criminal Justice*, p. 204.

64. H. Fletcher Moulton, "Circumstantial Evidence," in W. Teignmouth Shore, *Crime and Its Detection*, vol. 1 (London: Gresham, 1931), p. 151. He suggests that this is the case even if the accused declined to give evidence, as this would create suspicions in the minds of the jurors. See Stephen, *History*, p. 383, noting how Donnellan declined to address issues raised by the prosecution in his statement to the court.

65. The central problem in the evaluation of evidence is the burden of proof, and the modern burden of proof was not established until 1935. However, I do not propose to discuss this here. See Rupert Cross, *The Golden Thread of the English Criminal Law: The Burden of Proof* (New York: Cambridge Univ. Press); Alex Stein, "From Blackstone to Woolmington: On the Development of a Legal Doctrine," *Journal of Legal History* 14 (1993): 14; Shapiro, *"Beyond Reasonable Doubt."*

66. *Trial*, p. 9. This issue has been addressed in an important book by Lisa Rodensky, *The Crime in Mind: Criminal Responsibility and the Victorian Novel* (New York: Oxford Univ. Press, 2003). She argues that the Victorian novel experimented to an unprecedented degree with the representation of the interior world of individuals and that this had a substantial influence on legal understandings of interiority. However, she also argues that this exposes the epistemological limits of the law, in that the trial cannot reconstruct the thoughts of the accused person in the same way as the novelist but must rely on inference and circumstantial evidence.

67. See Cairns, *Advocacy*; Bentley, *English Criminal Justice*, chap. 24.

68. *Davidson v. Stanley*, 2 M & G at 727, 133 *E.R.* at 939. Stephen, *General View*, p. 169, was of the opinion that the judge should not conceal his opinion from the jury. In the case of Florence Maybrick (1889), his charge to the jury, over two days, was widely regarded as having swayed them toward conviction.

69. *Trial*, pp. 163–164. Though on a reading of his direction his view is quite clear.

70. See Martin J. Wiener, *Men of Blood: Violence, Manliness and Criminal Justice in Victorian England* (Cambridge: Cambridge Univ. Press, 2004), pp. 242–255.

71. Kenny, *Outlines*, pp. 132–140.

72. Tobin, closing speech, *Trial*, pp. 148–149.

73. Muir, opening speech, pp. 7–8, closing speech, p. 155; see also pp. xxii and xxviii.

74. Turner, "The Mental Element"; see also Stephen, *General View*, p. 69.

75. See Wiener, "Judges v. Jurors."

76. On sodomy trials, see H. Cocks, "Trials of Character: The Use of Character Evidence in Victorian Sodomy Trials," in *The Trial in History*, vol. 2, *Domestic and International Tribunals, 1700–2000*, R. A. Melikan, ed. (Manchester, UK: Manchester Univ. Press, 2003); on rape trials, see Conley, *Unwritten Law*.

77. See, generally, Bentley, *English Criminal Justice*, p. 238.

78. *R. v. Cole* (1810) in Bentley, *Select Cases from the Twelve Judges: Notebooks* (London: John Rees, 1997).

79. *Trial*, p. 12.

80. Possibly because of adverse press coverage before the trial. See Tobin, opening speech, *Trial*, p. 79; see also Emily Jackson's testimony, p. 26, Marion Curnow's testimony, p. 28, William Long's testimony, p. 31, and Adeline Harrison's testimony, p. 77.

81. See Muir, closing speech, p. 154.

82. *Trial*, pp. 103, 105–106, summarized at pp. 154–156. "But the most amazing feature of the trial was the absolute coolness and imperturbability of Crippen in the long and terrible cross-examination." *Trial*, p. xxxii. It is also included in a volume titled *Notable Cross-Examinations*, Edward Wilfred Fordham, ed. (London: Constable, 1951).

83. *Trial*, p. 165.

84. James Oldham, "Truth-Telling in the Eighteenth Century English Courtroom," *Law and History Review* 12 (1994): 95, 100–101. He identifies Evans's appendix to his translation of Pothier on Obligations (1806) as the best pre-Bentham discussion of the issue. The question is not new, but it had hitherto been considered that guilt would straightforwardly manifest itself in physical symptoms. See, e.g., Gaskill, *Crime and Mentalities*, chap. 6, citing Michael Dalton, *The Countrey Justice* (London: A. Islip for the Societe of Stationers, 1618), p. 226.

85. *Strong Representations*, chap. 1, esp. at pp. 39–40, discussing Bentham and Burke.

86. The issue is considered from a theoretical perspective in Peter Brooks, *Troubling Confessions: Speaking Guilt in Law and Literature* (Chicago: Univ. of Chicago Press, 2000).

87. *Trial*, e.g., pp. 105–106, 112–115.

88. *Trial*, p. 155.

89. Ibid., pp. 165, 173.

90. Carlo Ginzburg sees this as the emergence of a new epistemological model. See "Clues: Roots of an Evidential Paradigm," in *Clues, Myths and the Historical Method*, John and Anne C. Tedeschi, trans. (Baltimore: Johns Hopkins Univ. Press, 1989), pp. 96–125.

91. "[I]n each case, infinitesimal traces permit the comprehension of a deeper, otherwise unattainable reality," ibid., p. 101.

92. Though this does not mean that people avoided liability, as the expansion of the crime of manslaughter took up the slack. See Wiener, *Men of Blood*, chap. 7; Farmer, *Criminal Law*, chap. 5. It is also important to note that a concern with preventing wrongful convictions could go hand in hand with a desire to facilitate prosecution, as was recognized in the debates leading to the 1898 act.

93. Cf. Bender, *Imagining the Penitentiary*, p. 221, on Adam Smith and the reasonable man as an interior personification of juridical presence. Smith's metaphor is theatrical, but the mode of representation is entirely mental. Bender accounts for an emergent order based on guilt rather than shame and marked by the introjection of impersonal norms as character.

94. The term is taken from Mari Matsuda, *The Memory of the Modern* (New York: Oxford Univ. Press), p. 103.

THREE

"An Inducement to Morbid Minds"

Politics and Madness in the Victorian Courtroom

JOEL PETER EIGEN

Sometime after taking tea with her roommate Charlotte Whale and retiring for the night, Sarah Proctor turned around in bed, lifted a massive water jug out of its basin, and crashed it down on her friend's skull with such violence that, according to witnesses who arrived at the scene, "some of the brain was protruding." Although animated by a horrifically gruesome killing, Proctor's eventual prosecution contained so many standard features of a Victorian insanity defense that one could almost be forgiven for thinking the trial patently ordinary. Hardly an element of by-now conventional medical and lay testimony was missing: delusion, epilepsy, unconsciousness, and violence undertaken "without any reason" were each mentioned in court. A physician testified, "It is a feature of epilepsy that the person may have a sudden attack, and will then do most extraordinary things unconsciously, and may commit any crime that would occur to them"; another witness left the distinct impression that even so grotesque an assault on a friend was not unsurprising for someone with a delusion that there were persons "who wanted to do her an injury."[1] To complete the expected division of courtroom labor, there was also a prison surgeon on hand to reinforce the medical testimony that this had indeed been a sudden attack—in effect, a crime committed "unconsciously." As it turned out, the only feature Sarah Proctor did not share with hundreds of allegedly insane offenders tried earlier in the century at London's Old Bailey was her verdict: "Guilty of the act, but insane at the time."

At first glance, the jury's unusually worded finding seems only a nominal departure from the English court's traditional special verdict of not guilty on the grounds of insanity. The consequence of both verdicts was the same: indeterminate detention. Unlike insanity acquittals before 1800—when defendants were simply released from custody—nineteenth-century verdicts grounded on mental derangement carried automatic commitment to a prison, and, in time, an asylum, effectively incarcerating the defendant "at the pleasure of the Sovereign." If the end result remained identical, one wonders why Parliament went to the trouble of enacting the Trial of Lunatics Act in 1883, altering the wording but not the effect of the special verdict. What difference did it make if Sarah Proctor were found guilty but insane at the time, rather than not guilty on the grounds of insanity?

As it turns out, the exact wording of her verdict made little practical difference to the defendant but a great deal of difference to contemporary attempts to chronicle the law's response to the expanding medical specialization in mental derangement. While the effort to capture the common law's changing disposition to courtroom claims of aberrant mental states recognizes the dramatic moments afforded by unexpected verdicts and anomalous dispositions, today's historian of the jurisprudence of insanity would do well to exercise a healthy self-restraint in proclaiming the *ruling* precedent, the most *influential* type of witness, the most *effective* defense strategy. One has but to consider the lore that surrounds the most famous of Victorian insanity defendants, Daniel McNaughtan. Although every newly minted attorney in England and the United States since 1843 has been able to quote the McNaughtan Rules and confidently assert their defining role in trials of the mentally deranged, the criteria that were supposed to inform all future jury deliberations were rarely if ever invoked by name or in substance in subsequent courtroom testimony and instructions to the jury.[2] Their totemic status in legal education notwithstanding, the McNaughtan Rules rarely played a prescriptive role in nineteenth-century insanity trials. To appreciate the influence of any particular legal case or judicial pronouncement, insanity trials must be examined in the aggregate, allowing the historian to view at a distance the twists and turns of defense and prosecutorial strategy, the calling of specialist witnesses, and the striking of a judicial posture.

Although the trials of McNaughtan and several other noteworthy insanity defendants have been thoroughly reported and analyzed, today's students of the court are fortunate to have available narrative accounts of the universe of criminal trials, heard at London's central criminal court, the Old Bailey, from the mid-seventeenth to the early twentieth centuries. Enterprising publishers in this period realized the morbid fascination that criminal proceedings enjoyed among the London populace and thus dispatched shorthand writers to record courtroom testimony verbatim, transcribe it, and sell the resulting narratives on the street the next day. Known as the *Old Bailey Sessions Papers* (*OBSP*; also known as *Proceedings of the Old Bailey*), these narratives provide daily and often detailed account of trial testimony, occasional instructions to the jury, and, in time, "highlights of legal points and practice," particularly innovative rulings regarding verdicts or significant departure in trial procedure that the editors chose to underscore.³ For the purposes of this chapter, the years 1760 to 1900 were surveyed, producing over 700 trials at which the mental state of the accused was put forward for the jury to consider in its determination of guilt.⁴

Considered against the backdrop of this universe of cases, the wording of Sarah Proctor's verdict represents not merely the latest in a series of hundreds of insanity trials heard throughout the nineteenth century but an opportunity to glimpse a change in jurisprudence relative to the crimes of allegedly mad defendants. These changes in legal thinking surfaced in response to the expanding claims made by medical witnesses to discern the nature of madness and were often triggered by a series of assassination attempts that reached as high as the throne. Current scholarly attempts to chart the emergence of forensic psychiatry in early modern England have focused on the rise of asylum superintendence in general and mad-doctors in court in particular. Fortunately, we have long since progressed beyond a time when medical men engaged in the lunacy trade were deified or demonized, showered with praise for their pioneering professionalism or cynically dismissed as market-hungry entrepreneurs. Instead, one has come to appreciate the promise of courtroom testimony to examine wider cultural assumptions about the mind's infirmities, their supposed effect on self-control, and the legal significance of such alterations for the central question of criminal responsibility.

While securing a professional niche in the courtroom was doubtless an appetizing prospect for some medical men, it is nonetheless true that the early forensic psychiatrist was not the only courtroom actor with a budding professional interest in the mad business. Defense lawyers were no less curious about the shifts in lay beliefs regarding mental derangement, since these were the community attitudes jurors were most likely to import into the courtroom. And it was the fit between cultural attitudes and the diagnosis rendered by the medical practitioner that was of most concern to both the nineteenth-century defense lawyer and today's historian of law and medicine.⁵

It was also of interest, apparently, to Parliament. Since 1760, medical men had been appearing at the Old Bailey to deliver their opinions on the defendant's mind and—occasionally—his brain. Their task had been to report the presence of head injuries, fevers, and organic disturbances in general and to aver their likely psychological consequences for the defendant's mind. In his testimony, the medical man described himself as guided by external things as the "indices of things unseen." The source of these external assaults expanded in time from physical injuries and fevers to states of social and emotional upheaval. And the mental processes intruded on expanded to implicate the law's central concepts of the will: intention and the exercise of choice. Regardless of the changing substance of a medical witness's testimony, the imagery he employed increasingly pointed in one direction: the defendant's doubtful retention of human agency. If self-control were lost, if the defendant were indeed a "mere instrument in the hands of Providence" (curiously, the words of an eighteenth-century judge, not a Victorian alienist), no criminal culpability could attend the action.[6]

This chapter investigates the political attempts to accommodate the changing scope of medical testimony and wider cultural notions about mental derangement by examining three concerted efforts to acknowledge and incorporate changing perceptions about madness in the prosecution and disposition of allegedly mad offenders. Accommodation, of course, is a variegated phenomenon; lawyers, judges, lawmakers, governmental figures—*and* Queen Victoria— were all drawn into the nation's debate regarding the proper moral and legal response to a defense of insanity. By examining the background for these three moments in a change in criminal justice policy, one can appreciate the courtroom's own evolving conception of popular psychology and the proper grounds for prosecuting and incarcerating the seriously deranged.

1. The Criminal Lunatics Act of 1800

The attempt to strike a balance between punishing the wrongdoer while still acknowledging the reality of serious mental disturbance dates to at least the thirteenth century, when Henry II's legal scribe, Henri de Bracton, articulated the mental element required to ascribe culpability to action as *voluntas nocendi*, "the will to harm." A concern with intention, or *mens rea*, was not of course unique to de Bracton: one finds the pronouncement "madmen have no will" as early as AD 533 in *Justinian's Digest*.[7] Still, de Bracton is the first English lawyer to explicitly incorporate the will into the common law, offering an early sign of the "thing unseen"—human agency—into criminal responsibility.

The earliest forms of recognized mental pathology did not involve the will per se but rather understanding and awareness. *Mens rea* from its earliest days in England spoke to the nature of intention: what it was the actor meant to do. More directly, it spoke to what the actor chose to do—specifically, his choice to do evil. Only someone who understood the nature of his act and the likely consequences of his behavior could be said to have acted purposefully, that is, with resolve—with intention. The wording of the first acquittal in 1505—"the felon was of unsound mind. Wherefore it was decided that he should go free"—is frustratingly ambiguous concerning the *reason* for the acquittal, although a century later, the common law's thinking can be grasped in a subsequent ruling: "no felony or murder can be committed without a felonious intent and purpose."[8] Also missing from the 1505 verdict is any clue to the meaning of "unsound mind" or indeed what sort of actions could be both lethal yet devoid of intent and purpose. Matthew Hale's eighteenth-century treatise, *The History of the Pleas of the Crown*, endeavored to distinguish "partial" from "total" insanity in an effort to specify the extent of derangement necessary to render an action nonvoluntary for purposes of law. Only a total want of memory, a total lack of understanding, met the requirements of law.[9] This standard of global derangement echoed back to de Bracton and continued through Lord Coke: madmen "cannot be guilty ordinarily of capital offenses . . . their actions are in effect the condition of brutes."[10]

The image of a nonthinking, nonreasoning brute makes its appearance in the Old Bailey in 1723 with the wild beast test; jurors were instructed to acquit if the defendant resembled "an infant, a brute, or a wild beast." Although hardly a nuanced, much less a practical, standard, the "test" was in fact the first criterion offered to juries to calibrate the extent of derangement sufficient to acquit. Several decades later, the standard of global derangement inherent in the wild beast imagery was affirmed in the 1760 trial of Earl Ferrers, when the solicitor general reminded the jury that "a partial degree of insanity, mixed with a partial degree of reason" would not suffice for an acquittal. If the defendant retained a "faculty to distinguish the nature of actions; to discern the differences between good and evil, then upon the fact of the offence proved, the judgment of the law must take place."[11]

The trial of Earl Ferrers not only affirmed that a total insanity alone would rise to the level of legal significance but served as the first case in which a mad-doctor testified to assert insanity's status as a medical disease. Unfortunately, the thrust of Ferrers's defense had been to characterize his distress as "occasional madness," a seriously flawed strategy in an age in which only a "total want of reason" would rise to a level sufficient to support an acquittal. Indeed, with such an exacting standard, it seems hard to understand why any medical witness was thought to be needed at all. How difficult could it have been to spot a "total want of reason"? Who could fail to recognize a wild beast? Little was "unseen" in eighteenth-century madness for a medical expert witness to be needed; as Roy Porter concluded, eighteenth-century madness was "spectacularly on view . . . doubts about nature's legibility troubled few."[12] Not surprisingly, when medical witnesses appeared in the later nineteenth century—and infrequently at that—their medical diction was anything but precise. The defendant was "delirious," "insensible," "out of his wits."[13] Madness throughout the 1700s was thus lodged in an all-encompassing, amorphous state of confusion. The capacity to choose to do evil was precluded by an inability to think clearly.

There was nothing particularly mysterious in such depictions of derangement and nothing apparently threatening about releasing persons so afflicted. The jury's decision to acquit on the grounds of insanity was treated as any other acquittal: the defendant was free to leave the court. Very occasionally one finds a notation indicating that a judge recommended release to family members to ensure their unfortunate relative's security, but this was an afterthought, not judicial policy. All this would change in 1800 with the passage of the Criminal Lunatics Act of 1800. It remains one of the ironic twists in the history of the common law that the agent who precipitated Parliament's reaction to innovative and legally threatening conceptions of mental derangement should have been a lawyer, not a man of medicine. And he was not merely a lawyer but the man who was to become England's solicitor general, Thomas Erskine.

Had he been tried under an eighteenth-century notion of insanity, James Hadfield would certainly have faced conviction. There was little likelihood that a carefully planned assassination attempt foiled only by poor marksmanship could have been attributed to confusion, delusion, or insensibility. And there was little chance that a jury would believe the defendant incapable of appreciating the consequences of the killing. Hadfield's plan all along had been to effect his own death by committing treason, thereby ushering in the Second Coming since his own death at the hands of the state would mimic Christ's execution. Since political assassination constituted high treason—with capital punishment the likely sanction—Hadfield was afforded legal representation, the very able and capable young attorney Thomas Erskine. Recognizing the yawning gap between total madness and his client's methodically executed crime, the attorney introduced delusion as the essence of madness and with deft precision tailored the notion of a circumscribed madness to Hadfield's bizarre and yet totally "logical" behavior. The maniacal pursuit of his object was not to be thought of as the partial insanity Hale had excluded from the common law: Hadfield was instead completely deranged when his mind was turned to the one subject of his religious delusion.[14]

Could anyone who peered at the world through a lens so profoundly refracted by delusion ever be said to have *chosen* his action? Does choice not rest on understanding, after all? As insanity moved from a consideration of the defendant's antics to an inquiry into the distortion of his ideas, retaining a capacity for intentional action took on new urgency in courtroom deliberation and Parliamentary debate as well. Hadfield would not turn out to be the first defendant at the Old Bailey to be acquitted for his crime, but his verdict would be unique. While the jury considered his guilt, Parliament hastily passed legislation to ensure that all future Hadfields would remain in the hands of the state. The Criminal Lunatics Act of 1800 contained among its provisions the special verdict of not guilty on the grounds of insanity. Heretofore only a simple "not guilty" had been recorded, resulting in the defendant's release. Instead, the 1800 act mandated the "acquitted defendant to be kept in strict custody, in such place and in such manner as the court shall see fit, until His Majesty's pleasure be known."[15]

It is difficult to know how much to ascribe Parliament's speedy action to the innovative testimony offered in Hadfield's state trial. Late eighteenth-century criminal justice had witnessed neither a sudden increase in the incidence of insanity pleas nor conspicuous success of the defense. Medical witnesses did not appear in court with escalating frequency; no more than one in ten insanity trials featured the testimony of a mad-doctor.[16] Further, there had been no discernible change in the content of the medical testimony or a shift in the images the lay witness brought into court. Parliament's action seems rather to reflect a combination of Hadfield's particular target and the innovative (and frankly threatening) nature of the defense strategy. This was the second attempt on the king's life, although the first was not particularly menacing. The shooting in the Drury Lane Theatre was much more frightening, and the prospect that the would-be assassin could receive a total acquittal and be summarily released was more alarming still. And yet English sovereigns and their prime ministers were never free from attack; one rather suspects that something more urgent had animated Parliament's action.

Erskine's conception of delusion introduced a qualitative departure in the common law approach to the level of mental derangement that had legal significance regarding culpability. A madness circumscribed to one subject, permitting the afflicted to go unnoticed and to pursue his object with cunning and single-minded purpose, could not have resembled less the eighteenth-century delirious rambler. It was one thing to acquit a defendant who was so far *gone* that no reasoning and thus no choice could attend his action; it was quite another to ask a jury to enter into the thought world of the distracted and to find a seemingly purposeful action to have been involuntary. If Hadfield was reacting to his delusive universe as the sane reacted to theirs, and if he *chose* to sacrifice himself for the betterment of humanity, how could such selfless action constitute a moral wrong? How could his delusory construction of events surrounding his crime permit the inference of a choice to do evil? Parliament could not preclude the introduction of delusion into the courtroom—nor label it as "partial insanity" and forbid its entrance according to Hale's historic treatise. It could, however, ensure that Hadfield's acquittal would not be followed by freedom.

Ultimately, Parliament's action was not prompted by a struggle between practitioners of medicine and law; it rather appears to us today as a political maneuver enacted to counter a courtroom innovation spearheaded by the defense attorney. Although he tried to limit delusion's influence in future criminal defenses by stipulating that a direct, logical connection had to exist between the delusion and the crime, Erskine's introduction of circumscribed derangement would have its own unseen consequences: an expanded role for the medical witness.

2. "Out of the Pale of Self Control"

Although it might seem a logical inference to consider Hadfield's crime as the *expected* product of a delusion concerning the instrumental role he would play in Christ's return, Erskine did not explicitly endow the defendant's delusion with a force all its own. In some respects the defendant's delusive imagination resembled the traditional category of delirium: confusion, misunderstanding, an inability to appreciate the *legal* wrongfulness of his action. Hadfield's calculated actions leading up to the shooting seemed to belie the notion of full-blown delirium, and yet the jury deemed him incapable of intentional choice. The effort to connect delusion to specious reasoning would soon be replaced by the testimony of a new generation of forensic psychiatric witnesses who would shift the focus of courtroom testimony from occluded intellect to a diseased will.

Changes in English medical testimony reported in the *OBSP* in the early decades of the nineteenth century followed the emergence of *médecine mentale*, a school of French clinical medicine whose founder, Philippe Pinel, introduced the diagnosis of *manie sans délire* to typify a "clear thinking" madness in which the afflicted were carried away by abstract fury. His circle of acolytes extended the possibility of an autonomous force propelling the sufferer into involuntary crime by employing newly coined species of insanity known as *monomanie homicide* and *monomanie instinctive*.[17] Although monomania found a more ready home in French courts than in their English counterparts, a review of nineteenth-century medical testimony at the Old Bailey yields the same image of an autonomous force: an insistent, propelling agent produced by a delusion, not the defendant's will. Continuing Erskine's effort to employ medical concepts to courtroom advantage, an attorney in 1812 followed up a medical witness's mention of delusion by asking (indeed, asserting), "The old delusion, acting on his mind, will lead him to do any act?" When the physician answered, "Undoubtedly it will," the attorney was quick to ask, "Not conscious that he is doing wrong?" to which the doctor answered, "Most likely."[18]

The imagery of a force propelling the defendant into crime was not confined to an insanity of intellectual derangement alone. In addition to the currency of Pinel's ideas among medical circles, the developing school of phrenology also revealed a shift in explanatory locus from the processes of human thought to the (blind) influence of instincts and propensities. Criminal acts committed by an otherwise kind and gentle person could thus be traced to pathological development of the brain's constituent organs of self-preservation, of sexual gratification, or of cunning. Phrenology provided a most efficient explanation for a seemingly inexplicable crime: stealing unwanted items, killing a beloved infant, shooting at the sovereign for no reason at all.[19] Commenting on the cerebral organs of a convicted murderer, George and Andrew Combe employed unambiguous language ascribing involuntary behavior to materialist pathology: "[his] mental faculties . . . acting like so many limbs of an automaton . . . by the diseased energy of his large [organ] or Destructiveness, he could not refrain from murder."[20]

He could not refrain from murder? At precisely whose (or what) instigation had the actor committed the killing? Whether the seat of the impelling force was lodged in a cerebral organ or free-floating "murderous rage"—"I couldn't help myself; it was stronger than me"—the focus of medical theorizing and courtroom testimony had begun to challenge directly the cornerstone of the law's mental criterion for ascribing criminal culpability: the will to harm. The issue was no longer whether confusion had effaced the accused's capacity to choose; the issue was whether the defendant was indeed the author of the crime.

For all the attention paid to the will in the various schools of nineteenth-century medical psychology, there is a certain ambiguity regarding the will's *essential* nature. To the phrenologist, the will was "powerless" when a specific organ of the brain, implicated in a particular crime, was diseased. To the followers of David Hartley's associationism, the will was no longer "restrained by judgment" when reason was dethroned.[21] To Common Sense philosophers, violent passions could "overcome" the will, propelling the morally insane into horrific acts that often invited their own self-destruction.[22] Who but a madman would commit a crime that ensured detection and his own punishment? Regarding the morally insane, the only "will to harm" one could speak of with confidence was their will to *self*-harm.

By far the most curious fate for the will resided in a form of insanity that depicted the will itself as diseased. Originally described in the medical writings of Pinel's student, Etienne-Jean Georget, the curious malady known as "lesion of the will" made its entrance into the English courtroom during the trial of Edward Oxford, indicted for shooting two pistols at Queen Victoria's carriage in 1840.²³ With no possible motive—indeed, with no reason at all for targeting the Queen—"I might as well shoot at her as anybody else"—Oxford stood trial at Old Bailey and was eventually acquitted.²⁴ Although it would be unwise to try to account for any one jury's decision by focusing exclusively on a particular medical term, it would be just as foolish to ignore the elective affinity between inexplicable criminality and autonomous cerebral function: "[A] propensity to commit acts without apparent or adequate motive under such circumstances is recognized as a particular species of insanity, called in medical jurisprudence, *lesion of the will*." The witness then quotes one of his asylum patients, "I have no unsatisfied wish . . . I have nothing at all to impel me to the act but a strong impulse" (emphasis in the original).²⁵ Such testimony rendered the defendant almost a bystander at his own crime. It was no longer the defendant but an autonomous will that aimed and fired the pistols. Not even a delusion had animated the crime; it was only an impulse.

The final trial in this series is the celebrated case of Daniel McNaughtan, whose acquittal for the murder of Edward Drummond—mistaken for the prime minister—brought together a blind, compelling force and the familiar forensic term *delusion*. Robert Peel's would-be assassin, however, did not suffer from the sort of circumscribed distraction that had ushered in nineteenth-century forensic medicine. McNaughtan's delusion had quite simply robbed him of human agency. Jurors learned that the unfortunate Scotsman's derangement had left him "out of the pale of self control"; his "moral liberty destroyed . . . the commission of the act [was] placed beyond his moral control." Such a delusion, medical witnesses informed the court, "carries a man quite away . . . nothing short of a physical impossibility would prevent him from performing an act which his delusion might impel him to do."²⁶

McNaughtan's eventual acquittal prompted the House of Lords to summon the trial judges and ask them a series of questions regarding the prosecution of defendants alleging insanity. Coming so soon after Oxford's assault on the Queen three years earlier, the latest assassination attempt was doubtless the precipitating factor in this unusual political initiative. These two acquittals and the dynamics that characterized both trials were not anomalous, however; in the years that separated McNaughtan (1843) from Hadfield (1800), the participation of medical witnesses in insanity trials had grown exponentially and the first forensic-psychiatry term had emerged. *Delusion*, the medical diagnosis most frequently invoked by early nineteenth-century mad-doctors in supporting an insanity plea, described a state of mental confusion that increasingly carried an ineluctable consequence: volitional chaos.²⁷ Mistaken beliefs, after all, are fueled by fear: of family conspiracy, of myriad physical ailments, of political prosecution. To believe oneself to be under mortal threat was to seek the removal of one's tormentor or to save one's child from a slow death in hell. Mothers who strangled their children to save them from the devil or husbands who killed wives they believed to be poisoning them presented the court with actions that seemed not merely ordained by mistaken beliefs but impelled by a force beyond the defendants' own choosing. Does anyone freely *choose* to kill her own child?

The trial judges' answers to the questions posed by the House of Lords became known as the McNaughtan Rules, whose most prominent feature was the restriction of insanity to cognitive—not volitional—impairment.[28] An inability to "know right from wrong," to "know the nature and consequences of the act," was articulated as the jury's legitimate criterion for assessing evidence brought in support of an insanity plea. The restrictive focus on cognitive processes conspicuously excluded mention of delusion's (inevitable) "spur to action," a theme increasingly prominent in medical testimony. Medical witnesses, of course, could not easily be muzzled, nor could lay witnesses be prevented from transporting all sorts of cultural ideas into the courtroom. Vigorous defense attorneys, for their part, could likewise not be precluded from introducing any and all conceptions of human functioning that might fit the evidence of a particular trial. But at the end of each trial, the jury would henceforth receive an instruction from the judge that framed insanity in strictly "knowing" terms. Just as the Criminal Lunatics Act of 1800 reveals the state's interest in retaining custody of acquitted insanity defendants, so too the McNaughtan Rules were initiated by the House of Lords to retain the common law's traditional focus on intention: the will to harm. Human behavior was to be considered a function of human choice, not the involuntary product of an autonomous delusion with a *mind* of its own.

Also similar to Parliament's intervention in criminal justice during the Hadfield decision, the reassertion of the common law's historic conception of culpability after *McNaughtan* was not in reaction to some fundamental rivalry between law and medicine, between an entrenched judiciary confronting ambitious asylum physicians cum expert witnesses. Medical men did not speak with one voice; the existence of an insanity confined to moral chaos, devoid of intellectual incoherence, was pointedly rejected by some members of the medical community—in court and in print. Further, courtroom testimony that framed aberrant behavior as the *inevitable* product of delusion was often prompted—when not actually extracted—by an enterprising defense attorney. It is nonetheless true that jurists as well as lawmakers were growing visibly alarmed at the introduction of hypothetical states of being that "carried the defendant quite away," destroying moral liberty, self-control, and, in the process, criminal accountability. It is difficult not to see the initiation of the McNaughtan Rules as a defensive move on the part of certain members of the judiciary and the House of Lords to constrain jurors from considering seriously such dubious and dangerous concepts as lesion of the will and moral insanity and to draw their attention squarely to the one question of "knowing." Did the defendant understand that she had a knife in her hand; did she understand the consequences of stabbing her child?

3. "The Brain Stands Still; and Muscular Action Goes On"

With a historical sensibility, one has come to realize that the effort to limit insanity's meaning to cognitive impairment was doomed to fail. Not only were medical witnesses by the mid-nineteenth century beginning to find a professionally self-conscious voice—"I answer as a physician," responded Dr. John Birt Davis during the 1840 trial of Edward Oxford when asked if he was appearing in court "as a physician, or from your experience as a Coroner, or as a Magistrate, or merely as a member of society"—but efforts to circumscribe the jurors' inquiry failed to appreciate the protean face of madness.[29] In one age, the melancholic captures public attention; in another, irresistible impulse predominates. And in the years following the law's attempts to draw a circle around madness as intellectual confusion, a further extension of mental distraction entered into the courtroom in the person of the sleepwalker, the automaton, and the epileptic. This was the Old Bailey's first acquaintance with a series of defendants who would present the enigmatic state of *unconsciousness*. The jury's response was a verdict no less puzzling.

In an age of salon hypnotists, music-hall mesmerizers, spiritualists, and animal magnetizers, it would strike us today as odd *not* to have encountered "absent," "missing," and machine-like defendants in the London courtroom.[30] As it happened, efforts by individual judges to hold the line against ever more ambitious medical testimony seems in retrospect a futile gesture once the jury was confronted with a type of defendant whose mental function revealed no delusion, no "lesion of the will," no moral insanity. Indeed, as one medical witness forcefully asserted, "the complaint is not characteristic of insanity in the slightest way, the patient may be perfectly sane and fall into that condition . . . any act which is begun before the fit may be continued . . . it is not looked upon by the profession as insanity in any form."[31] Dr. Edward Merrion, physician to London's Hospital for Disease of the Nervous System, was appearing at Old Bailey in the defense of Elizabeth Carr, on trial for the mortal wounding of her infant daughter. Carr had entered the kitchen with her daughter in one hand and a carving knife in the other. Intending to slice off a piece of bread and some butter, the mother had fallen into a fit of epileptic vertigo and, unconsciously, tragically, sliced off the daughter's hand instead. In time, the infant died of her wounds.

Like the sleepwalker, the automaton, and defendants described as "quite absent," Elizabeth Carr exemplified the features of a new cohort of unconscious defendants. Although the Old Bailey jurors had heard of unconscious states earlier in the nineteenth century, these states of "unknowing" behavior had been tied to falls, accidents, and head wounds of all kinds. In the second half of the nineteenth century, however, it was the somnambulist who served as the avatar of a new, global conception of nonvoluntary behavior, both in and out of court. Medical testimony regarding unconscious criminality reached its greatest expression in the trials of the particular form of epilepsy I have just mentioned. *Vertige épileptique*, first described in French medical texts fifteen years earlier, was introduced into the English courtroom in the 1876 trial of Elizabeth Carr.[32] After a convulsive fit, some epileptic patients had been known to "return," to engage in coherent conversations and perform dexterous feats, only to reveal by a second fit that this *vertige*—this period of "absence"—had been very much part of the attack. No memory of the period between the two fits remained, no ability to recall conversation or any activity undertaken. It was as if the described activity and communication had happened to someone else.

Existing medical reports of unconscious behavior often relied for support on culturally familiar accounts of soldiers marching while asleep or musicians continuing to perform while falling into a deep trance. Both in medical texts and in courtroom testimony one learned of decapitated centipedes whose trunks continued to move inexorably forward.[33] Evidence of such a continuity of action bolstered the courtroom narrative of how the unfortunate mother, for example, could have *intended* to cut off a piece of bread, only to mistake the infant's wrist for the loaf. "They are purely automatic acts," the physician informed the court, "the [defendant] is perfectly unconscious . . . she does not know it herself."[34] Although the physician forcefully rejected the idea that the defendant's mental state qualified as insanity "in any way," it would not have been unexpected for the jurors to return a finding of not guilty on the grounds of insanity. Throughout the nineteenth century, the *OBSP* reveal juries returning such verdicts, even when the defense attorney had not raised the issue of mental derangement. In the trial of Elizabeth Carr, however, the jury returned with a verdict that no one expected: "Not guilty on the grounds of unconsciousness."

The judge immediately announced his intention to write to the Home secretary to explain the anomalous verdict and also his decision to detain the prisoner, much as he would have elected to do had she been acquitted on the grounds of insanity. But he could not keep epileptic vertigo out of the courtroom in subsequent trials nor preclude future juries from finding defendants not guilty on the grounds of unconsciousness. Five months after this singular verdict was entered into the *OBSP* (and nominated by the volume's editor to be highlighted in the "Index of legal points and practice"), another defendant's odd and *fatal* behavior was attributed to epileptic vertigo. Describing the global nature of this automatic state, a physician informed the court that "the memory is a blank, the brain stands still, and muscular action goes on."[35] Although this defendant did not escape conviction, today's historian of law and medicine notes with interest that the judge instructed the jury to consider whether the defendant "labor[ed] under such an affliction of Providence that he was for the moment deprived of consciousness to such an extent that he was a mere automaton from an attack of epileptic vertigo."[36]

And his instructions were not unique. Two years after the jury acquitted Elizabeth Carr on the grounds of unconsciousness, a judge presiding in a case of a sleepwalker who bashed his son against the bedroom wall—believing him to be a wild beast attacking his son—advised a jury, "[Y]ou should return a verdict such as this . . . that he was in a state of unconsciousness of the act he was committing by reason of the condition of somnambulism, and that he was not responsible."[37] Clearly not all judges were viscerally opposed to a defense of "unconsciousness," but then not all members of the judiciary "leaned against" defendants alleging insanity either. There were, however, unmistakable signs of judicial disquiet at the prospect of acquitting and releasing defendants whose crimes were placed "beyond their control," powerless to intervene against a morbid propensity, finding themselves engaged in crimes that were not of their choosing. To articulate the courtroom's proper response to the specter of purportedly *involuntary* crime, Parliament would need to fashion a new response.

4. "An Inducement to Morbid Minds"

By the time Sarah Proctor came to trial for the willful killing of her roommate in the case that began this chapter, the Old Bailey had grown familiar with medical testimony regarding the mental and behavioral effects of epilepsy. The specter of sudden attacks, unconscious and extraordinary behavior, and an all-encompassing state of utter oblivion were the same images used to describe *and* account for the tragic actions of the mother and the bread knife ten years earlier in the same courtroom. Sarah Proctor's condition might have closely resembled the hapless mother's, but her verdict did not. Notably, she was not found not guilty at all: insanity was fundamental to the jury's finding but so was guilt. In the years following the Old Bailey's initial flirtation with acquittals on the grounds of unconsciousness, political forces were at work to reassert the common law's interests in questioning where derangement separated from blame.

It was a truism of criminology in the 1960s that political assassinations and insanity defenses went hand in hand: the best way to deflect attention from deeply felt political grievance was to redirect the public's attention away from the intended target and on to the alleged pathology of the would-be assassin. Persecution delusions or hallucinatory orders from the Evil One *must* have animated the attack, not the corruption or cruelty of the king or president. Decades later, this was true of the commentary surrounding the attempted assassinations of Ronald Reagan and Gerald Ford and the elaborate pathographies constructed to fit the life and motivation of John Hinckley and Squeaky Fromm, respectively. Seen against the backdrop of successive changes in thinking about insanity in the nineteenth century, such contemporary experience finds a certain historical resonance. It is certainly true that throughout the nineteenth century major shifts in the courtroom division of labor—seen most conspicuously in the rise of an advocacy defense bar, but also in the arrival of the mad-doctor in court—accompanied the introduction of states of mental functioning that implicated the will directly, positing a defendant more missing than malevolent. But it is also undeniable that all three efforts by Parliament to clarify the common law's position regarding insanity took place in the immediate aftermath of politically motivated attacks. The Criminal Lunatics Act of 1800 followed the attempt on the life of George III, the McNaughtan Rules were introduced following the effort to kill Robert Peel, and Queen Victoria was not about to sit still following a third attack on her life.

Unlike the two earlier assaults, in which the would-be assassins had failed to load the weapons with ammunition, the third attack on Queen Victoria (1882) featured a man with a fully armed pistol who fired directly at her. Wrestled to the ground by a strapping Etonian wielding only a trusty umbrella, Roderick Maclean eventually came to trial for treason and, like the Queen's earlier would-be assassins, was found not guilty on the grounds of insanity. Following this third acquittal, the Queen communicated her displeasure, taking issue, among other things, with the apparently conventional belief regarding the inability of the insane to constrain their actions. In a letter from Windsor, she wrote, "Punishment deters not only sane men but also eccentric men, whose supposed involuntary acts are really produced by a diseased brain capable of being acted upon by external influence." It was in fact the knowledge of a likely acquittal that "encourage[d] these men to commit desperate acts." The courts' reinstating the likelihood of a conviction, she believed, "will terrify them into a peaceful attitude."[38] The Queen's view of popular psychology found receptive minds in both Houses and eventually resulted in the Trial of Lunatics Act (1883), which changed the wording for insanity-based verdicts from an acquittal to a conviction.

As mentioned earlier, little practical significance in terms of the consequences of the verdict attended this change: after 1883, just as before, those found guilty but insane faced the same indeterminate detention at the pleasure of the sovereign. But this was a most singularly worded verdict, one that would appear to elide defective mental state with the capacity to exercise intentional choice. Since the thirteenth century, the common law had weighed the culpability of an act with the mental state required to choose the act. Accordingly, the severely deranged and the extremely young could allege that a state of mental functioning belied the possession of *mens rea*. There was no question that something tragic had occurred, something eminently regrettable—perhaps even fatal. But without the requisite resolve to commit a legal transgression that could rest only on a sufficient understanding of the nature and consequences of one's action, something *criminal* had not taken place. It would make as much sense to transform other special verdicts to read, "guilty, but self-defense," or "guilty, but *doli incapax*."

It would be well to remember, however, that the exact wording of the 1883 special verdict was "guilty of the act but insane at the time," not "guilty of the crime but insane at the time." The legislators apparently finessed the question of culpability without *mens rea* by finding alleged lunatics guilty of a (simple) physical act—which was only a question of mechanics. As in any affirmative defense, the *actus rea* is freely admitted; most defendants did not deny wielding the knife or throwing the child into the Thames. This separation of mental contemplation from physical execution was apparently palatable as jurisprudence to members of Parliament because *Hansard's Parliamentary Debates* reveals no unease regarding the centuries of English law that were being effectively effaced. From all appearances, the act seems to have sailed through with no opposition: "It had been thought better that this alteration of the law should be made, and there was no reason [voiced] against it."[39] The relief at the palace was duly noted in a letter from the Queen to Mr. Gladstone dated August 23, 1883. "The Queen is especially glad that this Act altering the Criminal Law respecting Lunatics has been passed, and in so quiet a way."[40]

Tempting as it might be to think that Queen Victoria and Mr. Gladstone had slipped something past Parliament, the reasoning behind the bill affords today's legal historian with a glimpse into the legislators' decision to correct the conventional belief that no risk attended the crime of the madman. Indeed, it had been the law's *removal* of the threat of punishment that had served, in Gladstone's opinion, as "an inducement . . . to morbid minds for the commission of crime by an apparent declaration of innocence in the teeth of the facts."[41] One therefore begins to sense a concerted effort on the part of lawmakers (and doubtless the sovereign) to employ the language and imagery of Victorian psychiatry to their own advantage. In their spirited defense of medicine's proper role in insanity trials four years earlier, noted authors J. C. Bucknill and Daniel Tuke had written, "The opinion of the physician is really required in difficult cases . . . the [symptoms] may be almost illegible to the inexperienced eye."[42] The skillful alienist, the authors contended, understood "the laws of the mind, which are as regular as any other natural laws."[43]

The physician's words were not prudently chosen. Medical witnesses during the trial of Edward Oxford, Queen Victoria's first would-be assassin, had used similar wording, the need to "compare particular cases, more likely to be looked to by medical men," to support a claim for their privileged status as expert witnesses. Following this third attack on her life, the Queen was not inclined to accord medicine exclusive jurisdiction to articulate the catalogue of external things influencing madness. When she wrote of "external" influences acting on the diseased brain, she deliberately expanded the universe of fears that might act on brain to include the fear of punishment.

In a concerted way, the Queen and Parliament attempted to reappropriate the "things unseen" in medical testimony—the agency of human will—and bring it back within the realm of traditional common law principles. If will could be discerned in conspicuous, behavioral acts, its absence should be just as apparent. The eighteenth-century wild beast could be spotted by anyone; the delirious were alarmingly public by virtue of their conversational chaos and physical histrionics. The essence of delusion, however, was its recondite character; only the skilled clinician knew to "protract the discourse [revealing that] the map of his mind will point out that the smallest rivulet flows into the great stream of his derangement."[44] But it was the eventual investing of delusion with an irresistible spur to action that brought medical testimony into direct conflict with legal notions of human agency. In effect, it was delusion that did the choosing, not the defendant; a lesion of the will that let loose a morbid propensity to kill, an epileptic state that rendered the afflicted unconscious as the vertiginously spinning automaton picked up the knife. Who could be found culpable when the defendant *inside* was missing?

Rather than challenge this conception of the mind directly, Parliament chose to proffer its own conception of derangement, grounded in the era's transcendent belief in the centrality of deterrence for inducing behavioral control. If medical writers and witnesses could allude to the role of "external influences as the indices of things unseen," the common law could add fear of punishment as its own influence on the "thing unseen": human choice. Medical psychology, after all, has neither a monopoly on the definition for social deviance nor on the methods one might employ to force conformity. Whether the specter of an eventual finding of guilt could be grasped by the mind of the delusional and operate in such a way as to lead the sufferer away from crime because of the opprobrium attached to a formal conviction was anybody's guess. But how delusions worked in the mind of the afflicted and how it was possible for the unconscious to pursue seemingly intentional acts was anybody's guess as well, although there were medical authorities in court to affirm the possibility, indeed, the reality of involuntary action.

Lawmakers by the end of the century decided to stake their own claim to what the common law was *for* by trying to wrest the jurisprudence of insanity away from the budding partnership of criminal defense law and claims to medical expertise. Moral and social philosophers earlier in the century had articulated the foundation of deterrence as the prevailing rationale for punishment. With the 1883 Trial of Lunatics Act, Parliament reaffirmed its commitment to this rationale, even in the face of and, perhaps, especially because of the conception of human agency that was issuing forth from the witness stand. This third attempt by Parliament to frame questions of accountability and derangement reminds today's historian of law and medicine that the forces that shaped the common law's evolving approach to insanity and related aberrant mental states was likely to involve a cast of characters beyond those engaged in the immediate courtroom battles. Among the "external factors influencing the things unseen" there was also the political world in which the increasingly powerful professions of law and medicine operated.

In retrospect, it seems that the only tangible impact that England's political class could claim was the first intervention: the enforced detention of insanity acquittals. By the time lawmakers tried to reassert their view of the common law—with the McNaughtan Rules and the 1883 Trial of Lunatics Act—the significant forces shaping the workings of criminal justice had passed to the emerging professions of adversarial defense bar and asylum medicine cum forensic psychiatry, demonstrating the limits of even the palace and Parliament to influence the practice of day-to-day courtroom law.

Notes

1. *Old Bailey Sessions Papers* (*OBSP*), 1887–1888, Case 556, Eighth session, 179.
2. Joel Peter Eigen, "Delusion's Odyssey: Charting the Course of Victorian Forensic Psychiatry," *International Journal of Law and Psychiatry* 27 (2004): 395–412.

3. For a discussion of the historical utility of the *OBSP*, see the two seminal articles by John H. Langbein, "The Criminal Trial before the Lawyers," *University of Chicago Law Review* 45 (1978): 263–316, and "Shaping the Eighteenth-Century Criminal Trial: A View from the Ryder Sources," *University of Chicago Law Review* 50 (1983): 1–136. The most recent appraisal of the *OBSP* as the most important source we are likely to have for reconstructing crime and justice in early modern England was made by Peter King, *Crime, Justice, and Discretion in England, 1740–1820* (Oxford: Oxford Univ. Press, 2000), p. 221.

4. The trials from 1760 to 1843 have been examined in detail in Joel Peter Eigen, *Witnessing Insanity, Madness and Mad-Doctors in the English Court* (New Haven, Conn.: Yale Univ. Press, 1995). Trials from 1843 to 1876 were the subject of a second volume by Eigen, *Unconscious Crime: Mental Absence and Criminal Responsibility in Victorian London* (Baltimore: Johns Hopkins Univ. Press, 2003).

5. The late emergence of the role of full-advocacy defense is the subject of David J. A. Cairns, *Advocacy and the Making of the Criminal Trial, 1800–1865* (Oxford: Clarendon Press, 1998). Further investigation of the emerging role of the defense attorney in England and the forging of standards of forensic proof can be found in Barbara J. Shapiro, "'To a Moral Certainty': Theories of Knowledge and Anglo-American Juries, 1600–1850," *Hastings Law Journal* 38 (1986): 153–193.

6. *OBSP*, 1784, Case 388, Fourth session, 546.

7. Nigel Walker, *Crime and Insanity in England*, vol. 1, *The Historical Perspective* (Edinburgh: Edinburgh Univ. Press, 1968), p. 27.

8. Ibid., pp. 26–31.

9. Matthew Hale, *The History of the Pleas of the Crown* (London: E. and R. Nutt and R. Gosling for F. Gyles, 1736), see esp. pp. 30–37.

10. For a discussion of the importance of human reason to de Bracton's construction of the insane as "brutis," see Anthony Platt and Bernard Diamond, "The Origins and Developments of the 'Wild Beast Concept' of Mental Illness and Its Relation to Theories of Criminal Responsibility," *Journal of the History of the Behavioral Sciences* 1 (1965): 360–365.

11. Quoted in Nigel Walker, *Crime and Insanity in England*, vol. 1, *The Historical Perspective* (Edinburgh: Edinburgh Univ. Press, 1968), p. 62.

12. Roy Porter, *Mind-Forg'd Manacles: A History of Madness in England from the Restoration to the Regency* (Cambridge, Mass.: Harvard Univ. Press, 1988), p. 35.

13. Eighteenth-century medical testimony is examined in Eigen, *Witnessing Insanity*, pp. 134–136.

14. The most comprehensive study of the Hadfield trial will be found in Richard Moran, "The Origin of Insanity as a Special Verdict: the Trial for Treason of James Hadfield (1800)," *Law and Society Review* 19 (1985): 487–519. An official report of the case, complete with Erskine's use of delusion in Hadfield's defense, can be found in 40 Geo. III, *State Trials* 27, 1316–1317.

15. *An Act for the Safe Custody of Insane Persons Charged with Offenses*, 40 Geo. III, c. 94.

16. Eigen, *Witnessing Insanity*, pp. 26–28.

17. Philippe Pinel, *A Treatise on Insanity*, D. D. Davis, trans. (Sheffield: W. Todd for Cadell and Davies, 1806). The various forms of monomania are discussed in J. E. D. Esquirol, *Mental Maladies: A Treatise on Insanity*, E. K. Hunt, trans. (Philadelphia: Lea & Blanchard, 1845). The most comprehensive treatment of the French school can be found in Jan Goldstein, *Console and Classify: The French Psychiatric Profession in the Nineteenth Century* (Cambridge: Cambridge Univ. Press, 1987).

18. *OBSP*, 1812, Case 527, Sixth session, 333.

19. A comprehensive survey of the influence of phrenology on early nineteenth-century English culture is offered in Roger Cooter, *The Cultural Meaning of Popular Science: Phrenology and the Organization of Consent in Nineteenth-Century Britain* (Cambridge: Cambridge Univ. Press, 1984). Cooter examines the influence of monomania to phrenology in "Phrenology and British Alienists, ca. 1825–45," in *Madhouses, Mad-Doctors, and Madmen: The Social History of Psychiatry in the Victorian Era*, Andrew Scull, ed. (Philadelphia: Univ. of Pennsylvania Press, 1981), pp. 58–104.

20. George Combe and Andrew Combe, trans., *On the Functions of the Cerebellum*, by Drs. Gall, Vimont, and Broussais (Edinburgh: Machlachlan & Stewart, 1838), pp. 166–167.

21. Thomas Arnold, *Observations on the Nature, Kinds, Causes and Prevention of Insanity* (London: Phillips, 1806). David Hartley's seminal text is *Observations on Man, His Frame, His Duty, and His Expectations* (London: S. Richardson, 1749). A useful contemporary meditation on delusion and associationism can be found in John Johnstone, *Medical Jurisprudence of Madness* (Birmingham: J. Belcher, 1800). The ambiguous nature of the will in the "cementing of ideas" can be found in James Mill, *Analysis of the Phenomena of the Human Mind* (London: Baldwin & Craddock, 1829).

22. James Cowles Prichard, apparently the originator of the moral insanity concept, describes a derangement of feelings in *A Treatise on Insanity and other Disorders Affecting the Mind* (London: Sherwood, Gilbert & Piper, 1835) and *On the Different Forms of Insanity in Relation to Jurisprudence, Designed for the Use of Persons Concerned in Legal Questions Regarding Unsoundness of Mind* (London: Hippolyte Ballière, 1842).

23. Etienne-Jean Georget, *De la folie: considérations sur cette maladie* (Paris: Crevot, 1820) and *Discussion médico-légale sur la folie; ou aliéanation mentale, suivie de l'examen du procès criminel d'Henriette Cornier et de plusieurs autres procès* (Paris: Migneret, 1826).

24. *OBSP*, 1840, Case 1877, Ninth Session, 506.

25. Ibid., p. 507.

26. *OBSP*, 1842–1843, Case 874, Fifth Session, 760–763.

27. The emergence of delusion as both the term of preference for early nineteenth-century medical witnesses and as the conceptual basis for testimony that separated them from lay witnesses is described in Joel Peter Eigen, "Delusion in the Courtroom: The Role of Partial Insanity in Early Forensic Testimony," *Medical History* 35 (1991): 25–49.

28. The five questions asked of the McNaughtan judges are given in *McNaughtan Case*, 10 Clark and Finnelly, 200, 203–214 (1843).

29. *OBSP*, 1840, Case 1877, Ninth session, 495. For a discussion of a series of cases that reveal dawning professional consciousness among mad-doctors in court, see Joel Peter Eigen, "I Answer as a Physician," in Michael Clark and Catherine Crawford, eds., *Legal Medicine in History* (Cambridge: Cambridge Univ. Press, 1994), pp. 167–199.

30. For a recent, comprehensive treatment of the age of mesmerism in England, see Alison Winter, *Mesmerized: Powers of Mind in Victorian Britain* (Chicago: Univ. of Chicago Press, 1998).

31. *OBSP*, 1875–1876, Case 413, Eleventh session, 496–497.

32. Among the many sources of nineteenth-century clinical medicine devoted to epilepsy, several examine the curious phenomenon of *vertige* and its application to unconsciousness. Among these are Jean-Pierre Falret, "De l'état mental des épileptiques," *Archives Générales de Médecine*, 16–18, 5th Series (Paris: Bechet, 1860–1861); Armand Trousseau, *Lectures on Clinical Medicine, Delivered at the Hôtel-Dieu, Paris*, P. Victor Bazire, trans. (London: New Sydenham Society, 1867); Esquirol, *Mental Maladies*.

33. The story of the centipede is retold by William B. Carpenter in *The Doctrine of Human Automatism: A Lecture Delivered before the Sunday Lecture Society, 7 March 1875* (London: Sunday Lecture Society, 1875), p. 14, and again invoked during the trial of Elizabeth Carr, *OBSP*, 1875–1876, Case 413, Eleventh session.

34. *OBSP*, 1875–1876, Case 413, Eleventh session, 496.

35. *OBSP*, 1876–1877, Case 246, Fourth session, 459. Memory appears to have been invoked here as a conceptual shorthand for the general capacity to perceive and reflect; it was actually only one of several functions of the mind popularized by the nineteenth-century school of faculty psychology. Insanity, for followers of this tradition, was a defect in the cognitive capacity of the mind, a disturbance in its innate, inductive faculties. These hypothesized powers of attention, comparison, imagination, *and* memory actively sorted, arranged, and stored the ideas that were the basis of knowledge. When the passions or the emotions disturbed the mind's capacity to compare ideas (and, consequently, to recognize a fantasy for what it was), insanity ensued. In the preceding quote, and in Matthew Hale's characterization of insanity as a "total want of memory" (cited earlier), the failure of memory stood for a breakdown of the mind's capacity to process ideas and to recognize what was transgressive about their character. Today, memory denotes a particular mental faculty; in earlier psychological depictions of the mind, its absence appears to represent an index of generalized delirium. A good introduction of the nineteenth-century view of faculty psychology and insanity can be found in John Conolly, *An Inquiry Concerning the Indications of Insanity With Suggestions for the Better Protection and Care of the Insane* (London: J. Taylor, 1830).

36. *Times of London*, Feb. 9, 1877, 5–6.

37. *HM Adv. v. Fraser* (1878), 4 Couper 78:70–78. For a report of the medical witness who testified in support of the defense of sleepwalking, see Dr. Yellowlees, "Homicide by a Somnambulist," *Journal of Mental Science* 24 (1878): 451–458.

38. Quoted in Walker, *Crime and Insanity*, p. 189.

39. T. C. Hansard and Great Britain Parliament, *Hansard's Parliamentary Debates*, vol. 283. Aug. 16, 1883 (London: 1883, p. 922).

40. Victoria, Queen of Great Britain, *The Letters of Queen Victoria: A Selection from Her Majesty's Correspondence and Journal Between the Years 1862–1885*, George Earle Buckle, ed. (London: Murray, 1928), p. 439.

41. Quoted in Walker, *Crime and Insanity*, p. 189.

42. J. C. Bucknill and D. H. Tuke, *A Manual of Psychological Medicine*, (London, J.&A. Churchill, 1879), p. 439.

43. Ibid, p. 402.

44. John Haslam, *Medical Jurisprudence as It Relates to Insanity, According to the Laws of England* (London: Hunter, 1817), p. 18.

FOUR

The Meaning of Killing

GUYORA BINDER

The modern lawyer thinks of homicide as a crime of result. To convict a suspect of homicide, the prosecution must prove she committed an act causing the death of another, accompanied by a culpable mental state. Because the modern lawyer is attuned to the many ways human decisions can contribute causally to a death, culpability seems the more important determinant of liability. The extent of the actor's awareness that she is imposing a risk of death determines which deaths are homicides and also determines the gravity of the homicide offense. Above a certain threshold, she is guilty of murder.

The law conceived homicide very differently in seventeenth- and eighteenth-century England, but the common law's deference to the authority of tradition has made it difficult to grasp the nature and extent of the transformation. In the treatise literature of the seventeenth and eighteenth centuries, murder was defined as unlawful killing with malice aforethought, express or implied.[1] This formulation seems familiar and intelligible to the modern lawyer. Killing seems to correspond to the modern offense element of causing death, and malice appears to be a somewhat opaque term for whatever culpable mental states were deemed sufficiently heinous to warrant murder liability. This is how English and American lawyers have been taught to read these terms since the late nineteenth century, when J. F. Stephen, Victorian England's leading criminal jurist, proposed a codification of homicide as a crime of result.

In his masterful history of English criminal law, Stephen concluded that the traditional term *killing* had always meant "causing death directly, distinctly, and not too remotely," whether by act or omission.[2] Stephen acknowledged that older law required that death be ascribable to some definite bodily injury but held that this requirement reflected the necessity of precision in pleading combined with a more primitive state of medical knowledge. Thus, he reasoned, the seventeenth century would have seen indictments for killing by witchcraft, if only courts had a clearer understanding of how sorcery produced death,[3] while modern medical knowledge would permit a court to convict a murderer who caused death by startling a coronary patient.[4]

Stephen summarized four centuries of development by analyzing *malice* into five alternative mental states: intent to kill, recklessness of a probability of death, intent to cause grievous bodily harm, the intent to commit any felony, and the intent to resist arrest or incarceration.[5] In his Criminal Code Commission Draft, Stephen absorbed the latter three mental states into the second mental state, reckless indifference.[6] Thus, Stephen interpreted malice as a variety of different expectations with regard to a resulting death.

Stephen's reformist aims gave him every reason to emphasize continuities between the traditional "malicious killing" formula and his modern conception of homicide as culpable causation. But his equation of killing and causation leaves us with a puzzle: if killing meant causing death by any means whatsoever, why did seventeenth- and eighteenth-century English law regard killing as inherently malicious? According to Blackstone, malice aforethought was entailed by the act of killing, unless the killer could demonstrate an excuse such as self-defense, provocation, insanity, mistake, or accident.[7] Since defendants had no right to counsel during this period,[8] this allocation of the burden of proof left them in dire straits once a killing had been proven. And this was more or less by design: the early modern felony trial was not a test of the prosecution's evidence but a test of the defendant's character, somewhat in the nature of an ordeal. Its dramatic purpose was to surprise the defendant with manifestly inculpatory facts that would provoke him to bare his soul. He would be forced to either explain his innocence or confess his guilt.[9] So Stephen's account compels us to wonder why the mere causation of death would have seemed so inculpatory. Why was this element, rather than malice, the crucial filter separating homicides from other deaths?

Stephen's own answer, that far fewer human causes of death were known to science in the seventeenth century, merely reframes the question. If science was a less efficacious and influential institution and had little to say about human responsibility for death, why presume that seventeenth-century Englishmen conceptualized killing in scientific terms, as a cause? Malcolm Gaskill concludes that "medical expertise did not play a significant role in English investigations until the early nineteenth century,"[10] while seventeenth-century coroners and magistrates were still determining charges on the basis of testimony about dreams, ghosts, and magical portents.[11]

George Fletcher has offered a more promising approach to this puzzle of the inculpatory significance of killing at common law. In *Rethinking Criminal Law*, Fletcher found three different "patterns" of liability in the history of Anglo-American criminal law, prioritizing acts, intentions, and harms, respectively. Fletcher presented homicide as the paradigmatic offense in the "pattern of harmful consequences." He noted that in the early history of the common law even killers excused on grounds of accident or self-defense were subject to forfeiture of their goods. He reasoned that causing death, even blamelessly, "desecrated" the sanctity of life, thereby "tainting" the perpetrator and imposing an obligation to expiate the sin.

Fletcher's method had the merit of seeking the cultural meanings behind the doctrinal forms of liability. Yet his search for continuities between past and current law induced him, like Stephen before him, to equate killing with the modern concept of *causing*. This drew him into difficulties that he gamely acknowledged. Fletcher conceded that far more human actions have fatal consequences than have ever attracted the attention of the criminal law.[12] Further criteria are needed to determine which human contributions to death will be "tainted" as sacrilegious. Fletcher noted that the modern solution to the problem of proliferating causation is to tie causal responsibility to culpability, so that acts cause only their foreseeable harms. Yet this solution poses the further problem that "given modern notions of liability based on culpability of acts, it is particularly difficult to explain why the occurrence of death matters" at all.[13] If we need criteria of culpability to determine which fatal acts are killings, we have not explained why proof of killing could obviate inquiry into culpability.

Fletcher's difficulties stemmed from his insistence that homicide exemplified a uniquely result-oriented "pattern of harmful consequences," distinct from the act-oriented "pattern of manifest criminality" characterizing other crimes. Fletcher derived this pattern from a revisionist history of larceny. He argued that the emergence of the new category of larceny by trick in the late eighteenth century was not simply an expansion of larceny to encompass betrayals of trust in the marketplace. It ultimately involved restructuring the elements of larceny, substituting a subjective element, fraudulent intent, for the formerly requisite objective element of trespass in the taking. This restructuring, Fletcher argued, suggested the emergence of a new conception of theft as a "subjective" crime of secret intention and the decline of an older conception of theft as a "manifest" crime of provocative conduct, a breach of the king's peace.[14]

If we "rethink" killing as a kind of act rather than a result, we may be able to explain the transformation of homicide from unexcused killing to culpable causing as a similar transition from manifest to subjective conceptions of criminality. But what was it about the act of killing that made malice manifest? And what was meant by malice if it could be presumed from the act of killing? We will try to answer these questions by examining a sample of homicide cases tried at London's Old Bailey courthouse between the late seventeenth century and the early nineteenth century, with special attention to the means of causing death.

A clue to the traditional meaning of killing is provided by Fletcher's examples of medieval killings excused on grounds of accident: victims running into the paths of arrows or stumbling onto unsheathed swords.[15] These accidental deaths appeared to be killings because they resulted from wounds inflicted with weapons. During this era *kill* meant "to strike or throw" and did not necessarily denote the extinction of life.[16] It appears that something of this earlier meaning remained in the age of Hale and Blackstone. Killing ordinarily required striking the body and inflicting a fatal wound or injury. According to Hale, *killing* meant "giving a mortal stroke,"[17] for "death without the stroke or other violence makes not the homicide."[18] Accordingly, "If a man either by working on the fancy of another or possibly by harsh or unkind usage puts another into such passion of grief or fear, that the party either dies suddenly, or contracts some disease, whereof he dies . . . it cannot come under the judgment of felony, because no external act of violence was offerd, whereof the common law can take notice, and secret things belong to God."[19] The common law, this passage implied, concerned the king's peace. It was concerned with violence that could be publicly observed and that could challenge the security of public space and the authority of the king over it—particularly the violent use of weapons.

Modern discussions of causation in criminal law trace their origins to Hale, who formulated the year-and-a-day rule, and wrestled with the problems of intervening actors and aggravating medical treatment.[20] Yet Hale's entire discussion of these problems presupposed a "mortal stroke" to start the proverbial chain of causation. Hale did include other forms of deliberate cruelty among the acts of violence that could constitute homicide: "starving," "poisoning," "strangling or suffocation," and even "exposing a sick or weak person or infant unto the cold to the intent to destroy him" and "imprisoning a man so strictly that he dies."[21] Yet for Hale and his contemporaries these were metaphoric extensions of the paradigmatic case of a mortal wound. Malcolm Gaskill recounts how seventeenth-century witnesses sought to corroborate their suspicions of poison by reporting dramatic physical symptoms like those evident in stabbings: "poison was described breaking out of the body as swelling and even wounds."[22]

Hale's idea of malice was closely related to his concept of killing as a fatal wounding. Malice was "the intention to do harm,"[23] which even if it "did not rise so high as death, but only . . . to beat the party," might suffice for murder.[24] Here Hale followed Dalton[25] and Coke, who defined express malice as the intent to "kill, wound, or beat."[26] Blackstone also acknowledged that express malice included the intent to "beat another in a cruel and unusual manner," without the intent to kill:[27] "As when a park-keeper tied a boy, that was stealing wood, to a horse's tail, and dragged him along the park; when a master corrected his servant with an iron bar, and a schoolmaster stamped on his scholar's belly."[28] Blackstone argued that the "bad heart" these acts expressed made them "equivalent to a deliberate act of slaughter,"[29] but it seems that malice required only intent to wound or injure rather than intent to cause death.

Fletcher speculated that the common law's attitude to killing had religious overtones: that it was seen as a kind of desecration or pollution. And indeed, the idea of the royal peace was an outgrowth of the medieval Peace of God movement, which granted the nobility exclusive authority and responsibility to bear arms while subjecting armed conflict to clerical regulation.[30] Death was readily accepted in a culture sustained by faith in eternal salvation, but unauthorized violence breached a sacred boundary that defined legitimate authority in feudal society. In the more fluid society of the early modern period, the pacific Christian ethic would be challenged by a neoclassical ethic of martial honor, particularly among those with aspirations to gentility.[31] This ethic required ready resort to weapons to prove one's courage and nobility in the face of any challenge.[32] Yet puritanical religion would point to murder as a particularly graphic representation of the sin that threatened all. In the seventeenth century, suspicious neighbors could persuade coroners and magistrates to charge murder by reporting that a victim's corpse suddenly bled at the touch or the sight of the suspected killer. Indeed, Dalton approved such evidence, and coroners sometimes organized such "ordeals of the bier."[33] In such a world, murder was not a causal relationship but a tear in the social fabric, a spreading stain of sin. Like the ordeal of the trial, the ordeal of the bier made guilt manifest, dramatically reenacting the killer's act of bloodshed. Homicide was, in Gaskill's phrase, a "crime of blood."[34]

This focus on mortal wounds was perhaps dictated by the distinctive procedural context of homicide cases during the early modern period. Homicide cases were usually initiated by a coroner. Yet coroners lacked resources or incentives to investigate:[35] they were usually passive recipients of accusations and evidence from their communities.[36] Their original function was to collect amercements for the crown from communities that failed to report murders or apprehend murderers. The threat of a fine for nonreporting encouraged reporting obvious murders, but a levy for inquests discouraged reporting in ambiguous cases.[37] In general, inquests were confined to cases of violent death, where the condition of the body made foul play obvious to a layman.[38] The indictments issued as a result of coroners' inquests typically charged murder even if the coroner's jury had approved a lesser charge.[39] Perhaps murder could be presumed in any case of homicide because the coroner's jurisdiction and attention extended only to cases that looked like murder—that were "manifestly" malicious killings.

In any case, we will see such a sanguinary conception of killing in the Old Bailey cases, organized around the core case of a fatal blow struck with a weapon. Strangling and poisoning were of course included within this concept of killing, but such stealthy modes of violence were rare in a society that used violence as an idiom for expressing anger and vindicating status. Inflicting a fatal wound with a homely household implement might be a killing but probably not a murder. A weaponless beating might qualify as a killing but would pose a problematic case in a hierarchical society that accepted corporal correction of subordinates. The cruel treatment or neglect of dependents would be an even less likely case of criminal homicide. And certainly not every human cause of death was a killing, even if careless. For example, a collision knocking a carriage into a ditch and thereby causing a trapped passenger to drown would not ordinarily be referred to as "killing." A killing required an act culturally recognizable as a violent assault. This is not to say that causation of death was no part of killing. Many a murder case turned on medical testimony about causation, particularly in the later decades examined. But the issue was the one identified by Hale: whether death resulted from a violently inflicted wound or injury.

Our cases will suggest that the categories of murder, manslaughter, and accidental death were distinguished primarily on the basis of differences in conduct rather than mental states. Murder generally required an unprovoked and fatal attack with a weapon. Very few of the murder cases we will examine show a clearly focused intent to kill. Rarely does an assailant methodically attack until a victim expires. Instead the victim is left alive to languish, complain, and—conveniently—name his killer.[40] Yet the use of a weapon manifested malice in the colloquial sense of ill will. A murder was an act of war, expressing overt enmity. Even manslaughter was generally an armed assault with provocation or an unprovoked assault with some humble and homely implement. Convictions on the basis of mere carelessness were quite rare. Thus, neither offense required intent to kill, but both offenses required manifest hostility.

1. *Homicide at the Old Bailey*

For purposes of this study, I have examined a cross-section of the homicide cases reported in the *Proceedings of the Old Bailey* between 1674 and 1834.[41] These consist of a total of 245 homicide cases, consisting of all reported homicide cases from every tenth year, beginning in 1680. Of these, about 51 percent, or 125, resulted in acquittals for all homicide offenses. About 29 percent, or 72, resulted in manslaughter convictions. About 18 percent, or 43, resulted in murder convictions. There is little variation in these percentages before the end of the eighteenth century. After 1790, however, only 2 of 47 cases ended in murder convictions. In counting these cases, I treat each defendant as a separate case.

Five cases ended in convictions for the statutory offense of infanticide. Strictly speaking, this was not a homicide offense, since liability required only proof that an unmarried woman had concealed the birth of a newborn and that the newborn was dead.[42] In the eighteenth century, popular opinion turned decisively against this statute. Convictions under it became rare and were usually based on evidence that might support a murder conviction.[43] In our sample, there were no convictions for statutory infanticide after 1710, although there was a 1760 murder conviction for stabbing a newborn to death.[44]

The Old Bailey reports include the language of the indictments. The typical indictment for murder specifies that the defendant assaulted the victim with a certain weapon, with malice aforethought, causing a wound of a certain size in a specified location on the body, from which the defendant died. They might conclude that the defendant was charged with "willful murder" but would not more precisely specify intent to kill. By contrast, the 1750 indictment of William Archer for attempted murder did specify that he shot with intent to kill.[45] This suggests that intent to kill was not seen as a necessary element of murder. *Malice* apparently meant nothing more than its ordinary meaning: "hostility, or a desire to harm."

Unfortunately, the Old Bailey reports rarely include the jury instructions. They include at least summaries, and often transcripts, of the testimony at trial. Thus I will be using these reports to infer the law by correlating fact patterns revealed in the testimony with verdicts. I will first examine cases resulting in murder liability, finding that these generally involve an intentional unprovoked blow with a weapon that happens to prove fatal. In other words, the intention to attack the body with a weapon, rather than the intention to kill, made a death into a murder. Next, I will examine cases yielding manslaughter. These were of four general types: (1) provoked intentional blows with lethal weapons that proved fatal; (2) intentional blows with tools or household implements, sometimes unprovoked; (3) unarmed blows that proved fatal, usually unprovoked; and (4) recklessly inflicted blows that proved fatal. There were also numerous acquittals arising from cases of the third and fourth type, and I will compare the acquittals to the convictions. I will conclude that even where manslaughter was based on an unintentional blow, a hostile attitude was an important predictor of liability.

In this study, I am treating the entire time span from 1680 to 1830 as one period, even though there were undoubtedly changes in the applied law of homicide over this time. The sample of cases I am using is simply too small to determine these changes with any reliability. Nevertheless, this sample gives us a rough picture of how killing was conceived in England before the development of scientific element analysis in the nineteenth century. It suffices to show that the concepts of killing and malice prevailing during this period differed from those that prevail today, and this difference warrants more exhaustive investigation of the transformation of English homicide law over time.

2. Murder Cases: The Contours of Malice

The murder cases in our sample show some discernible patterns. Let us first consider how death was brought about in these cases. Cases of intentional wounding—or, rather, assaults with potentially injurious weapons—generally resulted in murder liability if unprovoked. The use of a weapon was almost a sine qua non for murder during this period. Of the forty-three murder convictions, thirty-nine involved the use of some kind of weapon. Twenty-two of these used a sword or knife, although in one case the weapon was thrown rather than held in the hand. There were nine shootings, two beatings with staffs, and one axe murder. The five remaining cases involved the opportunistic use of homely implements. Two defendants collaborated in a fatal beating with a poker. Dennis Rearden attacked his wife with a saw, which choice he regarded as exculpatory, wondering at his trial what sane person would use such an instrument to kill.[46] One frustrated mistress felt compelled to try a variety of tools in disciplining her recalcitrant maid: a whip, a hot poker, and finally a hammer.[47] John Foster, chimney sweep, clubbed Margaret Shovel with a broom handle.[48]

Of the four weaponless murders, one was a poisoning: Elizabeth Cranberry put arsenic in her father-in-law's porridge, after an argument in which he threatened to put her out of his house.[49] We can think of this poison as equivalent to a weapon. Elizabeth is unlikely to have known that the dose would suffice to kill her father-in-law and may not have intended to do more than sicken him. Yet the use of such a notoriously lethal poison was alarming and unambiguously, albeit stealthily, hostile. The remaining cases were two stranglings[50] and the 1790 murder conviction of Thomas Masters for beating his lover's six-year-old daughter Mary, causing numerous wounds, including a perforated bowel. Ordinarily, a beating without a weapon would have been manslaughter, but the frailty of the victim and a cruelty and force far in excess of what was customary in correcting a child made it murder. Masters claimed that he had struck the child only once and that the fatal injury resulted from a fall against a piece of furniture. Such indirectly caused deaths often produced outright acquittals. But the medical evidence belied his account of events, and he was convicted of murder.[51]

The prevalence of stabbing cases among the murder convictions raises a question that bears on my claim that an intentional blow with a weapon obviated any proof of intent to kill. This concerns the 1611 statute of stabbing, which removed the benefit of clergy for fatal stabbings of victims who had neither drawn a weapon nor struck a first blow.[52] According to Blackstone, this statute imposed murder liability without regard to malice aforethought.[53] Perhaps, then, these numerous stabbing cases should be seen not as evidence of the content of the common law concept of malicious killing but as exceptions to it.

But these stabbing cases were not, by and large, prosecuted under the statute of stabbing. Among the twenty-two reports of murder convictions arising from stabbing in our sample, only two were indicted under the statute of stabbing and both were also indicted under the common law. In one of these cases, Edward Richardson was convicted of common law murder but acquitted of statutory stabbing.[54] Jane Griffin was convicted of both common law murder and stabbing.[55]

It appears that during the sampled period the statute of stabbing was interpreted as going no farther than the common law. Thus, a 1666 meeting of judges at Serjeant's Inn concerning the trial of Lord Morley held that the statute was only a declaration of the common law aimed at clarifying that provocation required a blow or armed attack.[56] In a notorious 1743 case, the fifteen-year-old William Chetwynd was indicted both for common law murder and under the statute for his fatal stabbing of an older schoolmate in a scuffle over a cake. Although the defendant had the knife in his hand to cut his cake, his blow did not appear to be accidental. Attorneys for Chetwynd argued that the victim's taking of Chetwynd's cake was a trespass, sufficient for provocation at common law, and that application of the statute should be barred by any act constituting provocation at common law.[57] A panel of judges convicted Chetwynd of manslaughter only, based on the jury's special verdict.[58] In any case, Blackstone's concern about the statute was not that it might impose liability on some who did not intend to kill but that it might define provocation too narrowly. Despite these misgivings, however, he concluded that "the benignity of the law hath construed the statute so favorably in behalf of the subject, and so strictly when against him, that the offense of stabbing stands almost on the same footing, as it did with the common law."[59]

I suspect that rather than departing from the common law conception of malicious killing, the statute of stabbing *informed* it, providing judges and juries with paradigmatic images of killing and provocation.

Beyond the use of a weapon, how much evidence of intent to kill do we find in these cases? One case offered direct evidence of intent: Francis Nicholson, a carpenter, agreed to murder John Dimblebe for forty shillings, succeeding on his fourth attempt, by striking him several blows on the head with an axe.[60] Several cases offered circumstantial evidence of intent to kill. Tobias Butler and his accomplice waited for a Mr. Simonds and stabbed him to avenge an insult to a young woman.[61] Francis Stirn apparently bought pistols shortly after Richard Matthews threw him out of his home, sought out Matthews, and shot him in the chest at close range.[62] William Odell strangled his wife Elizabeth with a rope and concealed her body in a pond.[63] Also, some forms of assault are so final as to leave little doubt as to the perpetrator's intentions. Thomas Fox killed his fellow soldier by cutting his throat "from ear to ear."[64] Ann Hullock cut her newborn infant's throat, nearly severing the head, and concealed its body in a privy.[65] Dennis Rearden used a saw to hack open his wife's skull, although he claimed this was evidence of irrationality rather than murderous resolve.[66]

In most cases, however, the only additional evidence is the fact that the weapon hit a vital spot.[67] Often the circumstances of a quarrel make it difficult to infer anything more than an intent to hurt or wound. Thus, John Kein was drunk and abusive when his wife visited him in jail. They quarreled and he stabbed her in the throat.[68] John Thrift, angered that three passing men had called him for a convict, pursued them with a cutlass and struck Patrick Farrel a fatal blow on the head. The only issue at trial was whether the victim and his associates had struck Thrift first.[69] At the end of an evening of drink and dominoes, James Hartley stabbed his fellow soldier George Scott in the belly, in a dispute over the bar bill.[70]

Sometimes there was even less evidence of intent. Daniel Jackson shot his wife in the back as they alighted from a coach and looked for a shop at which to sell the pistol. The circumstances strongly suggested an accident, but there was testimony that Jackson had beaten his wife in the past and that she had expressed fear of him.[71] A drunken Morrice Fitzgerald joined with others in stopping a sedan chair and harassing its passenger. When a watchman came up to interfere, Fitzgerald stabbed him in the shoulder, and the wound proved fatal.[72] Thomas Clements, a butcher, argued with his colleague William Warner over a fine tongue Warner had promised to a customer. In his annoyance, he took up a handy knife and threw it at Warner, hitting him in the belly.[73] Most such workplace assaults with tools resulted in manslaughter liability; unfortunately for Clements, a butcher's tool is a knife, and this was apparently enough to convict him of murder. The gentle Mr. Doughty stabbed a coachman who followed him into another gentleman's house to demand his fare but then secured him medical treatment. The wounds appeared superficial and the coachman appeared to recover; but then he died, with the cause not clearly determined.[74] Edward Richardson stabbed John Marlow in the groin "upon some slight occasion."[75] That murder liability turned on the intent to strike a blow, rather than the intent to cause death, explains why so little evidence of intent was required for accomplice liability. For example, Roger Swiny drew a sword to menace an arresting bailiff but was held liable as an accomplice when his companion fatally stabbed the bailiff in the chest.[76]

A few murder cases arose from duels. Should we treat these as intentional killings? Participation in a duel implies a resolve to assault one's antagonist but not necessarily to kill, as duels were not always fatal. If a duel was fairly conducted, a resulting death was usually ruled a manslaughter during this time period.[77] But two murder cases in our sample involved dishonorable duelists, who struck prematurely. Edward Ely, a ship's petty officer, threatened his friend and fellow officer Charles Bignall with a duel if he did not sign over his share of a prize that he had agreed to sell Ely. On the appointed day, while negotiating the terms of the duel, Ely suddenly drew his sword and attacked. Bignall then drew as well, and both men were wounded, but Bignall got the worst of it, including a fatal wound in the chest.[78] Edward Clark shot Thomas Innes at a prearranged duel as the latter was about to take aim, and he was found guilty with a recommendation for royal mercy.[79]

Some cases offered evidence of gross indifference to human life rather than intent to kill. Frances Deacon, suspecting her maid Mary Cox of theft, tortured her to elicit a confession, eventually striking her on the head with a hammer. Mrs. Deacon refused to provide Mary with medical attention, saying she would have killed her if she had not confessed.[80] Jane Griffin, who stabbed her maid Elizabeth Osborn in the left breast, had on a previous occasion stabbed her in the arm, whereupon Jane was heard to say she would butcher her eventually and that no one would think Elizabeth worth hanging anyone over.[81] Richard Merridy, whose blade missed his victim, somehow inflicted a wound one and half inches deep in his victim's eye with the handle of his sword. He expressed satisfaction with the fatal result, saying it was no more sin to kill such a man than to kill a dog or cat.[82] When John Foster clubbed his victim, she protested that she thought he had murdered her, whereupon he struck her twice more.[83] Matthew and Patrick Kennedy went on a rampage, with two or three others, clubbing everyone they saw. Matthew struck John Bigby a fatal blow with an iron poker, while Patrick beat his companion.[84]

Should we treat these cases as evidence that gross indifference to human life was seen as one form of malice in seventeenth- and eighteenth-century England? Not necessarily. All of these cases involved intentional batteries with deadly weapons. Of course, stabbing a victim in the gut recklessly imposes a risk of death. But this does not mean that malice required the reckless imposition of a risk of death. If an assailant intentionally stabbed a victim, there was no need to prove his awareness that the victim might die. Moreover, if reckless indifference to human life was the core idea of murder, we might expect to see many cases of murder where the victim risks the infliction of a fatal blow, as by throwing a dangerous implement toward a victim. But in fact such cases appear in our sample and were usually treated as manslaughter. Similarly, we might expect to see numerous murder cases arising from release of a dangerous natural force, such as fire, or a dangerous animal. The treatises do mention a seventeenth-century case of dragging a youth behind a horse,[85] and a sixteenth century case of an abandoned newborn who died from the attack of a predator rather than from starvation or exposure.[86] But such cases were rare. Finally, we might expect to see murder liability arising from callous child neglect or medical quackery. But such cases were treated as manslaughter at most. Thus, while the seventeenth- and eighteenth-century treatises mention murder by risk taking, it appears that murder was seldom charged on this theory in their day.

To what extent did murder liability depend on causing death in resisting arrest or in attempting a felony? A few of our murders occurred in the course of resisting arrest. The official status of the victim does not seem to have been an element of liability but may have precluded claims of provocation. John Watkins and Edward Whittaker were both convicted of murder when they scuffled with a watchman who tried to stop and question them, and Watkins struck the watchman a fatal blow on the head with his staff. The jury rejected the defendants' claim that the watchman struck the first blow.[87] We have noted that Roger Swiny and his brother drew swords against bailiffs to prevent the arrest of a companion.[88] John Bennet shot, during a hue and cry, a pursuer who was seeking to apprehend him as a robber.[89] Patrick McCarty fatally stabbed William Talbot, a court bailiff, in the side as Talbot attempted to arrest him in execution of a writ.[90] John Smith fatally stabbed in the heart a police officer who tried to stop and question him and his companions.[91] Nothing was made of this context at the trial. In no case did the indictment specify that the killing took place in resisting a lawful arrest. This did not appear to be an element of the crime.

The commission of other felonies also played almost no role in determining which homicides were graded as murders. Fatal robberies appear to have become more common in the last few decades of the eighteenth century, and this is reflected in our sample. In 1770 Charles Stevens, Henry Holyoak, and Henry Hughes were held liable for murder as a result of their robbery of John Shaw. Holyoak and Hughes demanded Shaw's money. When Shaw refused and drew a knife, Stevens came up and shot him in the belly with a blunderbuss. Holyoak, who carried a pistol, was heard to say the shooting was "well-done." Hughes carried a cutlass. Here the threat involved in the robbery ties Hughes and Holyoak to the fatal assault, but complicity in that assault would have made them liable whether or not robbery was involved.[92] Also in 1770, Peter Conoway and Michael Richardson were convicted of murder. They had stopped two men, demanding their money. When both victims resisted, each robber shot a victim, one of whom died.[93] Again, the robbery makes clear that the two shootings were in furtherance of a common project, but it does not seem necessary for characterizing the killing as murder. In 1790 three Italian sailors, Jacintho Phararo, Anthoni Murrini, and Stephen Apologie robbed their traveling companion, another sailor named Josephi, stabbing him, hiding his body, and dividing his possessions.[94] In none of these cases did the indictment specify that the killing took place in the course of a felony, indicating that proof of such a felony was not seen as necessary for murder liability in these cases.

These results accord with the conclusions of my previous research on the emergence of felony murder liability, which dates this as a later phenomenon.[95] I found that a few "felony murder" convictions were reported in Stephen's day, although they always involved a violent assault or an act dangerous to life. However, scholars have yet to identify actual cases of felony murder liability in England before the nineteenth century. My own review of all murder convictions reported in the Old Bailey Proceedings disclosed no convictions before the end of the eighteenth century in which a felonious context made murder out of a death that otherwise would have been manslaughter or accident. Nor were questions at trial aimed at eliciting evidence of felonious motive. For example, in a 1718 case, John Price was interrupted in the act of raping and robbing Elizabeth White, who died of wounds to her head, throat, and abdomen. The testimony and questions at trial were directed only to proving the fatal assault rather than the theft or the rape.[96] Price's case is usefully contrasted with the 1773 case of *R. v. Lad*, overturning a murder conviction for the death of a nine-year-old girl after a rape for failure to allege that Lad inflicted a mortal wound during the rape.[97] Although a broad felony murder rule was proposed in several eighteenth-century treatises,[98] and approved hypothetically in a couple of cases,[99] it does not seem to have been put into practice. Of course, if a robber fatally stabbed a victim, he was liable for murder whether or not he intended to kill. But this was because the stabbing expressed malice, not because the felony implied it. The felony became relevant only to preclude a claim of self-defense or provocation if the victim had attacked first, in resistance to the robbery. On the other hand, if the robber carelessly and fatally ran down a pedestrian while riding off with the loot, he would not have been charged with murder since he would not have used a weapon or intentionally inflicted a wound.

3. Manslaughter Cases: Grounds for Mitigation

The means of causing death are reported in seventy-one of the seventy-two manslaughter cases in our sample. These cases fall into four distinct categories. The largest group involved intentional batteries with conventionally lethal weapons, mitigated on grounds of provocation. Provocation could consist of striking an unarmed blow, drawing a weapon (where the defendant had the opportunity to retreat), or agreeing to armed combat (provided the defendant did not strike prematurely). In rare cases, adultery could serve as provocation. A smaller group of cases involved batteries with more innocuous kinds of objects and tools. Here evidence of provocation was often dubious or nonexistent. A third group consisted of intentional unarmed batteries, which were often unprovoked. Finally, about a quarter involved carelessly inflicted injuries. Cases of these latter two types were somewhat dubious manslaughters, by which I mean that such cases also often led to acquittals. Accordingly, I will compare manslaughter convictions and acquittals arising from these two types of cases in this section. I propose that intentional unarmed fatal batteries and carelessly inflicted fatal injuries were dubious as manslaughters because they were dubious as *killings*.

A total of twenty-eight of our manslaughter cases were stabbings or shootings,[100] almost all provoked in some way.[101] Several of these killings were provoked by a blow.[102] As we have seen in the Chetwynd case, a trespass such as an attempted theft, unauthorized entry, or unlawful restraint might substitute for a blow.[103] Occasionally, such a thin claim of provocation could combine with a dubious claim of involuntary manslaughter to mitigate an armed battery. Such a case arose in a dispute over the hiring of a coach. One party attempted to prevent defendants from boarding the coach. Defendants drew, a scuffle ensued, and the victim received a stab wound that the assailant claimed was unintentional.[104]

Other armed killings were mitigated on grounds of a challenge or agreement to fight, whether the elaborately staged duel of the gentlemanly class or the more spontaneous "sudden quarrel" of the lower orders. In these kinds of cases both defendant and deceased provoked each other and both could have avoided confrontation by retreating.[105] In one case, witnesses testified that the deceased drew first and thrust his sword at the defendant James Smith twice before Smith drew and that Smith was not in a position to retreat. Yet Smith accompanied the deceased out into the street when the deceased called for him, with sword bared, which may have inclined the jury to view the case as one of combat by agreement rather than self-defense.[106] Roger Mansuer told a similar story. Insulted by a letter Mansuer had written him, James White came to Mansuer's chambers and called him out. After desultory efforts to mollify White, Mansuer began to insult him again. He then accompanied White outside where White drew on him, and Mansuer fatally stabbed him. Again, the jury classified this as manslaughter rather than self-defense.[107] Similarly, David Murphey was convicted of manslaughter for stabbing Ulysses Lynch after Lynch challenged him to fight with swords and threatened to cane him in public if he refused.[108] Sometimes a provocation narrative would combine a provoking blow with combat by agreement.[109]

Juries would sometimes discount dubious self-defense claims to provocation and convict of manslaughter.[110] In one such case, the jury used a manslaughter verdict to express that the defendant gave cause for the victim's attack. Edward Harrison enraged John Jacob by persisting in seeing his wife. Jacob drew on Harrison and pursued him to his door, where Harrison drew and defended himself, giving Jacob a mortal wound. Harrison followed all the requisites of self-defense, but the jury obviously viewed his familiarity with Jacob's wife as itself provocative.[111] However, only one case in our sample actually treats adultery as adequate provocation, mitigating an armed killing to manslaughter.[112] Such a claim was also offered in another case arising from an unarmed beating but was probably not needed.[113]

Our second category consists of eleven manslaughter convictions arising from fatal intentional batteries with more homely kinds of objects. One of these cases, a stabbing with scissors during a prolonged fight between two women, presented straightforward evidence of provocation.[114] But in other cases, juries accepted weak evidence of provocation. Thus, a group of four defendants, taking offense to an Irishman's presence, dragged him out of a tavern and beat him with a poker, sticks, and a brick. They offered dubious evidence that he had earlier thrown a brick at one of them and that he had agreed to fight them. But the jury may well have had doubts about the causal connection between the beating and the victim's later death: the victim was apparently well enough the next day to go to a dance, where he sustained a bad fall when the floor collapsed.[115] Another murky case involved a tavern outside of which a crowd of ruffians habitually stopped and harassed passersby.

John Higgs rode by, accompanying a wagon, and was pulled off his horse and struck. A few moments later Higgs got a spade from his wagon, sought out one Michael Fitzgerald who had apparently been among those who had stopped him, and struck him on the head. Fitzgerald languished for three weeks and then died. The judge in the case opined that the tavernkeeper was ultimately to blame for permitting such a disorderly situation and directed a verdict of manslaughter.[116]

In several cases, juries did not require evidence of provocation at all and chose manslaughter on some other ground. Juries applied manslaughter liability to deaths resulting from unprovoked beatings with a stick[117] and a pewter mug.[118] Interestingly, another case involving a *provoked* fatal beating with a pewter mug yielded a complete acquittal.[119] One defendant, a bailiff, turned and struck a child who protested the arrest of her father a single blow with a cudgel.[120] The blow was not provoked, but its intentionality may have been somewhat attenuated. Moreover, such a blow would probably have been seen as a completely appropriate exercise of authority if it had not been an armed one or if the child had physically rather than verbally restrained the bailiff. An additional two convictions arose from an intentional, unprovoked stabbing with a pitchfork. The defendants denied the act and the jury may have been uncertain about their guilt.[121]

Our third category consists of thirteen convictions arising out of completely unarmed assaults. Many similar cases led to acquittal, however. Homicide cases arising from unarmed assaults vary along two important dimensions: the directness of the link between battery and fatal injury, and the presence or absence of provocation.

Let us first consider deaths resulting directly from a punch, kick, or stomp. Nine manslaughter convictions arose from such cases. Only three involved physical provocation.[122] As noted earlier, one defendant claimed provocation based on the victim's infidelity.[123] Five convictions were based on deaths resulting directly from unprovoked blows.[124] Moreover, in several such cases causation was successfully disputed, and the defendant was acquitted outright.[125] I infer that an unarmed blow was not considered malicious, so that mitigation on the basis of provocation was unnecessary. In addition, an unarmed blow was considered harmless, and often appropriate, so that judges, juries, and medical witnesses were far less ready to assume a causal link to death.

Next let us consider cases in which death resulted indirectly, from an assault that caused a fatal fall. Manslaughter was found in four such cases, none involving provocation. In two cases, a blow caused the fall, and in two it was caused by a push.[126] But many similar cases led to acquittal. Two such acquittals involved victim-provoked assaults.[127] In one such case the schoolmaster John

Barney struck his inattentive twelve-year-old pupil William Poole, knocking his head against a brick chimney. He explained that such corrections were necessary, for Poole was "dull by nature," that he had endured the chore of teaching him "with as much gentleness of temper as possible," and that he "did not expect this would have any worse effect than former corrections of the same kind."[128] In two such cases, questions of causation were raised,[129] and in one the prosecution failed to establish that the little girl a sentry kicked was the same who died.[130] In two cases, a fatal fall resulted from a pull or push rather than a blow.[131] The high rate of acquittal in these fatal fall cases supports the conclusion that jurors understood *killing* to mean death resulting directly from an intentionally inflicted blow, preferably with a weapon. An unarmed blow was considered an appropriate way to express anger among equals of low status or to assert governing authority within hierarchical relationships.

Our final category of manslaughter consists of deaths resulting from carelessly inflicted injuries. In this category also, acquittals are as prevalent as manslaughter convictions. On the other hand, careless or dangerous acts were almost never murder. Eighteenth-century Englishmen apparently saw a great difference between an intentional blow with a weapon and the reckless handling of a weapon. An unintended shooting was never murder and might not even be manslaughter. Throwing a dangerous implement in anger was generally manslaughter. Even a dangerous act was unlikely to be treated as manslaughter, however, unless it expressed hostility. Negligent child care, for example, would not result in manslaughter liability. A cart accident might be manslaughter, but only if it involved an assault or particularly egregious negligence.

In our sample, there were nine cases where the defendant inflicted a mortal injury by handling a dangerous implement in a careless and hostile way. Various objects were thrown in anger: shears,[132] a shovel,[133] a brick,[134] a soldering iron,[135] a mallet,[136] and an iron heater.[137] One defendant swung a boat hook in anger in a crowd after being hit with a firecracker, striking a child in the head.[138] Another brandished a red-hot poker at a lazy coworker, unwittingly sinking it deep into his gut.[139] All nine of these deaths were ruled manslaughter. None resulted in murder liability. This is strong evidence that the concept of *extreme-indifference murder* had little traction in English law during the period studied. Consider the case involving the iron heater: Charles Perry apparently threw the heater at his common law wife after she spat at him, striking his infant daughter, who was nursing at her mother's breast, "through the child's head."[140] The defendant's act seems comparable to the extreme-indifference murder punished in the landmark U.S. case of *Mayes v. People*.[141] Mayes came home drunk and angry and threw a mug at his wife and daughter, breaking an oil lamp his wife was carrying. The broken lamp ignited the defendant's wife, who died of burns. It seems clear that this kind of reckless hostility would not have been considered malice in eighteenth- or early nineteenth-century England. On the other hand, none of these cases were considered mere accidents. In each case, the defendant's recklessness and hostility made the resulting death a culpable homicide.

There were five unintended shootings in our sample. Two resulted in manslaughter liability. William Gravestock, a youth, was convicted of manslaughter when he aimed a pistol in jest at his friend Mary Feney and, believing the gun not loaded, pulled the trigger.[142] John Marrey was liable when he accidentally discharged a pistol in his room, killing his partner Martha Slade.[143] On the other hand, Francis Kettleby, keeper of a debtor's prison, was not liable for manslaughter despite greater recklessness. Kettleby's neighbor kept a prison for prisoners of war, who periodically escaped. When he heard several of these prisoners of war in his attic, fearing robbery, Kettleby shot through a hole in the ceiling, hoping to frighten them, just as one of them stumbled into the path of the bullet.[144] One defendant was acquitted for accidentally hitting a victim while shooting on a firing range,[145] and another was acquitted for a hunting accident where it was unclear whose gun hit the victim.[146] While firing a gun was arguably more dangerous than throwing a tool, shooting was proper and orderly under some circumstances. By contrast, throwing a tool bespoke ungoverned passion and violated the order of home and workshop.

One important modern category of homicide consists of deaths resulting from child neglect. However, no such deaths were punished as homicides in London during the sixteen years surveyed. One defendant dropped his infant son out a window,[147] one defendant mistook a bottle of poison for a bottle of medicine and so administered poison to his son,[148] and one family friend gave a toddler a large glass of rum with fatal results.[149] A woman paid to board and care for an infant was charged with manslaughter when the emaciated baby died of apparent starvation.[150] All four were acquitted.

The sample includes one case of manslaughter arising from medical malpractice in the last year surveyed, 1830. The fashionable physician John St. John Long had many well-born ladies among his patients, who protected themselves against tuberculosis by regularly breathing mysterious vapors at his office. Another of his innovative treatments involved rubbing a caustic ointment on the backs of patients to produce a burn, which would require regular dressing and examination. In the case of poor Catherine Cashin, however, the wound festered and mortified while Dr. Long offered nothing but enthusiastic prognoses up to the night of her death.[151] This modern-seeming case probably reflects a newer understanding of homicide as culpable causation, but jurors may have seen the case as a killing: a death resulting from a deliberately and unjustifiably inflicted wound.

Vehicular accidents were often the occasion for homicide indictments at the Old Bailey. There are sixteen such cases in our sample: eight manslaughters and eight acquittals. Three of the manslaughters were really unprovoked unarmed batteries, where the victim fell under the wheels of a moving cart.[152] In two of these cases, the assailant could perhaps have assisted the fallen man and failed to do so.[153] Two manslaughter convictions arose from conduct that might be viewed as reckless. In one, a driver willfully drove his cart forward while a victim tried to halt the cart by holding the horses.[154] In the other, a coachman ran down a pedestrian while racing another coach.[155] The remaining three convictions were cases where inattentive drivers simply ran down pedestrians.[156]

The acquittals include a provoked unarmed battery resulting in a fatal fall under the wheels of a cart.[157] This result is consistent with the treatment of such batteries where vehicles were not involved. Two acquittals involved collisions with carts rather than pedestrians, and a third involved a collision with a post, causing a passenger to fall off the coach.[158] It seems to me that these results fit with the more lenient treatment of assaults causing fatal falls as opposed to assaults directly inflicting fatal injuries. To the eighteenth-century mind, running down a pedestrian might seem an act of violence, a kind of assault, where a collision with a vehicle or some other obstacle was merely an accident. The remaining four acquittals were simple run-over cases without strong evidence of the defendant's negligence.[159]

These results suggest to me that jurors and probably courts remained ambivalent about imposing criminal responsibility for careless conduct and were far more likely to punish it if it included some expression of hostility.

Conclusion

Our survey of homicide cases at common law reveals how dramatically reformers like Stephen had reoriented English homicide law by the end of the nineteenth century. Of Stephen's five alternative forms of malice—intent to kill, intent to injure, reckless indifference, intent to commit a felony, and intent to resist arrest—four were practically irrelevant in the Old Bailey. The intent to commit a felony or to resist arrest made no difference except in defeating a provocation claim. Reckless indifference to a risk of death might support manslaughter liability, particularly if it involved an element of hostility or anger, but it almost never sufficed for murder. As for intent to kill, the center of modern homicide law, it was almost completely peripheral in the seventeenth and eighteenth centuries. It would be relevant only if a defendant managed to invent some subtle way of dispatching a victim that did not manifest a desire to inflict bodily harm. Intent to kill was more than the common law required. Of Stephen's five components of malice, only the intent to injure resembled the meaning of malice in the era of Hale and Blackstone.

What, then, did the eighteenth-century lawyer mean by the proposition that malice could be presumed from the fact of killing? He did not mean that all acts causing death were killings or that all killings were presumed intentional. Homicide was not just a crime of "harmful consequences" but required that death be produced by a "manifestly criminal" act. *Killing* meant causing death by violence: by intentionally battering a person with a weapon, producing a wound or injury. Such an attack manifested overt enmity. It literally expressed malice, in a language intelligible to all. It demanded the attention of royal officials by desecrating the king's peace. Necessarily, then, malice could be presumed from killing, absent some account about why an armed attack did not mean what it is conventionally taken to mean. It was a defensive or retaliatory response, or it was an accident or mistake, or it was an act of madness. By shifting the burden onto the defendant to excuse an apparently malicious act, the law of homicide conformed to the pattern of manifest criminality.

Notes

1. William Lambarde, *Eirenarcha; or, Of the Office of the Justice of the Peace* (New York: Da Capo Press, 1970), pp. 240–250 (originally published 1588); Edward Coke, *Institutes of the Laws of England*, vol. 3 (London: E. & R. Brooke, 1794), p. 47; William Blackstone, *Blackstone's Commentaries*, vol. 4 (Oxford: Clarendon Press, 1769), p. 195.

2. James Fitzjames Stephen, *A History of the Criminal Law of England*, vol. 3 (London: Macmillan, 1883), p. 3.

3. Ibid., p. 4.

4. Ibid., p. 5.

5. Ibid., p. 80 (quoting digest, art. 228).

6. Ibid., pp. 80–81.

7. Ibid., p. 201.

8. Allyson N. May, *The Bar and the Old Bailey, 1750–1850* (Chapel Hill: Univ. of North Carolina Press, 2003), pp. 20, 176. Although it was not until the 1830s that prisoners gained a right to counsel, and that counsel could address the jury, some defendants had the assistance of counsel in examining and cross-examining witnesses beginning in the 1730s. Ibid., p. 26; J. M. Beattie, *Crime and the Courts in England, 1660–1800* (Oxford: Clarendon Press, 1986), pp. 356–357; John Langbein, "The Criminal Trial before the Lawyers," *University of Chicago Law Review* 45 (1978): 263, 312.

9. May, *Bar and the Old Bailey*, p. 20; Beattie, *Crime and the Courts*, pp. 341, 348–350; J. H. Baker, "Criminal Courts and Procedure at Common Law, 1550–1800," in *Crime in England, 1550–1800*, J. S. Cockburn, ed. (Princeton, New Jersey: Princeton Univ. Press, 1977), p. 37 (quoting Ferdinando Pulton, *De Pace Regis et Regni* [London: Professional Books, 1973], pp. 184–185 [originally published 1609]); Cynthia Herrup, *The Common Peace: Participation and the Criminal Law in Seventeenth Century England* (Cambridge: Cambridge Univ. Press, 1987), pp. 131, 141–142. Of course, prosecutors, who were usually private parties, were also often without counsel—although beginning in the early eighteenth century, prosecution counsel was common in murder cases; Clive Emsley, *Crime and Society in England, 1750–1900*, 2d ed. (London: Longman, 1987), p. 152.

10. Malcolm Gaskill, *Crime and Mentalities in Early Modern England* (Cambridge: Cambridge Univ. Press, 2000), p. 254.

11. Gaskill, *Crime and Mentalities*, pp. 231–233.

12. George Fletcher, *Rethinking Criminal Law* (Boston: Little, Brown, 1978), p. 363.

13. Ibid., p. 361.

14. Ibid., p. 59–122.

15. Ibid., p. 359–360.

16. *Oxford English Dictionary* (Compact Edition, 1971).

17. Matthew Hale, *History of the Pleas of the Crown*, vol. 1 (London: E. Rider for T. Payne, 1800), p. 425 (originally published 1736).

18. Ibid., p. 426.

19. Ibid., p. 429.

20. Ibid., p. 428.

21. Ibid., p. 431–432.

22. Gaskill, *Crime and Mentalities*, p. 261.

23. Hale, *History*, pp. 44–45.

24. Ibid., p. 49.

25. Michael Dalton, *The Countrey Justice* (London: A. Islip for the Societie of Stationers, 1619), p. 220.

26. Edward Coke, *Institutes of the Laws of England*, vol. 3 (London: E. & R. Brooke, 1794), p. 51.

27. *Blackstone's Commentaries*, vol. 4, p. 199.

28. Ibid., p. 200.

29. Ibid.

30. Guyora Binder, "Angels and Infidels: Hierarchy and Historicism in Medieval Legal History," *Buffalo Law Review* 35 (1986): 527; Georges Duby, *The Three Orders: Feudal Society Imagined* (Chicago: Univ. of Chicago Press), 1981.

31. Jeremy Horder, *Provocation and Responsibility* (Oxford: Clarendon Press, 1992).

32. Ibid.

33. Malcolm Gaskill, *Crime and Mentalities*, pp. 227–230.

34. Ibid., p. 203.

35. Ibid., pp. 246–247, 266.

36. This much was true of magistrates and constables as well. Frank McLynn, *Crime*

and Punishment in Eighteenth-Century England (London: Routledge, 1989), pp. 18–19; Beattie, *Crime and the Courts*, pp. 59–66. Modern police did not begin to develop until the 1830s (in 1829 in London), which is no doubt one reason why, in the eighteenth century, crime of all kinds had to be "manifest" to the community to come to the attention of the courts. The situation was somewhat different in London, however, where watchmen took a more active role in policing and investigation than elsewhere. Beattie, p. 70; Leon Radzinowicz and Roger G. Hood, *A History of English Criminal Law and Its Administration, from 1750*, vol. 2 (London: Stevens, 1948–1986), pp. 171–201. In addition, in the latter half of the eighteenth century, some London magistrates, notably Henry and John Fielding, began to employ professional investigators. McLynn, *Crime and Punishment*, pp. 32–35.

37. Gaskill, *Crime and Mentalities*, pp. 246–247, 250.
38. Beattie, *Crime and the Courts*, p. 80.
39. Ibid., p. 80.
40. Ibid., pp. 233–235. Gaskill points out that witnesses probably fabricated many of these dying declarations to implicate suspected killers. But, if so, they saw no tactical disadvantage in conceding that the suspect had left the victim alive.
41. These are available at http://www.oldbaileyonline.org. These were popular journalistic accounts of trials, which, however, came to be used increasingly by lawyers late in the eighteenth century. My citations to these materials will identify them by the surname of the defendant and the trial reference number, which consists of the year, month, day of publication, and order of appearance in that day's edition.
42. 21 James I, c. 27 (1624).
43. Beattie, *Crime and the Courts*, pp. 117–124; R. W. Malcolmson, "Infanticide in the Eighteenth Century," in *Crime in England, 1550–1800*, J. S. Cockburn, ed. (Princeton, N.J.: Princeton Univ. Press, 1977), pp. 197–198.
44. *R. v. Hullock*, t17600521-17.
45. t17500425-24.
46. Rearden, t17800028-7.
47. Deacon, t16900226-1.
48. Foster, t17400709-32.
49. Cranberry, t17200427-43.
50. Badham, t17400709-2; Odell, t17600910-38.
51. Masters, t17900424-1.
52. 1 Jac. I c. 8.
53. *Blackstone's Commentaries*, vol. 4, p. 193.
54. Richardson, t16900226-25.
55. Griffin, t17200115-35.
56. 84 E.R. 1080, J. Kelyng, "A Report of Divers Cases in Pleas of the Crown," 1708 at 55.
57. Chetwynd, t17431012-28.
58. John L. Raynor and G. T. Crook, *The Complete Newgate Calendar*, vol. 3 (London: Navarre Society, 1926), pp. 129–131.

59. *Blackstone's Commentaries*, vol. 4, p. 193.
60. Nicholson, t16801013-4.
61. Butler, t16800226-10.
62. Stirn, t17600910-19.
63. Odell, t17600910-38.
64. Fox, t16900226-21.
65. Hullock, t17600521-17.
66. Rearden, t17800028-7.
67. E.g., Riley, t17500912-61 (belly); Pursel, t17700711-37 (heart); Welch, t17901208-1 (gut).
68. Kein, t17200427-28.
69. Thrift, t17500425-29.
70. Hartley, t18000219-10.
71. Jackson, t17401204-6.
72. Fitzgerald, t17200712-15.
73. Clements, t17400416-33.
74. Doughty, t16800707-8.
75. Richardson, t16900226-25.
76. Swiny, t16800115-7.
77. This, according to Horder, was "chance-medley manslaughter," which remained an offense distinct from voluntary manslaughter based on provocation until the middle of the nineteenth century. Jeremy Horder, "The Duel and the English Law of Homicide," *Oxford Journal of Legal Studies* 12 (1992): 28–29.
78. Ely, t17201207-37.
79. Clark, t17500425-19.
80. Deacon, t16900226-1.
81. Griffin, t17200115-35.
82. Merridy, t16900022-11.
83. Foster, t17400709-32.
84. Matthew Kennedy, Patrick Kennedy, t17700221-44.
85. *Blackstone's Commentaries*, vol. 4, p. 199; Hale, *History*, p. 454.
86. *Blackstone's Commentaries*, vol. 4, p. 197; Hale, *History*, p. 432.
87. Watkins, t16801013-2; Whitaker, t16801013-3.
88. Swiny, t16800115-7.
89. Bennet, t16901210-55.
90. McCarty, t17601022-17.
91. Smith, t18300916-5.
92. Stevens, Holyoak, Hughes, t17700630-47.
93. Conoway, Richardson, t17700711-35.
94. Phararo, Murrini, Apologie, t17900416-1.
95. Guyora Binder, "The Origins of American Felony Murder Rules," *Stanford Law Review* 57 (2004): 59.
96. Price, t17180423-24.

97. 168 *E.R.* 150 (K.B. 1773).

98. William Hawkins, *A Treatise of the Pleas of the Crown*, vol. 1 (New York: Arno Press, 1972), p. 86 (originally published 1716); Michael Foster, *Crown Law* (London: E. Brooke, 1776), p. 258.

99. *R. v. Plummer*, 84 *E.R.* 1103 (K.B. 1701); *R. v. Woodburne*, 16 St. Tr. 53 (Suffolk Assizes 1722).

100. Twenty-six of the twenty-eight were stabbings.

101. The exceptions are two related cases where proof of identity was weak, and the jury compromised on a manslaughter verdict. Roxell, Ruttey, t16900430-30.

102. *R. v. Scroop*, t16800115-2 (provoked by tankard flung at head); *R. v. Stark*, t17401204-18 (soldier stabs superior, provoked by caning); *R. v. Knapp*, t17500530-21 (deceased tried to force his way into defendant's house with two others late at night, then threw stones at defendant, who pursued him and stabbed him with a cutlass); *R. v. Jones*, t18101205-49 (deceased pulled defendant's hair and shook him, while he was cutting his dinner with a knife; he struck with the knife in his hand, as deceased was in the act of striking him with a fist); *R. v. Roberts*, t17600709-21 (mounted defendant whipped deceased wagoneer's horses, believing wagon was trying to cut off a cart he was escorting; occupants of wagon cursed him, and he struck them with whip. Deceased got off wagon and chased defendant with stick, striking him; defendant brought sword down on deceased's arm, which medical testimony indicated was probably striking defendant); *R. v. Tomkins*, t16900226-23 (victim struck defendant with a switch while they were practicing shooting).

103. The case of *R. v. Knapp*, cited in the previous note, exemplifies this category as well, as the victim tried to force his way into the defendant's home.

104. *R. v. Floyd* and *R. v. Jones*, t16900226-5, *R. v. J——V——and J——E——*, t16900226-6.

105. Joseph, t18100919-32 (deceased challenged Portuguese sailors to fight, was part of a group that attacked defendant, and stabbed in the belly another Portuguese sailor to whose aid defendant came); Humphreys, t16900717-16 (defendant claimed they both drew during an argument and that deceased struck first); t16901015 (both drew during an argument; jury disbelieved self-defense claim); W—— W——, t16901210-17 (sudden quarrel, both drew); Fort, t17000115-15 (deceased struck defendant, both drew and wounded each other); Hill, t17200907-47 (sitting together in a booth at an inn, defendant and deceased got into a political argument and both drew; defendant convicted of manslaughter, acquitted under the statute of stabbing); Fitzgerald, t17300228-29 (quarrel in a tavern, defendant drew first and challenged deceased, who then drew); Vanrosendall, t16900226-18 (defendant shot victim, claiming that victim had drawn on him, but some evidence indicated he could have avoided confrontation).

106. Smith, t17200602-16

107. Mansuer, t17200712-40.

108. Murphey, t17300828-30.

109. A drunken Margaret Burke was keeping the occupants of a rooming house awake with her raving. An annoyed William Armstrong entered her room and beat her. She

shouted that if he tried it again she would stab him, and he charged into her room, saying he would teach her a lesson, at which she stabbed him in the upper chest. Burke, t17707 11-36; Sheldon, t16900605-2 (deceased struck defendant on head, after which both drew).

110. N—— Y——, t16900115-7 (defendant admitted killing, claimed victim had born him a grudge and set upon him, but there were no witnesses to corroborate his account).

111. Harrison, t16800421-3.

112. Grifein, t18100919-56 (victim was Grifein's wife, rather than her paramour).

113. Lowe, t17800510-58.

114. Wilson, t17601204-13.

115. Callaghan, Mary Donovan, William Donovan, Daniel Donovan, t18200918-29.

116. Higgs, t17700711-38.

117. Hopton, t17500117-18 (unprovoked).

118. Gratrix, t17100906-21.

119. Flanaghan, t17701024-59.

120. Bailey (unnamed), t16800526-6 (grade of homicide of which he was convicted was not specified, but did not appear to be murder).

121. Meeres and Cock, t16900717-13.

122. Haswell, t18000219-11 (provoked: deceased struck defendant for cheating at dominoes, they then fought by agreement); Woolley, t18000219-12 (defendant struck first blow, then they fought by agreement); Francklin, t17300408-40 (defendant and deceased were observed fighting. Medical evidence as to how death came about was inconclusive).

123. Lowe, t17800510-58 (defendant kicked and stomped his wife, rupturing her bladder; claimed her infidelity as provocation).

124. Jones, t17400903-31 (deceased was beaten and kicked, apparently without provocation or much resistance); Stroud, t17501205-60 (no provocation); Brannon and M'mahoan, t17700711-57 (no provocation); McCarthy, t18300916-251 (defendant kicked his wife in the stomach and chest without provocation).

125. Scot, t17000115-16 (unprovoked punch; causation disputed); Smith, t17600227-29 (unprovoked punch, question of causation); Thomas, Eyres, t17780223-10 (unprovoked beating of probable rape victim; causation question, death possibly from exposure); Cooper, t17900223-10 (unprovoked beating and kicking of wife; emphatic medical testimony that victim's bowel disorder due to some unidentified disease rather than a blow; directed verdict of acquittal); Burns, t18300708-134 (unprovoked punch, death after fifteen weeks).

126. Benbrook, t17400116-24 (defendant punched deceased without provocation, deceased fell back against stone steps, fracturing his skull); Bird, t17400709-10 (defendant struck his wife without provocation, who fell against metal bin, striking head); Goulding, t18300415-225 (defendant pushed his pregnant wife, or possibly pulled her out of bed, so that she fell and miscarried, with fatal consequences); Denallan, 16900115-13 (without provocation, defendant pushed victim, who died from the resulting fall).

127. Dawes, t18001203-68 (victim initiated fight without weapons, death probably from fall); Dukes, t18300708-71 (defendant and victim fell during scuffle, victim hit head).

128. Barney, t17701024-55 (schoolmaster hit pupil, whose head knocked against chimney).

129. Hamp, t18100411-39 (defendant punched victim, who fell, but causation of death uncertain); Hale, t18300916-154 (defendant shoved victim, who fell, breaking hip; causation questioned).

130. Hodgson, t18300916-152 (sentry kicked girl swinging on a chain, she fell, cracking her head; no eyewitness to the assault identified the body of the girl who died).

131. Broophy, t18200112-43 (defendant pulled pregnant wife from bed, she fell and hemorrhaged); Lanaway, t18201028-67 (defendant pushed victim, who fell, striking head).

132. Gibbons, t16801013-5 (unprovoked).

133. Hammond, t16901015-31 (without provocation, threw shovel at pig, hit deceased).

134. Coats, t17200712-1 (without provocation, threw brick at child; defendant heard to say victim wasn't dead yet, but she hoped he did die).

135. Williams, t17300513-26 (no provocation).

136. Puryer, t18100606-30 (no provocation).

137. Perry, t18300114-161 (no provocation beyond spitting).

138. Roundson, t17601204-12.

139. Rothery, t18000217-16 (no provocation).

140. Perry, t18300114-161.

141. *Mayes v. People*, 106 Ill. 306 (1883).

142. Gravestock, 16900430-32.

143. Marrey, t17700221-69.

144. Kettleby, t17101206-42 (verdict of chance medley, effectively an acquittal at that time).

145. Parker, t16900226-20.

146. Ockendon, t17201207-49.

147. Cullam, t17600227-32.

148. Catling, t18000402-38.

149. Haily, t18300708-65.

150. Acor, t17900424-26 (medical witness speculated that the baby may have died of tuberculosis).

151. Long, t18301028-112.

152. Westwood, t16800707-5 (defendant struck victim, who fell under wheels of cart); Smith, t17500530-32 (cart driver knocked victim down and his cart went over victim's leg); Skelton, t18200112-42 (defendant struck driver who fell under the moving wheel of his own cart).

153. Smith, t17500530-32; Skelton, t18200112-42.

154. Bragg, t17100906-9.

155. Tompion, t17701024-52.

156. Wolley, t17700711-39 (drunk driver fell off cart, which ran over a child); Hulcup, t17900915-71 (carter negligently ran over victim's leg, there being room to pass);

Bradfield, t18200628-37 (driver rode on horse instead of driving, cart collided with another, victim fell off that other cart).

157. Lee, t17300704-56 (fight between two drivers: victim carelessly hit defendant's horse, defendant punched victim, victim whipped defendant, who punched victim. Victim fell under the wheels of his own cart).

158. Ellison, t18301028-176 (defendant's coach collided with another while passing, victim fell off other coach to death); Marshall, t18300415-168 (carriages collided); Williams, t17900113-60 (driver of coach hit post in fog; victim fell off coach).

159. Cox, t17100906-3 (chance medley when cart horse ran over child without negligence); Langford, t16900903-16 (cart allegedly struck child, but question regarding driver's identity); Drury, t18300916-252 (cart ran over deaf man; defendant may have tried to warn him, provided aid after the collision); Layborn, t18300527-112 (ran over victim with carriage).

FIVE

"An Extraordinarily Beautiful Document"

Jefferson's "Bill for Proportioning Crimes and Punishments" and the Challenge of Republican Punishment

MARKUS D. DUBBER

1. Introduction

It might be supposed that the American Revolution spawned a wave of humanitarian reforms of the criminal law in light of the animating principles of the Revolution, notably a deep respect for the rights of individuals, including those convicted of crime, and a republican commitment to the ideal of self-government. That was not the case.

In fact, the Founders showed remarkably little interest in the criminal law as a problem of governmental power, though they did have occasion to consider its usefulness in suppressing dissent in the young Republic.[1] They instead took the power to punish for granted, as an obvious aspect of the states' all-encompassing power to police their internal affairs. There was no republican theory of criminal law, no *American* criminal law that shed the deeply hierarchical and preconstitutional nature of English criminal law in favor of enlightened, or at least revolutionary, principles of justice. American criminal law instead remained a vestige of a patriarchal system of criminal law, in which the sovereign disciplines wayward members of his state household if, and as, he sees fit, without meaningful constraints on his punitive discretion.

There was no American Beccaria, no American Bentham (or Eden), no American Feuerbach, not even an American Voltaire. While there were occasional calls for criminal law reform, they rarely went beyond vague urgings to move beyond the English Bloody Code. Actual changes in the law were limited to reducing the number of capital offenses (from 180 or so to a dozen or a handful, depending on the state) and then building prisons to house the convicts whose lives were spared as a result.

No comprehensive vision of a republican criminal law was ever laid out. Even the meager proposals to restrict, but not to eliminate, capital punishment were oddly divorced from the political ideals of the American Revolution. They were *unoriginal, arepublican,* and ultimately *apolitical.* They added nothing to the ideas, or the specific reform proposals, that had become commonplace in Europe—including in England itself—since at least the mid-eighteenth century. The one explicit provision in the Bill of Rights dealing with the problem of punishment, the Eighth Amendment's prohibition against "cruel and unusual punishments," adopted without debate and repeated as constitutional boilerplate in state constitution after state constitution, was lifted straight from the English Bill of Rights of 1689[2] (which itself was based on the Magna Carta[3]), a source that not only predated the American Revolution but was as English a document as could be found.[4] Whatever theoretical veneer was occasionally used to cover the pedestrian, uninspired, and unambitious reform proposals of the time consisted of unexplored citations to Beccaria's 1764 bestseller *On Crimes and Punishments,* which soon appeared in several English translations.[5] No effort was made to connect Beccaria's deterrence theory of punishment to republican principles. No suggestion was made that his views on criminal law were either particularly suited to American political ideals or, for that matter, inconsistent with the English system or any other monarchy, however despotic and however devoid of anything resembling the Magna Carta. (Bentham, the obsessive English systematizer of Beccaria's thought, certainly didn't find any such inconsistency, nor did P. J. A. Feuerbach, the drafter of the influential and deterrence-based Bavarian criminal code of 1813.[6])

Proposals for criminal law reform in the early Republic, however, were not only unoriginal and arepublican. More important, they were *apolitical.* To the extent that those convicted of criminal offenses[7] attracted the attention of reform-minded Americans, they were regarded as objects of pity, rather than as legal subjects. Religion was, in the end, the driving force behind actual reform. While the Magna Carta and Beccaria might appear in general calls for criminal law reform, the main engine behind the construction of prisons, the most visible change in American criminal law after the revolution, was Christian benevolence, not a sense of justice. What little American criminal law reform there was consisted of a private act of Christian charity, rather than a public performance of political obligation. It was not a recognition of offenders' individual rights or of principles of equal justice but sprang from the belief that those wretched creatures who, succumbing to the temptations of sin or (particularly in the case of some debtors) merely falling on hard times, committed crimes were God's children, too. The central institution in the reform of American criminal law in the late eighteenth century was not the government (state or federal), but the Philadelphia Society for Alleviating the Miseries of Public Prisons. The main proponents of reform were not republicans (or federalists) or Whigs (or Tories)—they were Quakers (and members of a smattering of other Christian denominations, including Unitarians and Methodists); they were not affiliated with political parties but with churches.

Most notable, however, is not that American criminal law reforms in the wake of the revolution were unoriginal, arepublican, and apolitical—but that they were largely nonexistent. They were nonexistent precisely because the question of state punishment for crime was regarded as neither political nor republican nor original. While the European Enlightenment recognized that the "invention of autonomy"[8] and the discovery of the self-governing subject required a new justification for punishment, the American revolutionaries who announced the birth of a new American science of politics based on the ideal of self-government continued to view punishment as an entirely unproblematic exercise of sovereign power over offenders who were literally at the mercy of the state. The same revolutionaries who went to war under the banner of no taxation without representation; who railed against outlawry, attainder, and "corruption of blood" in English law; and who included an explicit prohibition of bills of attainder in the federal Constitution had no qualms about retaining provisions disenfranchising criminal offenders.[9] Between 1776 and 1821, eleven state constitutions explicitly denied persons convicted of certain offenses the right to vote. By 1868 that number had grown to twenty-nine.[10]

In the following, we will set the stage for a close reading of Jefferson's "Bill for Proportioning Crimes and Punishments in Cases Heretofore Capital" of 1779, unquestionably the closest thing to an attempt at criminal law reform in light of republican principles, by locating it within the context of the broader discourse on the foundations of government in the early Republic as well as religion-based criminal law reform projects of the time. We will then turn to the bill itself, highlighting its disappointingly unfulfilled promise of an American system of criminal law.

2. *Police, Law, and Punishment*

To appreciate how Americans of the early Republic thought—or did not think—about the question of state punishment, it is helpful to invoke two modes of governance that were prevalent in political thought at the time but fell from view over the course of the nineteenth century: police and law.[11] Americans conceptualized punishment as a question of police rather than of law. Punishment as an exercise of the power to police, however, was not subject to the principles constraining government through law. The principles often bundled under "the rule of law" did not apply to state action in general but to state action in the form of law. Police actions, by contrast, were by definition, and often by design, exempt from these principles, which ultimately derived from a political conception that viewed the state as the guarantor of the rights of its autonomous constituents, who consented to the exercise of state power against themselves.

At the time, law and police represented two distinct, and radically different, modes of governance. *Police* was thought of as the householder's authority over members of his household reproduced constructively at the level of the political sovereign, regarded as the *pater patriae*, governing the state as his quasi family. In Blackstone's definition, quoted word for word in scores of American texts, including court opinions until the 1960s,[12] "the public police and oeconomy" meant

> the due regulation and domestic order of the kingdom: whereby the individuals of the state, like members of a well-governed family, are bound to conform their general behaviour to the rules of propriety, good neighbourhood, and good manners: and to be decent, industrious, and inoffensive in their respective stations.[13]

Law, by contrast, was thought to consist of those abstract rules that govern the relationship among equal persons, or citizens. This was a revolutionary and potentially radical notion. The sovereign-as-paterfamilias who guides, and corrects, his *familia* was no longer. The "head of state" was removed, leaving the body to govern itself or, more precisely, leaving the body to govern itself under the rule of *law*. "In America, the law is king," in Thomas Paine's words.[14]

From the perspective of police, then, punishment appears as a question of household discipline, employed by the superior sovereign against his inferior disobedient subject. As such, it may be subject to self-imposed and self-policed limitations of prudence, expedience, and perhaps mercy, but not of justice.[15]

Moreover, as a question of police, punishment is at best a technical bureaucratic concern and as such is neither particularly interesting nor important, at least to a revolutionary or political philosopher.[16] Adam Smith listed "public security" among the "objects of Police," but found it, along with "cleanliness," to be "too minute" to warrant his attention.[17] (His interest in "the opulence of the state," by contrast, led to the *Wealth of Nations*.)

As a matter of public safety, punishment as police is concerned with the disposal of human threats and thus is no different in kind than the establishment and maintenance of a dog-licensing scheme or, perhaps, the control, disposal, and destruction of dangerous or stray animals.[18] As a matter of public health (or "cleanliness"), punishment as police concerns itself with disposing of human waste or, less dramatically, "purifying the circulation" of the community.[19]

As a matter of household discipline, punishment as police raised issues of the proper management of human, and nonhuman, resources, the subject of traditional "economics."[20] These concerns of good governance—how should the wise, good, competent householder treat his wife, children (whether male, female, minor, or adult), slaves, dogs, cattle?—were precisely the questions that the modern science of politics had abandoned as uninteresting and irrelevant. Now that state power derived from the consent of the governed and that the objects of power were also its ultimate subjects, the question of the mechanics of managing the state's human resources was no longer the only, or even the central, question of politics but a subsidiary one that could be delegated to bureaucrats and state technocrats. Governance as household discipline was not the subject of laws; it was a matter of discretion, the rules of which might occasionally be distilled in directives, guidelines, and missives.

To say that government by police is not subject to the rule of law is not to say that it is not subject to rules, or at least guidelines, of any kind. After all, these rules occupied the minds of classical economists (in the private sphere) and classical political thinkers (in the public sphere) for millennia and generated guidebooks of governance as diverse as Marcus Aurelius's *Meditations*,[21] Machiavelli's *The Prince*,[22] and, in colonial America, slave owners' "plantation manuals and rule-books, . . . enforced with whipping and other punishments, including death."[23]

There have always been good and bad ways of running a (quasi) household; and there have always been good householders and bad ones. The rules governing the management of households large and small, public and private, however, are not principles of legitimacy, or of right; instead, they are guidelines of prudence, or of efficiency. They allow one to evaluate the quality, or competence, of the householder; they say nothing about the legitimacy, or justice, of his management. They are business principles, not legal principles. They focus on the subject of governance, not on the object, and maintain a categorical distinction between the two. In government by police, there is a manager and there are the managed, there is a governor and there are the governed. The objects of government were not conceived of as bearers of rights, who were entitled to respect as persons capable of self-government, but as resources in the hands of the subject of government; they were part of the householder's household, along with other resources, human and nonhuman.

Within this view of government as economics, or household management, punishment was discipline or correction for offenses against the peace of the household, and therefore ultimately against the householder. Private (micro) household discipline in turn was subject to rules enforced by the public (macro) householder. Even in medieval law, the lord's authority to discipline his serf did not extend to depriving him of "life or limb," or "slaying or maiming" him, at least in theory.[24]

The limitation of the micro householder's authority over his family-household itself reflected the householder's integration into the sovereign's state-household. The lords were thus reduced to the status of overseers who enjoyed disciplinary authority over their charges only within the limits set by the macro householder. An excessively violent lord was subject to the sovereign householder's discipline as a bad overseer or administrator.[25]

The traditional remedy for the loss of life or limb was, fittingly, an appeal in the royal courts, in the nature of a complaint by the king's man that the lord had exceeded his disciplinary authority over him.[26] Excessive discipline violated the peace of the king's macro household, to which both discipliner and disciplined belonged. An appeal against a lord in the royal courts thus served as a, presumably painful, reminder of his equality with the villein vis-à-vis their common master. The implication of extending royal protection to villeins—and slaves—for the inferior status of masters was as clear to English lords in the twelfth century as it was to Virginia plantation owners in the eighteenth.[27] Consider, in this regard, an eighteenth-century missive from the English King to his Virginia colony, in which the King expresses his displeasure with the failure to prosecute masters who had killed their slaves: "[A]t the time, the Slave is the Master's Property he is likewise the King's Subject, and that the King may lawfully bring to Tryal all Persons here, without exception, who shall be suspected to have destroyed the Life of his Subject."[28]

Destroying the life of a member of the king's macro household affected the king's householder authority in two ways. Most immediately, it deprived the king of a resource, an object of household governance.[29] What's more, it represented the assumption by a member of the king's macro household of a power—in fact, the most awesome power—reserved for the supreme paterfamilias, the power of life and death. If anyone had the authority to take the life (or limb) of a member of the household, it was the king (whether or not he enjoyed that power courtesy of yet another, and yet more powerful, householder, God). Faced with the fact of death, the very least the king could do to exercise his prerogative over life and death—the *ius vitae necisque* of the Roman paterfamilias—after the fact, so to speak, was to apply it to the person who had assumed it, the offender. Whether he pardoned him or disciplined him, in one way or another, through physical pain or monetary fine, was entirely within his discretion.[30]

Whatever limitations the macro householder imposed on the micro householder's discipline of members of his micro household thus themselves reflected the political rather than the legal nature of the system of punishment.[31] The householder's power to discipline was emphatically *not* limited by any rights possessed by the objects of his discipline. The only protection against abuse by one householder could come from another, superior, householder.

The patriarchal underpinnings of punishment were rarely made explicit by Anglo-American commentators in the late eighteenth and early nineteenth centuries. For a noteworthy exception, consider the following essay, which—though not addressing the legitimacy of criminal punishment in general—frames the propriety of a particular criminal sanction, the death penalty, as a question of good patriarchal governance:

Cicero calls his country "*Parens communis*"—what should we think of a parent who corrects his child by putting him to death? "The case of a civil ruler and his subject," says a sensible and energetic writer,

> is much like that of a father and his minor son. If the son behave himself unseemly, the father may correct him. If after all due admonitions, and corrections, the son should prove to be incorrigible, the father may expel him from his family, and he may disinherit him; but may not *kill* him. All civil as well as parental punishments ought to be mild, humane, and corrective; not vindictive, inhuman, and extirpating. They ought to be merciful, not rigorous; proportionate to the crime, not excessive; and tend to the reformation of the delinquent, but not to his destruction; and should be inflicted with reluctance, love, and affection; not with passion, hard-heartedness, and asperity. The highest encomium that can be bestowed on good rulers is when we style them *the fathers of their subjects, and the protectors of their rights*.[32]

This passage touches on many of the central aspects of patriarchal punishment, that is, punishment as police. The punisher is the father (or at least the *parens*). The punished is not only a member of his family but a minor, thus twice inferior to the head. Crime is analogized to "unseemly behavior," and punishment to "admonitions" and "corrections." A distinction is drawn between types of offenders, with the "incorrigible" ones being singled out for special treatment—expulsion. Glossing over the practice of *noxal surrender*, in which the paterfamilias, instead of paying reparation, turned over an offending member of his *familia* so that the victim may exact whatever punishment (including death) he deemed appropriate, the argument suggests that the rejection of capital punishment flows directly from the limitations inherent in the very nature of "paternal punishment." Note, however, the flexible nature of these limitations: paternal punishments *ought* to be mild, merciful, reformative, and—importantly—"proportionate to the crime"; they *should* be inflicted with love, "not with passion, hard-heartedness, and asperity." The normative import of these prudential guidelines stems not from a grounding in principles of justice, or the rights of the punished, but from the image of the "good ruler" and, presumably, whatever interest in others' contemporaneous or posthumous approval the ruler happens to muster.

Also noteworthy is the conflation of the realms of police and law, of prudence and justice, or rather the denial of the existence of a distinct realm of law in the first place. For the "good rulers" are not only "fathers of their subjects," but also "protectors of their rights." Here even the "rights" of the patriarch's "subjects"—a term used to mark the inferiority of household members vis-à-vis the householder, rather than their status as self-governing persons, or legal subjects—are within the protection of the householder. Even the rights of the punished are internal to the household, rather than the source of external constraints on the householder's power. The language of rights is (still) the language of police.

The reference to proportionate punishment deserves attention if only because calls for proportionality in punishment were common among those who turned their attention, however briefly, to matters of criminal law reform at the time (see, for instance, Jefferson's "Bill for Proportioning Crimes and Punishments," discussed in detail later). For now, suffice it to say that calls for proportionality as a rule of thumb are not inconsistent with a view of punishment as police. To see the connection between police and proportionality, it's useful to consider the question of proportionality alongside the final, and most fundamental, limitation identified in the quoted passage, that punishment "should be inflicted with reluctance, love, and affection; not with passion, hard-heartedness, and asperity." Proportionality as a guidepost of police—unlike proportionality as a requirement of law—does not arise from any right of the punished. Instead it reflects the punisher's discretionary assessments of what is prudent given the circumstances, of what he *should* do, rather than of what he *may* do.

As a matter of prudence, the punisher-householder may well decide to adopt a general rule of proportionality when meting out discipline. If his interest lies in deterring future acts of ill discipline, he may well feel that punishments should be roughly proportionate to offenses insofar as excessive *anticipated* punishments (the anticipated pain of which significantly outweighs the anticipated pleasure associated with the offense) might have an undesired chilling effect on desirable behavior. Similarly, even if excessive *inflicted* punishment might succeed in deterring undesirable behavior (and only that), it might prove to be inexpedient because it may reduce the punished's productivity, and therefore the welfare of the household, the maximization of which a good householder seeks.[33] Similarly, the householder might decide, with Bentham, that matching the quality of punishment and crime will enhance the punishment's efficacy. Bentham distinguished between various forms of this type of proportionality, including "The same Instrument used in the Crime as in the Punishment," "For a Corporal Injury a similar Corporal Injury," "Punishment of the Offending Member," and "Imposition of Disguise assumed." So arson should be punished by proportionate, and analogous, burning, carefully calibrated to the offender's act.[34]

In some, extraordinary, cases policing may be so ineffective, and the connection between means and end so unfathomably remote (as evidenced, for instance, by a tendency to inflict grossly disproportionate—and therefore counterproductive—punishments) that one might suspect incompetence on the part of the policer (rather than, say, recalcitrance on the part of the policed). While inexpediency by itself ordinarily remains comfortably within the householder's margin of discretion without compromising his supreme authority, *extreme* inexpediency may—at least in theory—amount to evidence of *unfitness* on the part of the householder or quasi householder. In colonial America, for instance, the master in his management of the slave as a household resource was presumed to act for the well-being of his household, the plantation. This presumption, however, was not irrebuttable, at least in law if not in fact.[35]

The use of measures "so great and excessive to put life and limb in peril, or where permanent injury to the person was inflicted" provided evidence of that "malicious and wrongful spirit" that marked the policer as unfit for his supervisory post.[36] In the context of quasi-patriarchal discipline on board of a ship as enforced by the captain against his crew, "clear and unequivocal marks of passion on the part of the captain," punishment "manifestly excessive and disproportionate to the fault," and, for our purposes most interesting, the use of "unusual or unlawful instruments" likewise revealed that the disciplinary measure wasn't in fact disciplinary at all, but motivated by the policer's self-regarding interest in gratifying an evil impulse,[37] suggesting that his "heart is wrong."[38]

Note that from the perspective of these traditional limitations on the policer's power over his inferiors, the familiar constitutional prohibition of "cruel and unusual" punishment appears as an *internal* limitation on the state's power to police, inherent within the power itself. As a police matter, cruel and unusual punishment is prohibited because it reveals an improper, self-regarding motive on the part of the punisher, not because it interferes with a

..ght of the punished.³⁹ The Eighth Amendment, after all, was copied from the decidedly preconstitutional English Bill of Rights of 1689; in fact, a proportionality limitation appeared already in the Magna Carta, not to mention the ius commune.⁴⁰

3. Christian Police and Criminal Law

There was nothing republican (or original) about the patriarchal police model of government. On the contrary, the revolution was a complete and utter rejection of the idea of police. The revolution was based on ideals of self-government, equal rights, and personhood, which were not only entirely inconsistent with the deeply hierarchical police model of government but arose out of a critique of that very model. Americans were tired of being policed by the English sovereign-householder. They didn't mind taxation; they went to war over taxation *without representation*. They sought law and autonomy, instead of police and heteronomy.

It is all the more puzzling that the revolutionary generation would see nothing problematic in retaining a system of criminal law as police that treated criminal offenders exactly the way they had been treated by the king of England. The solution to the puzzle lies in the fact that they saw criminals as radically different (or as irrelevantly similar), not as autonomous legal subjects but as objects of police discipline. More generally, once they took over power it turned out that they didn't object to government as police as long as they were doing the policing. Hence the continued subjugation, and disenfranchisement, of women, paupers, and, of course, slaves.⁴¹ Autonomy under law was the revolutionary ideal, except for those incapable of governing themselves, offenders chief among them.⁴²

But at least the police model frames the problem of government in general, and of punishment in particular, as a problem of state action. The police model may elevate household governance to the macro level, but it does not deny its public nature—a police action is by definition a state action, even if it is one beyond the scope of legitimation.

The same cannot be said for the many criminal law reform proposals of the time that were couched in *religious* terms.⁴³ Churches, of course, were also traditionally regarded, and governed, as households.⁴⁴ And perhaps religion-based criminal law reforms can be seen as attempts to improve the governance of wayward souls as members of a particular church or religious community. But the American state was no church and none of the proponents of religion-based criminal law reform suggested otherwise. Moreover, membership of criminal offenders in a particular church (or any church) was not a prerequisite, explicit or implicit, for their qualification as objects of reform. Still, it is worth noting that the particular nature of the reforms proposed, and implemented, tended to reflect the church membership and religious beliefs of their advocates. In fact, one might think of the prison reforms pushed by adherents of various Christian denominations (Quakers, Unitarians, Methodists) as attempts to construct prisons as churches—and even families—comprising the inmates and their guards (and ministers), with each church-family reflecting the theological precepts of the respective denomination.[45] But while (constructive) membership in a church, and subjection to its governance, might have been the intended *result* of religion-based reform proposals, it was not a prerequisite of it.

Offenders attracted the attention of religious reformers not as fellow church members but as Christian brothers (and sisters), as fellow children of God. Private charities, rather than the state or even churches, took up their plight. The reformers didn't view themselves as superior to the objects of their charity. "There but for the grace of God go I" was the driving sentiment, reflecting a sense of equality not based on equal political rights but on common fallibility. The 1787 constitution of the Quaker-dominated Philadelphia Society for Alleviating the Miseries of Public Prisons, the most successful of the crime charities, is very instructive in this regard:

> When we consider that the obligations of benevolence, which are founded on the precepts and example of the author of Christianity, are not cancelled by the follies of crimes of our fellow-creatures; and, when we reflect upon the miseries which penury, hunger, cold, unnecessary severity, unwholsome apartments, and guilt, (the usual attendants of prisons) involve with them, it becomes us to extend our compassion to that part of mankind, who are the subjects of these miseries, by the aids of humanity, their undue and illegal sufferings may be prevented: the links, which should bind the whole family of mankind together under all circumstances, be preserved unbroken: and, such degrees and modes of punishment may be discovered and suggested, as may, instead of continuing habits of vice, become the means of restoring our fellow-creatures to virtue and happiness.[16]

This "benevolence" and "compassion" toward "our fellow-creatures" was entirely Christian. As such it was private rather than public, discretionary rather than obligatory, religious rather than political, and (though broadly familial) had nothing to do with either police or law. Criminal law reform thus was not the state's concern but a matter of individual conscience.

While the details of Christian charity (and the variations among the denominations) may be safely ignored in the present context, the role of benevolence and compassion is worth considering in greater detail. The Christian reformer *identifies* with the offender—he regards him as a "fellow-creature" or, more precisely, as a fellow child of God. He does not identify with him as a fellow citizen, a fellow person, or a fellow holder of (equal) rights. The identification is religious: it is both apolitical and arepublican. The offender has no political or legal claim to the Christian reformer's attention; he is but the happy beneficiary of the reformer's Christian charity.[47]

This faith-based charity is entirely private and entirely discretionary. As such, it can dissipate at any moment. It may be not only temporary and fickle but also arbitrary and discriminatory. In fact, the zeal of early American prison reformers waned fairly quickly after the objects of their most intense compassion, debtors, were first housed separately from other inmates and then freed of criminal sanctions altogether.[48] Once the prisons had been emptied of the good prisoners, those "worthy characters . . . reduced by misfortune," leaving only the bad ones, the "wretches who are a disgrace to human nature,"[49] it may have been considerably more difficult to muster the requisite compassion. The distinction between the two groups of prisoners also roughly coincided with distinctions of social class, with the debtors' (former?) social class more closely resembling that of the reformers.[50]

The nature of the identification with the punished is of great significance. Any normative judgment, including—most important in the present context—the ascription of criminal responsibility, requires empathy, that is, putting oneself in the shoes of the object of one's judgment.[51] Empathy in turn presupposes the recognition of a relevant point of identification with the other as well as the willingness to identify with him in fact. Without identification between judge and judged, and between punisher and punished, punishment becomes an exercise of heteronomous oppression, which merely reaffirms the inferiority of the punished, thus excluding him from the class of persons capable of self-government, that is, the political community of citizens. It becomes an alegitimate act of police beyond the realm of justice.[52]

Only the identification with the punished as a fellow potentially autonomous citizen is consistent with the legitimation of punishment in light of republican principles. Other types of identification, such as among "fellow-creatures" or children of God or Quakers or merchants or Philadelphians, are irrelevant even if they may improve the punished's plight, at least in the short run. Similarly, the refusal to identify with *some* offenders—be they labeled "wretches who are a disgrace to human nature," "incorrigible" offenders, or "persons, who are guilty of enormous crimes"[53]—precludes legitimation of their punishment.

Given the immense difficulty of this identification in cases of horrific crime, legitimating punishment of the most odious offenders presents, paradoxically, the greatest, not the least, difficulty. As we'll see, even those who had an inkling of the special and novel challenge punishment posed in a republican government as a rule fell well short of this task.

Having discussed the two prevalent approaches to the question of crime and punishment prevalent during and after the American Revolution, patriarchal police and Christian charity, which were unoriginal, arepublican, and—in the latter case—also apolitical and utterly failed to appreciate, never mind address, the dramatic challenge of devising a legitimate system of republican criminal law, we will now turn to the first and best effort to derive a system of criminal law from the basic principle of political legitimacy driving the foundation of the American Republic, self-government or autonomy: Thomas Jefferson's Virginia "Bill for Proportioning Crimes and Punishments in Cases Heretofore Capital" of 1779.

That effort was a spectacular, and telling, failure.

4. Jefferson on Crime and Punishment: Deter, Reform, Exterminate

Jefferson's stab at criminal law reform fell short in several respects. One is apparent on its face: The "Bill for Proportioning Crimes and Punishments in Cases Heretofore Capital" was limited in scope, dealing with punishments, not with crimes or principles of criminal liability, and only with punishments for a very few offenses at that, namely, capital ones.[54] Jefferson's ambition did not exceed those of other reform proponents of the time: he was largely content to reduce the number of capital offenses from the universally criticized Bloody Code, without, however, proposing to do away with capital punishment altogether.[55]

Most important, the bill made no serious effort to achieve its stated goal of "deduc[ing] from the purposes of society" a principle of proportionate punishment, never mind a comprehensive system of republican criminal law. Rather than setting out a republican approach to criminal law consistent with the political principle of self-government that alone could legitimate state action, Jefferson ended up drawing on Anglo-Saxon dooms to retain such penalties as ducking and whipping, while making general reference to the need to deter potential offenders through "long-continued spectacles" of penal servitude, to "reform" offenders "committing an inferior injury," and to "exterminate" anyone "whose existence is become inconsistent with the safety of their fellow citizens," albeit only as "the last melancholy resource."[56]

In the end, the substance of Jefferson's bill provides a sketch of punishment as a matter of good governance, rather than as a matter of right, suggesting that Jefferson did not differ from his fellow architects of the new Republic in continuing to conceive of punishment as a matter of police, rather than of law. Jefferson's bill did not come close to laying the foundation for the continuing process of critique in light of principles of justice without which republican punishment cannot be legitimated.

A. PUNISHMENT AND OTHER POLICE MATTERS

Jefferson was well familiar with the distinction between governance by police and by law. Among the bills Jefferson drafted for the Virginia Committee for the Revision of the Laws, which also included the punishment proportionality bill (no. 64), was "A Bill for Amending the Constitution of the College of William and Mary, and Substituting More Certain Revenues for Its Support" (no. 80). This bill called for, among other things, the establishment of a chair of "law and police" as one of eight professorships at the College of William and Mary, the first holder of which was Jefferson's former teacher and now fellow law revisor, George Wythe.[57] The chair was to cover both "municipal" and "oeconomical" law: municipal law, or law in the narrow sense, included "common law, equity, law merchant, law maritime, and law ecclesiastical," whereas "oeconomical law," or police, encompassed "politics" and "commerce."[58]

This aspect of Jefferson's reform of William and Mary has received scant attention.[59] One noteworthy exception is Herbert Baxter Adams who, writing in 1887, emphasized the parallels between Jefferson's reform and Continental police academies. By the late nineteenth century, however, the distinction between police and law had been lost to such an extent that Adams found it necessary to explain the notion of police to his readers:

> This was much the same as the modern science of administration, which is just beginning anew to creep into our university courses in America. What the German would call *Polizeiwissenschaft*, and what the Greeks termed πολιτεία, was taught for nearly a century at the college of William and Mary under the head of "*police*." That name would probably suggest nothing but constabulary associations to most college faculties in these modern days.[60]

While the proportionality bill in the end remained mired in a pre-Revolutionary, prerepublican concept of punishment as police, it began with high ambitions of placing the punitive power of the state on principles of law. As

Jefferson reports in his *Autobiography*, he felt upon his return from the Inaugural Congress to his home state of Virginia that

> our whole code must be reviewed, adapted to our republican form of government, and, now that we had no negatives of Councils, Governors & Kings to restrain us from doing right, that it should be corrected, in all it's parts, with a single eye to reason, & the good of those for whose government it was framed.[61]

As chairman of the revision committee, which also included Wythe, Edmund Pendleton, George Mason, and Thomas Lightfoot Lee, Jefferson had an opportunity to put this ambitious plan into action. At a meeting on January 13, 1777, the committee settled certain basic principles of form and substance and divided up the work. Jefferson took responsibility for revising the first of three periods of English statutory law and the law of descents. Mason originally was assigned the criminal law, among other things. Upon Mason's resignation from the committee shortly after the meeting, Jefferson added the criminal law to his list of things to do.[62]

Although they did not exclude it from their comprehensive revision enterprise, neither Jefferson nor his fellow revisors expressed any particular interest in criminal law reform in light of republican principles.[63] According to Jefferson's *Autobiography*, the committee members assembled only a short and vague list of "leading principles" to guide the revision of Virginia's criminal laws: "On the subject of the Criminal law, all were agreed that the punishment of death should be abolished, except for treason and murder; and that, for other felonies should be substituted hard labor in the public works, and in some cases, the Lex talionis."[64]

Mason's notes, the only surviving record of the 1777 meeting, are a bit more extensive on the subject (perhaps because the criminal law was among his responsibilities), at least in that they specify in somewhat greater detail which noncapital punishment was to attach to some of the formerly capital crimes ("Forfeiture, Fine, Labour in public-works, such as mines, Gallies, Saltworks, Dock-Yards, Founderies, and public manufactories"[65]). At the same time, they contain no reference to the *lex talionis*, an omission that is all the more surprising given Jefferson's remarkably strict adherence to this principle in the bill and his later complaint that he was forced to do so in light of the committee's specific instructions on this point.[66]

Otherwise, the bill follows Mason's notes, though it does dispense with pardons altogether, an issue the committee decided to "defer to be consider'd at the next meeting." Opposition to the pardon power of the executive was widespread at the time as it was regarded by many as a vestige of the sovereign king's prerogative, and as a particularly clear instance of his patriarchal police power, which—as we've noted—included not only the power to punish but also the power to amerce, that is, in his mercy to refrain from (physical) punishment (in exchange for payment of a fine).[67] Here too it is noteworthy that Jefferson, upon his assumption of the governorship in 1779, himself made frequent use of the pardon as his executive prerogative; he regularly issued conditional pardons for offenders under sentence of death provided they worked in the lead mines or other public works.[68]

At the outset it is important to place the bill within the context of the revision project as a whole. The bill was, after all, not an isolated effort to reform the criminal law of Virginia. It was one of 126 bills prepared by the committee of revisors, and, as we've noted, Jefferson took on the subject of criminal law only after Mason's resignation. It would therefore be a mistake to read it as an outgrowth of Jefferson's particular interest in, or concerns about, the criminal law of his home state. Other subjects were much closer to his heart, including "the law of Descents," which "fell of course within my portion," as well as bills dealing with freedom of religion, freedom of the press, and public education, also subjects in which Jefferson took a particular interest. The contrast between these bills—including, for instance, those calling for the abolition of entail and primogeniture, which he regarded as aristocratic remnants inconsistent with the principles of a republic of equal self-governing citizens, modeled after his idealized vision of Anglo-Saxon society before the Norman conquest—and the proportionality bill could not be starker. The former provide a powerful illustration of what Jefferson could achieve when he was indeed committed to reviewing an area of the law and adapting it "to our republican form of government." By contrast, the proportionality bill is uninspired and undermotivated.[69]

The bulk of the 126 bills comprising the "revision of the laws" addressed mundane affairs of government and were no more ambitious than the proportionality bill. Bills such as those "directing the course of descents," "for the more general diffusion of knowledge," and "for establishing religious freedom" were the exception, not the rule. The proportionality bill was flanked by bills "concerning guardians, infants, masters, and apprentices" (no. 60), "to enable guardians and committees to perform certain acts for the benefit of those who are under their care" (no. 61), "for the restraint, maintenance and cure of persons not sound in mind" (no. 62), and "for registering births and deaths" (no. 63), on one end, and by bills "for punishing persons guilty of certain forgeries" (no. 65), "concerning treasons, felonies and other offences committed out of the jurisdiction of this commonwealth" (no. 66), and "concerning truces, safe conducts, passports, licenses, and letters of marque" (no. 67), on the other. In fact, the vast majority of the bills dealt with matters of police, rather than of law, including

- military discipline (no. 5)
- poor relief (no. 32)
- strays (no. 39)
- horned cattle, horses, deer (nos. 41–43)
- licenses for tavern owners and attorneys (nos. 45, 97)
- public roads and ferries (nos. 46, 47)
- "mill-dams and other obstructions of water courses" (no. 48)
- burial of dead bodies on board ships (no. 49)
- public storehouses (no. 50)
- slaves, servants, runaways, mulattoes, aliens (nos. 51–54, 56)
- the sale of "unwholesome meat or drink" (no. 76), the spread of small pox (no. 77), and quarantine (no. 78)[70]

A bill dealing with the disposal of criminal offenders as a question of police fit far better into this typical (diverse, bureaucratic, mundane, comprehensive yet incomplete, unsystematic, ahuman) list of police regulations[71] than the occasional right-based bill, such as the bill "for establishing religious freedom," which provided that no one should be compelled "to frequent or support any religious worship, place, or ministry whatsoever" and that "all men shall be free to profess, and by argument to maintain, their opinions in matters of religion."

B. COKE, NOT BLACKSTONE

The punishment proportionality bill has been largely ignored by historians. It did not pass; but then neither did the much-analyzed (and much-praised) freedom of religion bill.[72] A better explanation is that the bill was anachronistic, haphazard, incomplete, and altogether disappointing. Jefferson simply showed very little interest in the subject of criminal law. With nothing to say about the substance of the bill, he turned to its form. The best thing that could be said about his effort was that it was pleasing to the eye. In the words of Dumas Malone, one of Jefferson's many distinguished biographers, the manuscript of the bill is "an extraordinarily beautiful document":

[Jefferson] attached notes in Anglo-Saxon characters, in Latin, old French, and English, attesting the meticulous carefulness of his procedure. [He] placed them in columns, parallel with the text, after the manner of his old law book, *Coke upon Littleton*; and, as in the work of the old master, they frequently encroach upon the text. The penmanship is beautifully clear, and no other document that Jefferson ever drew better exhibits his artistry as a literary draftsman.[73]

Jefferson's "conscious imitation of the form of old legal treatises" went so far as to affect his spelling. As Julian Boyd points out in his edition of Jefferson's papers:

[I]n the first part of [the manuscript] TJ spelled the word "forfeit" as he was accustomed to do; he changed suddenly to "forfiet," going back to the beginning of [the manuscript] to alter the spelling from "forfeit" to "forfiet." From that point on . . . the word is spelled "forfiet" as if it had always been TJ's habit to do so.[74]

Boyd goes on to note that in the

exfoliation of notes and citations, drawn from classical authors and the ancient Anglo-Saxon laws, as well as such modern penologists as Beccaria, TJ was not so much creating a memory-saving device as he was yielding to the temptation to indulge in pedantic ostentation. . . . This mass of notes and citations, as well as the labored and artificial imitativeness in the form of the MS, may be partly responsible for [Malone's] judgment that "during the years 1776–1779, he gave more time to this bill than to all the rest together."[75]

Boyd's overall assessment of the bill is harsh, refreshingly straightforward, and also very quotable:

The preamble of this Bill stated in superb language the enlightened ideas of Beccaria and others; but the terms of the law that TJ proposed did little more than restate generally accepted practices concerning capital offenses. In respect to crimes of mayhem, the reliance upon the *lex talionis* [by providing that the maimer "be maimed or disfigured in like sort"] contrasts shockingly with the liberal thought of the age.[76]

Jefferson himself seems to have sensed the bill's shortcomings. Already in 1778, before the bill was presented to the legislature as part of the revision package, he wrote to Wythe that the talionic principle, which plays such a central role in the bill, "will be revolting to the humanised feelings of modern times" and "needs reconsideration."[77] In his *Autobiography* he professed that "[h]ow this . . . revolting principle came to obtain our approbation, I do not remember."[78] While he told Wythe that he had followed "the scale of punishments settled by the Committee," there is, as we have seen, no mention of an agreement on the talionic principle in general or on specific talionic penalties in the only surviving record, Mason's notes.

Jefferson did not care for criminal law, nor did he know very much about it, nor did he have any ideas about how to reform it. So he procrastinated and engaged in the contemporary equivalent of playing with fonts and margins and footnotes, and then—to waste further time—prepared a copy of the manuscript.[79] The primary use he had for the criminal law reform bill was to practice his penmanship.

For inspiration, on both substance and form, he turned to "the old master," his beloved Coke. To copy Coke's habit of writing marginal comments so extensive and independent of the main text as to amount to a second, parallel, text was one thing. To also copy the *substance* of Coke's seventeenth-century work was another. That Jefferson would consult Coke to learn about the substance of criminal law was no accident. Jefferson learned his common law from Coke, whom he admired as a true master of the common law. As he put it in a letter to his friend Madison in 1826,

> You will recollect that before the revolution, Coke Littleton [referring to Coke's first Institute, criminal law being treated in the third] was the universal elementary book of law students, and a sounder whig never wrote, nor of profounder learning in the orthodox doctrines of the British constitution, or in what were called English liberties.

Jefferson thus read—and copied—Coke not only because it was the trusted authority on the common law but also because he shared what he considered Coke's whigism, which he contrasted with Blackstone's "toryism": [W]hen his black-letter text, and uncouth but cunning learning got out of fashion, and the honeyed Mansfieldism of Blackstone became the students' hornbook, from that moment, [the legal] profession . . . began to slide into toryism.[80]

In Jefferson's view, Blackstone's *Commentaries*, unlike "the deep and rich mines of Coke, Littleton," had been "perverted . . . to the degeneracy of legal science."[81] Rather than digest the common law and capture its gnarly detail and what Jefferson saw as its stubborn, and always fact bound and therefore restrained, commitment to the preservation of the liberties of Englishmen, the *Commentaries* pretended to systematize and scientize the material with "elegance" but also without the Whig's fundamental distrust of central authority hidden behind an apparently abstract, and objective, system of legal principles.

And so instead of consulting the newfangled and dangerously facile and ambitious Blackstone, Jefferson got his criminal law from the modest Coke, who focused on the past, rather than the present, never mind the future. The result was a bill that amounted to a willfully unsystematic and reactionary replication of Coke's "learned and authoritative 'jumble.'" The bill didn't just draw on medieval law. Much of it consists of *quotations* from medieval law texts in the "margins," so much of it in fact that it qualifies as a partial replica of a medieval legal document. Coke is cited and quoted no fewer than twenty-two times; Bracton's thirteenth-century tract *De legibus et consuetudinibus Angliae*, ten times; Hale's seventeenth-century criminal law treatise, seventeen times; and last but not least, Anglo-Saxon dooms from the ninth and tenth centuries (in the original Anglo-Saxon), *twenty-five* times.[82] By comparison, Blackstone is cited (never quoted) eleven times, mostly in string citations along with other sources, which is a remarkably small number given the *Commentaries*' dominance as the leading treatise *and textbook* on the common law at the time.[83]

Just as remarkable, the entire bill contains only four minor string citations to Beccaria, none of which have anything to do with Beccaria's celebrated theoretical argument in *On Crimes and Punishments*.[84] (Montesquieu and Pufendorf score only one citation each.) Boyd's harsh words about Jefferson's bill, therefore, are not quite harsh enough. To say that Jefferson's copious notes drew "from classical authors and the ancient Anglo-Saxon laws, as well as such modern penologists as Beccaria" is at least misleading insofar as it obscures the relative irrelevance of the latter compared to the former. Counting charitably, the four citations to Beccaria are dwarfed by the seventy-four citations to "classical authors and the ancient Anglo-Saxon laws."

While Boyd is correct to point to the Dr. Jekyll–Mr. Hyde nature of the bill, whose benighted substance has nothing to do with its benign (if not entirely enlightened) preamble, it is both less and more than a restatement "in superb language [of] the enlightened ideas of Beccaria and others." Jefferson makes no reference to Beccaria or to his principle of "greatest happiness of the greatest number," which drives his penology (and Bentham's). Instead the preamble contains hints of what a republican criminal law might set out to achieve, or how a republican criminal law might be legitimated, even if it does not suggest what a legitimate republican criminal law might actually look like. (What follows the preamble makes it clear that Jefferson had no idea how to meet this challenge. He could not have believed that cribbing Coke and the Laws of Athelstan and Cnut was the answer.)

Before taking a closer look at Jefferson's preamble, clearly the most significant portion of the bill, the remainder of the bill deserves at least a quick look. Some highlights will suffice, since Boyd's judgment requires little elaboration. The death penalty was retained for treason (high and petit[85]) and murder. Other capital punishments were replaced by sentences of hard labor. Jefferson detailed what he had in mind for the "malefactors condemned to labour for the Commonwealth" in a separate bill (no. 68):

> [M]alefactors . . . shall be employed to row in the gallies of the commonwealth, or to work in the lead mines, or on fortifications or such other hard and laborious works, for the behoof of the commonwealth, as by the Governor and Council, in their discretion, shall be directed: And during the term of their condemnation . . . shall have their heads and beards constantly shaven, and be clothed in habits of coarse materials, uniform in color and make, and distinguished from all others used by the good citizens of this commonwealth; that so they may be marked out to public note as well while at their ordinary occupations, as when attempting to escape from the public custody.[86]

The bill provided for castration as the punishment for "rape, polygamy, or sodomy" (a woman instead was to suffer "cutting thro' the cartilage of her nose a hole of one half inch diameter at the least"). Murder by poison was punished by poisoning.[87] Maiming, as we've seen, was punished by maiming in kind.[88] Murder by dueling was punished by hanging, the dead body then to be placed in a gibbet—with further punishment for anyone who removed it and instructions to replace it.[89] Petit treason—the ultimate police offense of killing one's householder—was retained as a crime separate from and more serious than murder, punishable by hanging, followed by dissection by "Anatomists."[90] (There were several petit treason cases in eighteenth-century Virginia, all of them against slaves, resulting in horrific punishments.[91]) Other humiliating punishments such as ducking, whipping, and the pillory were retained, for offenses including witchcraft (!) and larceny.

Not all the medieval laws copied in the bill served to increase the severity, and brutality, of punishments. Prison escape, for instance, was not a crime in and of itself (except for the escapee's outside helpers); according to Jefferson's marginalia, it was "doubtful" whether breach of prison was a felony at common law.[92] Jefferson's gloss on this rule is consistent with the police model of punishment in that it focuses on the punisher's bad character, rather than on the punished's rights, and presumes the punished's inability to govern himself in the face of the "law of nature":

> It is not only vain, but wicked, in a legislator to frame laws in opposition to the laws of nature, and to arm them with the terrors of death. This is truly

creating crimes in order to punish them. The law of nature impels every one to escape from confinement.

Jefferson also proposed, or rather retained (as he saw it), restitution to the victim as a sanction in property offenses, in addition to a sentence to hard labor. Although Jefferson does not make this point in his marginalia, this latter feature of the bill is consistent with a view of criminal law that moves beyond the traditional police-based conception. In the traditional view, the object of criminal law was to maintain the householder's peace, which eventually was transformed into the "public" peace, once the "people" replaced the "king" as sovereign, at least in theory. Offenses against the householder's peace were offenses against the householder and his ability to maintain his peace, which was synonymous with that of his household.

This view of criminal law is, as we've seen, utterly incompatible with a republican system of government, which is based on the equality of all constituents of the political community and recognizes self-government, manifested through consent, as the only legitimation for coercive state action against any of these constituents.[93] Under this view, a crime is the violation of one person's right by another person, and the state's right to punishment is restricted to the protection of one person's right against violation by another.

Restitution of the loss suffered by one person, the "victim," at the hands of another, the "offender," is consistent with this, republican, view of criminal law, which regards the person, not the state-householder, as the paradigmatic victim of every criminal offense.[94] In fact, one way of framing the challenge of republican government is to ask why, and under what circumstances, state punishment is legitimate if restitution is possible, that is, if the victim's injury can be remedied without the infliction of punitive pain on the offender.

Elsewhere Jefferson is very clear about his view of the role of government in a republic, although he did not draw any explicit conclusions for a republican system of criminal law. In 1816, for instance, he argued that "[n]o man has a natural right to commit aggression on the equal rights of another; and this is all from which the laws ought to restrain him."[95] In fact, he advocated an early version of Mill's harm principle when, as early as 1776, he observed in his "Notes on Locke" that "[l]aws provide against injury from others; but not from ourselves"[96] and, a little later on in his *Notes on the State of Virginia*, that "[t]he legitimate powers of government extend to such acts only as are injurious to others."[97] Jefferson mustered this argument in support of his calls for religious freedom and freedom of expression ("[I]t does me no injury for my neighbour to say there are twenty gods, or no god. It neither picks my pocket nor breaks my leg."⁹⁸) without, however, connecting it to the broader question of the legitimacy of state punishment or the scope of criminal law.

C. THE PREAMBLE'S PROMISE

The perfect place for Jefferson to sketch the foundations, and limitations, of state punishment was, of course, the preamble to his criminal law bill. And the preamble does contain a number of suggestive remarks that deserve comment.

Jefferson begins by acknowledging that crime "frequently happens," a welcome recognition that must be the starting point for any account of criminal law. By contrast, political theory today has nothing to say about the challenge of punishment because it has consciously limited itself to questions of ideal theory under conditions of perfect compliance.⁹⁹ The problem of punishment, however, arises only in the event of noncompliance. Already in a 1776 letter to Pendleton, Jefferson rejected "[t]he fantastical idea of virtue and the public good being a sufficient security to the state against the commission of crimes, which you say you have heard insisted on by some."¹⁰⁰ In other words, Jefferson realized that even if an ideal theory had been developed, and implemented, the problem of crime would not cease to exist, leading—in his mind—to the need for retaining a system of punishment even after the establishment of a republican government. He went on to explain, however, that his ambitions in reforming such a system of punishments were strictly limited. "It is only the sanguinary hue of our penal laws which I . . . object to. Punishments I know are necessary, and I would provide them, strict and inflexible, but proportioned to the crime. Death might be inflicted for murther and perhaps for treason . . . Rape, buggery &c. punish by castration."¹⁰¹

A republican system of punishment, Jefferson continued in the preamble, must be "deducible from the purposes of society," the "principal" purpose being to "secure enjoyment" of men's "lives, liberties and property."¹⁰² Crimes, however, are "violations on the lives, liberties and property of others." The criminal law's function is to "restrain" and "repress" them.

Here, then, are the rudiments of a republican theory of crime and the scope of criminal law, pieced together from the preamble and various remarks on criminal law Jefferson made in other contexts.

Victims of crime are individual persons. The state is authorized, and in fact obligated, to protect the basic rights of its constituents (life, liberty, property), if necessary through the use of punishments. These serve a repressive, rather than a retributive, function.

The state's punitive power, however, does not extend beyond the protection of the "lives, liberties, and property" of its constituents. It does not, as we've seen, reach beliefs or even acts that are not harmful to others nor does it reach conduct that is harmful only to the actor.

Repression of crime can be achieved in three ways: deterrence, reformation, and incapacitation ("exterminat[ion]"). So having offenders perform hard labor in public would transform them into "living and long continued spectacles to deter others from committing the like offences." Reformation is also "an object worthy the attention of the laws." Incapacitation is reserved for those "whose existence is become inconsistent with the safety of their fellow citizens."

Crimes are committed by "wicked and dissolute men resigning themselves to the dominion of inordinate passions." The preamble refers to offenders as "members of society" and "fellow citizens." Among offenders the person "committing an inferior injury" must be distinguished from others. He "does not wholly forfiet the protection of his fellow citizens, but, after suffering a punishment in proportion to his offence is entitled to their protection from all greater pain." From this entitlement derives the requirement of proportionality ("a duty in the legislature to arrange in a proper scale the crimes which it may be necessary for them to repress, and to adjust thereto a corresponding gradation of punishments").

Jefferson doesn't explain what distinguishes the good offender from the bad one, a problem of classification that continues to befuddle penologists to this day. (A version of this distinction not only figured prominently in the Philadelphia prison reform movement of the late eighteenth century but also, in a slightly more differentiated version, has been central to treatmentist penology since its inception in the late nineteenth century.[103]) It would seem that "wicked" offenders would be incorrigible. Those who are (only) "dissolute," however, might have a better chance of correction. Their reformation presumably would have them throw off the "dominion" of "inordinate passions," and exercise their capacity for self-government, by drawing on their reason or, perhaps, passions, provided they are ordinate; one such passion might be benevolence (or perhaps even a sense of *justice*), which was central to Jefferson's view of personhood.[104]

This reading of the nature of crime, and of criminals, would be consistent with the widespread disenfranchisement of offenders, on the grounds that they were not in a position to *exercise* their capacity for self-government (along with paupers, servants, slaves, and women), though some suggest instead that they lacked the capacity altogether (in which case it would be difficult to make sense of punishment as rehabilitation or correction since there would be nothing susceptible to correction).

Capital punishment runs afoul of the requirement of proportionality as framed by Jefferson to the extent it exterminates those who might be reformed and thereby "weaken[s] the state by cutting off . . . useful members." It also forecloses the aforementioned opportunity for deterrence through the use of public labor as an alternative punishment for corrigible offenders. What's more, "cruel and sanguinary laws" are self-defeating; instead of deterring, they arouse the benevolence of others "to withhold prosecutions, to smother testimony, or to listen to it with bias."

Jefferson does not call for the abolition of capital punishment. Specifically, he makes no mention of Beccaria's well-known argument that capital punishment violates the social contract because no one has agreed, or may agree, to subject himself to death.[105] In fact, Jefferson, as we have noted already, retains not only capital punishment but corporal punishment as well: "For rendering crimes and punishments therefore more proportionate to each other: Be it enacted by the General assembly that no crime shall be henceforth punished by deprivation of life or limb *except those hereinafter ordained to be so punished*" (emphasis added).

In the end, Jefferson's interest in the preamble was not to provide a legitimation of punishment in general, even if one could be cobbled together along the lines suggested. As his letter to Pendleton makes clear, punishment in his mind was simply necessary to provide "sufficient security to the state against the commission of crimes," without exploring the connection between "the security of the state" and the protection of its constituents against violations of their rights. Rather than legitimating punishment as a whole, Jefferson was content to address the problem of *excessive*, that is, disproportionate, punishment.

He did, however, recognize that the question of proportionality was worth consideration because certain offenders retained their status as fellow citizens or members of society despite their crime. This is a crucial insight and frames the problem of punishment as a question of politics in general, and one of law (as opposed to police) in particular. Punishment is not only justified in terms of protecting the rights of persons as legal subjects (rather than of enforcing the authority of the sovereign) but also constrained by the recognition that victims as well as offenders are legal subjects endowed with *the same rights*, the protection of which justifies their punishment.

Jefferson's view of punishment as a political problem, however, remained limited. It did not include those offenders, wicked or incorrigible or both, who had inflicted more than "an inferior injury" and thereby had revealed themselves to exist beyond the border of the political community. These outlaws, "whose existence is become inconsistent with the safety of their fellow citizens," were subject to being "cut off" from the state. Their execution posed no political problem; at best it might engage the public's benevolence when, as "the last melancholy resource," they are "exterminated." Outlawry, after all, also was a familiar feature of medieval English law—and one Jefferson did not hesitate to employ when he deemed it appropriate.[106]

Conclusion

Jefferson was right. For radical law reform in light of republican principles, most importantly the fundamental principle of self-government, there was no time like the present: "Our rulers will become corrupt, our people careless.... It can never be too often repeated, that the time for fixing every essential right on a legal basis is while our rulers are honest, and ourselves united."[107]

In the case of criminal law, this opportunity was missed. It is no accident that Jefferson wrote these cautionary words in the context of a discussion of freedom of religion, one of his central concerns. Neither Jefferson nor anyone else of his generation recognized, or addressed, the full force of the new republican challenge to the legitimacy of the state's inflicting punitive pain on the very persons from whom it derives its legitimacy, of depriving those of life, liberty, and property (and limb) whose "lives, liberties, and property" it exists to preserve.

While the preamble to his "Bill for Proportioning Crimes and Punishments in Cases Heretofore Capital" contains some hints about how a republican system of criminal law might be legitimated, the bill itself was a remarkable failure, an empty reprise of medieval dooms.

No other attempt to come to grips with the problem of republican punishment has been undertaken, never mind succeeded. The moment had passed. Edward Livingston's system of penal codes (including a Code of Crimes and Punishments, a Code of Procedure, a Code of Evidence, a Code of Reform and Prison Discipline, and a Book of Definitions), completed some fifty years later (in 1826), already was too far removed from the moment of revolutionary crisis to question the legitimacy of every form of state action under the new republican regime. Livingston hoped to succeed where his admired English master Bentham had failed, having bombarded American legislatures, governors, and presidents with codification offers for years, none of which bore fruit.[108] His codes ("framed on the great principle of utility!"[109]) resembled Bentham's in rigorously utilitarian approach, detail, scope, and length. They also met the same fate, one they shared with Jefferson's earlier half-hearted attempt at criminal law reform: none of them was enacted.[110]

Notes

1. In the Federalist Papers, for instance, Alexander Hamilton spoke of the need of government to hand out "a penalty or punishment for disobedience," *Federalist No. 15*, pp. 73, 78; *Federalist No. 21*, p. 106, and in particular "the disorderly conduct of refractory or seditious individuals." *Federalist No. 16*, pp. 81, 85. Here a "vigorous" government was needed to dispose of those "seditions and insurrections . . . that are, unhappily, maladies as inseparable from the body politic as tumors and eruptions from the natural body." *Federalist No. 1*, pp. 1, 3; *Federalist No. 28*, p. 146.

2. Compare "That excessive bail ought not to be required, nor excessive fines imposed, nor cruel and unusual punishments inflicted" (English Bill of Rights) with "Excessive bail shall not be required, nor excessive fines imposed, nor cruel and unusual punishments inflicted" (Eighth Amendment). The Eighth Amendment was not the only provision in the Bill of Rights to be adopted without debate. See Leonard Levy, *Origins of the Fifth Amendment: The Right against Self-Incrimination* (New York: Oxford Univ. Press, 1968), p. 411.

3. Magna Carta, chap. 20 ("A freeman shall not be amerced for a slight offense, except in accordance with the degree of the offense; and for a grave offense he shall be amerced in accordance with the gravity of the offense, yet saving always his livelihood, and a merchant in the same way, saving his merchandise, and a villein shall be amerced in the same way, saving his wainage; if they fall into our mercy. And none of the aforesaid amercements shall be imposed except by the testimony of reputable men of the neighborhood."); see also ibid. chaps. 21–22. The ius commune of the time apparently also recognized proportionality and the offender's resources as considerations relevant for the imposition of fines. R. H. Helmholz, "Magna Carta and the ius commune," *University of Chicago Law Review* 66 (1999): 297, 326–327.

4. See, generally, Anthony F. Granucci, "'Nor Cruel and Unusual Punishments Inflicted': The Original Meaning," *California Law Review* 57 (1969): 839.

5. For a typical example, see William Bradford's well-known 1793 *Enquiry How Far the Punishment of Death Is Necessary in Pennsylvania*: "The general principles upon which penal laws ought to be founded appear to be fully settled. Montesquieu and Beccaria led the way in the discussion. . . . [A] remarkable coincidence of opinion, among the enlightened writers on this subject, seems to announce the justness of their conclusions: and the questions which still exist are rather questions of fact than of principle." William Bradford, *An Enquiry How Far the Punishment of Death Is Necessary in Pennsylvania* (Philadelphia: T. Dobson, 1793), p. 3; see also *Annual Report of the Inspectors of the Philadelphia County Prison, Made to the Legislature* (Harrisburg, Pa.: J. M. G. Lescure, 1791), p. 54 (Beccaria's "opinions have the force of axioms in the science of penal law"); see, generally, Paul Spurlin, "Beccaria's *Essay on Crimes and Punishments* in Eighteenth-Century America," *Studies on Voltaire and the Eighteenth Century* 27 (1963): 1489.

6. On Feuerbach, see Gustav Radbruch, *Paul Johann Anselm Feuerbach: Ein Juristenleben*, 3d ed. (Göttingen: Vandenhoeck & Ruprecht, 1969).

7. As opposed to, say, criminal *suspects*, who did enjoy various procedural protections (see, e.g., Fourth through Sixth Amendments to the federal Constitution), all of which, however, were also unoriginal and arepublican in that they were, quite consciously, taken from English common law, as the rightful extension of the full rights of Englishmen to Americans, who had been shamelessly denied these rights by a corrupt monarch or parliament for too long. The challenge of republican punishment—and any other attempt to legitimate punishment—becomes more acute as the person moves through the penal process, from suspect, to defendant, to convict, to inmate, to condemned. See Markus Dirk Dubber, *The Sense of Justice: Empathy in Law and Punishment* (New York: New York Univ. Press, 2006), chap. 5.

8. See J. B. Schneewind, *The Invention of Autonomy: A History of Modern Moral Philosophy* (Cambridge: Cambridge Univ. Press, 1997).

9. U.S. Const., art. 1, §9. Note, however, that this provision is generally interpreted as motivated by separation-of-powers concerns, rather than as a protection of offenders' rights. On this reading, it was legislative attainders that the drafters meant to prohibit, rather than attainders in general (and judicial ones in particular); bills of attainder were prohibited, not attainder itself. *United States v. Brown*, 381 U.S. 437, 440 (1965) ("an implementation of the separation of powers, a general safeguard against legislative exercise of the judicial function or more simply—trial by legislature"). The Founders' rejection of attainder also was not as categorical as one might think. While Jefferson's "Bill for Proportioning Crimes and Punishments in Cases Heretofore Capital," to be discussed in greater detail later, provided that "[n]o attainder shall work corruption of blood in any case," it did not reject attainder in all cases. In fact, Jefferson himself in 1778 drafted a bill of attainder against "a certain Josiah Philips labourer of the parish of Lynhaven and county of Princess Anne" for treason, providing that "it shall be lawful for any person with or without orders, to pursue and slay the said Josiah Philips and any others who have been of his associates or confederates at any time . . . , or otherwise to take and deliver them to justice to be dealt with according to law provided that the person so slain be in arms at the time or endeavoring to escape being taken." See Thomas Jefferson, *Papers*, vol. 2, Julian P. Boyd et al., eds. (Princeton, N.J.: Princeton Univ. Press, 1950), pp. 189–193, 506–507.

10. Today, forty-eight states prohibit inmates from voting while incarcerated for a felony offense, thirty-five disenfranchise felons on parole, thirty-one disenfranchise felons on probation, and five deprive all offenders permanently of their right to vote. Alec C. Ewald, "'Civil Death': The Ideological Paradox of Criminal Disenfranchisement Law in the United States," *Wisconsin Law Review* 2002: 1045; *Felony Disenfranchisement Laws in the United States* (Washington, D.C.: Sentencing Project 2004), p. 1 (available at http://sentencingproject.org/pdfs/1046.pdf).

11. See, generally, Markus Dirk Dubber, *The Police Power: Patriarchy and the Foundations of American Government* (New York: Columbia Univ. Press, 2005).

12. See *Commonwealth v. Keller*, 35 D. & C. 2d 615 (Pa. Ct. Common Pleas 1964) (creating common law misdemeanor of "indecent disposition of a dead body").

13. William Blackstone, *Commentaries on the Laws of England*, vol. 4 (Oxford: Clarendon Press, 1769), p. 162.

14. Thomas Paine, *Common Sense* (New York: Penguin Books, 1986) (originally published in 1776).

15. On the distinction between prudence and justice, see Adam Smith's *Lectures on Justice, Police, Revenue and Arms*, delivered at Glasgow in the 1750s and early 1760s, where he differentiated between "political regulations" founded "upon the principle of *justice*" and upon the principle of "*expediency*," the latter being "calculated to increase the riches, the power, and the prosperity of a State." "Introduction," Adam Smith, *Lectures on Jurisprudence*, R. L. Meek, D. D. Raphael, and P. G. Stein, eds. (Oxford: Clarenden Press, 1978), pp. 1, 3 (quoting Dugald Stewart, *Account of the Life and Writings of Adam Smith, LL.D.* [Edinburgh: n.p., 1794]). Smith regarded jurisprudence as "the theory of the general principles of law and government," which had "four great objects": "Justice, Police, Revenue, and Arms." The object of "[j]ustice" in turn was "the security from injury"; "[p]olice" by contrast concerned itself with "cheapness of commodities, public security, and cleanliness." Adam Smith, "Jurisprudence, or Notes from the Lectures on Justice, Police, Revenue, and Arms delivered in the University of Glasgow by Adam Smith Professor of Moral Philosophy," in ibid., pp. 396, 398.

16. Instead of struggling to reconceptualize punishment in republican terms under the rule of law, the Founders simply relabeled it to reflect the change in police authority. See John Adams, "Thoughts on Government, Apr. 1776," in *Papers of John Adams*, vol. 4, Robert Taylor, ed. (Cambridge, Mass: Belknap Press of Harvard Univ. Press, 1977), p. 86 (questioning "[w]hy may not indictments conclude, 'against the peace of the Colony of and the dignity of the same?'" in place of the traditional reference to the king's peace). I am indebted to Robert Steinfeld for this reference.

17. Smith, p. 398.

18. See Markus Dirk Dubber, *Victims in the War on Crime: The Use and Abuse of Victims' Rights* (New York: New York Univ. Press, 2002), pp. 40–47 (exploring parallels between animal control and criminal law).

19. William Roscoe, *Observations on Penal Jurisprudence and the Reformation of Criminals* (London: T. Cadell and W. Davies, 1819), p. 152 ("A Penitentiary is ... in the community, what the lungs are in the human body, an organ for purifying the circulation, and returning it, in a healthy state, to perform its office in the general mass").

20. M. I. Finley, *The Ancient Economy* (Berkeley: Univ. of California Press, 1973), p. 17 ("The word 'economics,' Greek in origin, is compounded from *oikos*, a household, and the semantically complex root, *nem-*, here in its sense of 'regulate, administer, organize'"); see also Jean-Jacques Rousseau, *A Discourse on Political Economy* (Oxford: Oxford Univ. Press, 1994) (originally published in 1755).

21. Marcus Aurelius, *Meditations*, Gregory Hays, trans. (New York: Modern Library, 2002) (originally published in 167).

22. Niccolo Machiavelli, *The Prince*, W. K. Marriott, ed. (New York: Dutton, 1908) (originally published in 1515).

23. See Jonathan A. Bush, "Free to Enslave: The Foundations of Colonial American Slave Law," *Yale Journal of Law and the Humanities* 5 (1993): 417, 426. After the Enlightenment, "good police" became a sociological or ethical, rather than a political or moral,

question. See, e.g., Max Weber, "Politics as a Vocation," in *Essays in Sociology,* Hans Heinrich Gerth and C. Wright Mills, trans. and eds. (New York: Dutton, 1946), p. 77 (ethic of responsibility).

24. Frederick Pollock and Frederic William Maitland, *The History of English Law before the Time of Edward I,* vol. 1 (Cambridge: Cambridge Univ. Press, 1968), pp. 415–416, 437 (originally published in 1898); Paul R. Hyams, *King, Lords and Peasants in Medieval England: The Common Law of Villeinage in the Twelfth and Thirteenth Centuries* (Oxford: Clarenden Press, 1968), p. 127.

25. A fourteenth-century English text explains that "the king now had a kind of 'fee sutyl en noun de seigneurie' in each man, so that *the lord became a sort of mesne between the king and the serf whom he ought to treat 'pur lui enprower e ne nie dampner.'*" Ibid., p. 128.

26. Ibid., pp. 135–136.

27. Southern plantation owners, in fact, often thought of themselves as manor lords and as such "[n]ot only . . . assume[d] control over their households and slaves, they resented and opposed the intrusion into their own affairs." Michael Stephen Hindus, *Prison and Plantation: Crime, Justice, and Authority in Massachusetts and South Carolina, 1767–1878* (Chapel Hill: Univ. of North Carolina Press, 1980), p. 9 (South Carolina low country).

28. Arthur P. Scott, *Criminal Law in Colonial Virginia* (Chicago: Univ. of Chicago Press, 1930), p. 202.

29. See J. H. Baker, *An Introduction to English Legal History,* 3d ed. (London: Butterworths, 1990), p. 601 (excusable homicide "'contempt' to the king for depriving him of a subject").

30. If conversely the serf harmed his lord or otherwise gave him offense, he was subject to whatever discipline the lord deemed appropriate or, if the lord proved incapable of enforcing his authority in this way, to corporal punishment imposed by a court, usually including whipping. If he killed his lord, he was guilty of petit treason, punishable by execution with any number of qualifications, including drawing, quartering, dismemberment, and public display of the severed head. In America these punishments survived until the late eighteenth century, with the crime of petit treason not being abolished until well into the nineteenth century. See Dubber, *Police Power,* pp. 24–30.

31. On this use of "political," see *United States v. Hing Quong Chow,* 53 F. 233, 234 (E.D. La. 1892).

32. William Roscoe, *Observations on Penal Jurisprudence and the Reformation of Criminals* (London: Cadell, Davies & Arch, 1819), pp. 38–39 (quoting *Essays on Capital Punishments,* republished by Basil Montagu, Esq., in his *Opinions of Different Authors upon the Punishment of Death* [Buffalo, N.Y.: Wm. S. Hein, 1984], p. 159 [originally published 1811]).

33. Note, however, that excessive punishment would not be inexpedient simply because it is unnecessary to have the desired deterrent effect. The unnecessary suffering of the punished by itself is, unlike in Beccarian-Benthamite theory, which equally weighs anyone's utility and disutility, of no interest. See Jeremy Bentham, "Principles of Penal Law (Rationale of Punishment)," *The Works of Jeremy Bentham,* vol. 1, John Bowring, ed. (New York: Russell & Russell, 1962, pp. 365, 398 (originally published in 1830).

34. Jeremy Bentham, *The Rationale of Punishment* (London: C. & W. Reynell, 1830),

pp. 56–62 ("It would be necessary carefully to determine the text of the law, the part of the body which ought to be exposed to the action of the fire; the intensity of the fire; the time during which it is to be applied, and the paraphernalia to be employed to increase the terror of the punishment.").

35. Arthur P. Scott, *Criminal Law in Colonial Virginia* (Chicago: Univ. of Chicago Press, 1930), p. 299 ("almost unlimited").

36. *State v. Mabrey*, 64 N.C. 592, 593 (1870).

37. Joel Prentiss Bishop, *New Commentaries on the Criminal Law*, 8th ed. (Chicago: T. H. Flood, 1892), p. 532 (quoting *Butler v. McLellan*, 1 Ware 219, 320).

38. *United States v. Clark*, 31 F. 710 (E.D. Mich. 1887).

39. For a similar interpretation of the constitutional prohibition against ex post facto laws, see *Calder v. Bull*, 3 U.S. 386, 389 (1798) (ex post facto lawmaking "stimulated by ambition, or personal resentment, and vindictive *malice*").

40. See Helmholz, "Magna Carta."

41. See, generally, Robert J. Steinfeld, "Property and Suffrage in the Early American Republic," *Stanford Law Review* 41 (1989): 335.

42. As John Adams wondered aloud in defense of the continuing disenfranchisement of women, paupers, and criminal offenders: "It is certain in Theory, that the only moral Foundation of Government is the Consent of the People. But to what an Extent Shall We carry This Principle?" Letter to James Sullivan, May 26, 1776. *Papers of John Adams*, vol. 4, Robert Taylor, ed. (Cambridge, Mass: Belknap Press of Harvard Univ. Press, 1977), p. 208. A century before, the proposals of the English Levellers likewise stopped short of expanding the franchise to "women, children, criminals, servants, and paupers." Edmund S. Morgan, *Inventing the People: The Rise of Popular Sovereignty in England and America* (New York: Norton, 1988), pp. 68–69. I am indebted to Robert Steinfeld for this reference.

43. Cf. Grotius's theory of punishment, which had stressed the identity of humans in contrast to omniscient and omnipotent God. Hugo Grotius, *De Jure Belli ac Pacis* (London: J. W. Parker, 1853), bk. 2, chap. 20, § 4 (originally published in 1625).

44. See Dubber, *Police Power*, pp. 12–14, 60–61.

45. See Christopher Adamson, "Wrath and Redemption: Protestant Theology and Penal Practice in the Early American Republic," *Criminal Justice History* 13 (1996): 75.

46. "Constitution of the Philadelphia Society for alleviating the Miseries of Public Prisons" (May 8, 1787), *Reform of Criminal Law in Pennsylvania: Selected Enquiries, 1787–1819* (New York: Arno Press, 1972), p. 105. See also William Roscoe, *Observations on Penal Jurisprudence and the Reformation of Criminals* (London: Cadell, Davies & Arch, 1819), pp. 176–177 (reform "is founded on Christian principles, and applies the precepts of our religion to the conduct of our lives [and] considers a criminal as an unfortunate fellow-creature, led on to guilt through a great variety of causes, but capable by kindness, patience, and proper discipline, of being reformed and restored to society").

47. Note also the identity of reformer and offender in contrast to omniscient and omnipotent God. Grotius, bk. 2, chap. 20, § 4.

48. See, generally, Markus Dirk Dubber, "The Right to Be Punished: Autonomy and Its Demise in Modern Penal Thought," *Law and History Review* 16 (1998): 113.

49. Michael Meranze, "The Penitential Ideal in Late Eighteenth-Century Philadelphia," *Pennsylvania Magazine of History and Biography* 108 (1984): 431, 442 (quoting *Pennsylvania Gazette*, Sep. 26, 1787).

50. Cf. Michael Meranze, *Laboratories of Virtue: Punishment, Revolution, and Authority in Philadelphia, 1760–1835* (Chapel Hill: Univ. of North Carolina Press, 1996), pp. 60, 156, 176 (class tensions in late eighteenth-century Philadelphia).

51. See, generally, Dubber, *Sense of Justice*.

52. See Dubber, "Right to Be Punished," p. 113.

53. John E. O'Connor, "Legal Reform in the Early Republic: The New Jersey Experience," *American Journal of Legal History* 33 (1978): 95, 99 (quoting New Jersey Gov. William Paterson).

54. The latter limitation is often obscured by the fact that Jefferson's bill tends to be cited as "A Bill for Proportioning Crimes and Punishments."

55. English criminal law, as the governor of New Jersey, William Paterson, put it in 1793, "is written in blood, and cannot be read without Horror." See O'Connor, "Legal Reform in the Early Republic," pp. 95, 99.

56. Preamble.

57. Thomas Jefferson, "Notes on the State of Virginia" (1781), query xv, http://etext.lib.virginia.edu/toc/modeng/public/JefVirg.html; Thomas Jefferson, "A Bill for Amending the Constitution of the College of William and Mary, and Substituting More Certain Revenues for Its Support" (1779), http://members.tripod.com/~candst/jefflaw2.htm.

58. Herbert Baxter Adams, "The College of William and Mary," *A Contribution to American Educational History*, No. 1 (Washington, D.C.: Government Printing Office, 1887).

59. But see Christopher L. Tomlins, *Law, Labor, and Ideology in the Early American Republic* (Cambridge: Cambridge Univ. Press, 1993).

60. Ibid., p. 39n1.

61. Thomas Jefferson, *Autobiography*, http://etext.virginia.edu/toc/modeng/public/JefAuto.html, p. 37 (originally published in 1821).

62. See Jefferson, *Papers*, vol. 2, p. 316.

63. For (later) calls for republican reform more specifically focused on criminal law, see Kathryn Preyer, "Crime, the Criminal Law and Reform in Post-Revolutionary Virginia," *Law and History Review* 1 (1983): 53, 78 (in Jefferson's own Virginia, George Keith Taylor, speaking in support of criminal law reform after Jefferson's bill had failed, "charged his colleagues with passively submitting to a system 'calculated to awe and crush the humble vassals of monarchy' and urged them to revise the criminal law 'to comport with the principles of our government'"); Bradford, *Enquiry*, p. 5 (William Bradford, in a well-known abolitionist speech in 1793 before the Philadelphia Society for Alleviating the Miseries of Public Prisons, complained that "laws, the offspring of a corrupted monarchy, are fostered in the bosom of a youthful republic"); Adamson, "Wrath and Redemption," pp. 75, 93–94 (Thomas Eddy, a wealthy Quaker, pushed for the establishment of penitentiaries in New York in the 1790s on the grounds that New

York's colonial criminal law reflected "monarchical principles" and was "imperfectly adapted to a new country, simple manners, and a popular form of government").

64. Jefferson, *Autobiography*, p. 39.

65. Jefferson, "Bill for Proportioning," p. 325.

66. Letter to George Wythe, Nov. 1, 1778, ibid., pp. 229, 230.

67. On the pardon power, see James Wilson, "Executive Department," *Lectures on Law, The Works* (Cambridge, Mass.: Harvard Univ. Press, 1967), pp. 442–444 (originally published in 1804).

68. Preyer, "Crime," pp. 53, 68.

69. Jefferson also showed great interest in providing for freedom of the press and of religion. Neither his draft constitution for Virginia (1776) nor his subsequent proposals for a bill of rights for the federal Constitution includes any mention of an analogue to the prohibition of cruel and unusual punishments that later appeared in the federal Bill of Rights; both, however, contained provisions guaranteeing freedom of the press and of religion. See David N. Mayer, *The Constitutional Thought of Thomas Jefferson* (Charlottesville: Univ. of North Carolina Press, 1994), p. 155 (discussing Jefferson's correspondence with Madison in the early 1780s about the proposed federal bill of rights).

70. Jefferson, *Papers*, vol. 2, pp. 329–333.

71. For discussions of similar police lists over the centuries, including American regulations in the late eighteenth and early nineteenth centuries passed under the states' police power, see, e.g., William J. Novak, "Common Regulation: Legal Origins of State Power in America," *Hastings Law Journal* 45 (1994): 1061, 1076 (N.Y. legislature between 1781 and 1801); William J. Novak, *The People's Welfare: Law and Regulation in Nineteenth-Century America* (Chapel Hill: Univ. of North Carolina Press, 1996); Dubber, *Police Power*; see, generally, Mariana Valverde, *Law's Dream of a Common Knowledge* (Princeton: Princeton Univ. Press, 2003), pp. 157–163.

72. No records of, or newspaper reports on, the debate on the bill are available. Preyer, "Crime," pp. 53, 69–70. Madison suggested, however, that the consideration of the entire revision project came to a halt when deliberations reached the proportionality bill. Ibid., p. 69.

73. Dumas Malone, *Jefferson and His Time*, vol. 1, *Jefferson the Virginian* (Boston: Little, Brown, 1948), pp. 269–270 (commenting on "Bill for Proportioning Crimes and Punishments in Cases Heretofore Capital" [1778]).

74. Jefferson, *Papers*, vol. 2, p. 504.

75. Ibid., p. 505.

76. Ibid.

77. Letter to George Wythe, Nov. 1, 1778, Jefferson, *Papers*, vol. 2, pp. 229, 230.

78. Jefferson, *Autobiography*, p. 39 (originally published in 1821). The 1778 letter to Wythe cited in the preceding note might have refreshed Jefferson's memory; there he mentions two reasons for adopting the *lex talionis*: its common law roots and its simplicity ("The *lex talionis*, altho' a restitution of the Common law, to the simplicity of which we have generally found it so advantageous to return will be revolting to the humanised feelings of modern times.").

79. Jefferson, *Papers*, vol. 2, pp. 504–505.

80. Letter to James Madison, Feb. 17, 1826, *The Writings of Thomas Jefferson*, vol. 10, Paul Leicester Ford, ed. (New York: Putnam, 1892–1899), pp. 375–376; see, generally, Mayer, *Constitutional Thought of Thomas Jefferson*, chap. 1.

81. Letter to John Tyler, June 17, 1812, *The Writings of Thomas Jefferson*, vol. 13, Andrew A. Lipscomb and Albert Ellery Bergh, eds. (Washington, D.C.: Thomas Jefferson Memorial Association, 1904), pp. 166–167.

82. The medieval quotations in the bill are so extensive that the editor of Jefferson's papers had to employ the services of one "Professor Robert K. Root, Princeton University, for transcription of the Anglo-Saxon text." Jefferson, *Papers*, vol. 2, p. 504.

83. See, e.g., Robert A. Ferguson, *Law and Letters in American Culture* (Cambridge, Mass.: Harvard Univ. Press, 1984), p. 11 (*Commentaries* "rank second only to the Bible as a literary and intellectual influence on the history of American institutions").

84. See Paul Spurlin, "Beccaria's *Essay on Crimes and Punishments* in Eighteenth-Century America," *Studies on Voltaire and the Eighteenth Century* 27 (1963): 1489.

85. On high and petit treason (killing of one's macro and micro householder, respectively) as the ultimate police offenses, see Dubber, *Police Power*, pp. 24–30.

86. "A Bill for the Employment, Government and Support of Malefactors Condemned to Labour for the Commonwealth," Jefferson, *Papers*, vol. 2, p. 513. The bill wasn't passed. In his *Autobiography*, Jefferson writes that he later had second thoughts about this proposal, after an experiment in exhibiting prisoners "as a public spectacle" had proved unsuccessful in Pennsylvania. Jefferson, *Autobiography*, p. 41.

87. Kathryn Preyer notes that poisoning was generally associated with homicides committed by slaves and that it was the only type of homicide punishable by death in kind. Preyer, "Crime," pp. 53, 64. Note also that, as Coke points out, "of all felonies, murder is the most hainous, [a]nd of all murders, murder by poysoning is the most detestable." Edward Coke, *The Third Part of the Institutes of the Laws of England* (London: M. Flesher for W. Lee and D. Pakeman, 1644), p. 47.

88. "Whosoever on purpose and of malice aforethought shall maim another, or shall disfigure him, by cutting out or disabling the tongue, slitting or cutting off a nose, lip or ear, branding, or otherwise, shall be maimed or disfigured in like sort: or if that cannot be for want of the same part, then as nearly as may be in some other part of at least equal value and estimation in the opinion of a jury."

89. Trying to account for the brutal punishment for dueling, Preyer speculates that "unrestrained, unregulated individual combat might rend the bonds of social unity within the governing class and threaten social stability." Preyer, "Crime," pp. 53, 66. This explanation would be inconsistent with the preamble's limited view of criminal law as designed to protect citizens' "lives, liberties, and property" (discussed later) since the loser in a duel would be just as dead as any other homicide victim, with the exception that he had consented to his death (and thus seemingly entitling the winner to mitigation, if anything, not aggravation in punishment). It would be more consistent, however, with a view of punishment as police, which would regard the blatant interference with the

sovereign's monopoly of violence a particularly serious and egregious offense against his (or its) authority. Harsh punishment, and particularly demeaning punishment, for micro householders who engage in dueling (mere household members would simply fight, not duel, one another) thus would put them in their (inferior) place, reasserting the sovereign's supremacy.

90. On anatomy as a punishment enhancement, see Peter Linebaugh, "The Tyburn Riot against the Surgeons," in *Albion's Fatal Tree*, Douglas Hay et al., eds. (New York: Pantheon, 1975).

91. See Scott, *Criminal Law in Colonial Virginia*, pp. 161–162.

92. Jefferson, *Papers*, vol. 1, p. 502.

93. For a sample of Jefferson's frequent references to the significance of self-government and consent for the legitimacy of government, see Mayer, *Constitutional Thought of Thomas Jefferson*, pp. 22, 54, 70, 85.

94. See, generally, Dubber, *Victims in the War on Crime*, part 2.

95. Letter to Francis W. Gilmer, June 7, 1816, *The Writings of Thomas Jefferson*, vol. 10, Paul Leicester Ford, ed. (New York: Putnam, 1892–1899), p. 32.

96. "Notes on Locke and Shaftesbury," Jefferson, *Papers*, vol. 1, pp. 544, 546. The proportionality bill does away with forfeiture as punishment for suicide, though on the ground "[t]hat Suicide injures the state [!] less than he who leaves it with his effects." Ibid., p. 496.

97. Jefferson, *Notes on the State of Virginia*, query xvii.

98. Ibid.

99. See, e.g., John Rawls, *A Theory of Justice* (Cambridge, Mass.: Belknap Press of Harvard Univ. Press, 1971) (ideal political theory of well-ordered society); Jürgen Habermas, *Between Facts and Norms: Contributions to a Discourse Theory of Law and Democracy*, William Rehg, trans. (Cambridge, Mass.: MIT Press, 1996), p. xxxix (criminal law beyond scope of inquiry).

100. Jefferson, *Papers*, vol. 1, p. 505.

101. Ibid.

102. On the debate over the significance of the difference between protecting "lives, liberties and property" and protecting "life, liberty and the pursuit of happiness" (as Jefferson put it in the Declaration of Independence), see Mayer, *Constitutional Thought of Thomas Jefferson*, pp. 77–81.

103. See Dubber, "Right to Be Punished," p. 113.

104. For examples, see Mayer, *Constitutional Thought of Thomas Jefferson*, pp. 72, 73, 76, 77, 85, 104; see, generally, Dubber, *Sense of Justice*.

105. Cesare Beccaria, *On Crimes and Punishments*, http://www.la.utexas.edu/research/poltheory/beccaria/delitti/, chap. 28 (originally published in 1764) ("Did any one ever give to others the right of taking away his life? . . . If it were so, how shall it be reconciled to the maxim which tells us, that a man has no right to kill himself, which he certainly must have, if he could give it away to another?").

106. See note 9 (Jefferson's 1778 bill of attainder against Josiah Philips).

107. Jefferson, *Notes on the State of Virginia*, query xvii.

108. See Sanford H. Kadish, "Codifiers of the Criminal Law: Wechsler's Predecessors," *Columbia Law Review* 78 (1978): 1098.

109. Edward Livingston, *The Complete Works of Edward Livingston on Criminal Jurisprudence*, vol. 1 (New York: Nat'l Prison Assoc. of the U.S.A., 1873), p. 175.

110. Though "the Republic of Guatemala" apparently adopted "certain portions . . . into her own laws." Chief Justice Chase, "Introduction," ibid., p. vii.

SIX

The Myth of Private Prosecution in England, 1750–1850

BRUCE P. SMITH

1. Introduction

In 1820 Charles Cottu, counselor of the Royal Court of Paris and secretary-general of France's Royal Society of Prisons, published a lengthy account of criminal justice administration in England based on his recent firsthand observations of English felony proceedings.[1] Having been dispatched to England by the French government to study the phenomenon of trial by jury, Cottu was struck by several aspects of English criminal procedure, including the prominence of lawyers and the extent to which criminal defendants were permitted to remain silent both before and during trial.[2] But nothing confounded him more than the English reliance on private victims to prosecute criminal cases. In England, as Cottu observed, "the business of prosecution, instead of being performed on the behalf of the public by an officer appointed expressly for the purpose," was "committed entirely to the hands of the injured party." In English felony proceedings, the private victim of crime, rather than a public prosecutor, served as "the arbiter of the culprit's fate"—deciding "according to the state of his feelings" whether to "follow up the prosecution to the utmost rigor of the law, abate its severity by procuring a mitigated bill of indictment, or, by abstaining from complaint, pardon the crime altogether."[3]

Historians of English criminal justice administration have likewise contended that the prosecution of crime in England, at least through the mid-nineteenth century, remained "almost invariably the sole responsibility of the victim."[4] According to this well-settled view, the English state assumed routine responsibility for prosecuting cases of crime only after roughly 1850, when professional police forces increasingly assumed a role in initiating and managing prosecutions and when, in 1879, the office of Director of Public Prosecutions (DPP) was finally established by Parliament to prosecute the most serious cases of violent crime.[5] Before the mid-nineteenth century, as the leading scholar of the subject has contended, "the typical prosecution in England was . . . at the initiative of a private citizen who was the victim of a crime and who conducted the prosecution *in almost all cases*" (emphasis added).⁶ In this system, so we have been led to understand, "[i]f the victim refused to react, the judicial system remained inert and ineffective."⁷

Yet much as it perplexed Cottu, England's so-called system of "private" prosecution has remained a legal-historical puzzle. Compared with Cottu's France, other Continental jurisdictions, and even Scotland—all of which, to varying degrees, relied on public officials to initiate and manage criminal prosecutions—the English system of "private" prosecution appears anomalous.⁸ And the tardy development of public prosecution in England appears only more striking when compared with the case of the United States, whose urban and rural jurisdictions, by 1800, routinely relied on district and county attorneys to prosecute a range of criminal offenses.⁹

The apparent disinclination of the English state to involve itself in investigating crimes, collecting evidence, and prosecuting defendants is also peculiar given the considerable investment of the central government in other aspects of criminal justice administration in the late eighteenth and early nineteenth centuries. In the century after 1750, Parliament authorized a series of important and costly innovations in criminal justice administration, including the establishment of salaried magistrates in London (1792), professional police forces in London (1829) and the counties (1839), and the nation's first penitentiary (1816).¹⁰ Yet while Parliament authorized the payment of considerable sums to private prosecutors in the form of rewards and costs, it refused, until the last quarter of the nineteenth century, to enact legislation officially establishing a public prosecutorial office.¹¹ And when Parliament finally decided to act, it did so after at least eight decades of vocal and steady agitation by parliamentarians, criminal justice administrators, and legal commentators, who argued that public prosecution would render the response to crime in England more energetic, more reliable, and more effective.¹²

Why, then, did England's anomalous system of "private" prosecution persist for so long? My answer is deceptively simple: it didn't. Increasingly in the century after 1750, persons—at least in London—who were suspected of committing various forms of petty theft (the most commonly prosecuted type of offense in the metropolis) were *routinely* arrested, tried, and convicted by public officials in proceedings in which private victims often played little or no role. These proceedings occurred not in the felony courts that Cottu and the great majority of modern-day historians have studied, but in "summary" (i.e., nonjury) proceedings before magistrates, whose role in adjudicating cases of petty theft has long remained obscure. By construing petty thefts as misdemeanors and disposing of them summarily, magistrates supervised a system in which police officers initiated prosecutions and the suspects' own faltering testimony secured convictions—often without the active participation of private victims at all.

The role of private victims was especially attenuated when magistrates acted pursuant to statutes (or informal practices) that required persons found with suspicious goods in their possession to "account" satisfactorily for the goods or face summary conviction. In earlier work, I have demonstrated how these statutes lowered the burden of proof typically required to prove theft in the higher courts by requiring suspects to rebut what was, in effect, a statutorily mandated presumption of guilt.[13] In practice, as I have argued, these statutes addressed several challenges associated with detecting, initiating, and prosecuting cases of theft—especially in instances where the items that had been appropriated were difficult for private victims to identify as their own.[14]

In suggesting that public officials played a larger role in the process of prosecution than has been previously appreciated, this chapter focuses on an offense common in eighteenth- and early nineteenth-century London: the theft of lead. Ubiquitous, accessible, nondescript, and malleable, lead possessed several properties (in addition to its value) that made it a desirable target of appropriation. Widely used in the eighteenth- and nineteenth-century building trades, lead was readily available to persons involved in small-scale appropriations. Like other types of items routinely targeted by opportunistic thieves or workers—such as rope, coal, wood, or wool—lead was a nondescript substance whose ownership, once the substance was removed from its original site, was difficult to establish. Moreover, lead's softness, plasticity, and low melting point made the metal particularly easy to transform, easing its sale to secondhand metal dealers and further frustrating detection and prosecution. This chapter argues that the appropriation of lead and other fungible, bulk goods integral to the material culture of eighteenth- and early nineteenth-century London created considerable problems for England's model of private prosecution and encouraged public officials to involve themselves in detecting, investigating, and prosecuting crime in ways that historians previously have failed to recognize.

The chapter proceeds in four parts. Part 2 examines the prosecution of cases of metal theft at London's Old Bailey in the late eighteenth and early nineteenth centuries, identifying the weaknesses of private prosecution as a means of securing convictions for theft in the principal court for the trial of felony offenses arising in the city of London and county of Middlesex. Part 3 demonstrates how property owners and public officials sought to address the limitations of private prosecution by enacting statutes that criminalized the unexplained possession of certain types of goods and that relied heavily on public officials to detect, initiate, and manage prosecutions. To the extent permitted by the surviving sources, Part 4 then examines the scope and significance of what I have styled "public" prosecution in England in the century after 1750. The chapter concludes by suggesting how the "public" nature of misdemeanor theft prosecutions in late eighteenth- and early nineteenth-century London might revise our understanding of English criminal justice administration in this period.

2. Prosecuting Metal Theft at the Old Bailey

In claiming that prosecution in England remained overwhelmingly "private" until the later decades of the nineteenth century, historians, to be sure, have identified certain notable exceptions. In cases deemed by the central government to threaten the interests of the state—most notably, instances of alleged treason or sedition—governmental officials frequently involved themselves in compiling evidence and even in arguing cases at trial.[15] In cases of forgery and coining, the Bank of England and the Royal Mint—entities with strong ties to the central government—were similarly zealous in their approach to prosecution, routinely employing solicitors and trial counsel to help secure convictions.[16] On occasion, public officials also took steps to supervise the collection of evidence and the retention of counsel in certain high-profile cases involving crimes of violence.[17]

By contrast, historians have generally assumed that public officials played no prosecutorial role with respect to property-related offenses, which comprised the overwhelming majority of criminal prosecutions in eighteenth- and early nineteenth-century England. In the introduction to an influential set of essays on the history of criminal prosecution in England, for example, Douglas Hay and Francis Snyder have contended that prosecutions of "virtually all thefts" in England before 1850 "were left to the general public."[18] Focusing on practice in Sussex and urban Surrey before 1800, John Beattie has asserted that "[o]nly in rare cases did . . . local constables actively prosecute offenses against property."[19] And on the basis of his study of Essex, Peter King has concluded that "[b]etween 1740 and 1820 [law enforcement] officials only took responsibility for prosecutions involving property appropriation in *very exceptional circumstances*, such as major coining or forgery cases" (emphasis added).[20]

There can certainly be little doubt that prosecutions of theft-related cases in England's *higher* courts relied predominantly on private prosecutorial initiative, even in prosecutions, such as those alleging the theft of metal, that posed challenges for private property owners. Consider the case of Thomas

Jones and John Myers, who appeared at the Old Bailey in April 1824 charged with stealing two hundred pounds of lead and an equivalent amount of copper, which they had allegedly stripped from the outside of a house located in the City of London and owned by one Thomas Quarrill.[21] Quarrill, a lamp-maker, recounted at trial that he had visited the house with a constable, Lewis Fache, and another officer, Henry Turnpenny, after receiving "information" that the building had been targeted by metal thieves. When Quarrill arrived at the house, which he had purchased at auction, he "found all the gutters stripped of . . . lead, and eighty-four feet of water-pipe gone." After Turnpenny "heard a noise in the kitchen" and spotted a man in the "front parlour" with a "dark lantern," Fache discovered a second man in the basement "coal-hole." During the officers' ensuing search of the suspects and premises, they discovered a "latch key" on Jones, a "box of matches" on the floor, some lanterns, a can of oil, and a phosphorous bottle.[22]

When questioned, the two interlopers claimed that they had come into the house "for a night's lodging." According to the testimony of the officers, however, the two suspects had "made no answer" when asked why they had entered the home carrying lanterns that had been "darkened." At trial, Jones claimed in his defense that it had been "a very wet night" and the pair had spotted an "empty house, [with] all the windows broken" and had "[gone] in for shelter." Myers, for his part, offered no defense. Confronted by the testimony of several prosecution witnesses, Jones's feeble explanation, and Myers's silence, the jury convicted both men. The presiding judge sentenced each to a seven-year term of transportation.[23]

In the context of its time, the case of Jones and Myers would have appeared utterly unremarkable. In late eighteenth- and early nineteenth-century London, lead was a common object of appropriation and prosecutions involving the theft of lead (or other metals) were routine. To understand these phenomena, we must first comprehend the revolutionary transformation in London's built environment in the post-Restoration period. London underwent a profound rebuilding in the generations after the Great Fire of 1666 that relied heavily on building materials such as copper, iron, brass, bell metal, and lead.[24] Lead was used in the building trades in numerous ways, including for "roofs, guttering, flashes, hips, cisterns, rain and waste pipes, pumps, [and] glazing."[25]

Unfortunately for builders and building owners, lead was relatively easy to appropriate, transport, transform, and resell. Persons willing to climb walls or traverse roofs could reach gutters and pipes. Because of its pliable nature, lead (unlike iron or brass) could be easily stressed and broken by repeated twisting and bending. And because of its softness and low melting point, lead was also "the most easily recycled of all metals," capable of being readily resold—at least in London—to a number of secondhand metal dealers or plumbers.[26]

Not surprisingly, prosecutions of persons suspected of stealing lead were commonplace at the Old Bailey in the late eighteenth and early nineteenth centuries, averaging perhaps twenty to thirty per year from 1790 to 1830.[27] In circumstances where lead had not yet been affixed to a building, such as where it was stored at work sites or in ships' holds, persons accused of stealing lead could be prosecuted under the common law of larceny.[28] And while the misappropriation of items affixed to buildings ("fixtures") had not traditionally fallen within the common law of larceny,[29] Parliament enacted several statutes during the eighteenth century that considerably narrowed this loophole with respect to metal fixtures.[30] As early as 1731, for example, Parliament had made it a felony to steal (or to "rip, cut or break" with *intent* to steal) "any lead, iron bar, iron gate, iron palisade or iron rail . . . fixed to any dwelling-house, outhouse, coach-house, stable or other building . . . or to any other building."[31]

Considered from the perspective of criminal procedure, the trial of Jones and Myers would also have merited little notice because the two had been detected, arrested, and prosecuted in a manner completely consistent with the received understanding of how English criminal justice administration was supposed to operate. The victim (aided, it seems, by a neighborly tip) had detected that his property was at risk. The suspects had been arrested without difficulty. Quarrill had opted to prosecute rather than to overlook the wrong or to reach a settlement with the suspects.[32] The grand jury (which had heard evidence only on the prosecutor's behalf) had returned a "true bill" rather than standing in the way of prosecution.[33] The trial jury (after hearing the testimony and assessing the defendants' brief defense) had convicted the pair, no doubt after little or no deliberation. And the judge (untroubled by lawyers for either side) had entered a sentence that would incapacitate the convicts for a long time.

Cases involving the theft of metal tried at the late eighteenth- and early nineteenth-century Old Bailey reveal that the appropriation of metal was, at times, an operation that entailed considerable risk. The process of removing metal from buildings (by banging, prying, twisting, snapping, and dropping the stripped metal from upper stories) typically generated considerable amounts of noise, which could attract suspicious neighbors or night watchmen.[34] At times, buildings that appeared to be abandoned were actually occupied by persons who had been hired by owners to watch them.[35] Because lead thieves often sought access to gutters and other fixtures on upper stories or roofs, they were susceptible to being caught with no viable escape routes.[36] And persons who sought to remove lead fixtures typically required the use of tools such as hammers, wrenches, knives, or chisels; such devices, if found on suspects, could be offered as convincing evidence of actual or intended wrongdoing.[37]

Moreover, once successfully removed from a building, lead pipes and gutters were heavy, bulky, and relatively difficult to conceal.[38] Worse yet, lead that had been recently twisted to secure its removal often appeared shiny—giving it the illicit appearance of having been "freshly cut."[39] And because lead fixtures were typically affixed to buildings by a series of imperfectly spaced nails, the nail holes could often be matched hole by hole to their original sites, often by the very plumbers who had installed them in the first place. In January 1792, for example, the plumber John Lovejoy testified at the Old Bailey that he was "well satisfied" that the lead found in the defendant's possession had been stolen from the prosecutor, because Lovejoy had "compared" the lead with the site from which it had been purportedly stolen, and "it fitted exactly."[40]

On the other hand, property owners could also face considerable challenges in detecting thefts of lead and other metals and, even if detection occurred, in securing convictions at trial. Enterprising thieves frequently worked at night and targeted unoccupied buildings—protected, in many instances, from the eyes (if not always the ears) of nonresident owners and roving watchmen. If successfully removed from buildings, lead could be "disposed of" with "the greatest Safety" by selling it to "Buyers and Receivers," who promptly placed the metal on the market at prices "under the real Value."[41]

Even if a person happened to be confronted by a police officer while carrying a suspicious sack or pushing a barrow laden with metal, the officer still might have little way of determining the identity of the metal's lawful owner. Although printed advertisements and handbills might effectively reconnect property owners with unique possessions such as horses, pocket watches, or engraved silverware, it is doubtful that such notices were of much use in identifying the owners of nondescript, quotidian materials such as metal, wood, coal, or cloth—the frequent targets of opportunistic thieves.[42] And while persons could be indicted for stealing goods from "persons unknown," such prosecutions frequently foundered at the Old Bailey when victims failed to appear at trial to prosecute.[43] In April 1801, for example, Lord Kenyon directed a verdict of acquittal on behalf of Joseph Bailey, who had been charged with stealing two hundred pounds of sheet lead and four pounds of lead pipe, after the court determined that there was "no evidence to bring the charge home to the prisoner."[44]

The surviving records do not reveal why victims of alleged thefts failed to appear at trial to prosecute their cases. Yet while English law provided incentives to private victims to prosecute and ostensibly held them responsible when they failed to do so, many individuals victimized by theft appear to have been more interested in seeing their goods returned than in incurring the expense and inconvenience of attending trial in the higher courts.[45] Other potential prosecutors likely were deterred by their distaste for the often severe penalties meted out to convicted thieves in the higher courts.[46]

Even those persons victimized by the theft of metal who did appear at trial could face considerable evidentiary hurdles. As one commentator observed in 1751, "the Ease" with which the "Form" of lead and solder could be "changed" often made it "impossible" for property owners to prove the "Identity" of lead stolen from their premises.[47] In 1793, for example, John Percival and Christopher Spiller were acquitted of stealing lead after the prosecutor's star witness, a plumber, testified that, although he could say that the metal allegedly stolen by the defendants "fit[] the place [from which it had allegedly been stolen] exactly," the piece had been "out of [his] sight for four or six months" by the time he had conducted his inspection, making it impossible for him to swear that the metal found in the defendants' possession was indeed that of the prosecutor.[48]

Several of the difficulties associated with securing convictions in the high courts related not so much to evidentiary challenges inherent in proving the theft of metal but to the broader procedural protections associated with trial by jury. As John Beattie's research has revealed, even when property owners chose to prosecute in the higher courts, they still faced the prospect of securing a "true bill" from the grand jury, which declined to return such bills in roughly 17 percent of property-related cases prosecuted in the courts of Surrey from 1660 to 1800.[49] Trial juries, for their part, acquitted at even higher rates, acquitting in roughly 35 percent of the noncapital property-related cases tried during this period.[50] On other occasions, as noted earlier, trial judges themselves intervened to render directed verdicts of acquittal. In 1801 the presiding judge at the Old Bailey directed the acquittal of one James Marston, indicted for stealing "a brass cock" and twenty pounds of lead "fixed to a certain cistern" in the defendant's garden, on the grounds that the indictment should have detailed that the garden belonged to the victim's *"dwelling-house"* (emphasis added).[51] In a similar vein, Samuel Linsey was acquitted at the Old Bailey in February 1824 on charges of stealing eight pounds of brass after the metal in question was found to have been "composed of a mixed metal, and not of brass," thus creating a fatal variance between the indictment and the proof to be proffered at trial.[52]

To legal commentators like the London magistrate Patrick Colquhoun, "the Number of Chances which a Prisoner, although guilty, has of escaping

Justice" recommended sweeping reforms in English criminal justice administration, including a more professionalized approach to criminal prosecution.[53] Testifying before a parliamentary subcommittee in 1798, Colquhoun noted that victims frequently failed to prosecute because of "the Dread of Expense," the "Threats of the Culprit," or the prospect of being "bought off by corrupt Means." If private victims proceeded to trial, they often proved "unable or unwilling to sustain the Expense of Counsel to oppose the Arguments and Objections . . . offered on Behalf of the Prisoner." To Colquhoun, the solution by the close of the eighteenth century was clear: "placing the Prosecution of public Offences under the Charge of an Officer of the Crown, to give full Effect to public Justice, by extending to such Prosecutions that necessary Energy that does not at present exist, and never can exist under the present System."[54]

Similar calls to create a state-sponsored prosecutorial body continued through the first half of the nineteenth century and beyond. In the 1820s, Sir Robert Peel observed in the House of Commons that, if Parliament "were legislating *de novo*, without reference to previous customs and formed habits," it should "not hesitate to relieve private individuals from the charge of prosecution in the case of criminal offences justly called by writers upon law—*Public Wrongs*" (emphasis added).[55] Yet despite these pleas, England failed to adopt an official system of public prosecution until the last quarter of the nineteenth century. How could English criminal justice administrators—who continued to invest considerable financial and institutional resources in the processes of detecting, arresting, convicting, and punishing criminals—remain so removed from the critical stage of criminal *prosecution*?

3. Prosecuting Metal Theft in the Police Offices

To understand how the English system coped without a formal system of public prosecution for so long, we need to shift our focus from the modes of criminal procedure applicable at the Old Bailey to the ways that criminal justice administration actually functioned in London's *lower* criminal courts—particularly, in the city's "police" or "public" offices, which were established throughout the metropolis in 1792. Although only fragments of evidence survive from those tribunals before the 1850s, the surviving sources reveal that the magistrates and officers who worked in those grimy and crowded confines found ways to bypass the pitfalls of private prosecution that vexed theft-related prosecutions brought in the higher courts. One way that these public officials did so was by dramatically diminishing their reliance on private victims.

Consider, first, the case of Thomas Murray, a self-described dealer in metal who appeared at the Thames Police Office in October 1836 after having been found by police officers in the parish of St. Giles with four hundred pounds of lead in his possession.[56] The lead had apparently been "doubled up and beaten together in such size and shape as to be carried . . . under the clothes of the person conveying them," suspended there "upon a belt fastened round the body or . . . from the braces [i.e., suspenders] or neck."[57] When Murray appeared at the Thames Police Office, the attending magistrate instructed him to demonstrate "not only that he had purchased [the lead] but also that it [had] been bought under such circumstances as would remove the suspicion attached to it." In response, Murray claimed to "do a deal of business in the lead trade" and stated that he "[could not] speak to every piece of it."[58] After hearing Murray's explanation, the magistrate convicted him and fined him five pounds, noting that Murray had "passed very lightly over the strong points of the case against him."[59]

Several months later, in March 1837, the Home Office received a petition from one Lewis Leo, a "Collector of Broken Glass and Old Metal" living in the East London parish of Spitalfields. In his petition, Leo sought "the return of a Cart" that had been "forfeited" after Leo's servant, Henry Samuels, had been convicted summarily at the Queen's Square Police Office in December 1836 for "unlawful possession" of thirty-four pounds of brass.[60] When Samuels had first appeared at the Queen's Square Police Office on December 19, the attending magistrate had initially adjourned the case to give Samuels "an opportunity to produce evidence that the said Goods were fairly and honestly purchased by him." When Samuels had appeared at the police office two days later, he claimed to have "produced the Person from whom he had bought the said Metal." The magistrate had then examined Samuels's witness, "touching [on] the same," who claimed that the suspect had "bought the said Metal [from] her, and [who] also stated the person of whom she bought the same." Despite this showing, the magistrate convicted Samuels and ordered him to pay a forty-shilling fine or, in default of payment, to be "committed to the House of Correction for three weeks."[61]

It is possible to reconstruct the proceedings involving Murray and Samuels in some detail, even in the absence of surviving magistrates' notebooks, because both of these individuals filed petitions with the Home Office challenging their convictions. But while the postconviction record (and our corresponding knowledge) of these two cases is especially detailed, the underlying proceedings do not appear to have been exceptional. To the contrary, scores of similar cases dot the pages of the *Police Gazette*, the published record of day-to-day practice in the metropolitan police offices. The following brief entries from the *Gazette*, reflecting the business of the Thames Police Office during the time frame when Murray and Samuels were convicted, provide some sense of the frequency and typicality of summary proceedings involving persons suspected of metal theft:

November 26, 1836

JOHN SMITH, on re-examination, with stealing fifty-six pounds weight of lead, the property of some person unknown, at Westminster.—Discharged from this; but convicted of a misdemeanor, and fined five pounds.[62]

December 5, 1836

ABRAHAM BENDAHAM, with unlawfully possessing, at Whitechapel, two hundred and sixteen pounds weight of lead, which had been stolen.— Convicted of a misdemeanor, and fined forty shillings.[63]

December 24, 1836

JOSEPH BALDWIN, with possessing, at Shadwell, one piece of iron, four pounds weight of copper, eight pounds of lead, four pounds of metal, twenty-five pounds of rope, and other articles, which had been stolen.—Convicted of a misdemeanor, and fined five pounds.[64]

In all of these cases of metal theft, the magistrates in attendance at the Thames Police Office decided to adjudicate the cases summarily rather than sending them to trial at the Old Bailey.

In doing so, they likely relied on statutory authority dating back to the mid-1750s. As early as 1756, Parliament had passed a measure designed to counteract the "pernicious practice" of persons who stole metal "fixed to, or lying, or being in or upon houses, outhouses, mills, warehouses, workshops, and other buildings," or located in "ships, barges, lighters, boats, and other vessels."[65] According to the statute's preamble, private victims had found it difficult to detect, prosecute, and convict persons suspected of stealing metal because the thefts were committed "in such [a] close and clandestine manner, that there can be no witness or witnesses to the same, but such as who . . . are partakers of the offence." The measure passed by Parliament in 1756 authorized constables to detain and search "every person . . . who may reasonably be suspected of having or carrying . . . at any time after sun-setting, or before sun-rising, any lead, iron, copper, brass, bell-metal, or solder, suspected to be stolen, or unlawfully come by." If the suspect could "not produce the party or parties from whom he . . . [had] bought or received the [metal], or some other credible witness to depose upon oath [its] sale or delivery," he "[was to] be adjudged guilty" of a misdemeanor in summary proceedings and either fined or imprisoned.[66]

By permitting constables to search persons conveying goods deemed to be suspicious, and by authorizing magistrates to convict such persons summarily if the suspects failed to "account" for possession, the 1756 act resembled other penal statutes passed by Parliament designed to address thefts of goods that, by their nature, were difficult for owners to identify credibly at trial.[67] Reflecting on these statutes, as well as on the informal practices associated with them, the police magistrate James Traill testified to a parliamentary subcommittee in the 1830s that his fellow metropolitan magistrates habitually exercised summary jurisdiction over three broad categories of offenders against whom "a charge of larceny [was] implied": (1) persons "found conveying goods suspected to have been stolen, and giving no satisfactory account of them"; (2) persons "found upon [a] search warrant in possession of property suspected to [have been] stolen, and giving no satisfactory account"; and (3) persons "appearing to have had prior possession of property suspected to [have been] stolen, and having had reason to suspect it to have been stolen."[68]

Why did police officers and magistrates in London resort to summary proceedings in cases where persons were discovered by police officers conveying suspicious items? First, these statutes addressed the particular challenges faced by private property owners in detecting thefts of nondescript, bulk goods and testifying credibly to their ownership at trial. As the influential treatise writer Thomas Starkie succinctly observed in the 1820s, statutes authorizing magistrates to adjudicate cases summarily generally focused on "the protection of property much exposed, and . . . difficult to identify."[69] Although absentee property owners might fail to detect thefts of metal from their buildings, it was at least conceivable that a police officer might notice a person at night furtively carrying a sack packed with twisted lead or pushing a wheelbarrow filled with rain gutters.[70] And while victims of theft might strain to convince juries at the Old Bailey that mundane and seemingly indistinguishable property found in the defendant's possession was actually the prosecutor's, statutes that placed the burden on suspects to account satisfactorily for their possession of suspicious goods bypassed this evidentiary hurdle.

Second, penal statutes that addressed the theft of metal, wood, or other nondescript commodities typically clarified and expanded the formal powers of police officers in the areas of detention, search, and arrest. Writing in 1960, the legal scholar Glanville Williams correctly noted that statutes such as the Metropolitan Police Act of 1839—a direct heir to eighteenth-century statutes like the 1756 act targeting the misappropriation of metal—permitted police officers to detain and search persons reasonably suspected of conveying stolen goods without first arresting them.[71] Although Williams had difficulty understanding how such "detain and search" powers were more helpful to twentieth-century English police officers than their authority to search *incident* to an arrest, he noted that officers interviewed in the 1950s nonetheless considered the distinction to be meaningful and that "detain and search" powers may well have been even more important before 1850, at "a time when it was not clear how far the police could search arrested persons."[72] More dramatically, although English police officers traditionally could not arrest suspected misdemeanants without a warrant, penal statutes that extended summary jurisdiction over the misappropriation of metal, textiles, and wood typically dispensed with this requirement.[73]

Finally, and most importantly for our purposes, statutes that required suspects to "account" for possession of suspicious goods or face summary conviction permitted criminal justice administrators to dispense with private victims. Such cases could be initiated by police officers themselves rather than by private property owners, who might be disinclined to prosecute. And, even more importantly, such cases could be resolved through the magistrate's assessment of the defendant's explanation rather than through an assessment of the evidence offered by individual victims, which might be absent or unconvincing.

It is conceivable, to be sure, that the surviving records simply fail to note the activities of private victims in summary proceedings that required suspects to explain away presumptive evidence of guilt. Yet if private victims had initiated these cases and secured the ensuing convictions through their own testimony, we would surely expect to find some mention of these important facts in the surviving sources. To the contrary, the sources reveal public officials playing these prosecutorial roles. In the case of Murray, the officers who apprehended him initiated his prosecution merely by swearing to the circumstances of Murray's detection and apprehension.[74] Similarly, the magistrate who convicted Samuels did so after the suspect's witness failed to provide a convincing explanation. In such cases, as Colquhoun crisply noted, "the Examination of the Delinquent" provided all the evidence needed to secure a conviction.[75]

4. Reassessing the Myth

How frequently did criminal justice administrators in London resort to summary proceedings in theft-related offenses during the late eighteenth and early nineteenth centuries? And can such prosecutions truly be considered "public" in nature given the long-standing position among legal theoreticians that the English police, when exercising prosecutorial functions, act merely in their capacity as "private" citizens?[76]

Although the first question is difficult to answer with precision, some sense of the importance of summary proceedings can be gained by comparing the respective workloads of the police offices and higher courts in the early decades of the nineteenth century, when data from these institutions first became available. In 1832, for example, the Metropolitan Police took into custody 26 suspected murderers, 10 suspected arsonists, 6 suspected rapists, and 1,176 persons on charges of "unlawful possession" of goods.[77] Among the latter group of suspected thieves, most, undoubtedly, had their cases resolved summarily by magistrates. Indeed, a decade earlier, the magistrates at the Thames Police Office reported that they had averaged forty misdemeanor cases per month in the previous year ("very few of which [did] not include a felonious taking" of property), compared to only thirteen committals per month to the higher courts for all types of felony combined.[78]

The question of whether prosecutions of theft-related offenses in the police offices, which relied so heavily on the initiatives of police officers, should be considered "public" is more vexing. As suggested above, legal theorists have traditionally conceptualized the prosecutorial activities of the English police as "private" in nature, claiming, as did Sir James Fitzjames Stephen in the 1880s, that the English police engage in prosecutorial activities "in their capacity of private persons" and exercise "hardly any legal powers beyond those which belong to private persons."[79] In turn, efforts to characterize prosecutions in the police offices as "private" or "public" also encounter definitional difficulties. As David Lieberman has perspicuously noted, "[e]ighteenth-century English law utilized the terms 'private' and 'public' with a frequency and range sufficient to frustrate any precise or simple definition," and the terms have continued to bedevil legal scholars to this day.[80]

With this said, Lieberman makes clear that the term "public" was "routinely" defined in eighteenth- and early nineteenth-century England to "refer to *the institutions and agents of state authority*" (emphasis added).[81] Given the intimate involvement of London's police officers and magistrates in the administration of criminal justice in the late eighteenth and early nineteenth centuries, it is difficult to argue that summary proceedings that required suspects to "account" for possession were "private" in any meaningful way.[82] Hired by the central government, supervised by the Home Office, and salaried by the English Treasury, the magistrates and police officers who worked in the police offices possessed the attributes of "public" officials in any historic (or modern) sense of the term.

Conclusion

What are the implications for discovering the active engagement of the English state in the process of criminal prosecution in London in the century before 1850?

That public officials in England were intimately involved in the detection, investigation, and prosecution of crimes helps make the English system of prosecution appear less anomalous. For over a century, commentators have contrasted England's seeming indifference to public prosecution with the active prosecutorial role taken by public officials in other parts of Britain, the United States, and the European continent. Examples of such contrasts are abundant. In 1856 in testimony submitted to a parliamentary committee on public prosecution, the Scottish lord advocate contrasted criminal justice administration in Scotland and England by noting that criminal prosecution in Scotland "proceed[ed] upon the principle that it is the duty of the *State* to detect crime, apprehend offenders, and punish them, and [all] that independently of the interests of a private party" (emphasis added).[83] Reflecting on the contrast between the history of criminal prosecution in England and the United States, the legal historian Lawrence Friedman has hypothesized that "the concept of public responsibility for prosecuting criminals rang a bell in the colonial [American] mind" that simply failed to toll in England.[84] In turn, leading comparativists have observed that Continental criminal procedure traditionally sought "to apply state policy toward crime independent of the defendant's attitude toward the charges."[85] In truth, English criminal justice administrators in the late eighteenth and early nineteenth centuries also viewed crime—even crimes against property—as an important public policy problem. In a world that increasingly valued promptness and certainty of conviction and punishment, the state increasingly looked to police officers and magistrates to circumvent the failings of private prosecution.

In a short, brilliant, and regrettably overlooked essay written in 1955, Glanville Williams examined the curious survival in English legal theory of the concept of "private" prosecution. Reflecting on the practical realities of criminal justice administration in England, he castigated lawyers and legal commentators who claimed "absurdly" that England "ha[s] no public prosecutions," noting that "[t]hose who deny that England has a system of public prosecution do so on the verbal ground that a policeman or official who prosecutes" does so, as a matter of legal theory, "as a private person and not in pursuance of any official power." According to Williams, "[A] prosecution by a policeman or other official is brought in pursuance of superior orders or under statutory authority and at public expence, so that it is *unreal* to describe it as a private prosecution" (emphasis added).[86]

Historians have also been reluctant to embrace reality—though, to be sure, the reality of misdemeanor justice that they have ignored has by no means been easy to reconstruct. By contrast, English criminal justice administrators in the late eighteenth and early nineteenth centuries clearly understood the critical public role that they played. In the 1820s the police magistrates at the Thames Police Office urged the Home Office to extend their jurisdiction over suspected thieves operating on and near the Thames because of the difficulty of detecting losses, identifying goods at trial, and convincing private victims to delay their voyages for the purpose of attending trials at the Old Bailey.[87] These public officials knew what they were talking about. Thefts were hard to detect; fungible goods were hard to identify; and private victims, if left to their own devices, were all too prone to "set sail" and decline to prosecute. By resorting to summary proceedings that required persons suspected of theft to "explain away" their guilt, the English state developed a mode of criminal prosecution that was efficient, effective, and—most strikingly—victim-*free*.

Notes

1. Cottu published his account in French. Charles Cottu, *De l'Administration de la Justice Criminelle en Angleterre et de l'Esprit du Gouvernement Anglais* (Paris: H. Nicolle, 1820). An English translation was published the same year in the *Pamphleteer*, a journal published in London from 1813 to 1828. See Charles Cottu, "On the Administration of the Criminal Code in England, and the Spirit of the English Government," *Pamphleteer* 16, 1820. Cottu's account was published in England as a book two years later. See Charles Cottu, *On the Administration of Criminal Justice in England; and the Spirit of the English Government* (London: R. Stevens, 1822). An earlier version of this chapter was presented at the European Centre for the Study of Policing at the Open University, where Clive Emsley and Pete King provided particularly helpful feedback. I am also grateful to the volume's editors and other contributors for their valuable reactions.

2. France introduced criminal jury trials in 1791. See Bernard Schnapper, "Le Jury Français aux XIX et XXieme Siècles," in *The Trial Jury in England, France, Germany, 1700–1900*, Antonio Padoa-Schioppa, ed. (Berlin: Duncker & Humblot, 1987).

3. Cottu, *Administration of Criminal Justice*, p. 38.

4. Douglas Hay and Francis Snyder, "Using the Criminal Law, 1750–1850: Policing, Private Prosecution, and the State," in *Policing and Prosecution in Britain 1750–1850*, Douglas Hay and Francis Snyder, eds. (Oxford: Clarendon Press, 1996), pp. 16, 18. See also David J. Bentley, *English Criminal Justice in the Nineteenth Century* (London: Hambledon, 1998), p. 7. ("The prosecution of criminals was in the eighteenth and early nineteenth century regarded as a private rather than a public responsibility.")

5. As John Beattie has observed, "it was not until the second half of the nineteenth century... that the police had any significant involvement in the prosecution of criminal offences." J. M. Beattie, *Policing and Punishment in London, 1660–1750: Urban Crime and the Limits of Terror* (Oxford: Oxford Univ. Press, 2001), pp. 130–131. See also David Philips, *Crime and Authority in Victorian England: The Black Country, 1835–1860* (London: Croom Helm, 1977) (describing the early history of police prosecution in the nineteenth-century English Midlands). On the legislative origins of the DPP, see Philip B. Kurland and D. W. M. Waters, "Public Prosecutions in England, 1854–79: An Essay in English Legislative History," *Duke Law Journal* 1959:493–562. See also Paul Rock, "Victims, Prosecutors and the State in Nineteenth Century England," *Criminal Justice* 4 (2004): 331–354.

6. Douglas Hay, "Controlling the English Prosecutor," *Osgoode Hall Law Journal* 21 (1983): 168.

7. Peter King, *Crime, Justice, and Discretion in England, 1740–1820* (Oxford: Oxford Univ. Press, 2000), p. 17.

8. Writing in 1883, four years after the establishment of the DPP, Sir James Fitzjames Stephen offered the following comparative observations:

> In most countries the duty of making a preliminary investigation into the circumstances of an offence, collecting evidence for the trial, and managing the case in court, is in the hands of public officers. Throughout the Continent officers are to be found answering more or less to the French *Procureur Général*, *Procureur de la République*, and *Juge d'Instruction*. Even in Scotland the Procurator Fiscal and his officers have somewhat analogous duties.... In England, ... the prosecution of offences is left entirely to private persons, or to public officers who act in their capacity of private persons and who have hardly any legal powers beyond those which belong to private persons.

James Fitzjames Stephen, *A History of the Criminal Law of England*, vol. 1 (London: Macmillan, 1883), p. 493.

9. See Lawrence M. Friedman, *Crime and Punishment in American History* (New York: Basic Books, 1993), pp. 29–30; Carolyn Ramsey, "The Discretionary Power of 'Public' Prosecutors in Historical Perspective," *American Criminal Law Review* 39 (2002): 1309–1393; W. Scott Van Alstyne Jr., Comment, "The District Attorney—A Historical Puzzle," *Wisconsin Law Review* 1952:125–138. This is not to suggest that public prosecutors in the antebellum United States *monopolized* prosecutions. In certain jurisdictions, such as Philadelphia, prosecution by private individuals continued well into the nineteenth century. See Allen Steinberg, *The Transformation of Criminal Justice: Philadelphia, 1800–1880* (Chapel Hill: Univ. of North Carolina Press, 1989).

10. On the origins of the stipendiary magistracy in England, see David Philips, "'A New Engine of Power and Authority': The Institutionalisation of Law-Enforcement in England, 1750–1850," in *Crime and the Law: The Social History of Crime in Western Europe since 1500*, V. A. C. Gatrell, Bruce Lenman, and Geoffrey Parker, eds. (London: Europa Publications, 1980), pp. 155–189; Stanley H. Palmer, *Police and Protest in England and*

Ireland, 1780–1850 (New York: Cambridge Univ. Press, 1988); and Ruth Paley, "The Middlesex Justices Act of 1792: Its Origins and Effects" (PhD dissertation, Univ. of Reading, 1980). On the history of policing in London before 1850, see Andrew T. Harris, *Policing the City: Crime and Legal Authority in London, 1780–1840* (Columbus: Ohio State Univ. Press, 2004); Elaine A. Reynolds, *Before the Bobbies: The Night Watch and Police Reform in Metropolitan London, 1720–1830* (Stanford, Calif.: Stanford Univ. Press, 1998); and Clive Emsley, *The English Police: A Political and Social History*, 2d ed. (London: Longman, 1996). On the development of penitentiaries in England, see Michael Ignatieff, *A Just Measure of Pain: The Penitentiary in the Industrial Revolution, 1750–1850* (New York: Pantheon, 1978); and Randall McGowen, "The Well-Ordered Prison: England, 1780–1865," in *The Oxford History of the Prison: The Practice of Punishment in Western Society*, Norval Morris and David J. Rothman, eds. (New York: Oxford Univ. Press, 1995), pp. 79–109.

11. On the payment of rewards, see J. M. Beattie, *Crime and the Courts in England, 1660–1800* (Princeton, N.J.: Princeton Univ. Press, 1986), pp. 50–55.

12. The London magistrate Patrick Colquhoun argued forcefully on behalf of a "Crown prosecutor" in the late 1790s. See *Report of the Select Committee Appointed by the House of Commons, Relative to the Establishment of a New Police in the Metropolis, 1799* (London: R. Shaw, 1799), p. 79. In 1856 a parliamentary select committee specifically recommended the creation of a public prosecutor. See *Report from the Select Committee on Public Prosecutors: Together with the Proceedings of the Committee, and Minutes of Evidence, Parliamentary Papers 1856* (London: Her Majesty's Stationery Office, 1856). See, generally, W. R. Cornish, "Defects in Prosecuting—Professional Views in 1845," in *Reshaping the Criminal Law: Essays in Honour of Glanville Williams*, P. R. Glazebrook, ed. (London: Stevens, 1978), pp. 305–316; Allyson N. May, *The Bar and the Old Bailey, 1750–1850* (Chapel Hill: Univ. of North Carolina Press, 2003), pp. 194–197; and David J. A. Cairns, *Advocacy and the Making of the Adversarial Criminal Trial, 1800–1865* (Oxford: Clarendon Press, 1998), p. 174.

13. See Bruce P. Smith, "The Presumption of Guilt and the English Law of Theft, 1750–1850," *Law and History Review* 23 (2005): 133–171, and "Did the Presumption of Innocence Exist in Summary Proceedings?" *Law and History Review* 23 (2005): 191–199.

14. For a more expansive discussion, see Bruce P. Smith, "The Origins of Public Prosecution in England, 1790–1850," *Yale Journal of Law and the Humanities* 18 (2006): 29–62.

15. For example, the government played an important role in prosecuting members of the London Corresponding Society and other radicals in the 1790s. See E. P. Thompson, *The Making of the English Working Class* (London: V. Gollancz, 1963).

16. See Bruce P. Smith, "Plea Bargaining and the Eclipse of the Jury," *Annual Review of Law and Social Science* 1 (2005): 131–149 (citing unpublished work on the Bank of England by Randall McGowen). On the role of the Mint solicitor, see John H. Langbein, *The Origins of Adversary Criminal Trial* (Oxford: Oxford Univ. Press, 2003), pp. 115–120.

17. In 1799, for example, the solicitor general appeared at the Old Bailey to prosecute James Eyres, a coal-heaver accused of murdering an employee of the Thames Police

Office during a riot. Eyres, Proceedings of the Old Bailey, Jan. 9, 1799, t17990109-5. (The Proceedings of the Old Bailey [POB] are a searchable, online edition [www.oldbaileyonline.org] of the Old Bailey Sessions Papers, a published series of accounts, beginning in 1674, of trials at the Old Bailey. Citations to the POB include the defendant's name, the date, and the document's POB reference number.)

18. Hay and Snyder, "Using the Criminal Law," pp. 16, 18, 23.
19. Beattie, *Crime and the Courts*, p. 35.
20. King, *Crime, Justice, and Discretion*, p. 17.
21. Jones and Myers, POB, Apr. 7, 1824, t18240407-61.
22. Ibid.
23. Ibid.
24. See Timothy M. M. Baker, *London: Rebuilding the City after the Great Fire* (Chichester, U.K.: Phillimore, 2000); and Elizabeth McKellar, *The Birth of Modern London: The Development and Design of the City, 1660–1720* (Manchester, U.K.: Manchester Univ. Press, 1999). In stressing the prevalence of metal theft in Georgian England, I do not mean to underestimate the degree of the problem in the modern age. See "Scrap-Metal Theft a Growing Global Problem," FOXNews.com (Jan. 19, 2006), http://www.foxnews.com/story/0,2933,182188,00.html (discussing thefts of copper wiring and aluminum siding).
25. Roger Burt, "Lead Production in England and Wales, 1700–1770," *Economic History Review*, new ser., 22 (1969): 259.
26. Donald Woodward, "'Swords into Ploughshares': Recycling in Pre-Industrial England," *Economic History Review*, new ser., 38 (1985): 183. The melting point of lead is 327.5°C, making it relatively simple to melt in a small fire. By contrast, copper melts at more than three times that temperature (1083°C). Although English lead production expanded considerably in the eighteenth century to meet expanded domestic and foreign demand, such demand was also met "by the re-use of scrap, easily melted and re-cast" by plumbers or by secondhand metal dealers, who were widely believed to be engaged in the illicit receiving of stolen metals. Burt, "Lead Production," p. 260. On the expansion of the English lead industry in the eighteenth century, see Roger Burt, "The Transformation of the Non-Ferrous Metals Industries in the Seventeenth and Eighteenth Centuries," *Economic History Review*, new ser., 48 (1995): 23–45. For discussions of the presumed linkage between secondhand metal dealers and receiving stolen goods, see Patrick Colquhoun, *A Treatise on the Police of the Metropolis* (Montclair, N.J.: Patterson Smith, 1969), pp. 75–77 (seventh London edition originally published in 1806). See also "The Voluntary Examination and Confession of William Bartlett," POB, Feb. 13, 1753, msp17530221-1 (confessing to stealing four hundred pounds of lead from Tottenham Church and selling it "to one James Robinson who deals in old Iron in Church Lane White Chaple").
27. This is only a rough preliminary estimate. It is based on various word searches in the POB for the names of various metals, including "lead," "copper," "iron," and "brass."
28. "When a man takes any thing to which he has no right, with a felonious intent, and it is personal property, the offence is larceny." Robert Bevill, *A Treatise on the Law of Homicide and of Larceny at Common Law* (London: printed for W. Clarke & Son, 1799), p. 229.

29. "[I]f [the suspect] take any thing which is fixed to a building . . . it is not personal property; and therefore the person taking it cannot be guilty of larceny. . . . [But] when any thing fixed to a building is separated from it . . . it is larceny, in the same manner as if it had always been personal property." Ibid., pp. 278–279.

30. As a treatise directed to constables instructed in 1808, metal fixtures such as "lead upon a house, rails in a yard, and the like" were not considered the type of "property" protected by English criminal law, unless "particular Acts of Parliament . . . made them so." Society for the Suppression of Vice, *The Constable's Assistant: Being a Compendium of the Duties and Powers of Constables, and Other Peace Officers; Chiefly as They Relate to the Apprehending of Offenders and the Laying of Informations Before Magistrates* (London: F. and C. Rivington, 1808), pp. 15–16.

31. 4 Geo. IV, c. 33 1731. Persons convicted of the theft of lead or iron fixtures could be transported for seven years, as could those who bought or received such items "knowing the same to be stolen."

32. Quarrill's metal had been valued at seventy shillings, roughly two hundred pounds in modern-day terms. See "Measuring Worth, Purchasing Power of British Pounds from 1264 to 2005," http://www.measuringworth.com/ppoweruk/.

33. On eighteenth-century grand jury practice, see Langbein, *Adversary Criminal Trial*, p. 45.

34. In January 1803, for example, John Bowers, an officer who served as a member of the "patrol" on the City Road, testified at the Old Bailey that he had "heard something fall upon the floors" near the defendant's "unfinished house, for near an hour" and "at last . . . heard something fall very heavy." See White, POB, Jan. 12, 1803, t18030112-103.

35. For example, William Roach was convicted of stealing metal on the basis of the testimony of a carpenter who was sleeping in the prosecutor's house "to take care of it." Roach, POB, Dec. 4, 1805, t18051204-57.

36. But see Brown, POB, May 23, 1792, t17920523-88 (defendant "jumped off one story" of a building when approached).

37. See, for example, Bowman, POB, May 20, 1801, t18010520-5 (defendant discovered in possession of a chisel, as well as a knife—the latter, "a very capital instrument for cutting lead"); and Lucas and Crawley, POB, Oct. 28, 1789, t17891028-59 (defendant spotted using "a hammer and wrench" to remove lead from a gutter).

38. See, for example, Jones, POB, Feb. 23, 1785, t17850223-43 (defendant arrested wheeling a barrow with lead in the presence of a small boy "with a pig of lead in his apron," totaling fifty-one pounds); and Hawkes, POB, Sept. 12, 1798, t17980912-33 (defendant arrested with a quantity of lead on his back).

39. In 1801 an assistant constable named John Smith arrested Thomas Barton on Gray's Inn Lane after searching Barton's bag and determining that the lead contained therein "had the appearance of being fresh cut." Barton, POB, Apr. 15, 1801, t18010415-59.

40. Surrin, POB, Jan. 13, 1792, t17920113-27.

41. Member of Parliament, *Further Observations on the Buyers or Receivers of Stolen Goods, Particularly of Lead, Iron, Copper, Brass, Bell-Metal, and Solder . . .* (London:

H. Whitridge, 1751), p. 26. Relying on information allegedly provided to him by "a considerable Dealer in Rags and Old Iron," Colquhoun observed that "some of these dealers in old metals . . . keep men employed in knocking the broad Arrow or King's mark, out of the copper-bolts, nails, and bar iron, whereon it is impressed," "cutting such bar iron into portable lengths," and purchasing "pewter pots stolen from the Publicans, which they instantly melt down." Colquhoun, *Treatise on the Police of the Metropolis*, p. 77.

42. Not surprisingly, advertisements for horses and other easy-to-identify types of property predominated in contemporary newspapers and other periodicals. See John Styles, "Print and Policing: Crime Advertising in Eighteenth-Century Provincial England," in *Policing and Prosecution*, Hay and Snyder, eds., p. 60 (noting that "the most striking feature of . . . newspaper advertisements designed to secure information in the aftermath of a particular offence was the predominance of missing horses"). On advertising and other efforts to identify owners of stolen property in eighteenth-century England, see John Styles, "Sir John Fielding and the Problem of Criminal Investigation in Eighteenth-Century England," *Transactions of the Royal Historical Society* 33 (1983): 127; and King, *Crime, Justice, and Discretion*, pp. 57–62.

43. See, for example, Simmons, POB, Feb. 16, 1774, t17740216-29 (defendant acquitted after having been indicted for "stealing 40 lb. wt. of lead, value 4 s. the property of persons, unknown"). See also Bird, POB, Jan. 11, 1775, t17750111-56 (defendant acquitted after having been indicted for "stealing a hand-saw, value two shillings, and forty pounds weight of lead, value three shillings, the property of persons unknown").

44. Smith, POB, Apr. 15, 1801, t18010415-4.

45. "Uppermost in most victims' minds once the crime had been discovered was the desire to get their goods back as quickly as possible." King, *Crime, Justice, and Discretion*, p. 23. Under the so-called Marian committal statute, which dated from the 1550s, victims who brought their complaints to local magistrates were required to post a bond (or "recognizance") that could be forfeited if the complainant failed to prosecute—though such forfeitures appear to have been rare by the late eighteenth century. On the Marian regime, see John H. Langbein, *Prosecuting Crime in the Renaissance: England, Germany, France* (Cambridge, Mass.: Harvard Univ. Press, 1974). King observes that, "while about 10 per cent of prosecutors failed to bring indictments, less than 1 per cent were estreated [i.e., forfeited their recognizances]." King, *Crime, Justice, and Discretion*, p. 42.

46. For a treatment of such considerations in the context of capital sanctions, see Donna T. Andrew and Randall McGowen, *The Perreaus and Mrs. Rudd: Forgery and Betrayal in Eighteenth-Century London* (Berkeley: Univ. of California Press, 2001), p. 24 (noting that "[a] prosecutor might experience uneasiness at the thought of hurrying an acquaintance to death and a sensitivity to the judgments his neighbors might make").

47. *Further Observations*, p. 23.

48. Percival and Spiller, POB, Oct. 30, 1793, t17931030-67.

49. Beattie, *Crime and the Courts*, pp. 401, 402, and table 8.1.

50. Ibid., p. 425 and table 8.4. In Surrey, trial juries acquitted in 35.7% of noncapital cases at the assizes and 34.1% of cases at the quarter sessions.

51. Marston, POB, Feb. 18, 1801, t18010218-45.

52. Linsey, POB, Feb. 18, 1824, t18240218-59.
53. *Report of the Select Committee on New Police in the Metropolis*, p. 76.
54. Ibid.
55. Quoted in Leon Radzinowicz and Roger G. Hood, *A History of English Criminal Law and its Administration from 1750*, vol. 3, *Cross-Currents in the Movement for the Reform of the Police* (New York: Oxford Univ. Press, 1957), p. 259n2.
56. I provide further details of Murray's case in "Presumption of Guilt and the English Law of Theft, 1750–1850," *Law and History Review* 23:133.
57. *Police Gazette; or, Hue and Cry*, October 24, 1836, National Archives (NA): HO 62/18. See also William Ballantine and Thomas Clarkson to Samuel March Phillipps (under-secretary of State for Home Affairs), Dec. 6, 1836, Thames Police Office Letter Book, June 11, 1834–July 14, 1842, London Metropolitan Archives (LMA): PS.T/1/Letter book/3.
58. Ballantine and Clarkson to Phillipps, Dec. 6, 1836, Thames Police Office Letter Book, June 11, 1834–July 14, 1842, LMA: PS.T/1/Letter book/3.
59. A person who accompanied Murray was discharged. See *Police Gazette*, October 24, 1836, NA: HO 62/18. Reference to Murray's fine is contained in Phillipps to Thames Police Office, Dec. 2, 1836, Thames Police Office Letter Book, June 11, 1834–July 14, 1842, LMA: PS.T/1/Letter book/3. On the police magistrate's assessment of Murray's testimony, see Ballantine and Clarkson to Phillipps, Dec. 6, 1836, LMA: PS.T/1/Letter book/3.
60. "Petition of Lewis Leo, Praying the return of a Cart, forfeited by his servant on being Convicted of unlawful possession of Certain Metal," Mar. 1837, Home Office: Police Courts and Magistrates: In-Letters and Returns (Home Office In-Letters), NA: HO 59/8.
61. Gregoire to Home Office, Mar. 6, 1837, Home Office In-Letters, NA: HO 59/8.
62. John Smith, Nov. 26, 1836, *Police Gazette*, NA: HO 62/18.
63. Abraham Bendaham, Dec. 5, 1836, *Police Gazette*, NA: HO 62/18.
64. Joseph Baldwin, Dec. 24, 1836, *Police Gazette*, NA: HO 62/18.
65. 29 Geo. II, c. 30 1756.
66. Ibid.
67. Smith, "Presumption of Guilt."
68. Letter from James Traill to House of Commons Select Committee on Metropolis Police Offices, Dec. 1, 1837, in *Report from Select Committee on Metropolis Police Offices; with the Minutes of Evidence, Appendix and Index, 1837–38* (Shannon: Irish Univ. Press, 1970), appendix (originally published in 1838).
69. Thomas Starkie, *A Practical Treatise on the Law of Evidence, and Digest of Proofs, in Civil and Criminal Proceedings*, vol. 2, 2d American ed. (Boston: Wells & Lilly, 1828), pp. 840–841.
70. For an incisive discussion of the use of statutes to criminalize various forms of possession, see Markus Dirk Dubber, "Policing Possession: The War on Crime and the End of Criminal Law," *Journal of Criminal Law and Criminology* 91 (2001): 829 (discussing, among other statutes, an act passed by Parliament in 1851 authorizing a three-year

prison term for any person "found by Night having in his Possession without lawful Excuse (the Proof of which Excuse shall lie on such Person) any Picklock, Key, Crow, Jack, Bit, or other implement of Housebreaking").

71. Glanville Williams, "Statutory Powers of Search and Arrest on the Ground of Unlawful Possession," *Criminal Law Review* 1960:598.

72. Ibid., p. 606.

73. "In cases of Misdemeanor, the Constable cannot apprehend the offender without a warrant." Society for the Suppression of Vice, *The Constable's Assistant* (London: F. and C. Rivington, 1808), p. 19.

74. The submission of the magistrates to the Home Office at least suggests as much. It stated that officers were eligible for a portion of a penalty when "the facts sworn to by them are undisputed." Ballantine and Clarkson to Phillipps, Dec. 6, 1836, Thames Police Office Letter Book.

75. Patrick Colquhoun, *A Treatise on the Commerce and Police of the River Thames* (Montclair, N.J.: Patterson Smith, 1969), p. 279 (originally published in 1800).

76. As Lord Devlin observed, "[E]very *police* prosecution [in England] is in theory a private prosecution; the information is laid by the police officer in charge of the case, but in so doing he is acting not by virtue of his office but as a private citizen interested in the maintenance of law and order." Patrick Devlin, *The Criminal Prosecution in England* (New Haven, Conn.: Yale Univ. Press, 1958), p. 20.

77. *Number of Persons Taken into Custody by the Metropolitan Police, and the Result of the Charges in the Year 1832* (London: n.p., 1833). Arrests for the "victimless" crime of public drunkenness outpaced arrests for any other offense.

78. Letter from William Kinnard, John Longley, and Thomas Richbell to Home Office, Mar. 5, 1821, Thames Police Office Letter Book, Mar. 31, 1804–April 16, 1822, LMA: PS.T/1/Letter book/1.

79. See note 8.

80. David Lieberman, "Mapping the English Criminal Law: Blackstone and the Categories of English Jurisprudence," in Norma Landau, ed., *Law, Crime and English Society, 1660–1830* (Cambridge: Cambridge Univ. Press, 2002), p. 157. For suggestive modern treatments, see, for example, Randy E. Barnett, "Foreword, Four Senses of the Public Law—Private Law Distinction," *Harvard Journal of Law and Public Policy* 9 (1986): 267, and Duncan Kennedy, "The Stages of Decline of the Public/Private Distinction," *University of Pennsylvania Law Review* 130 (1982): 1349.

81. Lieberman, "Mapping the English Criminal Law," p. 157.

82. See William M. Landes and Richard A. Posner, "The Private Enforcement of Law," *Journal of Legal Studies* 1975:2n4 (describing the English police in the eighteenth and early nineteenth centuries as "licensed private enforcers" because they "looked to bounties, fines, and the like" to supplement their "nominal salaries by the state"). On the practices of informers in England, see M. W. Beresford, "The Common Informer, the Penal Statutes and Economic Regulation," *Economic History Review* 10 (1957): 221.

83. *Report of the Select Committee on Private Prosecutions*, p. 17 (cited in Rock, "Victims, Prosecutors and the State," pp. 331–354, 339).

84. Friedman, *Crime and Punishment*, p. 30.

85. Mirjan R. Damaška, *The Faces of Justice and State Authority: A Comparative Approach to the Legal Process* (New Haven, Conn.: Yale Univ. Press, 1986), p. 190.

86. Glanville Williams, "The Power to Prosecute." *Criminal Law Review* 1955:600.

87. Longley, Kinnard, and Richbell to Home Office, Mar. 5, 1821, Thames Police Office Letter Book, Mar. 31, 1804–April 16, 1822, LMA: PS.T/1/Letter book/1. Referring to their "imperative duty" to make "such a number of Summary Convictions," the magistrates urged that "no difficulties nor doubts ought to be thrown in the way of [these] powers" and that "the law upon which [summary convictions were] founded should be simplified as much as possible."

SEVEN

Hans Litten and the Politics of Criminal Law in the Weimar Republic

BENJAMIN CARTER HETT

Perhaps the most characteristically modern challenge for a legal system is that of establishing its legitimacy; and how a legal system draws lines between the concepts of *politics*, *law*, and *crime* will largely determine how, and to whom, its operations will appear legitimate. As the chapters in this collection show, in the last two centuries this challenge has been at the heart of such diverse issues as defining the nature of intention or justifying the laws of an imperial ruler. The challenge also becomes acute when courts try to identify a political criminal or police the operations of trial lawyers or judges. What sorts of arguments may a lawyer raise on behalf of a defendant? How is the scope of relevance defined? How does a legal system determine the acceptable parameters of a judicial decision—in other words, the point beyond which the judge is engaging in politics rather than law, or even, in rendering his or her decision, actively committing a crime?

These questions, difficult enough at the best of times, become vastly more complex when the legal system is operating as part of a regime that itself faces a serious crisis of legitimacy. Seldom has a system of criminal justice been faced with so many simultaneous crises of legitimacy as in Germany in the era of the Weimar Republic (1919–1933). The courts of Weimar Germany had not only to answer the basic questions of how to legitimate state coercion against individuals but at the same time to formulate answers in a nation divided as few ever have been along lines of class, politics, region, and religion. In this context, criminal trials regularly became the focus of bitter controversy.

Historical accounts of Weimar law have generally focused on two themes. An older line of literature deals with the *Vertrauenskrise der Justiz*—the "crisis of confidence in justice"—the result of a clash between a generally conservative-monarchist judiciary and a new democratic state with an increasingly democratically minded populace.[1] The crisis-of-confidence literature is really a branch of political history and has tended to present a simple, binary opposition between republicans and antirepublicans.² More recently, the intellectual-historical theme of the *Methodenstreit*, or "controversy over methods" in Weimar jurisprudence, has attracted a great deal of attention. This literature, too, tends to depict a binary opposition, in this case of legal positivism versus antipositivism. Its goal is ultimately to explain the largely supine attitude of the German judicial establishment to the masters of the Third Reich.³

But a close study of how arguments were actually deployed in Weimar Republic courtrooms casts doubt on the usefulness of these dichotomies—republican/antirepublican and positivist/antipositivist—for explaining the connections between law and politics in the years before Hitler and how legal arguments may have contributed to or detracted from political goals. Like much recent research on Weimar, the argument in this chapter seeks to move beyond a narrative highlighting "a model battleground between modern liberals and anti-modern authoritarians," to an appreciation of Weimar as "the fascinating foreground against which to track the dark shadows of modernity."⁴ Adding the dimension of legal argument immeasurably complicates the business of drawing up teams and analyzing which arguments may be ascribed to whom. Weimar's political spectrum was made up of a veritable rainbow, not simply of democrats and Nazis, but of monarchists who had come to accept the "reasonableness" of a parliamentary republic, national conservatives who knew that political modernization and a generous welfare state would be the most effective means of shoring up support for an adventurous foreign policy, Social Democrats who hated the Communists more than the Nazis, and "National Bolsheviks" who would let no "fascist" outdo them in denouncing "the slave treaty of Versailles" or the shackles of the "Young Plan" for the payment of Germany's First World War reparations. At the same time, the stakes in the legal *Methodenstreit* involved the very nature of law itself and its relationship to the politics and culture of the society in which it functioned.⁵ Drawing connections between positions in the theoretical disputes and those on the politics of the day is by no means simple; the connections are neither uniform nor obvious. But by considering the manner in which political arguments were carried out through law, and legal arguments through politics, as well as how these discourses blurred together, it is possible to cast new light on some old questions regarding the collapse of Weimar and the role of law in that collapse.

To probe these questions, this chapter focuses on two cases argued by the remarkable Weimar lawyer Hans Litten (1903–1938). The cases are the Eden Dance Palace trial of spring 1931 and the Felseneck case, which ran through most of 1932. Litten's cases offer an excellent vehicle for studying the intersections of law and politics in late Weimar. On the one hand, Litten was a self-consciously political lawyer, whose work inevitably raised questions regarding the politicization of law and the legalization of politics. His radicalism was itself a kind of standing challenge to the boundaries and assumptions of the legal culture in which he worked. At the same time, as we shall see, Litten's legal philosophy—insofar as it can be divined—was rather conservative, showing strong affinities to classic Enlightened legal thought, indeed to Enlightenment in the problematic sense of Adorno and Horkheimer. Finally, it is important to see what law, whose past is so often studied as intellectual history, looks like in action in the courtroom and to explore the often-hidden links between law in theory and law in practice. For these purposes, studying the work of a practicing lawyer is ideal.

Running through the rhetoric—from all sides—in the Eden and Felseneck cases, we find consistent oppositions between two pairs of concepts: crime versus politics, on the one hand, and politics versus law, on the other. Calling an event "political" as opposed to "criminal" implies, first of all, that it is a matter of collective action, whereas "crime" may be an individual affair. Second, a political event is one that is planned, purposeful, and rational, whereas a crime can be spontaneous, random, and irrational. But when we introduce the opposition of law and politics we see that the values shift. In this second operation, law takes on the qualities of order and rationality, and it is politics that becomes the realm of permitted violence, irrationality, and disorder. Tellingly, it is generally politics that is the inculpatory argument. To assess a violent action as a crime rather than politics is to lessen the responsibility for its commission, to take into consideration all the mitigating factors of human frailty. But when politics is juxtaposed to law, then politics becomes pejorative—the realm of (unlovely) passion and arbitrary caprice, while law is pristine, rational, and neutral. The relationships between these concepts, perhaps in some instances unconsciously assumed, nevertheless profoundly shaped the way the Eden and Felseneck cases were argued and decided.[6]

The first section of this chapter examines the Eden Palace case, while the second section looks at Felseneck. In the final section I make an argument about the links in these disputes between conceptions of law and politics and how a close study of them contributes to reconceiving the politics of criminal law in late Weimar.

1. Eden Dance Palace

On May 8, 1931, Adolf Hitler, still a prominent radical politician and not yet chancellor of the German Reich, testified as a witness at the criminal courthouse in Berlin-Moabit. The trial, the case against *Stief and Others*, or as it was more commonly known, the Eden Dance Palace trial, was of a sort that had become routine in Germany in the late Weimar years. Four members of the National Socialist *Sturmabteilung* (Storm Section), or SA, stood accused of forcing their way into a dance put on by a Communist hiking club and firing randomly at the participants. Three young men attending the dance were wounded, one of them seriously. Hitler was summoned both by Hans Litten, who represented the victims, and by the defense counsel for the SA men, although certainly with very different expectations of his testimony. Among the other witnesses that day were two former members of the SA, Walter Stennes and Ernst Wetzel, who had recently staged a dramatic revolt against Hitler's leadership of the National Socialist Party, fearing that Hitler had betrayed the revolutionary roots of Nazism to become just another bourgeois politician. With revolutionaries to the right and left of him—Litten, though commonly called a Communist, disliked the Communist Party of Germany (KPD) and claimed to be a revolutionary anarchist—Hitler gave evidence that day that consisted of an increasingly shrill and strained insistence on the legality of his National Socialist German Workers' Party (NSDAP).

In light of this political background, the real subject of *Stief* had nothing to do with what four SA thugs had done or not done at the Eden Dance Palace. Rather, the real subject was a conversation about crime, politics, and law in the context of a Germany sinking steadily into civil war. Nazi rhetoric in the preceding months and years had set some dangerous traps for Hitler. In an April newspaper attack on Walter Stennes, Hitler claimed that Stennes had contributed nothing more to the Nazi Party than "the formation of a few pitiful Roll-Commandos."[7] Nazi propaganda chief Joseph Goebbels had written a pamphlet a few years earlier calling for a "revolution" that would "chase the parliament to the devil" and found a new state "on the basis of German fists and German brains."[8] Hitler now had to explain how such statements could be reconciled with the party's repeated pious claims to legality, a prominent feature of Nazi propaganda since Hitler's refounding of the party in the wake of the failed Beer Hall Coup of 1924.

Hans Litten formally requested that Hitler be summoned to confirm three facts: that the Nazis had formed Roll Commandos, or "groups which carry out planned and organized attacks on political opponents with the goal of committing premeditated homicide"; that the Berlin *Sturm* 33, which had carried out the attack on the Eden Dance Palace, was such a Roll Commando; and that, as Litten wrote, "the criminal act which forms the subject of these proceedings, and numerous other criminal acts of a similar type, were planned and organized by the members of *Sturm* 33."[9] In the course of a three-hour examination, Litten forced Hitler into a series of awkward evasions and, finally, desperate rage.

If the Nazi Party was strictly "legal," why had Hitler charged Stennes with the formation of "pitiful" Roll Commandos within the party? Why had Goebbels advocated "beating the enemy to a pulp"? The court disallowed other questions. Litten wanted Hitler's opinion on whether the SA men had acted in self-defense in raiding the Eden Palace. He wanted the evidence of a senior civil servant from the Reich Interior Ministry concerning Nazi legality. He wanted to ask the SA witness Wetzel whether he thought inflammatory statements by Nazi leaders were to blame for other crimes similar to the attack on the Eden Palace and whether he thought that other SA leaders opposed Hitler's "legal" strategy. And he wanted to ask both Wetzel and Stennes if they believed a particular member of Sturm 33 had committed a political murder in January 1931.[10] The court gave the same reason for each refusal: the information sought was not relevant. "The ideas of wide circles of the NSDAP, or of its leadership, regarding the carrying out of its political struggle with legal or illegal means, permit no conclusion regarding whether the defendants have committed the criminal action with which they are charged."[11]

On May 22, exactly two weeks after Hitler's appearance, the court gave its judgment in *Stief*, convicting three of the accused SA men of minor offenses—breach of the peace and trespassing, with sentences of two and a half years' imprisonment—and acquitting the fourth. The court found that the men had attacked their political enemies "with great recklessness" but there was no evidence they had intended to kill them. Litten, representing the private prosecutors, had sought to hold the defendants to this more incriminating standard, arguing that the SA men had engaged in a "planned undertaking with the goal of intentional and premeditated murder of revolutionary workers." But the court found "the entire picture of the evidence" spoke against such a construction. The judgment emphasized the defendants' lack of rational planning. If the attack had been premeditated, they would have striven to cover their tracks, whereas in fact they had done "exactly the opposite." The precipitate nature of their attack could be seen, said the court, in the fact that most of them went out into the November night without hats or coats; and the evidence showed they were completely unfamiliar with the layout of the Eden Palace. "All of this," the court concluded, "speaks against the assumption of a planned attack," intended to lead to "a prepared and premeditated killing."[12]

Remarkably, in a case in which Nazi storm troopers had attacked Communists and the Nazi leader had been cross-examined by an anarchist, the court underplayed the political content of the trial. Certainly, it found that the defendants were "in the midst of a bitter struggle with the members of left-radical political groups," which had "often led to violent confrontations." But rhetorically emphasizing that the case was a crime—that is to say, disorder rather than politics—the court proclaimed that it was "not in a position to decide who bears the greater responsibility for these fights." An "inner disposition" of fear and hatred of the political opponent explained the objectively disproportionate violent response of the Nazis, and this inner disposition, "even if it is one-sided and unjustified," had to be considered as a mitigating factor in sentencing.[13]

The wounded Communists and the SA defendants all appealed the verdict to the Imperial Supreme Court in Leipzig. In his written appeal, Litten stressed the planning and organization of the attack; his argument made clear how much a decision about the relevance of evidence had to do with a decision about politics versus crime. If the trial court had permitted his questions about other crimes by members of SA Sturm 33, then it might have "drawn conclusions about the violent disposition of the SA in general, and of the members of *Sturm* 33 of the Berlin SA in particular." This would have permitted the further conclusion that "even those culprits who did not themselves carry firearms had the intention [*eventuellen Vorsatz*] to commit homicide."[14] In its efforts to downplay the political overtones of the case, the trial court's verdict had entirely and wrongly neglected Adolf Hitler's evidence. If the court had allowed Litten's question about the meaning of self-defense, Hitler might have claimed that the SA attack qualified. Such an answer could then have "shaken the court's belief in the National Socialist claim of a communist share in the responsibility for the constant conflicts." Litten's arguments about the court's refusal of his questions for Stennes and Wetzel emphasized the political role of the NSDAP leadership. In finding such questions irrelevant, said Litten, the court had contradicted itself. It had permitted him to ask Hitler about Goebbels' inflammatory writings and about an alleged promise to Reich Chancellor Brüning to dissolve the SA in return for a share of power. Thus the court itself had acknowledged that the "possible attitude of particular circles in the party leadership to acts of violence" was not "beyond all connection with the subject of the trial."[15]

But the most revealing of Litten's arguments was one ostensibly *in favor* of the Nazi defendants: he argued that the court should recognize them as *Überzeugungstäter*—"criminals by conviction."

What did this mean? The narrow issue at stake involved the conditions the convicted men would experience in prison. At a broader level, it is easy to see Litten's strategic interest in wishing the court to designate the storm troopers as political actors rather than random thugs. And at the broadest level, this matter of the defendants' "convictions" raised serious questions of the distinction between politics and law. Paragraph 20 of the German Criminal Code of 1871 specified that, where a code provision created alternative sentences of custody in a fortress or a penitentiary (the former, despite the ominous sound, much less onerous), a court could sentence a prisoner to penitentiary time only "if it is determined that the conduct which is found to be punishable arose out of a dishonorable cast of mind (*Gesinnung*)."[16] In the Weimar years, a similar provision was included in the Reich "Principles for the Execution of Custodial Sentences of 1923," in which paragraph 52 stipulated better treatment for prisoners upon an express finding by the trial court that the prisoner's "decisive motive" arose out of a subjective belief that he or she was "obliged to carry out the deed on the basis of moral, religious or political convictions."[17] In a revealing gloss on paragraph 20, one scholar wrote that "the culprit who acts out of honorable (*wertvollen*) motives must not be equated with the common criminal."[18] What was also striking about the *Überzeugungstäter* provision was its construction of the kind of deed and the kind of person that would fall under its terms. What mattered, according to legal scholar Wilhelm Budzinski, was not "the individual motive for the deed" but rather "the constant direction of the will." A political crime, then, was one that rested on a kind of structure, an order in the mind of the prisoner. Furthermore, Budzinski wrote, the modern political criminal was distinguished by three characteristics: he followed a party program; his "struggle against the prevailing order becomes a permanent condition"; and the cause of his struggle "lies in his social connectedness [*Bezogenheit*]." The modern political offender's actions were likely to derive less from his individual conscience than from his social integration [*Eingliederung*]; he was thus the "bearer of a group spirit."[19] But of course it was an open question whether there could ever be a consensus on the nature of honor amid the chaos of Weimar Germany. The undefined quality of an honorable (or dishonorable) cast of mind had, "especially in the stormy times during and after the war," led to "contradictory judgments in the higher courts," as Budzinski wrote with some considerable understatement.[20]

In the Eden case, paragraph 20 of the Criminal Code could not apply, as the offenses in question made no provision for custody in a fortress. Paragraph 52 of the "Principles" could potentially apply to the SA men, but the trial court found that they did not fit its terms. Although the court believed the men had "not acted out of a dishonorable cast of mind," it also found that their "decisive motive" did not arise out of a belief in their *duty* to attack the Eden Palace.[21] This finding was, of course, perfectly consistent with the court's downplaying of politics throughout the judgment, especially in light of Budzinski's emphasis on the social nature of the modern *Überzeugungstäter*.

It was logical, then, for Litten to object to this finding; and if his argument on appeal, along with the text of paragraph 20 itself, seemed to reverse the usual rhetorical valuation of politics and crime, his pretense of honoring the defendants' conduct as political rather than criminal was transparently disingenuous. "The private prosecutor," he wrote in his appeal, "has a justified interest in being protected from a violent political opponent through the highest possible sentence, but on the other hand has no interest in defaming the opponent beyond what is necessary." Rather obviously dodging the key question of a subjective belief in "duty," Litten argued that the court's finding in this regard stood "in crass contradiction" to its finding that "the conduct of the defendants is *only* comprehensible on the basis of their political convictions (which means that other motives cannot possibly be drawn into the realm of reasonable consideration), and further, that the political convictions of the defendants *determined* their conduct."[22]

On November 19, 1931, the Imperial Supreme Court denied the defendants' appeal, and for the most part denied Litten's. The most revealing passage of the judgment dealt with the trial court's disallowance of Litten's questions, because here the Supreme Court reflected on the meaning and scope of a political trial. It characterized the Eden case as an example of "*crimes and misdemeanors* against the public order, life and bodily security, of the kind that occupy the courts in ever greater numbers." Logically, then, it "was not a *political* case in the strict sense" (emphasis added). The court then found irrelevant "how the leader of a party in fact evaluated the deed, whether he was inclined to excuse it in some way, whether some subaltern leaders of a party rejected the commitment of the higher leader to a legal position, whether other similar breaches of the legal order were provoked by inflammatory statements of party leaders, [or] whether a subaltern leader received knowledge of the participation of a party member in the killing of a worker at another time and place." The court's rhetoric sought to preserve the purity of the laws of criminal procedure from the abusive introduction of politics: Litten's questions were suitable "only for delivering material for the party-political struggle." The laws of criminal procedure could not be "misused" for such "impermissible sidepurposes."[23] In a further revealing move, the Court took only one sentence to find that Litten's argument on behalf of the defendants' status as political criminals was unfounded. The reason: this was an administrative measure not subject to review by an appellate court.[24] Thus, in an important sense, it was not law.

Litten's work in the Eden Palace trial, then, can be seen on the one hand as an effort to establish a narrative resolving the disorder of a crime into the order of politics. At the same time, his private statements show he was just as concerned to impose the *higher* order of law on the chaos of (Nazi) politics. According to one report, flushed with triumph after his examination of Hitler, he boasted to his mother, "I did it! I made Hitler swear an oath to legality!"[25] After the trial, Hans's father, Fritz Litten, complained bitterly to his son about the personal and professional consequences to him of Hans's political advocacy. Hans replied that his work in the trial had been "less of a political than a general-legal sort: representing the interests of people who are prey for organized murder bands," a half-defensive explanation in which the characterization "general-legal" is clearly intended to refer away from the arbitrary caprice of politics toward the unobjectionable neutrality of law.[26] It is striking, then, that the Imperial Supreme Court rejected Litten's claims by trumping him: dismissing his arguments as political, mere efforts at unworthy propaganda, a violation of law's neutrality. Given the light sentences for the SA men, however, the net result of the Eden Palace trial and its appeal was a victory for the exculpatory claims of passion and disorder against the reasoned implications of political action: two courts had wished to see the former and screen out the latter.

2. Felseneck

The Felseneck case took up most of the year 1932 and would prove to be Hans Litten's last major battle against the NSDAP. Late in the evening of January 18, 1932, about 150 SA men left a meeting in the northern Berlin suburb of Waidmannslust and set out on a long and circuitous march, ostensibly as an escort for several members who lived in nearby Reinickendorf. Their route eventually took them past a cottage settlement (*Laubenkolonie*) called the Felseneck Colony. Such colonies were (and to an extent still are) a familiar part of the landscape of German cities. In some cases the colonies simply provided garden allotments for city dwellers. But in the hard years of the Depression, it was common for working-class people, especially the unemployed, to live permanently on them. Felseneck, in solidly working-class Reinickendorf-East, was known as a Communist Party stronghold, and one of its residents, 29-year-old Fritz Klemke, had drawn the special hatred of the local SA.[27] According to the most credible accounts, as the SA men neared the colony, they fanned out around it and attacked from all sides with stones and firearms. The colonists' own improvised night watch went into battle against the storm troopers. Soon two men were dead: one was Fritz Klemke, who was likely the primary target of the Nazi attack, the other an SA man named Ernst Schwartz. Several other people, including two police officers, were injured.[28] A mass trial for participants in the brawl—with a highly unrepresentative selection of sixteen colonists and eight SA men in the dock—began in April 1932, with Litten as defense counsel for the colonists.

In the context of Germany in 1932—a year in which five major election campaigns revealed growing support for the most extreme parties, the National

Socialists and the Communists, and a civil war was fought in nightly increments in the streets—such a trial could not help but raise the most fundamental challenges to the legitimacy of the law. On January 21, Joseph Goebbels's paper *The Attack* criticized a Berlin police memo that found that the SA bore the "political guilt" for the brawl, even if the "criminal guilt" was yet to be determined. *The Attack* posed a more profound question than its editors probably realized when it asked, "What does political guilt mean here?"[29] In an article headed "An incomprehensible separation: 'Political' and 'Criminal' Guilt," *The Attack's* correspondent wrote that "the police are not to determine who bears the political guilt" but rather are supposed to "investigate in a professional manner who was the attacker and who was the attacked." At a more grandly theoretical level, the article concluded: "It is obviously nonsense [*ein Unding*] to try to separate the 'political' from the 'moral' guilt for an attack that involves a bloody and murderous deed."[30] A few months later, Joseph Goebbels himself delivered a scathing criticism of a court that had acquitted several of Hans Litten's clients on charges of killing another SA man. This verdict showed, said Goebbels, that "the court was true to the letter of the law" but not to its spirit: the judges were too "objective" to see the truth. "The paragraph has carried away a victory over the true, gruesome facts of the case" was Goebbels's pathetic complaint. The "authoritarian state leadership" was too "objective" to impose "an atonement for [the crime] that would do justice to popular feelings."[31]

With so many defendants and a witness list running into hundreds, the Felseneck trial was destined to be long. But Litten was so persistent in his questioning, so unwilling to let any point go, so eager to summon ever more witnesses, that the judges and prosecutors began to complain that he was making the orderly conduct of the case utterly impossible. Litten enraged the authorities by alleging that the police had covertly assisted the SA men with their attack, providing not only an escort but also the weapon that killed Klemke. He claimed that the prosecutors, in their desire to convict Communists rather than Nazis, consistently misrepresented the colonists as the aggressors; and he accused the examining magistrates and the trial court itself of both bad will and incompetence. By August, the prosecutors were conspiring to expel Litten from the case, and their efforts to get rid of the troublesome lawyer brought the Felseneck trial, and indeed the politics of law in late Weimar, to a climax.

The prosecution conspiracy is attested to by a memo written in late July by Chief Prosecutor Sethe at Berlin's Superior Court III to his superior at the Court of Appeal. Sethe's memo was a list of complaints about both Litten and the trial judge, Superior Court Director Bode. Litten's endless questions to witnesses, said Sethe, had dragged the trial out to a length "out of all proportion to the material dealt with." But Director Bode had failed to take control. Indeed, in meetings with the prosecutors, Bode not only said that nothing in the Code of Criminal Procedure prevented a lawyer from carrying on as Litten had, he even praised Litten's lawyerly skills and knowledge. Sethe found all of this unacceptable. Either Litten or Bode had to go. Sethe thought the trial should be stayed and "continued under a more suitable president"; he also suggested his superior consider "what possibilities there are for the prosecution to save the wayward state of the trial."[32]

It is likely that senior prosecutors or ministerial officials subsequently approached Director Bode with Sethe's message. For on August 15, Bode's court issued an order expelling Litten from the trial. The court's sixteen-page ruling claimed that Litten had abused his position through exhaustive and repetitive questions and through allegations that responsible officials had favored the Nazi defendants. Since Litten was an experienced specialist in criminal defense, he had to know that his conduct was improper. He was obviously pursuing another purpose: the spreading of "unrestrained political propaganda" on behalf of the Communist Party, "for use against the state and its institutions." The court thought too highly of "the law-finding task entrusted to it" to allow "so irresponsible a defense counsel" to destroy "the dutiful work of the court and the other participants in the trial, and to allow the courtroom to become a playground of fanatical political passions." Thus it was the court's "well-founded duty" to "expel Advocate Litten as defense counsel from this proceeding."[33]

This was a remarkable step for a German court to take, and it was followed by an even more remarkable justification. "The jury court knows," the ruling continued, that its "unusual" measure "cannot be supported by a specific and express provision of the Code of Criminal Procedure." But the court believed it could "do without" any such support: "There are consequences that so necessarily emerge from a given situation, that they do not need an express statutory rule." For every legal proceeding there were "presumptions" so obvious that their incorporation in the statute was "superfluous," for "it cannot be assumed that the Code wishes a practical impossibility." To cover its bets, the court also argued that there was a provision in the Code that permitted the same conclusion "by analogy": paragraph 145 allowed the court to appoint a new defense counsel if the present one refused to carry on the defense. Certainly Litten had not *expressly* refused to defend any of his clients, but his behavior amounted to the same thing, as he had "refused to conduct the defense" in a manner befitting "an organ of the administration of justice." Still, the court was careful to point out that it did not put decisive weight on the argument by analogy.[34]

Now, as we have seen, Bode himself had earlier admitted that the code did not permit such a measure; and the tone of the ruling betrayed a good deal of judicial discomfort. Some of its criticisms of Litten were surprisingly mild (for instance, that his attacks on various officials would be more appropriate in an administrative complaint). The elaborate legal justifications of the court's actions, complete with the nervous reference to an argument by analogy, positively breathed self-doubt. All of this suggests that officials behind the scenes pushed Bode to make a decision he did not wish to make. Litten himself claimed that another senior judge had told him privately that an influential clique in the Berlin courts enjoyed "rumor-mongering" about him.[35]

The issue of the scope of a criminal defense was, and is, a perennially sensitive spot in German criminal procedure. Already by the turn of the twentieth century, aggressive young barristers were locking horns with a conservative legal establishment over how hard a lawyer should strive for an acquittal and how much time could be consumed in the (potentially) open-ended trials German procedural laws allowed. In many well-publicized cases, the German bar's stringent enforcement of professional norms sought to undo, not always successfully, the theoretically broad protections in the Code of Criminal Procedure—such as a defendant's right to remain silent or to ask for the recusal of a potentially biased judge.[36] Such arguments have continued to the present day, in the recent controversies over the so-called *Krawallanwälte*, with the fundamental issue remaining the same: is the system's promise of the defendant's rights only hypocrisy if such rights are seldom exercised, and even then only at the cost of considerable controversy?[37] Does the legitimacy of a trial rest on the thorough testing of the prosecution's case by an aggressive defense or instead on the commitment of all trial participants to an impartial investigation of the truth, unsullied by partisan concerns? Historically, the freedom with which German lawyers could conduct defenses closely followed the political openness of the German state, widening considerably from the quasi-authoritarian 1880s to the much more easygoing 1920s.[38] But after 1930, as Germany began to swing back toward authoritarian rule even before the advent of Hitler's chancellorship, the obstacles to aggressive criminal defense began to mount.[39] Litten, probably the most aggressive political counsel in Weimar Germany, felt the changes more than most.

Indeed, the court's admission that there was no statutory basis for its expulsion order gave Litten the opportunity for an aggressive response, one that raised another fundamental question of legal legitimacy. On September 2, Litten filed a request with the prosecutor's office that Bode and his two assistant judges be charged with "bending the law" (*Rechtsbeugung*).[40]

What does this mean? The offense of *Rechtsbeugung* is rooted in the efforts of German states in the age of absolutism to police the work of their judges. For "bending the law" is a criminal offense that *only* a judge or similar official can commit. Paragraph 314 of the Prussian Criminal Code of 1851 stipulated that "an official" who intentionally made himself guilty of "an injustice" in the course of the "conduct or decision of a legal matter" was to be punished with five years of hard labor.[41] The first parliament of the new German Empire returned the language to "bending of the law" (*Rechtsbeugung*) rather than "injustice" in drafting paragraph 336 (today § 339) of the Reich Criminal Code of 1871. Otto Henning, a doctoral student of Gustav Radbruch, wrote in his 1929 dissertation that this change "better expresses that only a breach of positive law, not a contradiction of the idea of justice, falls under this crime."[42] And here is the vital point. The Social Democratic lawyer and legal scholar Ludwig Bendix, writing in 1926, noted that the Reich Criminal Code viewed *Rechtsbeugung* "uncritically" from the standpoint of a "naive realism." This naive realism assumed that any good-faith observer *must* perceive the contradiction between the judge's improper construction of the law and the law as it stood in the code. This assumption, Bendix continued, rested in turn on a second one: that the law "whose bending stood in question" was a "purely logical system of legal norms with an inner logical consistency divorced from its object, [from] social life, and from the personality of the judge" and from his social milieu.[43] Was the judicial offense, then, a matter of law or of politics, and how were these concepts distinguished in German jurisprudence? The fierce academic as well as political controversies of Weimar had raised these question in the most unavoidable way. For Bendix, the offense of law bending had to serve a frankly political purpose as a weapon against the antidemocratic sentiments common in the judiciary. Bendix's proposal culminated in the proposition that a subsequent court should convict a judge of law bending if it found that the judge reached a decision on the basis of considerations "foreign to the judicial office, or hostile to a free state." Bendix also thought that a mental state of negligence, rather than conscious intent, should suffice for conviction.[44] Henning, on the other hand, advocated exactly the interpretation of law bending that Bendix condemned as naive: any "contradiction to the objective law." Henning assumed that the law was a realm free of politics, of all subjective and arbitrary judgments, with the offense of law bending serving as a kind of border patrol.[45]

The core of Litten's argument in his charge against Bode's court was simple: as there was no statutory basis for his expulsion, the judges had necessarily "bent the law" in reaching their decision. The court's open admission that "this measure . . . cannot be supported by a specific and express provision of the Code" allowed Litten to argue that this was "that rare case in which the facts of bending the law can be proven against three judges carrying out their official duties, not only objectively, but also subjectively."[46] Litten, who liked to say that as an anarchist he stood far to the left of Germany's Communist Party, thus appeared in this case as the champion of a conservative literalism in the construction of legal texts, in opposition to a court that seemed to pursue a far-right political agenda with the most up-to-date and progressive theoretical tools.

Litten's argument failed: after a complicated round of appeals, he was finally forced from the case in October 1932. The Felseneck trial ended inclusively in December, with the case stayed as the result of an amnesty.[47] German lawyers, and what remained of a liberal public sphere, were well aware of the significance of Litten's expulsion for civil liberties in Germany, and his case was one of the last major legal controversies before the advent of Hitler's chancellorship in January 1933.[48] Four weeks after Hitler came to power Litten was arrested; after five terrible years, he died in the concentration camp at Dachau in 1938.[49]

3. Enlightenment

In the argument thus far, I have presented two incidents from the legal career of Hans Litten and argued that they illustrate the crisis of legitimacy in criminal law in late Weimar Germany. Arguments about legitimacy were carried on through a rhetoric characterized by an ordering of concepts shared by all of the participants in the cases, despite vast differences in political ideology—in which crime bore the relationship to politics that politics in turn bore to law, the relationship of the disordered and irrational mirror image of a conception of purpose and rationality. In the Eden Palace case, Litten strove to portray the SA defendants as engaged in a planned and calculated political activity; two levels of court rejected this political interpretation of the event and opted instead for the exculpatory image of a crime, a disorderly and random action carried out by nonpolitical, admittedly crude, but forgivably frightened individuals. In the Felseneck case, Litten was driven from the trial by a court that had willfully opted for a political, that is, logically unconstrained construction of a legal text, to which Litten responded with the arsenal of law, of pure rational legal argument. In this final section of the chapter I wish to demonstrate the deeper significance of these arguments and what they might tell us about larger questions of the role of law in the demise of the Weimar Republic.

It is at this point that I wish to stress the connections between what the actors in these courtrooms were doing and the more ethereal realm of Weimar legal thought. Certainly I am not claiming that either Hitler or Litten were moved by theoretical considerations. Hitler's disinterest in matters of legal theory need hardly be stressed. Litten, despite his juristic brilliance, was no more engaged with such questions; according to his close friend Max Fürst, Litten once wrote in his diary, "When the ox in Paradise got bored, he invented jurisprudence."[50] But any politician or lawyer acts on the basis of assumptions, often unstated, about the relationship of law and politics. These assumptions help to explain both personal actions and what was at stake in these confrontations.

First, it is impossible to characterize the Eden Palace or Felseneck cases as in some way pitting supporters of the Weimar constitution against opponents of it: in both trials, probably everyone in the courtroom—Litten and his Communist clients no less than the prosecutors, the judges, and the Nazis—were opponents of the republic. "At the time . . . we were against democracy," wrote Max Fürst, an admission in which the "we" can be taken to include Litten himself.[51] Nor were these trials battles between elites and outsiders, modern conceptions of society and politics against premodern ones, or even one clearly defined social class against another. The battles here were about the legal politics of opposition, the relation of law to power, in a context in which *all* actors portrayed themselves as self-consciously modern.

Take the case of the "criminal by conviction." At its heart, this question went to the connections between law and morality, law and politics, and the legitimacy of state punishment, which had riled German criminal law scholarship for decades before the 1930s.[52] For Litten, the point was that punishment legitimately belonged at the top, with a much lesser degree of responsibility attaching to those whom he regarded as Hitler's poor and deluded followers. As Litten's friend Max Fürst recalled, Litten recognized that in cases like Eden and Felseneck "the culprits on both sides were workers," and his arguments targeted "the National Socialist Leaders, the agitators . . . and not just the unemployed workers . . . who [were] naturally especially vulnerable to the cheap solutions of National Socialism."[53] In other words, Litten aimed at a political, not a criminal-legal, victory; his attitude to the punishment of the SA men in the Eden Palace case (imprisonment solely a matter of the defense of his clients) closely tracked the pragmatic, utilitarian philosophy of criminal punishment advocated by the modern or sociological school of Franz von Liszt and Gustav Radbruch.[54] In fact, one indicator of Litten's integration into the broader world of German legal culture is that he was Liszt's godson.[55]

One can demonstrate other connections between Litten's cast of mind and patterns of argument and the broader questions that faced German law in late

Weimar. What is surprising about these connections is that they reveal a man who, far from holding legal views typical of the far left, was something of a jurisprudential conservative.

On the level of legal theory, the Weimar period was marked by the advance of various versions of antipositivist conceptions at law, at the expense of an embattled positivism. Legal positivism, in the Weimar-era German understanding, implied either a strict textualism in interpretation or an understanding of law as cleanly separable from morality, politics, custom, or sociological study.[56] The most sophisticated of Weimar positivists was Hans Kelsen, advocate of a *reine Rechtslehre*, or "pure theory of law." Kelsen was deeply influenced by neo-Kantian epistemology; his thinking was therefore largely a matter of drawing careful boundaries around necessarily distinct fields of inquiry. Law inhabited a realm of "ought" uncontaminated by the realm of "is." *Purity*, for Kelsen, meant "cleansed of all political ideologies and all natural-scientific elements." This was a neat and orderly theory, an "ideal of an objective science of law and the state," that could find general acceptance only in "a period of social equilibrium." Writing in 1934, Kelsen hoped that a younger generation would not lose its faith in such a science despite "the wild racket of our time." If that noise came largely from those, on right and left, with substantive agendas for "justice," Kelsen wrote coolly that "justice is an irrational ideal . . . not accessible to empirical perception [*Erkennen*]. To this is given only positive law."[57]

Weimar-era antipositivistic legal thinking had its roots in the work of some leading jurists of the late nineteenth century—above all Rudolf von Ihering—as well as in the thought of Nietzsche, Schopenhauer, and, perhaps most of all, Hegel. Since the first years of the twentieth century, thinkers of the Free Law or Sociological Jurisprudence schools had advanced the proposition that law was a radically historical substance that could never be contained within the dead letter of a legislated code. Thus law must constantly evolve, in part through the bold decisions of judges; for the Free Lawyers, the textualism advocated by jurisprudential conservatives was really just the continuation of politics by other means. Most characteristically, antipositivists argued that law must stay in constant touch with life, perhaps through drawing on the insights of the social sciences.[58] Before the First World War, German antipositivists were mostly left-liberals or moderate Social Democrats, and the leading figures were almost all of Jewish background. But this was not universally so: Carl Schmitt was already advocating a right variant before the war, and by the 1920s the flight of the nationalist right from positivism was becoming massive. Thus jurisprudential debates in Weimar took on an odd appearance, in which the insistence on life and historicity, the whole arsenal of Nietzschean or Hegelian argument, could emerge identically from the far left *or* the far right. Such a bastion of the national conservative judicial establishment as the *Deutsche Richterzeitung*, the official journal of the Association of German Judges, deployed criticisms of formalistic jurisprudence out of touch with life in articles with titles like "Judicial Correction of Obsolete Laws," "Morality and Law," and "Problems of Legal Decision-Making."[59] But Ernst Fuchs, a left-liberal Jewish advocate of free law, could also denounce the "thoroughly un-German spirit" of "legal mathematics" that had come to dominate Germany since "the rape of the German people through the reception of Roman law."[60] Consciously or not, here Fuchs was echoing the rejection of "materialistic" Roman law in the Nazi Party program.[61]

The essential point of antipositive theory was that politics and morals *had* to inform law, and thus antipositivists of right and left stood strongly against the neo-Kantians' celebration of reason and order and their drawing of careful, categorical lines. Shortly after Hitler came to power, Carl Schmitt, the most infamous of Nazi legal theorists, celebrated the achievement of Nazi jurists in overcoming the positivistic "tearing apart" of "law and economics, law and society, [and] law and politics."[62] In the essential dichotomies crime/politics and politics/law, we have seen that the Nazis always ended up on the first, the disorderly, side. Nazi jurists correspondingly put forward theories of disorder, if not indeed disorderly theories. Carl Schmitt made a surprising concession to Kelsen when he wrote that Kelsenite positivism was "plausible" in a "stable situation" in which one could safely neglect all "meta-legal" points of view.[63] For Schmitt, needless to say, Germany in the 1930s presented no such stable situation.

Now, what is odd about Litten's patterns of legal argument is that he did not, as a conventional left-radical antipositivist would have, pour scorn on "the shadowy, bloodless concepts" of "so-called justice" and "objective law."[64] And this at a time when it was virtually ubiquitous on right and left to do so; even the reactionary clique around Reich president Paul von Hindenburg was convinced that under modern conditions, a government needed a solid base of public support for its laws to be legitimate.[65] Instead, Litten's (implicit and unarticulated) legal philosophy was strikingly Kelsenite. Litten's argument against Bode on the matter of law bending follows Kelsen's analysis of the "gap problem." Theorists of the time were much engaged with the question of how a judge should deal with a "gap" in the law—in other words, a failure of the legislator to provide for a given situation. Bode's court was, in its own view at least, faced with such a gap: the Code of Criminal Procedure left it no express means of dealing with an obstructive defense counsel. And so Bode's court followed a Free Law prescription and boldly adapted the statute to its needs. But Kelsen wrote that the so-called gap problem was merely an "ideological formula" for situations in which the court found unacceptable the legislator's failure to provide a desired norm.[66] This was precisely Litten's position when he argued that by not expressly providing a court grounds for the removal of a defense counsel, the code implicitly refused such an option.

We have seen Litten's insistence on the legality as opposed to the politicality of his trial work; and there is one more route to demonstrate the neo-Kantian, Kelsenite positivism of his mind. If Litten wrote nothing on legal theory, he wrote extensively on art history and art theory. On these matters he had an all-encompassing and elaborately developed theory, at which he claimed to have arrived in 1924–1925, "the breakthrough year of 'my' art-theory."[67] From these writings one can form, by analogy, a clear impression of his jurisprudential assumptions. Fundamental to Litten's thinking on art were the definition of hermetically sealed categories and the drawing of consequences from the existence of those categories. His writings on art constantly played on the distinction between the "metaphysical reality" that was the subject of art, and the "physical means of expression" that were its tools. Physical reality could be studied with all of the tools of empirical science, but "we cannot receive those things that stand beyond the laws of logic with the tools of this logic." This approach coincides with a neo-Kantian division of the sciences of "is" from those of "ought," or of the natural from the cultural sciences. It meant that for Litten there was a clear line between art and nonart: a painting or a play or a composition that did not deal with the metaphysical was nonart.[68] Furthermore, criticisms of a theatrical production on the grounds that it misrepresented the text of the play were hopelessly misguided. Litten established something akin to a Kelsenite "pure theory of theater"; he disapproved of applying "extra-artistic principles" to the organizing of a theatrical work, a practice that was "unfortunately common today."[69] The historical understanding underpinning Litten's art theory was eighteenth century, decisively pre-Ranke, pre-Hegel, pre-Marx: he saw history as an endlessly repeating cycle of "cultural" and "anti-cultural" ages, with no notion of progress. For Litten, cross-temporal judgments on artistic validity were certainly possible, and he made them with defiant and idiosyncratic abandon.[70] This cast of mind put him very much in line with the ahistorical neo-Kantians and very much against the strongly historicist antipositivists. His was, in short, a classically *Enlightened* view.

And this, finally, is the key to Litten's trial work, the key to what was happening when he faced Hitler and argued so strongly against Director Bode. His opponents were those who set themselves most consequently against the Enlightenment. Neo-Hegelian legal thinkers like the young Karl Larenz or conservative Catholics like Carl Schmitt were the most vehement in their rejection of the rationality, utilitarianism, and individualism they associated with the Enlightenment. In the final analysis Litten, despite his claims to the contrary, was no wild-eyed anarchist; he was a champion of Enlightenment, albeit in its most radical and uncompromising form. Litten had a strongly didactic character. Friends' recollections of him stress his lessons about poetry, art, or politics: "He could never refuse Enlightenment when someone asked," wrote Max Fürst.[71] But Litten's version of Enlightenment was hardly benign. It was, indeed, marked by all of the coercive potential that Adorno and Horkheimer famously diagnosed. "Before us stands an image of human beings that is to become reality," Litten wrote in an essay on art for fellow members of the youth movement. "Knowledge only has purpose for us insofar as it serves education in accordance with this image." Although a freakishly cultivated man, who could recite the complete works of Rilke and many other writers from memory, Litten could be militantly philistine in his attitude to culture: "The enrichment of knowledge out of pure interest is an irresponsible waste of time," he wrote. He added a qualification, but it was the qualification of a political fanatic: "When the supply of knowledge appears necessary to us, then the selection is deliberately one-sided."[72] This is precisely the kind of Enlightened utilitarianism, rooted in Francis Bacon as well as Luther, that Adorno and Horkheimer criticized: "Knowledge that tendeth but to satisfaction, is but as a courtesan."[73] And Fürst recalled that Litten could easily reduce a debate to "friend versus enemy" and liked nothing more than dogmatically insisting on the worth or lack of worth of a human being, a recollection that would not surprise some who suffered from being on the wrong side of his ruthlessness in dispute.[74] Most successful trial lawyers are consummate pragmatists. Litten was not. The manner in which he framed his arguments was shaped by a faith that people only needed to be shown the truth to recognize it, and Litten appeared unable, or at least unwilling, to think about advocacy as persuasion of the reluctant.

Litten's courtroom battles, then, do not fit any of the standard dichotomies applied to law in the Weimar Republic. The Eden and Felseneck cases did not pit republicans against monarchists or Nazis; they did not set a positivism willing to accept immoral Nazi laws against a natural law committed to the rights of man (or for that matter a pro-Nazi antipositivism against a democratic, liberal positivism). Rather, as Peter Fritzsche puts it, one side here was as "modern" as the other.[75] The anti-positivists of the 1930s were riding the very latest wave of judicial thinking; ideas that law needed to be brought in touch with "life" or the "people" were close cousins of the Nazi argument that theirs was the truly social movement, an argument that recent research has found to have been compelling to millions of Germans.[76] Litten's positivistic attitude to law, though in some respects of an older lineage, spoke to an embrace of an Enlightened rationality very much of a piece with the celebrated classical modernity of Weimar. Conveniently, this understanding of law allowed him to oppose the irrationalism of the Nazis without at the same time positively affirming the Weimar constitution; his arguments could draw legitimacy from principles beyond the Weimar state and in practice be applied against that state as well (the targets of his first cases were Social Democratic officials rather than Nazi activists). Reflecting on what was at stake in these courtroom battles—a hypermodern Enlightenment against a hypermodern anti-Enlightenment—helps us as well to make sense of recent research on Weimar elections, which has moved steadily away from traditional class-to-ideology linkages to stress the importance of identities and myths in the political life of pre-Nazi Germany.[77] Rationalists and antirationalists both could stake claims to being "democratic" as well as modern; indeed, the Nazis piled up impressive vote totals in 1932 and 1933, at a time when Litten did not claim to be a democrat. As we naturally think of legitimacy being tied inseparably to democracy, this conclusion is disturbing.[78] Litten appears in the trials surveyed here as the advocate of a law legitimated by its *correctness*, its affinity to an Enlightened truth unconnected with either time or politics, a logical enough stance for a lawyer who wished simultaneously to oppose the existing state *and* its most threatening insurgency. That a modern liberal democrat will find little comfort in either approach only underscores the complexity of the legal battles fought out in Weimar's courtrooms.

Notes

1. Heinrich Hannover and Elisabeth Hannover-Drück, *Politische Justiz 1918–1933*, 2d ed. (Bornheim-Merten: Lamuv, 1987); Robert Kuhn, *Die Vertrauenskrise der Justiz (1926–1928): Der Kampf um die Republikanisierung der Rechtspflege in der Weimarer Republik* (Cologne: Bundesanzeiger, 1983), pp. 23–29.

2. See Peter Fritzsche, "Did Weimar Fail?" *Journal of Modern History* 68 (1996): 626–656.

3. See among others Peter C. Caldwell, *Popular Sovereignty and the Crisis of German Constitutional Law: The Theory and Practice of Weimar Constitutionalism* (Durham, N.C.: Duke Univ. Press, 1997); Arthur J. Jacobson and Bernhard Schlink, eds., *Weimar: A Jurisprudence of Crisis* (Berkeley: Univ. of California Press, 2000); Manfred Gangl, ed., *Linke Juristen in der Weimarer Republik* (Frankfurt: Peter Lang, 2003).

4. Fritzsche, "Did Weimar Fail?" p. 632.

5. Jacobson and Schlink, *Weimar*; Michael Stolleis, *A History of Public Law in Germany 1914–1945*, trans. Thomas Dunlop (Oxford: Oxford Univ. Press, 2004).

6. I was inspired to think about the tropes of order and disorder in criminal law by

reading Jules M. Owen, "Structures of Indirect Legal Argument in the Criminal Law" (SJD dissertation, Harvard Law School, 2003).

7. Constantin Goschler, ed., *Hitler: Reden, Schriften, Anordnungen. Februar 1925 bis Januar 1933, Band IV: Von der Reichstagswahl bis zur Rechspräsidentenwahl October 1930–März 1932*, Teil 1, "Oktober 1930–Juni 1931" (Munich: K. G. Saur, 1994), p. 257.

8. Litten to the court, May 5, 1931; LB A Rep 358-02 Nr. 98. *GStA beim Landgericht Berlin, Stief und Genossen*, Bd. 4, Bl. 117.

9. Hans Litten, *Beweisantrag*. Apr. 17, 1931. Ibid., Bl. 41.

10. Litten to the court, May 5, 1931; Trial Protocol, May 8, 1931. Ibid., Bl. 116–123.

11. Trial Protocol, May 8, 1931. Ibid., Bl. 120–121.

12. Judgment, June 2, 1931. Ibid., Bl. 189.

13. Ibid., Bl. 193–194.

14. Hans Litten, *Revisionsschrift*, July 16, 1931. LB A Rep 358-02 Nr. 98, *GStA beim Landgericht Berlin, Stief und Genossen*, Bd. 6, Bl. 123–124.

15. Ibid., Bl. 125–127.

16. Wilhelm Budzinski, *Der Überzeugungsverbrecher* (Leipzig: R. Naske, 1931), pp. 4–5.

17. "Grundsätze für den Vollzug von Freiheitsstrafen." RGBl 1923 II, pp. 263, 268.

18. Quoted in Budzinski, *Überzeugungsverbrecher*, p. 2.

19. Ibid., pp. 21–22.

20. Ibid., p. 6.

21. Judgment, June 2, 1931. LB A Rep 358–02 Nr. 98, *GStA beim Landgericht Berlin, Stief und Genossen*, Bd. 6, Bl. 195.

22. Hans Litten, *Revisionsschrift*. July 16, 1931. Ibid., Bl. 132.

23. Decision of the *Reichsgericht*, Nov. 19, 1931. Ibid., Bl. 159.

24. Ibid., Bl. 158, 160.

25. Quoted in Carlheinz von Brück, *Ein Mann, der Hitler in die enge Trieb: Hans Littens Kampf gegen den Faschismus. Ein Dokumentarbericht* (East Berlin: Union-Verlag, 1975), p. 20.

26. Hans Litten to Fritz Litten, June 17, 1931. BA-BL NY 4011. *Nachlaß Hans Litten*, Bd. 4, *Korrespondenz—Ausgehende. Briefe von Hans Litten an seine Eltern vor seiner Haftzeit 1931*, Bl. 5.

27. *Bericht*. Jan. 19, 1932. LB A Rep 358–01 Nr. 37. *Adam und Genossen (Felseneck)*, Bd. 37.

28. Ibid.

29. "'Die Nazis sind schuld'—an den gegen sie verübten Bluttaten!" *Angriff*, Jan. 21, 1932.

30. "Eine unfaßliche Trennung: 'Politische' und 'kriminelle' Schuld." *Angriff*, Jan. 21, 1932.

31. Joseph Goebbels, "Wir sind objektiv." *Angriff*, Oct. 8, 1932.

32. Sethe to GSTA KG, July 28, 1932. LB A Rep 358–01 Nr. 37. *Adam und Genossen (Felseneck)*. Handakten, Bd. II.

33. Ruling of the Jury Court, Aug. 15, 1932. Ibid., Bl. 21–30.

34. Ibid., Bl. 30–32.

35. Hans Litten, *Beschwerde*, Oct. 16, 1932. LB A Rep 358–01 Nr. 37. *Adam und Genossen (Felseneck)*. Bd. 12, Bl. 129–130.

36. Benjamin Carter Hett, *Death in the Tiergarten: Murder and Criminal Justice in the Kaiser's Berlin* (Cambridge, Mass.: Harvard Univ. Press, 2004), chaps. 2 and 3.

37. Markus Dubber, "American Plea Bargains, German Lay Judges, and the Crisis of German Procedure," *Stanford Law Review* 49 (1997): 547, 580.

38. Hett, *Death in the Tiergarten*, chaps. 2, 3, and "Epilogue."

39. Strikingly, historian Nikolaus Wachsmann has recently found a parallel process at work in the growing harshness of prison conditions in late Weimar. Nikolaus Wachsmann, *Hitler's Prisons: Legal Terror in Nazi Germany* (New Haven, Conn.: Yale Univ. Press, 2004), pp. 54–64.

40. Hans Litten, *Strafanzeige*, Sep. 2, 1932. LB A Rep 358 Nr. 1285, *Strafsache contra Bode und Genossen wegen Rechtsbeugung*.

41. Ursula Schmidt-Speicher, *Hauptprobleme der Rechtsbeugung. Unter besonderer Berücksichtigung der historischen Entwicklung des Tatbestandes* (Berlin: Dunker & Humblot, 1982), p. 51.

42. Otto Henning, *Die Rechtsbeugung im geltenden Recht und in den deutschen Strafgesetzentwürfen, unter besonderen Berücksichtigung der amtlichen Entwürfe eines allgemeinen deutschen Strafgesetzbuches von 1926 und 1927* (Heidelberg: Geissen, 1929), p. 15.

43. Ludwig Bendix, "Die Rechtsbeugung im künftigen deutschen Strafrecht," *Die Justiz* 2 (1926): 42–75.

44. Ibid.

45. Henning, *Rechtsbeugung*, 15, 17.

46. Hans Litten, *Strafanzeige*, Sep. 2, 1932. LB A Rep 358 Nr. 1285, *Strafsache contra Bode und Genossen wegen Rechtsbeugung*.

47. See, generally, LB A Rep 358-01 Nr. 37, *Adam und Genossen (Felseneck)*.

48. Tillmann Krach, *Jüdische Rechtsanwälte in Preußen. Über die Bedeutung der freien Advokatur und ihre Zerstörung durch den Nationalsozialismus* (Munich: C.H. Beck, 1991), pp. 82–87.

49. On Litten's imprisonment, see his mother's memoir: Irmgard Litten, *Beyond Tears* (New York: Alliance Book, 1940).

50. Max Fürst, *Gefilte Fisch und wie es weiterging* (Munich: Deutscher Taschenbuch Verlag, 2004), p. 264.

51. Fürst, *Gefilte Fisch*, p. 657.

52. Eberhard Schmidt, *Einführung in die Geschichte der deutschen Strafrechtspflege*, 3d ed. (Göttingen: Vandenhoeck & Ruprecht, 1995), pp. 294–295, 308–309, 372–381.

53. Fürst, *Gefilte Fisch*, p. 646.

54. Quoted in Budzinski, *Überzeugungsverbrecher*, p. 32.

55. Litten, *Beyond Tears*, p. 3.

56. Markus Dirk Dubber, "Judicial Positivism and Hitler's Injustice," *Columbia Law Review* 93 (1993): 1820–1822.

57. Hans Kelsen, *Reine Rechtslehre. Einleitung in die rechtswissenschaftliche Problematik* (Leipzig: F. Deuticke, 1934), pp. iii, vii–xix, 24.

58. Ibid.; Karl Larenz, *Methodenlehre der Rechtswissenschaft*, 6th ed. (Berlin: Springer, 1991), chaps. 3, 4.

59. Bernhard Ascher, "Richterliche Korrektur unzeitgemäßer Gesetze. (Art. 102 RV und § 4 RAO)," *Deutsche Richterzeitung*, Jan. 15, 1930, pp. 4–6; LGD Dr. Marx, "Sittlichkeit und Recht," *Deutsche Richterzeitung*, June 15, 1930, pp. 201–204; OLGP i. R. Dr. Levin, "Probleme der Rechtsfindung," *Deutsche Richterzeitung*, Oct. 15, 1930, pp. 325–328.

60. Ernst Fuchs, "Die 'Deutsche Richterzeitung' und die 'Justiz,'" *Die Justiz* 1 (1926): 251–252.

61. See Document 3, "The Program of the German Workers' Party," in *Nazism 1919–1945: A Documentary Reader*, vol. 1, *The Rise to Power 1919–1934*, Jeremy Noakes and Geoffrey Pribram, eds. (Exeter, UK: Univ. of Exeter Press, 1998), pp. 14–16.

62. Carl Schmitt, *Über die drei Arten des rechtswissenschaftlichen Denkens* (Hamburg: Hanseatische Verlagsanstalt, 1934), p. 65.

63. Ibid., pp. 31–32.

64. "Die Begründung des Freispruchs," *Welt am Abend*, Oct. 7, 1932.

65. See, for instance, Heinrich A. Winkler, *Weimar 1918–1933. Die Geschichte der ersten deutschen Demokratie* (Munich: Beck, 1993); Peter Fritzsche, *Germans into Nazis* (Cambridge, Mass.: Harvard Univ. Press, 1998).

66. Kelsen, *Reine Rechtslehre*, pp. 100–106.

67. Hans Litten to Sulamith Reuter, Mar. 26, 1935. BA-BL NY 4011, *Nachlaß Hans Litten*, Bd. 3, *Korrespondenz—Ausgehende*, Bl. 218.

68. Hans Litten, "Kunst," Dachauer Archiv DA 993, *Jüdische Häftlinge: Litten, Hans: Dokumente*.

69. Hans Litten, "Dichtung und Bühnenwerk: Eine grundsätzliche Bemerkung zum 'Fall Volksbühne,'" *Königsberger Hartungsche Zeitung*, Apr. 13, 1927 M. BA-BL NY 4011, *Nachlaß Hans Litten*, Bd. 2, *Aufzeichnungen zu Themen der Literatur und Kunstgeschichte aus der Zeit seiner Haft 1933–1937*, Bl. 9.

70. See Litten, "Kunst"; and generally the letters in BA-BL NY 4011, *Nachlaß Hans Litten*, Bd. 3, *Korrespondenz—Ausgehende*.

71. Fürst, *Gefilte Fisch*, p. 473.

72. Litten, "Kunst."

73. Quoted in Max Horkheimer and Theodor W. Adorno, *Dialectic of Enlightenment* (New York: Continuum, 1972), p. 5.

74. Fürst, *Gefilte Fisch*, pp. 515, 613.

75. See note 2.

76. Götz Aly, *Hitlers Volkstaat: Raub, Rassenkrieg and Nationaler Sozialismus* (Frankfurt: S. Fischer, 2005).

77. Jürgen Falter, *Hitlers Wähler* (Munich: Beck, 1991).

78. Indeed, an old line of literature sees the Nazis as the logical culmination of mass democracy. See George L. Mosse, *The Nationalization of the Masses: Political Symbolism and Mass Movements in Germany from the Napoleonic Wars through the Third Reich* (New York: H. Fertig, 1975).

EIGHT

Civilizing Darwin

Holmes on Criminal Law

GERALD LEONARD

The influence of Oliver Wendell Holmes in American law can be found in any number of areas, including, of course, criminal law. But little historical work has been done on this aspect of his writing.[1] Maybe that is because he turned to criminal law for the first time as something of an afterthought. His writings on the subject amount primarily to a single chapter in *The Common Law*[2] and a limited number of cases on the bench, in which he mostly carried through the arguments of his book. Moreover, in the stream of articles that he produced across the 1870s in preparation for writing *The Common Law*, he wrote hardly at all about criminal law. His interests lay elsewhere. Yet when he did finally come to assembling his great work, criminal law assumed a central place in the conceptual structure of his argument. And today his discussions of the "external," or objective, quality of the basic standards of criminal liability—both as author and as judge on Massachusetts's high court—remain fixtures in casebooks as well as in some of the substantive law of crimes.

The question for me, then, is why Holmes chose to write what he did about criminal law. What did he hope to accomplish with his criminal chapter and his subsequent judicial opinions? What was the state of thinking about law in general and specifically about criminal law as of 1880 or so that moved him to contribute as he did? And to what extent does an understanding of this context enhance understanding of the meaning of Holmes's writing?

The answers to these questions should begin with an understanding of Holmes's general intellectual commitments and context. In an age when the term *science* was coming to signify the emancipation of intellectual inquiry from the dogmas of a reigning Protestant theology, Holmes hoped to elucidate the ways law might join in that emancipation.[3] Relatedly, he sought to demonstrate the profound significance for legal science of the Darwinian revelation that human life rested on a timeless "struggle for existence," an insight particularly pertinent to that directly coercive branch of law, criminal law.

At the same time, while recognizing before the Realists that the Darwinian perspective might seem to expose law as a mere mask for power, he sought to demonstrate the persistent value of law in civilizing humans' inevitable conflicts. No one surpassed Holmes's willingness to expose the politics that informed judging, to remove the judge's apolitical and pre-Darwinian disguise. However, equally importantly, Holmes never wavered from his conviction that law, empty form though it may seem, brought a vital measure of peace to Darwinian struggle. It manifested, implemented, and reinforced a collective "sympathy" that saved lives and enabled a kind of peaceful social development that even the cynical Holmes cherished. In all this, the criminal law stood as law par excellence and thus the field in which these truths might be most starkly developed.

Space constraints render impossible a full development of all of the themes just intimated. This chapter will begin with a brief look at the mid-nineteenth-century Darwinian transformation in the very meaning of science, a transformation that supplied the essential context for Holmes's entry into the world of legal scholarship. The next short section will examine Holmes's writings of the 1870s to suggest the shape of his ideas about legal science, the importance of Darwinism, and the capacity of law to "civilize" a world understood in Darwinian terms. The bulk of the chapter will then analyze the essay on criminal law in *The Common Law*, which used these general ideas to extract a unifying principle of criminal law—prevention—from a sophisticated doctrinal analysis. Along the way, a few noteworthy criminal cases from his time on the Supreme Judicial Court of Massachusetts will help to illustrate Holmes's meaning. As a whole, the chapter will explain Holmes's commitment to a project of reconciliation between cold Darwinian science, on the one hand, and Victorian civilization, on the other, thus explaining the emergence of a theory of criminal law that continues to shape doctrine and practice even to the present day.

1. Science

Although legal thinkers had aspired to make law a science for some time before Holmes came along, Holmes was America's first thoroughgoing legal scientist of real distinction.[4] One or two of the more ambitious treatise-writers of the day might have disputed that claim, but of course Holmes was not interested in the sort of science dictated by the Protestant framework that had dominated American intellectual life into the mid-nineteenth century.[5] He did not seek to reduce law to an exercise in working out divine will or deductive logic.[6] Instead, Holmes identified himself with the rising, Darwinian sense of science as a matter of making predictions based on detailed investigation of patterns of natural causation and human choice, rigorously excluding the supernatural (including the divine) and the teleological from all analysis of causes and effects.[7] I should be clear that neither Holmes nor the rest of his generation learned what I'm calling "Darwinian science" simply from Darwin. The new science increasingly filled the air starting a decade or two before Darwin.[8] Nevertheless, Darwin stood as the greatest provocation to the defenders of the Protestant framework and the great symbol of science's emancipation from that framework.[9] Consequently, this chapter broadly uses the idea of Darwinism to indicate the intellectual orientation of the new-style intellectual as scientist as well as to indicate the emergent notion that the "struggle for existence" lay at the foundation of everything human.

With this outlook, Holmes determined to turn a scientist's eye on the common law. Convinced by Darwinism that a struggle for existence among individuals and thus among social groups underlay all human behavior, Holmes disdained questions of legitimacy,[10] which always seemed to rest on rash assumptions, inadequately grounded in the brute, inevitable realities of struggle and coercion. Specifically in criminal law, Holmes reacted sharply against German philosophy, as a major source of useless essentialisms; against the American treatise-writer, Joel Prentiss Bishop, for his reliance on an interventionist God and an inborn understanding of divine morality; and even against the English utilitarian, James Fitzjames Stephen, whom Holmes deemed insufficiently scientific.[11] Instead, Holmes built on John Austin's positivism and Henry Maine's post-Darwinian sense of contingency. He treasured the capacity of the law to civilize human struggle and coercion, to substitute the peaceful exercise of authority for open violence. But he warned against the unscientific supposition that law or legitimacy emerged from any place but humans' rightful self-preference and social struggle.

2. Holmes in the 1870s

His first major effort in the direction of legal science, an 1870 article called "Codes, and the Arrangement of the Law," actually declared, "Law is not a science but essentially empirical."[12] But Holmes did not thereby set himself against science, only against the deductive science that had long discouraged a truly fearless empiricism. He would have enough other occasions explicitly to embrace scientific approaches to law.[13] In "Codes," he meant to deny only that law could be understood by merely positing principles and deducing doctrine. Instead, it had to be investigated empirically and so arranged as to accurately reflect the law as it was, however divergent from imagined principles. That empirical problem—the problem of coming to a "philosophical" arrangement of the law as it actually was—would occupy him continually until publication of *The Common Law* in 1881.

In this initial run at the question, he addressed primarily John Austin, the most ambitious systematizer of the law before him and a man who enjoyed an impressive—if posthumous—vogue in the 1860s.[14] Austin's system rested on his famous definition of law as a command issued by the sovereign to his political inferiors. Although Holmes objected to this formulation in some respects, he embraced Austin's central claim that the only law that lawyers attended to and that, therefore, a scientist of the law need take account of, was the law that judges actually enforced.[15] This positivist suggestion that the law could and should be treated as a creature of human institutions, independent of any transcendent morality or divine intention, opened the door to unrestrained scientific inquiry in law. The importance, then, of Holmes's debut lay in his declaration of an intent to pursue a scientific arrangement of the law and his embrace for the most part of Austin's positivism.

Two years later, in a short Book Notice,[16] Holmes reaffirmed his positivism as he defined *law* simply as the lawyer's professional expectations of what the courts will do. The profession generated its expectations not by consulting Austin's sovereign but by assessing the genuine sources of decision, the likely motives of the judges. These would typically include precedent, custom, and statute. They would not include "the blandishments of the emperor's wife" or the like, not because of some preconceived notion of the extralegality of such factors, but because such motives were, as a matter of experience, "singular" and thus useless to the professional lawyer as predictors of judicial outcomes. In this effort, he was heartily supported by his British counterpart and friend, Frederick Pollock, the author of the article ostensibly under review in Holmes's book notice. Pollock wrote to him in 1874, "I thoroughly agree that the only definition of law for a lawyer's purposes is something which the Court will enforce."[17] Neither man thought that was the only possible definition of law—that would have been to essentialize the concept—but they agreed that what courts would do was the operative meaning of law for lawyers' purposes. Thus, as an independent field of inquiry, law took as its defining task the cold-eyed prediction of what courts would do, just as the hard sciences pursued theories that might predict natural sequences.

Moreover, in the same brief piece, Holmes introduced an idea that would prove essential to *The Common Law*'s account of criminal law: that the state's purpose to *prevent* certain kinds of behavior, as opposed to simply redistributing losses, distinguished criminal law from other kinds of law. Insofar as tort or contract liability, for example, was simply a matter of paying damages, all the court did was exact a price or, looking prospectively, offer each person an option to do or forbear subject to a tax. Criminal liability, as he implied here and would make explicit in *The Common Law*, was a different matter. There, the lawgiver acted to prevent conduct absolutely.

By the early 1870s, then, Holmes had set for himself the task of bringing science to law. By science he meant careful study of empirical detail, followed by induction of more or less broad classificatory principles that might arrange all the detail rationally. And the test of those principles lay in their ability to predict the outcomes—the classifications—of cases yet to come. More narrowly, he had suggested his belief that the central predictive principle of criminal law was prevention of harms to the community. This much, however, might not have distinguished him much from so-called classical legal thinkers like Harvard Law's Dean Langdell.[18] What would distinguish his brand of legal science from what had gone before was his Darwinism.

The first, somewhat enigmatic entry of Charles Darwin onto Holmes's stage came in "The Theory of Torts" (1873).[19] In this article, while continuing his work toward a philosophical arrangement of the law, he denied that the legal principles he was so assiduously working out could be counted on to provide a right answer to every case. He thus broke with so-called classicism and prefigured his famous remark that "[g]eneral propositions do not decide concrete cases."[20] He explained that a legal principle could dictate an outcome only for the extreme case on which all would agree, while there remained many hard cases to which more than one legal principle might apply. Over time the decisions established a line separating classes of cases from each other so that the legal professional was increasingly able to predict outcomes, but the process of establishing that line was not a simple, rational process, certainly not a matter of deduction from a priori principles. Rather, the question of how any particular line got drawn was "a question for Mr. Darwin to answer."[21] That is, although Holmes's main goal in this article was an early explication of the principle of the external standard, he offhandedly revealed his underlying philosophical position. Law, he suggested, was not a matter of logical structure but a matter of Darwinian struggle.

In the same year, he made essentially the same point in the very different realm of legislation in his comment on the British gas stokers' strike.[22] There he reproved the celebrated social Darwinist Herbert Spencer for simultaneously embracing evolution as a model for social analysis and claiming to identify illegitimate "class legislation" by deductive reasoning. Virtually all legislation was class legislation, Holmes wrote, and must be so as long as we remain in a struggle for existence. Amid such underlying struggle, there could be little or no social consensus, no deductive route to the interests of the whole, but only conflicting interests. Still believing that a new "arrangement of the law" to improve on Austin was a worthy ambition, Holmes began to bring into focus the inescapable, Darwinian insight that at bottom the law was as much a site of raw political struggle as was every other area of human endeavor.

To predict what judges would do, then, was to predict how that class of lawmakers would make policy. Still, the traditions of the law, including a deep-running respect for such conceptual arrangement as the judges could perceive, remained a central aspect of that policy making and rendered it distinct from electoral and legislative politics, where mere majority will might unabashedly hold sway. Judging might not have been the application of geometric rules, but it was nevertheless the application of law rather than will. Here was the "paradox of form and substance" that he elucidated in his article on common carriers.[23] Law could not escape Darwin's truths, but, as law, it might be able to civilize them.

3. *The Criminal Law in* The Common Law

A. HOLMES'S TARGETS

For reasons I have suggested, when Holmes finally turned to the criminal law, he reacted decisively against Kant and Hegel, against the Christian synthesis of criminal doctrine in Joel Prentiss Bishop's ambitious treatises, and even against his fellow Austinian, England's James Fitzjames Stephen. In the case of the Germans, Holmes derided the naked assertion that the state could never legitimately use a person as a mere means to an end. Whatever a priori theories of legitimacy the philosophers might want to propagate, the historical fact was that governments used persons as means to collective ends all the time, whether bodily (by drafting them into military service) or by seizing their property for public needs.[24] Kant could philosophize all he liked about some ideal state of affairs, but his philosophy was irrelevant to the study of law as it actually functioned, to the science of predicting when judges would authorize the state's use of force.

Bishop's problems, for Holmes, were somewhat different. Certainly the most accomplished writer of his time on American criminal law, Bishop turned out many editions of his *Commentaries on Criminal Law* starting in 1856, as well as many other treatises. And Holmes relied on Bishop's treatises in *The Common Law* as his chief source for American law. As lawyerly and accomplished as Bishop's work was, however, Holmes bridled at Bishop's attachment to the Protestant framework and his tendency to suggest that the law was a matter of God's will and the offender's personal intention to flout that will rather than straightforward calculations of public safety. Thus Bishop identified crime with evil individual choice, acts done with a bad conscience.[25] He claimed that "crime proceeds only from a criminal mind"[26] and that "the essence of an offence is the wrongful intent, without which it cannot exist."[27] He announced that mistake of fact must be a full defense "in every system of Christian and cultivated law."[28] He asserted that legal authority lay in "the voice of God speaking the language of abstract right"[29] and that defendants' ignorance of the statutes under which they were charged was normally irrelevant because the statutes reflected only the law that was already "'written in their hearts'" (quoting Romans 2:15).[30] Although Holmes criticized Bishop by name only once, for insisting that in attempt cases "an actual intent is all that can give the act a criminal character,"[31] his entire chapter on crime attacked views championed by Bishop.

As a follower of Austin's positivism, Fitzjames Stephen might have been counted on to separate law from morality a good deal more rigorously than Bishop, but in this respect he disappointed Holmes. Stephen declared his allegiance to Austin's command theory and frankly observed the reality and even desirability of "judicial legislation." But he manifested little ambition to bring science to law, little of Holmes's sense of law as a product of the Darwinian struggle for survival, and a reluctance to confront squarely the logic of the separation of law and morals.

In his landmark *A General View of the Criminal Law of England* (1863), Stephen described criminal law as a matter of "punishment"[32] and exhibited there, as elsewhere, a persistent belief in the objective superiority of Victorian Christian values.[33] In contrast to Holmes's exclusive focus on prevention, Stephen's commitment to deterrence was frequently colored by a retributive desire to give deviants from correct morals what they deserved. Thus he said that criminal law had two purposes. The first was prevention, but the second was that "it regulates, sanctions, and provides a legitimate satisfaction for the passion of revenge."[34] Noting that "malice may . . . be said to be a necessary ingredient in one form or other of all crimes whatever," he explained that, since criminal law could function only as long as it was generally consistent with "the moral sentiments of the nation," "it will be found in practice impossible to attach . . . any other meaning than that which properly belongs to [it] of . . . wicked."[35] Twenty years later, in his *History of the Criminal Law of England*, he explicitly identified morality in substantial part with individual "conscience,"[36] suggested a timeless rightness in using the criminal law not just to prevent harms but to "express" the "hatred" that criminals deserved, and made clear that this function was "beyond all question distinct from" prevention.[37] The criminal law, then, ultimately rested less on prevention than on a timeless, perhaps divine, morality that one should not look behind or seek to justify by its good effects.

Stephen and Bishop represented some of the best writing on criminal law available, but to Holmes they remained prescientific, plagued by assumptions about the law's necessary conformity to a priori morality or divine will. In contrast, Holmes offered a novel, scientific recasting of criminal law as nothing more or less than the positive public policy of the dominant interests, tempered by and manifested in the traditions and forms of law. The dominant interests in the Anglo-American tradition embraced such legal restraint on policy making not because Bishop's God or Kantian philosophy imposed that discipline but because they prized the benefits of civilization. These traditions and forms converted judging from mere ex post facto legislating—the accusation of the early American codifiers[38]—into disciplined and principled implementation of the (limited) "sympathy" felt by the civilized for their fellows. That sympathy, the mark of the Victorian "civilization" that Holmes quietly celebrated in *The Common Law*, defined the scope, purpose, and limits of law as a temporary and contingent agent of peace within the larger and more fundamental struggle for existence. But while this sympathy overlapped quite a bit with Victorian morality and tempered the more violent impulses of the dominant, the particular shape that law and sympathy would take—the doctrines they would produce—depended ultimately on the substantive needs and preferences of the dominant groups in society, not on a priori morality. And the particular shape that *criminal* law would take depended, as the sociology of law-production would practically guarantee, less on appealing principles of individual justice than on more vital interests in collective safety and prevention shared by the great bulk of society.

B. THE PREVENTIVE THEORY OF THE CRIMINAL LAW

Holmes opened his criminal law chapter by noting some plausible arguments for the claim that criminal law's purpose was to exact revenge, to punish the offender for "the condition of [his] heart or conscience."[39] Naming Stephen as one advocate of such a position, Holmes quoted Stephen's remark that "criminal law stands to the passion of revenge in much the same relation as marriage to the sexual appetite."[40] He further cited Hegel and Kant as the great expounders of the view that "there is a mystical bond between wrong and punishment," which was inconsistent with the use of man as a means rather than an "end in himself."[41] But he rejected that position and the "internal standard"[42] that he thought it implied, asserting further that "probably most

English-speaking lawyers would accept the preventive theory without hesitation."[43] Why? Primarily because the actual practice of government was and always had been to use men as means. Moreover, although government might sometimes let wrongdoing go unpunished if it could be confident that no further wrong would follow, "there can be no case in which the law-maker makes certain conduct criminal without his thereby showing a wish and purpose to prevent that conduct. Prevention would accordingly seem to be the chief and only universal purpose of punishment."[44] (It is important to note here that Holmes did not say that prevention was the only purpose of criminal punishment but that it was the only "universal" purpose, the only purpose that applied in every criminal case, as opposed to other plausible purposes, like retribution or rehabilitation, that might apply in some cases but not in all.)

He bolstered this proposition about the law as it was—apparently considering questions of legitimacy merely derivative of a properly scientific understanding of law and Darwinism—by turning to "some doctrines which cannot be satisfactorily explained on any other ground" than prevention. First, he claimed that the deliberate taking of even innocent life was not punishable "when it is the only way of saving one's own." This doctrine enabled him to argue that society broadly recognized that Darwinian "self-preference" unavoidably (and therefore rightly) shaped society and human behavior. Motivated by a primal need to defend one's own existence and interests, the individual and the group alike would all but inevitably put prevention of harms at the foundation of law. Here was a principle induced from (other people's) careful research about the world as it was, not from philosophical speculations about the world as it might be. Of course, in modern days, civilization had pleasingly removed us ever further from open confrontation; the "ever-growing value set upon peace and the social relations" tended to produce a rhetoric of equality and sympathy that would militate against sacrificing another merely for one's own interests.[45] But when up against it—when an individual's interests were sufficiently important or when they were at least comparable to the other's life—the law rightly conformed to the reality that such sacrificing of others was either rightful or inevitable or both and that, "a fortiori," the community as a whole must sometimes sacrifice the individual to its interests. In sum, the preventive theory not only undergirded the criminal law as it was but, given the insights of Darwinian science, practically dictated the character of state coercion.[46]

Holmes did admit that this supposed rule of law was not as clearly established as he might have hoped, but there was substantial evidence for his claim that it was the operative rule. Running against Holmes were such cases as *Dudley and Stephens*. Coming hard on the heels of Holmes's book, that British case raised the rhetoric of Anglo-Christian self-sacrifice above Darwinian reality to condemn the "custom of the sea"—the practice by which shipwrecked sailors regularly sacrificed the lives of some innocents to save the lives of others.[47] But the token sentences imposed in that case must have seemed like some vindication of Holmes's view of the genuinely operative law. So too, of course, had the authority that he had cited in *The Common Law*. His most interesting authority was the American shipwreck case of *U.S. v. Holmes*[48] (he must have quietly enjoyed that coincidence), in which the sailors in an overcrowded longboat ejected into rough seas at least fourteen men before the remaining castaways were rescued the next day. The judge charged the jury that these deliberate killings of innocents might be excused by the "law of necessity," a law that had to take into account such realities as the need for sufficient crew to manage the boat and the practicality (or not) of drawing lots. Note that the court both implicitly and explicitly rejected the claim that such extreme circumstances reduced all to the state of nature. The court would not say that law had no place when the struggle for existence became so immediate. Nor would Holmes. To the extent that society existed—even the society of a lifeboat—law might exist as well. Moreover, if law could be applied at all then it must in its nature do as much as the facts would allow to promote sympathy, equality, and peace—to civilize what would otherwise be open struggle—but only as much as the facts would allow. Law could not displace the struggle for existence and rightful self-preference; it could not criminalize even the sacrifice of the innocent when the security of the group was better served by that sacrifice than by an extension of sympathy to these innocents.

In making policy as to where such lines should be drawn, the judge (and jury) might simply have to legislate on questions of relative human value and the like, but in such a case legal rhetoric played an enormously important part in achieving peace and the benefits of civilization where open struggle would otherwise reign. Thus, in the case of the British sailor-cannibals, the newspapers justified the court's hortatory conviction of the sailors by explicitly holding out the fear that a contrary rule would indeed unleash an un-Christian "struggle for existence."[49] A court like this one might achieve its civilizing purpose by tricking its audience into thinking that the law was a matter of mechanical application of "abstract right." Judges often portrayed the law that way. But the law might achieve the same civilizing end by frankly advertising itself as a merely improved form of struggle, a relatively peaceful and satisfying alternative to life without legal discipline. Holmes portrayed the law this way. As Holmes remarked, "[N]o civilized government sacrifices the citizen more than it can help," but even the most civilized did indeed sacrifice that citizen when the welfare of the rest required it.[50]

More clearly established than the law of necessity was the rule that "[i]gnorance of the law is no excuse for breaking it,"[51] and Holmes turned to that rule next, arguing again that the criminal law openly sacrificed the innocent when necessary for prevention. He quickly disposed of Austin's explanation for this sacrifice of "justice to the individual," that is, difficulty of proof. More important, he offered his own terse but telling indication of the incentives that required the rule. Following his bald assertion that "every one must feel that ignorance of the law could never be admitted as an excuse" even when clearly proven, he observed that "to admit the excuse at all would be to encourage ignorance where the law-maker has determined to make men know and obey." If the public interest, "the larger interests on the other side of the scale" as determined by the dominant interest in society, depended on obedience to a rule, Holmes suggested, it hardly made sense for the government to offer the individual an incentive to ignorance of those rules.[52] Holmes did not expect the citizenry to devote its time to legal research,[53] and he did not think that the state ought to sacrifice innocently ignorant citizens willy-nilly. However, he did expect the citizenry to adopt an attitude of obedience and an alertness to the demands of morality and public policy that would generally keep it on the right side of the line. And if the state must choose between encouraging that sort of moral knowledge or, alternatively, encouraging a self-serving legal ignorance, the proper choice was obvious.

Holmes gave little indication of how he came to his analysis of the ignorance rule. Nor did he attend to any of the rule's exceptions. But a quick look at some nineteenth-century cases that Holmes could have read, as well as Bishop's and Stephen's brief discussions of the rule, suggests that Holmes may well have isolated the best available rationale for the rule—and thus the best predictor for future cases—from a range of fairly superficial arguments. Bishop, for example, should have been quite troubled by the rule, since he had gone some length toward identifying criminal justice with a requirement of self-conscious wrongdoing. (And, in fact, quite a few of the courts that resisted the full rigors of the rule cited Bishop's general statements to that effect in their support.[54]) But Bishop skated quickly past the rule, since he thought that criminal law was overwhelmingly "written in [our] hearts"[55] and since the few established exceptions would take care of most of the remaining potential for injustice.[56] But that was it. He could hardly have read the cases very closely without encountering the occasional injustice, according to his principles.[57] But he chose not to look too closely, since the rule seemed both indispensable and yet a "snare for the unwary" as Blackstone had already thought a century earlier.[58] As for Stephen, his *History* declared that knowledge of the law was never required for conviction except where a requirement of specific intention dictated otherwise, although, like others after him, he offered larceny as his only example of this supposedly general exception.[59] Some years later, in the second edition of his *General View*, he skipped the exception for crimes of specific intent and explicitly acknowledged the unreality of the presumption that everyone knew the law, yet, again, he offered no justification for this even more absolute version of the rule.[60]

What, then, did the courts have to say about this rule? The answer is mostly disappointing and must be severely abbreviated here. Sometimes, courts insisted on the rule despite what they recognized as obvious injustice simply because the rule was so well established. Justice Story operated this way in the frequently cited early case, *The Ann* (1812).[61] There, Story acknowledged that a mistake-of-law defense would reflect "good sense, and natural equity" but refused to permit it, simply because the strict rule was "agreeable to ancient principles" and unchallenged by any extant authority.[62]

Courts did sometimes make exceptions to the rule, particularly in cases of larceny and sometimes, crucially, where a public official was obligated to act in the face of legal uncertainty.[63] But mostly they rejected the defense with unelaborated, Austinian assertions of the utter impracticality of allowing mistake-of-law defenses to clog the system. Thus, the Alabama high court said that mistake of law was "never an excuse" or else "the administration of justice would be impossible, as every cause would be embarrassed with the collateral inquiry of the extent of legal knowledge of the parties."[64] Moreover, the Virginia bench offered, "It would certainly be a very difficult and doubtful question to be solved in every case" if knowledge of the law had to be proven.[65]

This sort of boilerplate endorsement of an absolute rule could hardly help a lawyer or legal scientist to predict outcomes—that is, to know the law—when in fact there were a number of exceptions to the general rule that did not bring criminal proceedings to a halt or raise insoluble problems of proof. A couple of cases, however, hinted at something more valuable. These cases did not work out careful justifications for the rule, but they offered a little more nuance while anticipating the Holmesian perspective. In a New York case, members of the Board of Police were convicted for removing an election inspector without notice and without the sort of exigent circumstances specified in the statute. They defended themselves by claiming a mistake of law, but the court held that the traditional rule was well justified, since a rule to the contrary "would, in many cases, prevent the restraining influence which the statute was designed to secure."[66] This bald reliance on prevention, or deterrence (as we now would say), found more nuance in *Boyett*, a North Carolina prosecution for voting in a constable's election without having lived the required time in the district. The North Carolina Supreme Court sustained the conviction over a claim that, at least in statutory offenses or on "collateral questions of law," the defendant ought to be able to prove his good faith.[67] The court held instead, "To allow ignorance as an excuse would be to offer a reward to the ignorant."[68] It would create an incentive for a defendant to "contrive to ground his conduct upon misapprehension or improper advice," and then "it would hardly ever be possible to convict."[69] A "reward to the ignorant" would encourage the tailoring of one's knowledge of the law (by way of "improper advice," for example) according to one's own interests. A strict refusal to accommodate such legal ignorance would encourage a true understanding of one's duties, if only to avoid liability.

But even a rationale that dictated a quite strict rule might also dictate particular exceptions. Thus the *Boyett* court noted that the defendant might rebut the presumption of knowledge if he could show that he had relied on "the judges of the election" in learning the pertinent law, because the rebuttal would have been done "in a manner contemplated by law."[70] Presumably, the court meant that, even though the result would still constitute a "reward" for the defendant's ignorance, its grounds would be circumscribed precisely to avoid creating an incentive to "contrive" ignorance. The court concluded by asking rhetorically, "Why make the exception and offer a reward for ignorance in this particular case?"[71] thus indicating a principle and a question that might predict future cases.

Holmes did not cite *Boyett* in *The Common Law*, but his own rationale for the exclusion of mistakes of law seemed to follow *Boyett* pretty closely. The emphasis was not on difficulties of proof or other unnamed problems of judicial administration but simply on prevention. And the first requisite of prevention was that the citizenry have sufficient incentive to "know and obey," to avoid the harms that the law sought to prevent. But, as I will explain later, much of the chapter argued that prevention depended not on the citizen's knowledge of the ins and outs of the law but on "knowing and obeying" the community's moral code. A strict rule on ignorance would create an incentive to practical moral knowledge, not impractical legal research; an indulgent rule would not so much preserve justice (for the innocently ignorant) as create an incentive for legal and moral ignorance and the harms such ignorance would encourage. Still, a proper structure of incentives called for some exceptions, arguably the very exceptions that were found in the cases. If the community meant to encourage persons to exercise control over property, for example, or to vote or otherwise to act in socially beneficial ways despite inescapable legal ambiguity, then closely circumscribed exceptions might be and were inserted into the structure of the incentives. Thus, unlike the Austinian boilerplate,

Boyett's implementation of the preventive principle seemed to offer some predictive value. Holmes did not go as far as *Boyett* in explicitly suggesting exceptions to the ignorance rule, presumably because he was less concerned with ignorance doctrine as such than with proving that the criminal law in fact punished for prevention more than for desert. However, his terse reliance on incentives—prevention could not afford to "encourage ignorance"—made sense of the doctrine's apparent subordination of individualized justice and, as *Boyett* illustrated, implied the right kind of exceptions.[72]

To this point, Holmes had argued that only prevention could unify the great body of the criminal law. Given his Darwinian view of law as bound to partial social interests, he might have abandoned the whole project of identifying a single unifying principle for any body of law. But he remained committed to a middle path, where principles might not reliably predict every outcome yet retain enough disciplinary power to civilize, in the interests of most segments of society, the judges' positive authorizations of force. From this point, Holmes delivered a series of sophisticated analyses of selected doctrines meant to establish the boiled-down, lawyerly version of this argument: that questions of criminal liability generally turned on the application of an "external standard," with occasional exceptions that were nevertheless assimilable to prevention.

The rule on ignorance of law exemplified this external standard, and Holmes now generalized his claim that "the actual personal unworthiness of the criminal alone" could not be the key to liability. "That consideration will only govern so far as the public welfare permits or demands."[73] Personal fault only mattered insofar as judges decided that public policy depended on it. And public policy, the "public welfare," did not refer to some objective assessment of the polity's welfare as a body, as he made clear enough elsewhere,[74] but only to those interests that controlled the governing institutions, disciplined by the forms of law. The criminal law, then, implementing a preventive policy, generally ignored "the condition of a man's heart or conscience" even more resolutely than did the noncriminal law, since it "aim[ed] more directly than any other [branch of law] at establishing standards of conduct."[75] Criminal law addressed those harms that the dominant interests meant absolutely to prevent, rather than just to tax. It therefore required each citizen not just to refrain from self-consciously malevolent action but also to avoid excessive risk-creation altogether. To permit seriously negligent conduct and merely apply a tax when bad consequences resulted was, in Holmes's analysis, too pregnant with the harms that criminal law existed to prevent.

This argument provoked critics then and now to charge that Holmes had utterly divorced the criminal law from morality.[76] But while Holmes eagerly emphasized the difference between the two, he was equally eager to insist that criminal law was in fact "founded on blameworthiness." Moreover, he seemed to think that it had to be (although for sociological rather than philosophical reasons). To suggest otherwise "would shock the moral sense of any civilized community," since to be "civilized" was to substitute more or less predictable and principled coercion for utterly arbitrary coercion. The relevant blameworthiness, though, was not that of the particular offender's "conscience" or "heart" but that of an "average member" of that "civilized community" when placed in the defendant's shoes. Prevention called not for restricting liability to those of bad conscience but to those who had failed to internalize and adhere to the morality of that "civilized community"—to "know and obey"—as well as its "average member" had. The community was "civilized" because it was moral: because it had a moral code that it imparted to its members and because it would not generally coerce its members in ways that that moral code would not predict. In fact, to enforce a law that was meaningfully stricter than that moral code—"or, to put it another way, a law which punished conduct that would not be blameworthy in the average member of the community"—would logically prove "too severe for that community to bear"[77] and thus counterproductive from a preventive perspective. It would only subvert the peace and the broad sense of security that law existed to promote. For that reason—maintenance of the community as a civilized entity in the eyes of its dominant group—and not for reasons related to trans-social justice to the individual, morality had to remain integral to the criminal law of any "civilized" community.

Holmes made this point again a few pages later when he noted that the law forbore punishing for consequences that "no one, or only some exceptional specialist, could have foreseen." That fact might have implied a rule of individualized blameworthiness, but Holmes explained otherwise: "[S]till the reason for this limitation is simply to make a rule which is not too hard for the average member of the community."[78] And, in summing up the chapter, Holmes again noted that the reason for refusing to punish "what would not be blameworthy in an average member of the community" was to avoid a rule that "practically was too high for that community"—that is, that simply would not prevent harms and promote civilization in that time and place.[79] Thus, while the occasional convict might well be "morally without stain, because he has less than ordinary intelligence or prudence," the average member of the community "will not, as a general rule, incur liability without blameworthiness."[80] The criminal law's harsh command to "know and obey" would guarantee that few would create excessive danger. And while the law's incentives would be tailored to accommodate the *average* person's frailties, the law could not regularly spare the innocent-of-conscience who nevertheless did create excessive danger, except at the expense of civilization.

Turning to murder doctrine, Holmes relied on Stephen's summary of the law to show the foolishness of Stephen's own claim that the "malice" required for murder amounted to "wickedness" rather than serious negligence. It was clear enough from Stephen's summary that malice did not imply a desire to cause suffering as such, nor even a desire to kill or cause grievous bodily harm, but only "knowledge that the act will probably cause death." But Holmes then went further, claiming with few citations that such "knowledge" was proven whenever the defendant had known all the circumstances necessary for "a man of reasonable prudence" to have foreseen the death, regardless of whether this particular defendant had actually foreseen any such thing.[81] For Holmes, this was a matter of common sense. Wasn't it obvious that a workman would be guilty of murder if he were to throw heavy beams from a rooftop at midday in one of London's busiest streets, even if this workman had never considered the danger?[82] And to take a real case that landed on Holmes's desk only three years later, wouldn't a self-styled doctor be guilty of manslaughter if, while genuinely attempting a cure, he were to douse his patient in kerosene until her skin burned away and she died?[83] To Holmes, at least, the answer was clear: "[T]he test of murder is the degree of danger to life attending the act under the known circumstances of the case"; actual awareness of likely death was unnecessary although, of course, adequate when present.[84]

The standard of liability for murder, then, was a kind of severe negligence.[85] Holmes resisted, however, the further step to strict liability. He acknowledged that the law as it was contained pockets of strict liability, even in murder, and that this doctrine was in tension with the theory of prevention (since the threat of punishment could not deter conduct that would appear safe to the average person). So how could he sustain his claim that prevention underlay all criminal doctrine? First, he maintained that strict liability was "intelligible as it stands,"[86] since there might be cases where the "legislator apprehend[ed]" excessive danger in certain conduct that the average person did not and so deemed it "desirable to make special efforts for the prevention of such deaths" or other harms. He did not discuss how strict liability would work as a "special effort" to improve deterrence, although modern readers will supply arguments about the educational function of the law or the elimination of opportunities for acquittals based on deception or hard-to-prove causal chains and the like. Rather, Holmes left the assertion dangling. But he also expressed his doubt that this aspect of British law and of Stephen's summary would serve as much of a predictor of the law in America: "I do not, however, mean to argue that the rules under discussion arose on the above reasoning, any more than that they are right, or would be generally applied in this country."[87] Recent scholarship indicates he predicted the law pretty well in the case of felony murder, since, however strictly the doctrine may often have been stated, it seems clear that convictions then and now have generally rested on evidence of at least severe negligence in the causing of the death.[88] And when he had occasion to write on the doctrine as a judge, he again observed the firmness of the authority for the rule as well as the cogent criticism, while also observing that the evidence made the doctrine superfluous in the case at hand.[89]

Note, though, that American courts did, in fact, apply strict liability in many cases, especially in liquor cases and other "regulatory" cases as well as cases of abduction and statutory rape.[90] Holmes joined in some of these without a whimper and wrote at least one opinion that extended the reach of strict liability rather aggressively. That opinion came in a prosecution for being in a gaming house when gaming implements were found. There, he appeared to come around fully to the utility of strict liability as a tool of prevention in at least some categories of offenses. Without explaining exactly why he found strict liability so unambiguously implied in the statute, Holmes spent a long paragraph explaining why it might be rational to convict the defendant without proof of "knowledge of the presence of the implements, or the character of the place."[91] He argued that the apparent purpose of the law was to prevent gambling; that in pursuit of that purpose the law might criminalize the preliminary fact of merely being in a gaming house; and considering the potential difficulties of proving a defendant's knowledge, might rely on the fact that people in gaming houses generally do know where they are.[92] Here, the principle of prevention ruled the day but without any reference to controlling precedent, without any exegesis of statutory language, without any consideration of the tempering principle of *The Common Law* that the necessarily hard rules of the law should nevertheless remain soft enough that the "average member of the community" can bear them—thus without any explanation of why a conventional mistake-of-fact rule would have failed to afford adequate prevention.

The rest of the chapter examined a handful of offenses in which prevailing doctrine seemed to focus on the defendant's actual state of awareness at the time of the offense. Holmes's challenge was to reconcile these doctrines, which might look like concessions to individualized justice, with the principle of prevention and the external standard.

In malicious mischief, for example, he acknowledged that the law might be read to require an actual intention and motive to cause harm "for the sake of the harm." But the reason was simply that the judges had deemed mere trespasses on property unworthy of criminalization since the owners could be compensated by the civil law easily and adequately. Trespasses accompanied by "spite," however, caused an altogether different harm that the law sought to prevent rather than simply compensate. Thus the judges punished only the harm they sought to prevent and not some other that needed only taxing.[93] Prevention remained at the core of the criminal law even if policy-making judges could rationally determine that an internal standard sometimes represented the best policy. Here, Holmes might have observed the limits of his science. From the evidence of extant criminal doctrine, he could and did induce a general principle of prevention, but that general principle could not alone predict the doctrine, the policy, that judges (and juries) would make. The full task required the far more sophisticated social science that Holmes later hinted at in "The Path of the Law."[94]

Still, if an internal standard might apply where the law was primarily concerned with a harm caused by a spiteful motive, such doctrines were relatively rare. Arson, a close cousin of malicious mischief, came quickly to be punishable wherever the defendant merely intended an unjustified burning, even though the motive was spite-free. As Holmes noted, the contrary doctrine had been defended: Bishop reported that courts had frequently found no arson when a prisoner burned a jail not specifically to burn the building down but only to facilitate an escape, a result in serious tension with what even Bishop took to be proper principles.[95] Further support for Holmes's application of the preventive principle was found in East's example of a man who burns his own house under circumstances making it very likely that nearby houses would burn too.[96] Convinced that the sensible, preventive result in these cases would soon win out, Holmes further argued that such a requirement of mere intention always put the law "on the high-road to an external standard."[97] In these examples and others, he asserted, the law would punish intolerable risk taking regardless of the actual state of the defendant's mind. But here he made the assertion in the face of a number of cases, sports though he may have thought them, that cast doubt on his science.

An internal standard might also apply in cases of attempt. It clearly did apply in cases of incomplete conduct, those cases where the defendant had taken too few steps to justify a conclusion that the natural consequence of the acts would be the completion of the offense. Holmes accepted that a showing of actual intention to do all necessary further acts was imperative. Only by that showing could one conclude that the defendant actually represented the sort of risk taking that the law meant to prevent. "The importance of the intent is not to show that the act was wicked, but to show that it was likely to be followed by hurtful consequences."[98] And the explanation for the specific-intent requirement in larceny—itself understood as a forever-incomplete attempt to deprive another of property—was precisely the same.[99]

But the preventive principle applied only problematically in cases of complete conduct, cases where the defendant had indeed done all such conduct as could be expected naturally to result in completion of the offense (e.g., pulling a trigger even though her or his aim turned out to be slightly off). In these cases, Holmes argued that the external standard should resume its place. Such a defendant had intentionally taken all the steps normally adequate to complete the offense, and, in so doing, had proven herself or himself as dangerous as one who had actually completed the offense. If the latter's dangerousness were to be judged by an external standard, then that of the former should be as well. The principle of prevention, therefore, militated for conviction for attempt, regardless of actual subjective intention to kill or internal blameworthiness. This position was in significant tension with at least the rhetoric of the law, but Holmes pointed to the doctrine that, even in attempt cases, a person might be taken to have intended the natural and probable consequences of her or his acts.[100] While Bishop insisted that such a rule was a mere rule of evidence, subordinate to the substantive requirement of subjective intention, Holmes countered that that understanding of the rule was "a mere fiction disguising the true theory."[101] Still, the courts' and commentators' persistent, Bishop-like rhetoric required Holmes to claim no more than "at least color of authority" for his reading of the rule.[102]

No doubt, here and elsewhere, Holmes sought not just to predict the law but actually to bind the law ever more closely to the "only universal" theory of criminal law, the theory that he thought the only tenably scientific one after Darwin. This effort to improve the law, to enhance its civilizing capacity by exposing and eliminating its anomalies, emerged clearly enough throughout *The Common Law*. But that element of reform did not detract from the more fundamental mission to extract the principles that would equip one to predict outcomes. The mixture of the two projects may even have been logically compelled. The behavior to be analyzed and predicted was that of human beings making judgments that, by the conventions of law, demanded to be characterized as sounder or less sound according to abiding standards. A rigorous separation between prediction of those choices and judgment as to the soundness of the possible choices was unlikely and maybe impossible. Only by making judgments as to the relative soundness of different cases might one begin to see which of those cases stood as the most likely predictors of future decisions. The descriptive and normative arguments implied each other. And yet one more giant step was implied: only by recognizing the limits of the predictive power of even the soundest, lawyerly decisions in a universe where the "struggle for existence" would ultimately prevail over any lawyerly argument, could one advance the predictive science even further, from a science of parsing and evaluating the soundness of appellate cases to an economics, a statistics, a social science of the ever-elusive law.[103]

Holmes did not have a chance as a judge to fight out the particulars of the attempt doctrine just discussed. He did have a number of opportunities on the bench, however, to develop his claim that judging was policy making, as well as his apparent preference that it should be done without disguise. Thus, again, while he insisted that principles and logic be adhered to as far as they carried, he taught his generation the fundamentally political, or legislative, nature of the substantive choices made by judges. So, in his discussion of attempt in *The Common Law*, he indicated pretty clearly the role and limits of logic. He considered the objective standard for "completed" attempts, discussed previously, a "logically" compelled consequence of his prior demonstrations of the preventive and external nature of basic criminal standards. But when turning to the conduct side of attempt doctrine, he recognized that judgments as to exactly how much conduct would convert *precriminal* preparation into *criminal* attempt were matters of "[p]ublic policy" or "legislative considerations." They could never be reduced to logic but only to judgments as to the levels of risk that a particular society (or its dominant interests) was willing to tolerate.[104] In this connection, he noted the example of an Alabama case of 1860 that had found an attempted rape by a slave on the basis of his merely chasing after a white woman, conduct that Holmes understood normally to be far from adequate for such a conviction. "No doubt the fears peculiar to a slaveholding community had their share in the conviction," he said, in a tone that recognized that every community had its own dominant groups and peculiar fears that dictated the substance of its judicial legislation as well as its statutory law.[105]

Some years later on the bench, he had the chance to elaborate on how policy might be made in an appropriately judicial fashion where the question was the sufficiency of the conduct in attempt cases. Two opinions he wrote on the law of attempt again illustrate his frankness about the judicial role. In the first, *Kennedy*, the defendant challenged his conviction for attempting murder by rat poison. Holmes in effect merged his dual claims of impossibility (too little poison in the indictment) and insufficient conduct (too little poison in the victim) into a single question: whether the defendant had come close enough to accomplishing a sufficiently alarming purpose that the courts might deem acquittal too dangerous. Again following *The Common Law*'s discussion of doctrine closely, Holmes observed that all cases of attempt could be understood as impossibility cases, since the defendant's purpose necessarily turned out to be impossible under the precise circumstances as they developed, but that the law punished attempts anyway if the conduct reached a point too close to the apprehended harm to be tolerated. The law tended to require quite a bit of conduct before it would find this standard met since "the aim of the law is not to punish sins, but is to prevent certain external results."[106] But that preventive principle, focusing on the quantity of risk created, left judges with quite a bit of policy making to do. If the defendant could point to cases where the impossibility of killing a man by shooting mistakenly at a post had produced acquittal, Holmes could point to cases where the picking of an empty pocket or an attempt to perform an abortion on an unpregnant woman had resulted in conviction. Messy as they were, the attempt cases yielded some important discipline in directing the judge to two primary considerations: how close the defendant had apparently come to accomplishing the offense before it proved impossible and the gravity of the harm threatened from the public's point of view.[107] Still, once a judge had read the cases and distilled the pertinent principles, a measure of policy making remained: "It is a question of degree," Holmes wrote in the other of his major attempt cases. And "the degree of proximity held sufficient may vary with circumstances, including, among other things, the apprehension which the particular crime is calculated to excite."[108] In short, attempt law was neither about punishing the sinful nor about excusing the lucky but about establishing what risk taking would be tolerated by judges and what would not, the judges speaking not for themselves but for the collective interests they took to be reflected in the statutes, the case law, and their own (inevitably partial) sense of the public's point of view.

Conclusion

The decisions in these last cases were arbitrary. Holmes did not suggest otherwise, even as he offered a framework for decision making in such cases. The sources of law lay in precedent and statute but also, inevitably, in simple judicial policy making, as he had said even more frankly in his discussion of attempt in *The Common Law*. It was, therefore, a bit ironic that Holmes concluded his criminal law chapter with a seductively neat summary of his argument for the centrality of external standards and the conformity of virtually all doctrine to that standard. The summary was so schematic, so neat, that a casual reader could be forgiven for thinking that she or he was momentarily in the hands of Langdell. But, just as Holmes was too much the Darwinian scientist to throw in with Langdell, so he was too much the lawyer to be the founder of Realism. For him, the principle of prevention really did distinguish the criminal law from other branches of law. The external standard really was the only lawyerly candidate for the basic standard of criminal liability. On the basis of such principles—and later (he would say) on the basis of rigorous social science as well—the law really could be known and predicted in meaningful degree. As a corollary, it could likewise be refined so as to give it even more of the coherence and predictability that made it law at all. Still, the final leap from such principles to outcomes of cases, sometimes trivial in size and sometimes across a huge chasm, always retained an element of arbitrariness or policy. When the judge determined exactly how he would authorize force and coercion, he was not the tool of God but the agent of one competitor or another in the struggle for existence.

The external, objective standard took center stage in *The Common Law* not because Holmes was a morally indifferent man but for just the opposite reason: because his reading of the sources of the law yielded up that standard as the only plausible candidate to render the criminal law—state coercion par excellence—predictable to the average person. And law was only law as long as it was reasonably predictable because only then did it serve its preeminent purpose: the preservation of (Victorian) civilization as the most peaceable iteration of Darwinian struggle that the world had yet known. Unlike so many moderns who might vainly criticize him from opposite directions—for supposedly draining morality from law, on the one hand, or for hypocritically defending the law that he had himself exposed as merely political—Holmes was able to celebrate law as the foundation of civilization without ever supposing it to be anything grander than a contingent human device for coping with Darwinian imperatives. That ability made Holmes one of the great products of and propagators of the Darwinian revolution in science and thus, for legal science and criminal law, a persistently influential figure more than a century later.

Notes

1. The main exceptions are the insightful but brief assessments in Mark DeWolfe Howe, *Justice Oliver Wendell Holmes*, vol. 2, *The Proving Years, 1870–1882* (Cambridge, Mass.: Belknap Press of Harvard Univ. Press, 1963), chap. 6; and G. Edward White, *Justice Oliver Wendell Holmes: Law and the Inner Self* (New York: Oxford Univ. Press, 1993), pp. 157–161.

2. Oliver Wendell Holmes, *The Common Law* (Boston: Little, Brown, 1881).

3. On this emancipation, see Jon H. Roberts and James Turner, *The Sacred and the Secular University* (Princeton, N.J.: Princeton Univ. Press, 2000); Louis Menand, *The Metaphysical Club* (New York: Farrar, Straus, Giroux, 2001); Philip P. Wiener, *Evolution*

and the Founders of Pragmatism (Gloucester, Mass.: P. Smith, 1969), chap. 1 (originally published in 1949).

4. See White, *Justice Oliver Wendell Holmes*, pp. 40–43; Thomas C. Grey, "Langdell's Orthodoxy," *University of Pittsburgh Law Review* 45 (1983): 1–53; Robert W. Gordon, "Legal Thought and Legal Practice in the Age of American Enterprise, 1870–1920," in Gerald L. Geison, ed., *Professions and Professional Ideologies in America* (Chapel Hill: Univ. of North Carolina Press, 1983), and his "Holmes' Common Law as Legal and Social Science," *Hofstra Law Review* 10 (1982): 722–726; M. H. Hoeflich, "Law and Geometry: Legal Science from Leibniz to Langdell," *American Journal of Legal History* 30 (1986): 95–121.

5. See Roberts and Turner, *Sacred and the Secular University*, pp. 1–25.

6. On deductive science, see, e.g., Hoeflich on Langdell and his forebears ("Law and Geometry"); on divine will, see, e.g., Stephen Siegel, "Joel Bishop's Orthodoxy," *Law and History Review* 13 (1995): 215–259.

7. On the new science, see Roberts and Turner, *Sacred and the Secular University*, pp. 28–29 and passim.

8. Wiener, *Evolution*, pp. 1–9.

9. Roberts and Turner, *Sacred and the Secular University*, pp. 28–29. Holmes himself, late in life, reflected that the source of his basic intellectual skepticism lay in a commitment to science that he absorbed even before Darwin's emergence. See Mark DeWolfe Howe, *Justice Oliver Wendell Holmes*, vol. 1, *The Shaping Years, 1841–1870* (Cambridge, Mass.: Belknap Press of Harvard Univ. Press, 1957), pp. 17–18.

10. Cf. chapter 5, Markus Dubber's contribution to this volume.

11. Holmes to Pollock, Mar. 25, 1883, in Mark DeWolfe Howe, ed., *Holmes-Pollock Letters: The Correspondence of Mr. Justice Holmes and Sir Frederick Pollock, 1874–1932*, 2d ed. (Cambridge, Mass.: Belknap Press of Harvard Univ. Press, 1961).

12. Oliver Wendell Holmes, "Codes, and the Arrangement of the Law," *American Law Review* 5 (1870): 4.

13. See, e.g., Holmes to Pollock, Mar. 25, 1883, and Mar. 4, 1888, in Howe, ed., *Holmes-Pollock Letters*; Oliver Wendell Holmes, "Law in Science and Science in Law," *Harvard Law Review* 12 (1899): 443–463.

14. Lisa Rodensky, *The Crime in Mind: Criminal Responsibility and the Victorian Novel* (New York: Oxford Univ. Press, 2003).

15. Holmes, "Codes," pp. 4–5.

16. Oliver Wendell Holmes, *American Law Review* 6 (1871): 723–725.

17. Holmes to Pollock, July 3, 1874, in Howe, ed., *Holmes-Pollock Letters*.

18. Classics of the literature on classical legal thought include Grey, "Langdell's Orthodoxy," and Duncan Kennedy, "Toward an Historical Understanding of Legal Consciousness: The Case of Classical Legal Thought in America, 1850–1940," *Research in Law and Sociology* 3 (1980): 3–24.

19. *American Law Review* 7 (1873): 652–663.

20. *Lochner v. New York*, 198 U.S. 45, 76 (1905) (Holmes dissenting).

21. "Torts," p. 654.

22. "The Gas-Stokers' Strike," *American Law Review* 7 (1873): 582–584.

23. "Common Carriers and the Common Law," *American Law Review* 13 (1879): 609–631.

24. Holmes, *Common Law*, pp. 42–43.

25. This simplifies Bishop a bit for present purposes. For a fuller and fairer account, see Gerald Leonard, "Towards a Legal History of American Criminal Theory: Culture and Doctrine from Blackstone to the Model Penal Code," *Buffalo Criminal Law Review* 6 (2003): 748–754.

26. Joel Prentiss Bishop, *Commentaries on the Criminal Law*, 2d ed. (Boston: Little, Brown, 1858), p. 259.

27. Bishop, *Commentaries*, p. 260.

28. Bishop, *Commentaries*, pp. 278–279.

29. Bishop, *Commentaries*, p. 2.

30. Bishop, *Commentaries*, p. 275.

31. *Common Law*, p. 66.

32. James Fitzjames Stephen, *A General View of the Criminal Law of England* (Cambridge: Macmillan, 1863), pp. 4–6.

33. K. J. M. Smith, *James Fitzjames Stephen: Portrait of a Victorian Rationalist* (Cambridge: Cambridge Univ. Press, 1988), chap. 6.

34. Stephen, *General View*, pp. 98–99.

35. Stephen, *General View*, p. 82.

36. James Fitzjames Stephen, *A History of the Criminal Law of England*, vol. 2 (London: Macmillan, 1883), p. 76.

37. Stephen, *History*, vol. 2, pp. 81–83.

38. Charles M. Cook, *The American Codification Movement: A Study of Antebellum Legal Reform* (Westport, Conn.: Greenwood Press, 1981).

39. *Common Law*, p. 50.

40. *Common Law*, p. 41.

41. *Common Law*, pp. 42–43.

42. *Common Law*, p. 40.

43. *Common Law*, p. 43.

44. *Common Law*, pp. 43–47, quotation at 46.

45. *Common Law*, p. 44.

46. *Common Law*, p. 47.

47. On this case and its context, see A. W. Brian Simpson, *Cannibalism and the Common Law: The Story of the Tragic Last Voyage of the Mignonette* (Chicago: Univ. of Chicago Press, 1984).

48. *U.S. v. Holmes*, 1842 U.S. App. Lexis 584, 26 F. Cas. 360 (1842).

49. Simpson, pp. 251–252.

50. *Common Law*, p. 43.

51. *Common Law*, p. 47.

52. *Common Law*, p. 48.

53. Cf. Jerome Hall, *General Principles of Criminal Law* (Indianapolis, Ind.: Bobbs-Merrill, 1947), pp. 349–350.

54. See, e.g., *State v. Cutter*, 36 N.J.L. 125, 126 (1873).
55. Bishop, *Commentaries on the Criminal Law*, vol. 1, 6th ed. (Boston: Little, Brown, 1877), p. 165.
56. Bishop, *Commentaries*, p. 168.
57. See, e.g., the outcome and discussion in *Halsted v. State*, 41 N.J.L. 552 (1879).
58. William Blackstone, *Commentaries on the Laws of England*, vol. 4 (Chicago: Univ. of Chicago Press, 1979) (originally published in 1769), p. 4.
59. *History*, vol. 2, pp. 114–115.
60. James Fitzjames Stephen, *A General View of the Criminal Law of England*, 2d ed. (London: Macmillan, 1890), p. 72.
61. 1 F. Cas. 926, 1 Gall. 62 (C.C. Mass. 1812).
62. See also *People v. Brooks*, 1 Denio 457 (N.Y. Sup. Ct. of Judicature, 1845); *Smith v. Brown*, 1 Wend. 231 (N.Y. Sup. Ct. of Judicature, 1828).
63. See, e.g., *Byrne v. State*, 12 Wisconsin 519 (1860); *State v. Reeves*, 15 Kan. 396, 399 (1875). More generally, see Bishop, *Commentaries* (1877), pp. 166–168.
64. *Gordon v. State*, 52 Ala. 308, 309 (1875). See also *Hemphill v. Moody*, 64 Ala. 468, 473 (1879).
65. *Wimbish v. Com.*, 75 Va. 839, 845 (1880).
66. *Gardner v. New York*, 62 N.Y. 299, 305 (1875).
67. *State v. Boyett*, 32 N.C. 336 (1849).
68. *Boyett*, at 344.
69. *Boyett*, at 345.
70. *Boyett*, at 345.
71. *Boyett*, at 346.
72. Cf. Holmes's opinion in *Com. v. Chance*, 174 Mass. 245, 252 (1899), quoting 1 East, P.C. 262, where the question was the standard for murder liability but where Holmes took the opportunity to justify objective standards generally. He pointed out that a defendant only had to consider "common social duty" and ask whether "a more circumspect conduct" than the one he chose was available to him, a perfect statement of the rationale for strict liability rules like the ignorance rule.
73. *Common Law*, p. 49
74. "Gas-Stokers' Strike," p. 584.
75. *Common Law*, p. 50. See also *Com. v. Pierce*, 138 Mass. 165, 176 (1884), where Holmes practically pasted this section of the book into the Massachusetts Reports.
76. Stephen, *History*, vol. 2, p. 79; Albert W. Alschuler, *Law without Values: The Life, Work, and Legacy of Justice Holmes* (Chicago: Univ. of Chicago Press, 2000).
77. *Common Law*, p. 50.
78. *Common Law*, pp. 56–57.
79. *Common Law*, p. 76.
80. *Common Law*, p. 51.
81. *Common Law*, pp. 52–57.
82. *Common Law*, p. 55.
83. *Com. v. Pierce*, 138 Mass. 165 (1884).

84. *Common Law*, p. 57.

85. Holmes himself explicitly recognized that the standard was a kind of "negligence." *Common Law*, p. 62.

86. *Common Law*, p. 58.

87. *Common Law*, p. 59.

88. Guyora Binder, "The Origins of American Felony Murder Rules," *Stanford Law Review* 57 (2004): 59–208.

89. *Com. v. Chance*, 174 Mass. 245, 252–253 (1899).

90. See Leonard, "Towards a Legal History."

91. *Com. v. Smith*, 166 Mass. 370, 375 (1896).

92. *Smith*, pp. 375–376.

93. *Common Law*, pp. 63–64.

94. Holmes, "The Path of the Law," *Harvard Law Review* 10 (1897): 469. Here, Holmes suggested that prediction must really depend on "the man of statistics and the master of economics" and the like, not just on traditional lawyer's skills.

95. *Common Law*, p. 64. Holmes cited 2 Bishop § 14, 6th ed., 1877, but it is necessary to read through to §§ 15–16 to get all of Bishop's account.

96. *Common Law*, p. 64 and n. 5.

97. *Common Law*, p. 64.

98. *Common Law*, pp. 66–68.

99. *Common Law*, pp. 70–74.

100. *Common Law*, p. 66 and n. 2.

101. Ibid.

102. *Common Law*, pp. 65–66.

103. Cf. Holmes, "Path of the Law," p. 469.

104. *Common Law*, p. 68.

105. *Common Law*, p. 69.

106. *Com. v. Kennedy*, 170 Mass. 18, 20–21 (1897).

107. *Kennedy*, p. 22.

108. *Com. v. Peaslee*, 177 Mass. 267, 272 (1901).

NINE

Bodies, Words, Identities
The Moving Targets of the Criminal Law

MARIANA VALVERDE

1. Introduction: Questions of Method

A historian would most likely approach the topic of homosexuality and law by way of a study of a particular period in a single country. A criminal law scholar interested in history would probably look for large-scale shifts in the logics of the criminal law. In contrast to both of these stances, this chapter is something like a historical sociology of the criminal law. I call what I do "sociology of law" not because I want to wave the flag of society to criticize lawyers' legalism but simply because I am interested in writing about legal developments without taking the categories of law and the boundaries of areas of law for granted. Yet, unlike most sociologists and social theorists, I do not see legal categories as secondary reflections of more fundamental struggles and interests. From an epistemologically agnostic perspective, drawn mainly from Nietzsche and Foucault, I endeavor to question received notions about society, at the same time and with the same analyses, that also displace and decenter law's claims about itself.[1] In addition, as Foucault did (and Max Weber well before him), I regard historical sociology as fundamental to any study of social relations, since studies of the present can proceed in a critical and reflexive manner only if and when we are first informed about the genealogy of the categories that we ourselves use as common currency.

If we are interested in making current familiar categories of governance seem strange by highlighting the contingency of such taken-for-granted entities as the individual,[2] the citizen,[3] the state,[4] and the gay person,[5] it is necessary to avoid repositing and thus renaturalizing the categories that are in question. Instead of beginning with existing categories and codes, it is more useful to consider concrete problems as they have actually appeared to various authorities.[6] If we look at eighteenth-century sodomy prosecutions only from the standpoint of modern homosexual identity, for example, all we can do is to ask whether they (the sodomites) were like or unlike modern homosexuals—a highly presentist question, even if some of the answers stress discontinuity.[7]

The question of method, often turned into a scholastic exercise by sociology's fetishism of methodology, is at bottom the simple question of beginning. How do we begin studying something? How do we then begin writing about it? In both research and writing, how can we work to capture the contingency and instability of the many "its" that are usually taken for granted, rather than reifying them through our own work? In a somewhat offhanded manner, Foucault described his own method as beginning with "problematizations," that is, with a particular issue (which to our modern eye might look like a jumble of issues) as it appeared to a set of governing authorities. From this perspective, since sodomy was clearly an issue for ecclesiastical and legal authorities, it deserves to be studied on its own. The scholar must suspend the question of the relation between sodomy and homosexuality. *Problematization* is just an idea, not a method (hence Foucault's refusal to elaborate an abstract methodology); but scholars such as Robert Castel, Paul Veyne, and Nikolas Rose have explored its possibilities somewhat systematically.[8]

In relation to regulating bodies, desires, and identities, the history of the criminal law in common law jurisdictions reveals that even if we limit our scope to something that is relatively concrete (men having sex with men), what looks like one issue turns out to be many. This is because this one issue has served (even if we look only at recent history) as the site or occasion for the formation of strikingly different, even contradictory, problematizations.[9] This lack of coordination, this absence of any accepted way to resolve or even manage contradictory views, is especially apparent in the United States, where the biblical category of unnatural sex coexists with both modern therapeutically produced psychic identities and legal entities generated through human rights claims. Concerning male-male desire and male-male sex, the oldest and the newest knowledges swirl around each other in a remarkably uncoordinated manner. The law of theft has certainly changed over time, and even murder has not always been the same (as Guyora Binder's chapter in this volume explains); but it is unlikely that even a contemporary Nietzsche could unearth anything like the proliferation of conflicting paradigms and problematizations that male-male sexuality has occasioned in other areas of criminal law.

For this reason, it is highly inappropriate to consider the legal regulation of sexuality as a special-interest topic. Weber showed that the study of religion did not have to be left to specialists. Similarly, we have learned from contemporary feminism and from Foucault's pioneering work that a problem space such as male-male sex can be a fruitful site for studies that reveal much about wider processes and techniques of regulation—and this is certainly the case even if one limits the analytic gaze to legal forms of regulation.

It is thus perhaps not so surprising that, in respect to the study of the criminal law, examining the curious and unpredictable trajectories of entities such as sodomy turns out to shed some new light on existing key theoretical issues in legal studies. Following are three such issues.

1. The manner in which regulations aimed at bodies and body parts turn out to target speech, not bodies, as if words describing a sexual act or a desire were of more concern to the state than eliminating behavior. This is a well-known feature of English buggery law; but it is alive and well today in the U.S. military, where, as Janet Halley's brilliant study shows, soldiers are just as likely to be dismissed for saying, "I am going to the Pride parade," than for doing anything.[10] This curious process puts in question traditional legal distinctions between expression and conduct.

2. It is important to study legal processes without presupposing or even beginning with the categories of law. This chapter highlights this by documenting the often contradictory and seemingly unpredictable relations between criminal law and other areas of law—not only human rights law and family law but also minor areas of law, such as liquor licensing and municipal ordinances. This finding puts in question law schools' habit of treating criminal law as self-contained.

3. In keeping with existing work on the constitutive effects of law, studying legal mechanisms deployed to govern certain forms of sexual speech and conduct reveals that regulatory strategies (legal, extralegal, or hybrid) sometimes bring into being new entities—the very entities whose existence is said to be the reason why regulation is required. The sodomite existed in Christian discourse well before secular statutes on sodomy, but other legal processes bring new sexual entities into being. Sexual orientation is often thought of as a personal experience, but it was created as a term useful for legal struggles;[11] so too, same-sex marriage is an experiential category as well, but one imbued with and formed by human rights legal consciousness.

These three issues can be separated analytically as evidenced in the preceding, but in the real world they are always intertwined in ways that are not predictable in advance. Thus, they will not receive separate consideration here, as they might in a more traditionally formatted theory article. Rather, they will be highlighted, as appropriate, as we go along, to help demonstrate how various legal developments in relation to sodomy, homosexuality, and sexual orientation can become occasions to develop our collective stock of theoretical insights.

The substantive portion of the chapter begins with the old English category of buggery, the crime said to be unique in that the offense in question was not to be named among Christians, as Blackstone famously put it. The silence injunction, paradoxical in itself, becomes downright incoherent when recent scholarship on the offense of blackmail is considered. It seems that it was precisely unauthorized speech about male-male sex that prompted Parliament to pass a law lending some protection to practicing homosexuals as well as to innocent parties—at roughly the same time that the net was being widened with indecency offenses whose prosecution involved much discourse about the very crime said to be unnamable. The performative character of legal speech has certainly been noted in work emphasizing how legal words unwittingly slide into extralegal actions.[12] However, what emerges as one considers the complex relation of blackmail and sodomy in English is something like the reverse of legal performativity: the legal regulation of bodies seems to lose sight of its object, becoming instead obsessed with words.[13]

The next part of the chapter considers the invention of the homosexual identity—an invention that law failed to recognize for a very long time, especially in the United States. We then consider how the proliferation of legal technologies such as antidiscrimination policies and ordinances eventually forced even the morally conservative Supreme Court of the United States to declare sodomy laws unconstitutional. While this 2003 decision was greeted as if it granted gay people equal rights, observers attuned to the heterogeneity of law noticed that the abolition of sodomy was accompanied by a flood of antihomosexual statutes. Defense of Marriage acts performed a new subordination of lesbians and gays—something that underscores the need to look at legal fields in their interaction rather than in their traditionally separate subdisciplines.

The recent eruption of same-sex marriage into headlines and courtrooms will not be discussed here, in part because its connection with the criminal law is somewhat tenuous. Nevertheless, the reader of this chapter would do well to keep today's media images of gay and lesbian weddings in mind as we go over earlier historical processes. As I write these lines, gays and lesbians can and do get married not only in Toronto's City Hall but also in several Protestant churches around the city. This fact, perhaps more unexpectedly revealing about gay desire than about Protestantism, underlines the sheer contingency of the discontinuous history outlined here. Our story begins with the common law dictum about the crime that must not be mentioned among Christians, undergoes a process of disciplinarization and secularization through modern psychological readings of identity, and ends up back in church, though with male-male sex now being redeemed not through enlightened science but through a sacrament.

2. Unnatural Acts and the Limits of Christian (English) Speech

A. BUGGERY AND BLACKMAIL: NAMING THE UNNAMABLE

Buggery was removed from ecclesiastical jurisdiction and created as a secular crime under Henry VIII. At this time buggery covered unnatural acts "with either man or beast," but sources suggest that anal sex involving two males had become the unnatural act par excellence by the late eighteenth century. The word *sodomy*, of Latin origin, seems to have been used largely synonymously with the earthier Saxon-origin word *buggery* for a considerably long period in English legal history. However, there are interesting semantic and legal divergences separating those two words, especially in the United States, where various jurisdictions gave largely unexplained twists to existing English statutes.

If sodomy and buggery are ill-defined categories, this is not only because of the semantic slippages occurring across time and across English-speaking jurisdictions. It is also because of something that is peculiar to the offenses in question, namely, the ancient English practice of naming it (whatever "it" might encompass) as the crime that ought not to be named—among Christians at any rate—a linguistic practice traditionally identified with Sir Edward Coke.[14] The phrase from Coke that is always cited is "peccatum inter christanos non nominandum," but the "peccatum" is usually omitted. The actual phrase, quoted in full by Blackstone but not by subsequent legal writers, is "peccatum illud horribile, inter christianos non nominandum." Most commentators remark on the paradox of naming the ineffable but do not comment on the fact that, in contradiction with the Tudor project of secularizing the criminal law, "sin" (*peccatum*) is the grammatical subject here, not "crime."

In Blackstone's text, sodomy is found immediately after a discussion of rape and "ravishment" concerned not with women, gender, or bodies but rather with the problem of false accusations against gentlemen. This worry about the power of words to challenge gender and class hierarchy was turned into—and partly concealed by—a legal question concerning evidentiary difficulties. Before saying anything about sodomy, Blackstone sets out an evidentiary principle that acts to sharply limit the scope of both rape and sodomy prosecutions, but especially the latter. Blackstone's limitation is worth noting because it runs against the grain of the usual gay-history (and critical-legal studies) practice of exaggerating the reach of the law's terror.

> What has been here observed, especially with regard to the manner of proof, which ought to be more clear in proportion as the crime is more detestable, may be applied to another offense, of a still deeper malignity; the infamous *crime against nature* [emphasis in original], committed either with man or beast. A crime, which ought to be strictly and impartially proved, and then strictly and impartially punished. But it is an offense of so dark a nature, so easily charged, and the negative so difficult to prove, that the accusation should be clearly made out: for if false, it [the accusation] deserves a punishment inferior only to that of the crime itself.

This exhortation to legal restraint is followed by the one passage that sexuality studies scholars love to repeat:

> I will not act so disagreeable a part, to my readers as well as to myself, as to dwell any longer upon a subject, the very mention of which is a disgrace to human nature. It will be more eligible to imitate in this respect the delicacy of English law, which treats it, in its very indictments, as a crime not fit to be named.[15]

An 1842 appeal-court case discussed by Les Moran, in which counsel for a Mr. Rowed succeeded in having the indictment thrown out because it did not properly name the criminal act, demonstrates very vividly the contradiction laid out clearly in Blackstone's text. At first sight, the indictment appears as overly wordy as any other legal document:

> being persons of nasty, wicked, filthy, lewd, beastly and unnatural dispositions, and wholly lost to all sense of decency and good manners, heretofore, to wit on . . . with force and arms at ____ in a certain open and public place there, called Kensington Gardens, frequented by divers of the liege subjects of our lady the Queen, unlawfully and wickedly did meet together for the purpose and with the intent of committing and perpetrating with each other, openly, lewdly and indecently, in the said public place, divers nasty, wicked, filthy, beastly, unnatural and sodomitical practices; and then and there unlawfully, wickedly, openly, lewdly and indecently did commit and perpetrate with each other, in the sight and view of divers liege subject of our said lady the Queen, in the said public place there passing and being, divers such practices as aforesaid to the

great scandal and disgrace of mankind in contempt . . . to the evil example . . . and against the peace.[16]

The rhetorical excess of the indictment, an effect of ordinary legal practice compounded by the effort to avoid the inherent vagueness of the sin that must not be named among Christians and the crime against nature, did not suffice to overcome the evidentiary problem named by Blackstone. The court agreed with defense counsel that the words, however numerous, did not actually name the act with terms effective in law. "[S]odomitical practices" was not proper legal English.[17]

The contradiction that sodomy prosecutors faced was not merely discursive. It extended to law enforcement. H. G. Cocks's recent survey of prosecutions for sodomy and male-male indecent assault shows that the late eighteenth-century campaign to seek out and punish vice, including upper-class vice, briefly gave rise to expanded prosecutions, but this trend was after some years halted and reversed. The reversal was due to a mix of factors, including mistrust of the new police among upper-class gentlemen unhappy with surveillance by social inferiors, existing judicial anxieties about blackmail, and the backfiring of Peel's generous court-cost policies for private prosecutors. Given all these factors, certain men, especially soldiers posted in Royal Parks in London, began to make a business out of accusing gentlemen of sodomy.

> The overall effect of these police practices, I suggest, was a policy of de facto toleration of private offenses. They [the police] would, of course still prosecute private offenses if discovered by individual officers or prosecutors, but generally did not pursue these offenses themselves. . . . In addition, a poorly prepared police case would often attract criticism from magistrates for risking indecent publicity without the certainty of conviction.[18]

The Blackstonian dilemma juxtaposes a desire to make sodomy into the worst crime with an equally strong desire to prevent the corruption of English law through speech about a taboo. This seems to have resulted not in carefully chosen state-controlled prosecutions of well-founded cases, as recommended by Blackstone, but rather in its opposite, namely, prosecutorial policies based simply on where the crime was committed.

If it was difficult for police and prosecutors to clearly and effectively name the offenses covered by buggery law, a certain category of criminals suffered no such difficulties when speaking about the abominable crime: blackmailers. McLaren's comparative study of sexual blackmail in Britain and in the United States offers an interesting finding. While U.S. nineteenth- and early twentieth-century newspapers documented many extortion attempts by scheming female prostitutes and their male coconspirators, English newspaper coverage of blackmail trials suggests that accusations of sodomy were the main, or even the only, source of most blackmailers' income.[19] Indeed, as McLaren points out, the very offense of blackmail was created specifically to deal with gentlemen's fears of accusations of male-male sexual activity. The "criminalization of blackmail" came about "because of concern with stigmatized homosexual acts"—or, more accurately, concern with private, financially driven speech about such acts.[20] This was not a passing phenomenon. McLaren's later chapters show that blackmail concerning homosexual activity was still very common in the 1930s and 1940s in Britain.

It is thus clear that the paradox arising out of English law's self-declared delicacy about sodomy and buggery survived well into the mid-twentieth century. It was complicated by the mutually constitutive links between the criminalization of one form of speech about sodomy (blackmail) and law's rather weak effort to use its own uneasy combination of silence and authorized speech to prosecute a few sodomites cavorting in public spaces.

B. THE RESIDUAL CATEGORY OF INDECENCY

Nearly all accounts of the legal history of male-male sex in Britain see the 1885 Labouchere Amendment to the Criminal Law Amendment Act, which created the offense of "gross indecency" as a male-male offense, as a crucial dividing point. The Labouchere Amendment, so the story goes, widened the net considerably by making it unnecessary to provide evidence of anal sex. The target was now the male-male bond, not so much a particular body part. All sexual activity between men was criminalized as gross indecency.[21]

The unexpectedly successful prosecution of Oscar Wilde in 1895 was and is the most famous example of what the new law could do.[22] Recent research in criminal records, however, suggests that the Labouchere Amendment was not a revolution but amounted merely to statute law catching up with the common law. Historians had long commented on the scarcity of sodomy prosecutions in the nineteenth century—both in Britain and in North America—but they had not undertaken the tedious task of combing through hundreds of indictments looking for men engaging in same-sex acts who were prosecuted for nonspecific crimes. H. G. Cocks's research shows that indecent assault was used to target nonconsenting sex and when an older man had sex with a boy (or girl) below the age of consent, but it was also used in numerous instances of consenting sex between two adult men.[23] For the purposes of indecent assault, whether men were kissing or having anal sex was immaterial. Consent was not very important either (a nonliberal choice of legal rationality that, as we shall see, was to a large extent preserved in the post-Wolfenden reforms of 1967). In addition, just as female prostitutes were often charged under the 1824 Vagrancy Act rather than being accused of sexual offenses specifically, so too men who had sex with men were also charged with vagrancy in a significant number of cases throughout the nineteenth century and into the twentieth.

The obsession with buggery, or more accurately the obsession with safeguarding the proper economy of speech and silence around buggery, appears to be one of those peculiarities of the English that defy functionalist explanations. By contrast, the legal categories of gross indecency and indecent assault—as well as the panoply of police and prosecution tactics enabled by these terms—spread easily around the British Empire. In Canada, for example, criminal justice historians tell us that sodomy prosecutions were virtually nonexistent. However, subsequent to the introduction of gross indecency into the 1892 Criminal Code of Canada, a great deal of effort went into police surveillance of males in public or quasi-public places and into prosecuting and jailing men who had engaged in mainly consensual sex.[24]

Although more research is needed, it seems that criminal statutes targeting "indecency" in its various forms have acted as a kind of ramp leading from the higher reaches of law (the criminal law) into a lower-level, little-documented legal territory populated by all manner of administrative as well as legal tools. Unlike the famous criminal cases heard by appeal courts, enforcement of minor legal rules leaves few traces either in public documents or in the published books of the law. It is thus not surprising that this terrain has been mapped only very partially—for example, in George Chauncey's study of "gay New York." Among other things, this groundbreaking book documents the importance of the state liquor authority in the governance of New York City male-male sexual life in the period after the repeal of prohibition.[25] Governing sexuality through liquor licensing left few traces, since individual gay persons were not targeted or even named—liquor authorities merely threatened to close down any licensed premises that catered to or simply tolerated homosexuals. Chauncey's findings underline the importance of studying records beyond the traditional history of criminal law research tools, namely, court documents and transcripts.

Despite the dearth of research, the existing studies do allow some tentative generalizations about the *longue durée* of state efforts to legally identify and stigmatize male-male sexual conduct. Sodomy turns out to be central at the level of appeal courts (and perhaps also within the judicial and legislative imaginaries, which in the United States seem rather stuck in biblical imagery). However, sodomy laws were not central in the lives of most men who had sex with men. Bill Eskridge's exhaustive search of criminal records and prison records shows that in the United States sodomy prosecutions were extremely rare before the 1890s. Even after this time (when many sodomy statutes were revised to expand their scope), most male-male sex was policed not through the felony of sodomy but through a variety of low-level legal tools: municipal codes, liquor licensing laws, vagrancy statutes at the state level, and indecency laws of various kinds. He concludes,

> Some but not many [men] were arrested for sodomy in the period around World War I. On the eve of World War II, however, a homosexual with an active social life had a good chance of spending time in jail, possibly for sodomy but more likely for misdemeanors such as disorderly conduct, lewd vagrancy, indecent exposure, lewd or lascivious conduct, indecent liberties with minors, loitering near a public toilet or schoolyard, or sexual solicitation.[26]

It is difficult to venture even tentative comparisons between the United States and England in regard to these low-level regulatory and coercive tactics, since English legal historians have focused on sodomy and buggery to the exclusion of low-level legal tools used to police sexuality and sexual minorities. However, at the level of the criminal law in the strict sense, while U.S. statutes governing sodomy and indecency all claimed to be solidly based on English law, some notable differences are detectable.

Two such differences are apparent on the face of statutes themselves: (1) the degendering of sodomy in the United States and (2) the late nineteenth-century U.S. preoccupation with sexual acts other than traditional English buggery. A full comparative analysis of relevant statutes is beyond the scope of this chapter, but the next section will attempt to lay out a few points that would need to be followed up in further research.

C. PROLIFERATING UNNATURAL ACTS: SODOMY IN AMERICA

In North America, neither sodomy nor indecency was exclusively masculine. No information on women's prosecution under sodomy and indecency statutes in Canada is available, but, in the United States, coerced or forced heterosexual sodomy—presumably involving claims about a man forcing "unnatural" sex on a woman—seems to have been particularly zealously policed in the 1970s and 1980s.[27] Even heterosexual couples in a consensual sex situation were sometimes prosecuted for sodomy in the United States, unlike in England.

If sodomy was not as closely linked to male-male sex in the United States as it was in England, so too the particular acts targeted by indecency and sodomy laws were also more numerous. Lesbian activity could be prosecuted in the United States (although it seems this rarely happened), unlike in England and Wales. Eskridge finds that California's lewd vagrancy statute, passed in 1872 together with a 1903 law criminalizing acts outraging public decency, constituted a strong net with which to catch all manner of moral and sexual deviants. Meanwhile, in New York, state police used a very broad disorderly conduct law to police behavior and appearance without having to meet the high evidentiary standards of sodomy prosecutions.[28] In addition, California, a leader in moral laws, chose to make oral sex a separate crime in 1915 ("oral copulation"). Other states also followed this approach (e.g., Vermont), but many others (in the period 1870–1920, roughly) created new nonspecific crimes that could be used to prosecute oral sex (e.g., Florida's unnatural and lascivious acts 1917 law).[29]

The rather obsessive and perhaps specifically puritan focus on particular sexual acts and particular body parts that characterizes U.S. sodomy laws was undercut by the growing influence of psychiatric discourses about "personalities" and "neurosis"—discourses which, among other effects, led to the passing of new criminal statutes against sexual psychopaths, which were sometimes used to persecute gay men.[30] Inquiries into psyche and desire were also increasingly important, in the postwar, cold-war era, in state institutions such as the diplomatic service and the military. These institutions pursued vigorous campaigns, now documented in some detail by historians, whose target was not the sodomite but the homosexual.

Despite being concerned with homosexual persons rather than with sodomitical acts, and thus existing in a different ontological plane than the old buggery prosecutions, one thing the postwar homophobic witch hunts had in common with the Coke-Blackstone tradition was their concern with the regulation of speech. That homosexuals were more likely to reveal state secrets to spies or to enemy governments was one of the main justifications for the antigay witch hunts of the 1950s. The other justification for targeting speech occurring in the proximity of male-male sex was the persistent fear of blackmail. Even if homosexual civil servants or military officers did not willingly blab the state's secrets to their lovers, they might become subject to enemy blackmail. Thus, in a further twist in the policing-of-language story, the homosexual propensity to treasonous speech was once again linked to their vulnerability to another form of unauthorized speech—blackmail. As in the story of English buggery, the regulation of deviant sexuality in the cold-war era is inseparable from the state's attempt to institute a particular economy of silence and discourse.

D. SODOMY AND ANXIETIES OF EMPIRE

Before we pick up the postwar story, it is appropriate to pause to ponder the significance of the fact that in the United States anal sex between men has not been privileged (either in law or in popular discourse) nearly as much as in England. The noncriminalization of lesbian sex in England is often attributed to extreme prudery or to the social invisibility of female-female sex, but it can also be read as a side effect of a persistent English obsession with men putting their penis in the wrong place. North American jurisdictions, as we saw, had colonial sodomy laws that were still enforced in the twentieth century; but at various points campaigns around oral sex, homosexual identity, dangers to children, and other even more heterogeneous concerns (communism, for example, in the 1950s) were superimposed on the classic buggery story. In England, however, anal sex persisted as *the* crime against nature (in law in the books, at any rate) well into the postwar era. As we shall see, despite the Wolfenden Committee's interest in constructing a new regulatory scheme based mainly on age, consent, and public and private distinctions, they could not bring themselves to strongly recommend the elimination of buggery.

To understand the English focus on buggery between men, it is necessary, I would argue, to think more seriously about the "among Christians" part of Coke's dictum, using the resources of postcolonial studies. English Victorian and imperial discourses on sexuality developed a taxonomy of vice in which certain races were presented as prone to (or even constituted by) characteristic vices. Chinese males were collectively addicted to opium smoking, black African males were prone to rape and other impulsive crimes, women of African descent were unchaste, and so forth. On its part, sodomy seems to have been associated mainly with the Orient: boy-love and buggery were the vices of the Arab and Turkish worlds, in the minds of nineteenth-century middle-class Englishmen. Historians have not paid attention to how this orientalist construction of sodomy affected the course of domestic prosecutions. But there are some indications that the Christians named in Coke's famous dictum, which in his own time set up a contrast between Christians on the one hand and pagans and heretics on the other, did a different kind of discursive work in the context of late nineteenth-century concerns about Empire. For example, in the course of a collective prosecution of men involved in a weekly drag ball in Manchester in 1880, defense counsel stated,

> But when the police . . . asked them [the jury] to say that in this city—not in Turkey or Bulgaria or some places where these odious practices were common—but in Manchester, this vice—a vice so hateful that it was unnamable among Christians . . .[31]

This is in keeping with offhand remarks found throughout both scientific and popular representations of sodomy. Havelock Ellis, the foremost turn-of-the-century sexologist writing in English, used an orientalist construction to support his theorization of "born inverts" or true homosexuals, who, he stated, are rarely found among "the lower races."[32] The psychologically sophisticated—if abnormal—invert was a product of the highest civilization. Sodomitical practices were very common in tropical countries[33] and among Arabs,[34] but the happy-go-lucky deviant sex of the uncivilized had nothing to do with the anxieties about normality of educated, civilized men. Ellis seems to have agreed with the views presented by his friend, the homosexual classical scholar John Addington Symonds. Symonds rebuked the German homosexual activist and writer Carl Heinrich Ulrichs for paying insufficient attention to forms of sexual conduct attributable to uncivilized habits and oriental vices rather than to a deep, inborn, specifically European psychic identity. In Symonds's (and Ellis's) view, "Turks" (a rather expansive category in this time period) engaged in sodomy because they were depraved beings who pursued any and all sexual pleasures.[35]

The orientalist construction of sodomy did not restrict sodomy to the geographic Orient. Christopher Lane's overview of homosexuality in late Victorian English literature tells us that E. M. Forster's 1922 short story, "The Life to Come," featuring a missionary who valiantly suppresses his erotic interest in an African prince who cannot understand why homoerotic passion ought not to be fulfilled, is likely based on an 1886 conflict in the kingdom of Buganda. The king of Buganda "executed converts to Catholicism and protestantism in reaction to European evangelism and its fervent denunciation of homosexuality. Before this massacre, British missionaries had warned their religious converts that they would not tolerate 'crimes against nature' [i.e., sodomy] in the court of Mwanga." The execution—or massacre—of about one hundred Christian Ugandans was apparently well publicized.[36] Forster's presentation of the African prince as unable to understand the missionary's insistence that unnatural sexual desire must be repressed for the sake of "the life to come" is in keeping with the views about Turks and their happy-go-lucky attitude to sexual experimentation (and to life generally) reported by Havelock Ellis and others.

3. Abnormal Identities and the Common Law

A. SEXOLOGY

Havelock Ellis's interest in sharply separating primitive sexual freedom (including sodomy) from the kind of inborn sexual identity found among "true inverts"—the classic homosexuals and lesbians discovered or invented in the

1860s–1880s period—has already been mentioned. Alongside primitive men and Turkish potentates, English criminals in all-male prisons and public-school boys are also said to be prone to the vice of sodomy but not necessarily to the modern psychological abnormality of homosexuality. In keeping with the influential views of his German predecessor, Richard von Krafft-Ebing,[37] Ellis states as a proven fact that same-sex erotic experimentation in schools is "a spurious kind of homosexuality; it is merely the often precocious play of the normal instinct, and has not necessary relation to true sexual inversion."[38]

The case histories collected by Krafft-Ebing, Ellis, and a handful of other pioneers of the science of sexology (the texts used by Foucault to construct his famous argument about the sharp break between the sodomite and the modern homosexual)[39] generally feature middle-class professionals and upper-class men. In keeping with Freud's insistence on breaking with asylum mental medicine in favor of middle-class personalized therapy, Ellis underlines the importance of studying sexual abnormality, not among the convicts and asylum inmates who had furnished Victorian medicine with its subjects, but among the noninstitutionalized and the educated.

An interesting light is shed on the discontinuity between sodomite vice and homosexual identity by the fact (not yet noticed by commentators) that Ellis's lengthy and sophisticatedly introspective case histories feature many homosexuals or inverts who make a point of stating that they share the view that sodomy or buggery is a degrading practice. A couple of his twenty or so case histories involve men who admit to having liked buggery at least on occasion, but on the whole the inverts in question, while generally concluding their stories with a plea to have same-sex love (among men at any rate) recognized as a worthy form of love, disavow sodomites. Some of them explicitly state they abhor buggery. Others (perhaps due to being steeped in the Greek and Roman classics at school) do not share the Blackstonian revulsion but are still very concerned to differentiate the abnormal but nevertheless worthy invert from the vicious sodomite. Typical of this latter approach is the man whose autobiography is reported as case 6.[40]

> I have never had to do with actual pederasty, so called. My chief desire in love is bodily nearness or contact, as to sleep naked with a naked friend; the specially sexual, though urgent enough, seems a secondary matter. Pederasty, either active or passive, might seem in place to me with one I loved very devotedly and who also loved me to that degree—but I think not otherwise.... I cannot regard my sexual feelings as unnatural or abnormal, since they have disclosed themselves so perfectly naturally and spontaneously within me.

This kind of attempt to validate love among men, while relying to a greater or lesser extent on the discursive resources provided by a classical education, also relied, less consciously, on an implicit contrast between uncivilized Orientals and Englishmen. The Englishmen (and a few Germans and Americans) featured in Ellis's text scrutinized their inner selves in classic Protestant fashion and pursued same-sex love, including some sex if that was what their inner selves, their inborn nature, required.

Numerous scholars have told the story of sexology—in Britain and internationally—and it need not detain us here.[41] What has not been pointed out, however, is that the effort to construct the homosexual (the usually cultured born invert) as abnormal but nevertheless admirable may have unwittingly contributed to supporting the buggery law and its natural law focus on "nasty" bodily practices that are criminal by their very nature, not because of inappropriate situations. The Napoleonic code, for example, criminalized only indecent sexual acts committed in public, leaving the private sphere free. In England, however, buggery law continued the natural law logic, paying little attention to the public-private distinction or for that matter to consent. In addition, of course, after the Labouchere Amendment of 1885, virtually all same-sex acts were subject to prosecution even if committed in private.

The sexologists, in Britain and on the Continent, mainly supported law reforms that would favor the well-behaved, well-educated, nonsodomitical homosexuals who did not frequent parks and public toilets. Opposing paragraph 175 of the new German criminal code was a central focus of Continental sexology. While in Britain law reform efforts were less public, sexologists decried the gross indecency provisions.[42] Nevertheless, sexologists such as Ellis, while keen to legitimate the law-abiding and often artistic born invert, did nothing to challenge the buggery law. It seems that the Blackstonian specter of buggery as the unspeakable crime continued to haunt progressive sexologists—and even self-declared homosexuals.

B. THE HOMOSEXUAL APPEARS IN/TO ENGLISH LAW:
THE WOLFENDEN COMMITTEE

It was only in the 1960s that serious reforms of sex and morals laws were successfully undertaken in most common law countries—in England and Wales in 1967, in Canada in 1969, and in those American states that adopted the Model Penal Code's suggestion that sodomy laws be repealed, around 1970. For England and Canada, one of the main resources guiding and justifying this sweeping reform was the Wolfenden Committee, entrusted in 1954 with the task of modernizing prostitution laws and laws governing male same-sex conduct.

The Wolfenden Committee enthusiastically took up the medical and psychiatric discourse of the time, which suggested that inborn homosexuals could not help who they were and that it was useless and cruel to criminalize a condition that, while abnormal, was compatible with contributing to society. Wolfenden and his colleagues embraced the modernizing discourse of shining the light of science into every corner and speaking openly about every issue. Yet the Blackstonian injunction about delicacy persisted. As Les Moran shows, keen to protect the delicate eyes and ears of the committee's (female) secretarial staff, Wolfenden instituted a rhetorical practice that reenacted the very Victorian delicacy he claimed to eschew. In their internal memos, homosexuals were "Huntleys" while prostitutes were "Palmers"—euphemisms based on the popular brand of tea biscuits Huntley & Palmer.[43]

The Wolfenden Committee's report led eventually to the Sexual Offenses Act of 1967, which marks the first appearance of the word *homosexual* in English statute law. That the 1967 act marks the historic decriminalization of sex between two consenting adult men in private (lesbian sex had never been criminalized in English law, unlike in the United States) is well known. What is less well known, however, is that the category of buggery—based on a natural law logic ranking of natural and unnatural uses of the body—was not eliminated in favor of an enlightened scheme focusing on age, social harms, and privacy rights. The crime of buggery continued to exist.

Instead of poring over the act, it is useful to refer to Lord Diplock's authoritative interpretation of it, in a case appealed to the House of Lords. In 1982 Lord Diplock pointed out that in the 1967 act the traditional category of buggery had been split into four separate (and now exclusively male and homosexual) offenses. The first was the life offense of buggery—referring to buggery (by an adult man) with a boy under the age of sixteen. Neither the consent of the young person nor the location of the offense was relevant for this offense. The second kind of buggery was the ten-year offense. This referred to an adult man committing buggery with a male over sixteen without his consent. (That this was called buggery rather than rape only confirms the point made earlier about the peculiar English fascination with buggery). The third type of buggery was the five-year offense, where the accused is an adult male and the other party is a male between the ages of sixteen and twenty who did consent to the act. The final offense, which also attempts to govern modern homosexuality but mainly reproduces the old buggery law, targets homosexual erotic activity in parks and toilets. The two-year offense concerns two men over twenty-one who are engaging in consenting sex in nonprivate settings.[44]

The *Courtie* case suggests that at least some of what had fallen under the lesser category of gross indecency since 1885 would now be prosecuted as buggery: a peculiar result, given the Wolfenden discourse on the need to make English law more responsive to the inborn but well-behaved homosexual. Les Moran's comment is apposite:

> Lord Diplock's observations suggest that the juxtaposition of the decision to retain buggery and the decision to fragment the penalties applicable to it in the name of erasing its significance as a distinct offense has had a dramatic effect. Rather than producing the insignificance or disappearance of buggery, the reforms have been interpreted as an amplification of the presence of buggery in the law, creating four different offenses of buggery where only one existed prior to the 1967 Act.[45]

The Wolfenden Committee's expressed wish to make law flow along more modern lines of power and knowledge by relying on age categories, social harm, and the public-private distinction thus remained only very partially realized. Age, consent, and privacy were important indeed, but only in distinguishing between different modes of buggery.

C. RECONCILING LEGAL TRADITION AND MODERN DISCIPLINARY
KNOWLEDGES: THE U.S. SUPREME COURT INVENTS
"HOMOSEXUAL SODOMY"

The Foucaultian account of the formation of the homosexual identity in the late nineteenth century has been revised in significant ways by social historians documenting forms of erotic life that fit neither the sodomite nor the homosexual categories.[46] But the Foucaultian opposition of the act-based governance that made sodomy into a sin or crime and the identity-based governance that probed and constructed homosexual psychic identities is also challenged when one studies the development of law. That sodomy continued to exist and do a great deal of governing work in the United States until 2003 was not a fact that Foucault could have accounted for very easily.[47] And as we have seen, in England, the Wolfenden attempt to put aside the legacy of buggery in favor of a construction of homosexuals as an abnormal but not wholly criminal minority ended up, as it struggled with the straitjacket of legal parameters, proliferating buggery categories rather than ending them. In English-speaking legal systems, then, contrary to what Foucault predicted, natural law categories (buggery, sodomy) were not replaced by modern psychological categories (the invert, the homosexual).

In the United States, despite the huge success of the modern psychological category of homosexuality after World War II, sodomy continued to preoccupy legal actors to a remarkable extent for many decades. The *Bowers v. Hardwick* case of the 1980s was a crucial lightning rod, drawing into law both old Christian conceptualizations of unnatural sex and modern notions of homosexual identity, so a brief discussion of this case is in order.

By 1986, after several decades of conflicting moves—liberalizing moves repealing sodomy laws in some states and Moral Majority moves strengthening sodomy laws in other states—United States sodomy law was in a serious state of fragmentation. Some states, mainly in the north, had no sodomy laws whatever. Seven states had reformed their sodomy laws to make sodomy between men and women legal while still considering sodomy between two men criminal. In some states, by contrast, different-sex sodomy was made a misdemeanor, while same-sex sodomy remained a felony. In Georgia all sodomy was considered a felony, regardless of gender, until 1998.[48] The test case heard by the Supreme Court was an appeal concerning the constitutionality of the Georgia statute.

It needs to be noted that, despite the common use of the terms *gay* or *homosexual* to refer to those targeted by sodomy law, whether the men who are having sex are homosexuals does not matter in black-letter law (as pointed out by numerous gay commentators but also by Cass Sunstein[49]). Sailors or prison inmates defining themselves as heterosexual could be prosecuted for indulging in sex with their fellows as easily as homosexuals. But given the dominance of the modern homosexual identity in the post-1950s period, criminal justice actors thought of sodomy laws as targeting homosexuals, rather than men who have sex with men.[50] Moreover, on its part, the gay movement made sodomy laws into a central concern for homosexuals as a distinct group.

Reinforcing this "gaying" of sodomy laws, the Georgia prosecutors in the *Hardwick* case refused to allow a different-sex couple to join the constitutional challenge to sodomy laws as such initiated by Michael Hardwick. The married couple that claimed that they felt an imminent threat of prosecution whenever they engaged in a sexual activity they liked was found to have no standing, since the state of Georgia had an official policy to never prosecute different-sex couples for sodomy. In other jurisdictions (Canada, for example, or most of Europe), government prosecutors would be very unwilling to admit that they used a facially gender-neutral law to prosecute only homosexuals. However, in the United States acknowledging institutional homophobia by having an explicit policy to not prosecute different-sex couples engaging in anal sex worked as an argument in the statute's favor, since after the 1960s there was no public support for prosecuting married heterosexual couples for engaging in anal sex.

The charge of sodomy that was laid after the police claimed to have caught Hardwick and another man having sex became technically moot, when prosecutors decided not to pursue the sodomy charge laid by the police. Nevertheless, the appeals continued, in part because of the gay movement's politicization of this prosecution but also because the government of Georgia and the courts persisted in separating homosexuals from heterosexuals, even though the statute itself was strictly neutral as to gender.

Given that the statute was gender neutral, how was the gay-straight divide drawn, then? In the texts of the Supreme Court justices upholding the Georgia law, one sees no argument to the effect that sodomy among self-proclaimed gay people, or between men of any sexual orientation, causes more social harm than the same acts being enjoyed by different-sex couples and is thus deserving of a gender-specific prosecution policy. But what is more surprising is that the nonreproductivity of same-sex couples, considered as a crucial fact for legal purposes in Christian circles, also goes unmentioned. This latter omission is no doubt attributable to the Hardwick court's unwillingness to directly tackle existing precedents on abortion and contraception. However, the fact remains that the texts elaborated by the justices in the majority are peculiar in the context of philosophies of the criminal law. They speak about neither harm nor nature, which are historically the two main rationales for using the criminal law to govern sexuality. The justices speak only about history—a rather mythical history that pretends that old buggery statutes were actually aimed at modern homosexuals.[51]

The main point of all the majority judgments is that homosexuals are inherently outside the scope of privacy rights and cannot derive any comfort from the relevant decisions around contraception and abortion. Canadian Prime Minister Pierre Trudeau had famously said, when introducing the sweeping 1969 criminal code reforms, that "the state has no place in the bedrooms of the nation." In 1986 the U.S. Supreme Court found that the coercive power of the state need not be kept out of the bedrooms of people like Michael Hardwick—that is, people who are construed as "homosexuals" solely on the basis of having committed a certain act that some heterosexual couples also admit to having committed.

Yet the homosexuals haunting the *Hardwick* court are not merely defined by that particular act—they are not sodomites like their eighteenth-century predecessors. They are modern homosexuals, who effectively organize politically as a group and go to court to demand their rights—even when they are no longer actually being prosecuted, as happened in Hardwick's case. As law-review and media comment on the decision pointed out, moral conservatives on and off the Court were feeling, at the height of the so-called culture wars, that they had to fight to regain control over the media, universities, and other institutions, and they tended to portray gay people as powerful and well-organized enemies posing a real threat to American culture through their very existence. Nevertheless, the legal case at hand concerned sodomy—not homosexuality and not gay rights. It was only by forcibly marrying, so to speak, the old biblical category of sodomy to the modern homosexual identity that the court's majority was able to conclude that "the issue presented is whether the Federal Constitution confers a fundamental right upon homosexuals to engage in sodomy."[52]

A further confusion was caused by the fact, not mentioned by the Supreme Court, that Mr. Hardwick was enjoying oral sex, not anal sex, when the police barged into his apartment. This was technically sodomy in Georgia, but it is obviously not a specifically male or homosexual practice; the "gaying" of the case, however, swept these factual difficulties under the rug.

A few years later, the U.S. Supreme Court was faced with a very different kind of "gay" case. The voters of Colorado, spurred into ballot box action by the Family Values Coalition, had forced the state legislature to pass an amendment to the state's constitution that barred political activity designed to amend antidiscrimination ordinances and policies to include "sexual orientation."[53] The amendment (amendment 2) was badly drafted: it reenacted Jim Crow mechanisms for keeping African Americans politically disenfranchised even after they gained formal voting rights, but with homosexuals as the target group. The state legislature was and is free to deny gay and lesbian Americans the right to marry and various other rights, but denying a whole group equal participation in the political process was something that even conservative courts would be unlikely to uphold.

Nevertheless, there was much surprise when the Supreme Court of the U.S. not only struck down the amendment as unconstitutional but also went so far as to state that the amendment amounted to the exercise of animus against a minority. Legislative bodies are not obligated to grant legal protection to every group, but targeting a specific identifiable group (rather than a behavior) goes quite contrary to the grain of American post-Reconstruction law, the court stated.

What is most important from our point of view is not the interesting game of analogical reasoning comparing blacks and gays that the case stimulated but rather the fact that the decision (*Romer v. Evans*)[54] made no mention at all of *Bowers v. Hardwick*.[55] Many commentators found this omission inexplicable; but this omission can be seen as underlining the fact that there is no single *homosexual* of or in law in general—there are many different sexualized entities and issues coexisting in a legal universe that is in turn highly fragmented. The civil rights logic of the voting-rights cases that courts had to reread when ruling on amendment 2's constitutionality is, in black-letter terms, quite irrelevant to the criminal law. Given the sharp separation between U.S. law on voting and other political rights, on the one hand, and the criminal law, on the other, it is not paradoxical that sodomy laws could continue to be enforced even as American gays and lesbians were told that the state, while not granting them equal rights, would refrain from persecuting them—other than with sodomy laws.

It was the leading natural law thinker on the court, Justice Antonin Scalia, who refused to countenance the law's ability to do different things with different knowledges. As far as he was concerned, if *Bowers v. Hardwick* proclaimed that homosexual sodomy is evil, it follows logically that there is nothing objectionable about hating those who commit this evil, namely, homosexuals: "Of course it is our moral heritage that one should not hate any human being or class of human beings. But I had thought that one could consider certain conduct reprehensible—murder, for example, or polygamy, or cruelty to animals—and could exhibit even 'animus' toward such conduct."[56]

Scalia was demanding a consistency that is simply not historically present, in U.S. law or in law in general. He writes as if *Romer v. Evans* were a statement declaring, "Gay people are okay." However, this is not so. One of the key features of human rights law is that it can proceed quite nicely without making ontological or moral claims about identifiable groups. In earlier work, I have documented that whether most gay people are gay by nature or gay by choice is not a question that human rights tribunals or courts are at all keen to debate.[57] Neither do courts need to ask if gays are morally worthy, since banning discrimination does not entail praising the group in question. As the Supreme Court accurately noted in the Colorado *Romer* case, antidiscrimination law merely prohibits the state from facilitating animus against minority groups; nothing requires states to actually value minority cultures. While human rights law often does serve to actually promote multiculturalism, this happens only if civil-society groups or politicians choose to use it in this manner. At the level of strictly legal effects, human rights law works with a very thin conception of subjectivity and of social identity that, in the case of homosexuals, can effectively bracket both moral discourses about sodomy as unnatural and psychological discourses about sexual identity.

4. *The Logic of Human Rights and the End of American Sodomy: A Case of Conflict of Laws*

The study of conflict of laws presupposes that the conflicts worth studying are those among jurisdictions. U.S. law students who take a conflicts class may thus ponder the fate of a Massachusetts married lesbian couple who move to Florida, a state that refuses to recognize same-sex marriages performed in other jurisdictions. What they will not have an opportunity to formally study, however, is what happens when people who stay put nevertheless become subject to contradictory rules because of conflicts between different juridical fields.[58] Law's habit of considering only certain authorized legal antecedents (the relevant line of cases) when ruling on a specific situation often acts as the broom in this sort of situation. A notable sweeping-under-the-carpet operation is found in the *Romer v. Evans*[59] decision, which avoids reconciling the continuing criminalization of gay male sex with the suddenly felt need to ensure that gay Americans are not denied access to the political process.

This conflict of laws at the Supreme Court is by no means the only one affecting gays and lesbians, however. In some liberal strongholds gays and lesbians, now protected by municipal ordinances and by private-company benefits plans recognizing same-sex couples, were by the late 1990s insisting on being granted the right to marry and the right to have civil partnerships recognized if marriage proved impossible. Eventually civil unions would be allowed in several states, including California and Vermont; same-sex marriage came to a bad end in Hawaii,[60] but Massachusetts would defy the prevailing Supreme Court moralism to the extent of legalizing marriage in 2003 (*Goodridge v. Department of Public Health*).

The political action that brought about civil unions and proposals for same-sex marriage caused a huge backlash among the well-organized forces of moral conservatism, who succeeded in passing a spate of largely symbolic backlash statutes driven by nothing but the very animosity that *Romer* supposedly declared unconstitutional: Defense of Marriage acts.[61] But as same-sex marriage—its specter much more than its reality—came to dominate the legal and political discourses around *sexual orientation* and *homosexuals*, a case from Texas suddenly shifted attention from the novel and still fuzzy image of the happily married same-sex couple back to the ancient legal terrain of sodomy law.

Unlike the facially gender-neutral Georgia statute at issue in *Bowers*, the Texas statute prohibited only homosexual sodomy. In the light of *Romer*, this selectivity appeared as a flaw rather than as a constitutional virtue. To make a long story very short, the Supreme Court, despite being full of moral conservatives, decided that the statute was unconstitutional (*Lawrence v. Texas*).[62] The court explicitly ridiculed the *Bowers* court's version of "millennia of moral teaching." Relying on an amicus brief by historians of sexuality, the court found that the United States is remarkably lacking in historic laws against homosexuals; at the time the Constitution was written, it targeted nonprocreative sex, not homosexuals. History and tradition were thus sidelined to make room for an argument that did not quite recognize homosexual privacy rights (perhaps because of internal disagreements about abortion rights) but that, sidelining privacy, concluded that the Constitution's promise of "liberty" makes laws such as the Texas sodomy statute unconstitutional.

The *Lawrence v. Texas* decision put an end to the centuries-old tradition focused on that sin or crime that must not be named among Christians. In putting an end to this tradition, however, the judgment paradoxically enacts the delicacy of law even better than its predecessors do. It speaks about sodomy statutes and sodomy prosecutions—but remains wholly silent about the conduct targeted by law. "The conduct referenced in *Bowers*" is the phrase chosen. By referring meaning wholly to an earlier (and quite incoherent) legal text, this curiously empty phrase manages to not name the crime in question even better than Blackstone ever did. Thus, the long-standing semantic troubles caused by law's paradoxical relationship to speech about buggery are not so much resolved here as reenacted. The court admits it doesn't really know how to name the activity criminalized by sodomy statutes—is it gay sex? Is it anal sex among men? Is it any kind of anal sex? And what about oral sex? The headaches are endless, and so the court primly writes, "the conduct referred to in Bowers."

The decision, however, is not lacking in passion and feeling. Unable to repeat, in the context of a secular twenty-first-century society, Blackstone's invective against sodomites, but equally unable to truly put Blackstone behind it and embrace gay pride discourse, the court chooses to wax eloquent about something else altogether, namely, liberty. The decision's passionate discourse about American liberty has the effect of quietly averting law's gaze completely from the body.

A. FROM SODOMITES TO VICTIMS OF CRIME

While few jurisdictions have followed Canada's lead in explicitly recognizing (in a 1996 sentencing statute) homophobia as an aggravating factor in violent crimes, nevertheless the identity "victim of hate crime" is readily available to gays and lesbians throughout Europe and North America.[63] Without entering into the details of the category of hate crime and its application to gay bashing, a short reflection on this phenomenon will serve as the conclusion to the chapter.

Many observers note that with the decline of the welfare state and the general lack of trust in state authorities characteristic of neoliberal mentalities, citizenship is no longer exercised in the name of state-building projects. Rather, citizenship is exercised in the more defensive guise of speaking up as victims of crime, potential or actual.⁶⁴ It is perhaps then not surprising that gay and lesbian activism in English-speaking countries affected by such neoliberal trends—and having had the example of women's groups advocating for harsher sentences for male abusers—has spent much time and energy on gay-bashing and homophobic harassment. Without entering into the debates about whether focusing on hate crimes necessarily implies collaborating with right-wing law-and-order agendas, here it will simply be noted that the existence of a broad-based campaign about homophobic hate crime illustrates a larger process, namely, the amazing flexibility of legal consciousness and legal mechanisms. The hate-crime debates show that even before they became fully decriminalized, the groups that the common law always regarded as potential criminals could suddenly audit for the role of victims of crime. The contemporary hate-crime struggles normalize and desexualize gay people. As, drawing on other experiences, it comes to be said that, like blacks, Asians, and women, gay people are often victims of hate, gay people lose their sexual rebel aura and come to be seen as innocent citizens subject to cultural prejudices.⁶⁵ This construction completely reverses the traditional construction of sodomites and homosexuals as defined by their passions and desires. In the hate-crime scenario, the passion is all on the side of the (homophobic) offender. The gay person is merely a victim, and in criminal law discourse generally, victims have no passions other than fear (and sometimes revenge).

Fear of crime, then, that key contemporary specter uniting neoliberals and neoconservatives, now comes to play a constitutive role in the construction of the gay citizen, as Les Moran and Bev Skeggs have recently shown, in an empirical study of gay experiences and feelings about urban space and safety.⁶⁶ The implications of this for future constructions of sexual minorities are not yet apparent. One can wonder, however, whether the long tradition of defiant sexual desire and subversive attitudes toward morality and toward conventional rules about using public space that sodomites, homosexuals, and modern gays share will manage to survive in the face of this new respectability. This is even more relevant as the victim-of-crime subjectivity comes to be increasingly aided and abetted by the other great source of respectable citizenship in the postwelfare neoliberal era: marriage.

The sexual rebels who pioneered gay male subjectivity, from Oscar Wilde to Jean Genet—and for that matter Michel Foucault—would not believe their eyes if they were to rise from the grave to read today's newspaper accounts of heavier sentences for homophobic offenders and celebrations of gay marriages. Legal history is unpredictable indeed.

Notes

1. Mariana Valverde, "'Which Side Are You On?': Uses of the Everyday in Sociolegal Scholarship," *Political and Legal Anthropological Review* 26 (2003): 86–98.
2. E.g., Nikolas Rose, *Inventing Ourselves* (Cambridge: Cambridge Univ. Press, 1996).
3. E.g., Lauren Berlant, *The Queen of America Goes to Washington: Essays on Sex and Citizenship* (Durham, N.C.: Duke Univ. Press, 1997).
4. E.g., Philip Corrigan and Derek Sayer, *The Great Arch: English State Formation as Cultural Revolution* (Oxford: Blackwell, 1985).
5. Mariana Valverde, *Law's Dream of a Common Knowledge* (Princeton, N.J.: Princeton Univ. Press, 2003), chaps. 4 and 5.
6. Cf. Paul Veyne, "Foucault Revolutionizes History," in *Foucault and His Interlocutors*, Arnold Ira Davidson, ed. (Chicago: Univ. of Chicago Press, 1997).
7. David Halperin, *How to Do the History of Homosexuality* (Chicago: Univ. of Chicago Press, 2002).
8. Robert Castel, "'Problematization' as a Mode of Reading History," in *Foucault and the Writing of History*, Jan Ellen Goldstein, ed. (Oxford: Blackwell, 1994); Veyne, "Foucault Revolutionizes History"; Rose, *Inventing Ourselves*; Nikolas Rose, *Powers of Freedom: Reframing Political Thought* (Cambridge: Cambridge Univ. Press, 1999); Valverde, *Law's Dream*.
9. The history of the regulation of female-female eroticism and sex has only been very partially explored—and the criminal law is not a good site for these explorations, since even in jurisdictions that (unlike England and Wales) criminalized lesbian relations, neither law enforcement nor cultural-political authorities concerned with law were ever seriously worried about such relations. Legal arenas are thus not very likely to prove fruitful research sites for lesbian history projects. Indeed, a major discontinuity between our present and the past is that today sexual orientation, a gender-neutral liberal category, erases distinctions between men and women quite radically, whereas in the past the gender distinction was paramount.
10. Janet Halley, *Don't: A Reader's Guide to the Military's Antigay Policy* (Durham, N.C.: Duke Univ. Press, 1997).
11. Valverde, *Law's Dream*.
12. Judith Butler, *Excitable Speech: A Politics of the Performative* (New York: Routledge, 1997).
13. Cf. Halley, *Don't*.
14. Leslie Moran, *The Homosexual(Ity) of Law* (London: Routledge, 1996), p. 33.
15. William Blackstone, *Commentaries on the Laws of England*, vol. 4 (Oxford: Clarenden Press, 1769), chap. 15, pp. 215–216.
16. *R. v. Rowed*, 1842, quoted in Moran, *Homosexual(Ity)*, p. 38.
17. Writing indictments for sodomy was a fraught task. H. G. Cocks's detailed study of criminal records comments that "indictments for sodomy were marked 'misdemenaour', 'b——y', or 'assault with intent etc', as though even the clerks could not bring themselves to refer to the acts by name. Proceedings of these trials were not recorded in

the bound volumes produced by the Central Criminal Courts which covered all other criminal trials in exhaustive detail." H. G. Cocks, *Nameless Offenses: Homosexual Desire in the Nineteenth Century* (London: I. B. Tauris, 2003), p. 79.

18. Ibid., pp. 51, 53.

19. Angus McLaren, *Sexual Blackmail* (Cambridge, Mass.: Harvard Univ. Press, 2002), p. 9.

20. Ibid., p. 11.

21. Judith Walkowitz, *Prostitution and Victorian Society* (Cambridge: Cambridge Univ. Press, 1980); Jeffrey Weeks, *Sex, Politics and Society: The Regulation of Sexuality since 1800* (London: Longman, 1989).

22. Richard Ellman, *Oscar Wilde* (New York: Viking, 1987).

23. Cocks, *Nameless Offenses*, pp. 25–30.

24. Steven Maynard, "'Through a Hole in the Lavatory Wall': Homosexual Subcultures, Police Surveillance, and the Dialectics of Discovery: Toronto 1880–1930," *Journal of the History of Sexuality* 5 (1994): 207–242; Steven Maynard, "Horrible Temptations: Sex, Men, and Working-Class Male Youth in Urban Ontario, 1890–1935," *Canadian Historical Review* 78 (1997): 191–235; David Kimmel and Daniel Robinson, "Sex, Crime, Pathology: Homosexuality and Criminal Code Reform in Canada, 1949–1969," *Canadian Journal of Law and Society* 16, no. 1 (2001): 147–165.

25. George Chauncey, *Gay New York: Gender, Urban Culture, and the Making of the Gay Male World, 1890–1940* (New York: Basic Books, 1994).

26. William Eskridge, *Gaylaw: Challenging the Apartheid of the Closet* (Cambridge, Mass.: Harvard Univ. Press, 1999), p. 43.

27. See appendix C2, reported sodomy cases, in Eskridge, *Gaylaw*, p. 375.

28. Ibid., p. 31.

29. See www.sodomylaws.org.

30. Estelle Freedman, "'Uncontrolled Desires': The Response to the Sexual Psychopath, 1920–1960," in *Passion and Power: Sexuality in History*, Kathy Peiss, Christina Simmons, and Robert A. Padgug, eds. (Philadelphia: Temple Univ. Press, 1989), pp. 199–225.

31. Cocks, *Nameless Offenses*, p. 72.

32. Havelock Ellis and John Addington Symonds, *Sexual Inversion* (London: Wilson & Macmillan, 1897).

33. Ibid., p. 22, citing Sir Richard Burton.

34. Ibid., p. 81.

35. Ibid., p. 265.

36. Lane, 1995, pp. 161–162.

37. Richard von Krafft-Ebing, *Psychopathia Sexualis: With Especial Reference to the Antipathic Sexual Instinct, translated from the 12th German Ed.* (New York, Scarborough/Stein & Day: 1965).

38. Ellis and Symonds, *Sexual Inversion*, p. 82.

39. Michel Foucault, *The History of Sexuality*, vol. 1, *An Introduction* (New York: Vintage, 1980).

40. Ellis and Symonds, *Sexual Inversion*, pp. 46–47.
41. Weeks, *Sex, Politics and Society*; Lucy Bland, *Banishing the Beast: Sexuality and the Early Feminists* (London: New Press, 1995); John D'Emilio and Estelle Freedman, *Intimate Matters: A History of Sexuality in America* (New York: Harper & Row, 1988).
42. Weeks, *Sex, Politics and Society*.
43. Moran, *Homosexual(Ity)*, p. 92.
44. *Courtie*, 1984, cited in Moran, *Homosexual(Ity)*.
45. Moran, *Homosexual(Ity)*, p. 30.
46. Chauncey, *Gay New York*; Halperin, *How to Do the History of Homosexuality*.
47. Nevertheless, recent evidence does not invalidate Foucault's analysis. As David Halperin wisely reminds us, Foucault's famous contrast between acts of sodomy and homosexual identity did not claim that this contrast amounted to a real-life revolution that overthrows the old regime. "Such a misreading of Foucault can be constructed only by setting aside, and then forgetting, the decisive qualifying phrase with which his famous pronouncement opens: 'As defined by the ancient civil or canon codes', Foucault begins, 'sodomy was a category of forbidden acts.' . . . Foucault is speaking about discursive and institutional practices, not about what people really did in bed." *How to Do the History of Homosexuality*, p. 29. We can add, or what police, judges, and prosecutors did in their policing work.
48. Eskridge, *Gaylaw*; Janet Halley, "Reasoning about Sodomy: Act and Identity in and after *Bowers v. Hardwick*," *Virginia Law Review* 79 (1993): 1721–1804; www.sodomylaws.org.
49. Cass Sunstein, "Sexual Orientation and the Constitution: A Note on the Relationship between Due Process and Equal Protection," *University of Chicago Law Review* 55 (1988): 1161–1179.
50. The nonmedical, purely behaviorist category of men who have sex with men was featured in the Kinsey studies of the 1950s. But it seems to have fallen into disuse, overshadowed by the more powerful figure of the homosexual, until in the late 1980s public health and epidemiological professionals, for purposes of AIDS research and prevention, reinvented the man who has sex with men.
51. Eskridge, *Gaylaw*, pp. 149–160; Markus Dubber, "Homosexual Privacy Rights before the United States Supreme Court and the European Court of Human Rights: A Comparison of Methodologies," *Stanford Journal of International Law* 27 (1990/1991): 189–214; Halley, "Reasoning about Sodomy"; Kendall Thomas, "The Eclipse of Reason: A Rhetorical Reading of *Bowers v. Hardwick*," *Virginia Law Review* 79 (1993): 1805–1832.
52. *Bowers v. Hardwick*, 478 U.S. 186, 190 (1986).
53. Evan Gerstmann, *The Constitutional Underclass: Gays, Lesbians, and the Failure of Class-Based Equal Protection* (Chicago: Univ. of Chicago Press, 1993).
54. 517 U.S. 620 (1996).
55. 478 U.S. 186 (1986).
56. 517 U.S. at 636.
57. See Valverde, *Law's Dream*, chap. 5.

58. Pierre Bourdieu's concept of *juridical field*, has been used by many sociolegal scholars to advantage, but in my view we need to recognize that legal networks contain a large number of juridical fields with distinct internal logics. Pierre Bourdieu, "The Force of Law: Toward a Sociology of the Juridical Field," *Hastings Law Journal* 38 (1987): 805–853. The boundaries of juridical fields, I would argue, are not necessarily coterminous with those of established areas of law, but up to a point, black-letter distinctions (such as criminal vs. civil) do form fields.

59. 517 U.S. 620 (1996).

60. Jonathan Goldberg-Hiller, *The Limits to Union: Same-Sex Marriage and the Politics of Civil Rights* (Ann Arbor: Univ. of Michigan Press, 2002).

61. Evan Gerstmann, *Same-Sex Marriage and the Constitution* (Cambridge: Cambridge Univ. Press, 2003).

62. *Lawrence v. Texas*, 539 U.S. 558 (2003).

63. Leslie Moran and Bev Skeggs, *Sexuality and the Politics of Violence and Safety* (London: Routledge, 2004).

64. Jonathan Simon, "Megan's Law: Crime and Democracy in Late Modern America," *Law and Social Inquiry* 25, no. 4 (2000): 1111–1150; Markus D. Dubber, *Victims in the War on Crime* (New York: New York Univ. Press, 2004); Berlant, *Queen of America*.

65. Cf. Jonathan Goldberg, ed., *Reclaiming Sodom* (New York: Routledge, 1994).

66. Moran and Skeggs, *Sexuality*.

TEN

Criminal Law at a Fault Line of Imperial Authority
Interracial Homicide Trials in British India

MARTIN WIENER

[T]he British Power in India is like a vast bridge over which an enormous multitude of human beings are passing, and will (I trust) for ages to come continue to pass, from a dreary land, in which brute violence in its roughest form had worked its will for centuries—a land of cruel wars, ghastly superstitions, wasting plague and famine—on their way to a country of which, not being a prophet, I will not try to draw a picture, but which is at least orderly, peaceful, and industrious, and which for aught we know to the contrary, may be the cradle of changes comparable to those which have formed the imperishable legacy to mankind of the Roman Empire. The bridge was not built without desperate struggles and costly sacrifices. *Strike away either of its piers and it will fall*, and what are they? *One of its piers is military power: the other is justice*, by which I mean a firm and constant determination on the part of the English to promote impartially and by all lawful means, what they (the English) regard as the lasting good of the natives of India. Neither force nor justice will suffice by itself. (emphasis added)

—JAMES FITZJAMES STEPHEN, 1878

As the sociocultural history of law, particularly of criminal law, has rapidly developed in recent years, so also of course has the history of colonialism. This chapter addresses the area in which these two fields of study intersect— the place of criminal law in the history of British colonialism, or it might with equal reason be put, the place of colonialism in the larger history of British criminal law. Until recently, the two histories had little to do with one another. The only kind of law thought relevant to empire was constitutional, and the imperial dimension was simply absent in even the most intellectually innovative histories of criminal justice (such as E. P. Thompson's *Whigs and Hunters* or David Garland's *Punishment and Welfare*—or indeed, my own writings[1]), which paid no attention to "Greater Britain." Fortunately, however, that mutual neglect is now ending, as several of the contributions to this volume, including this chapter, illustrate.[2]

What has most struck this student of criminal justice history within the British Isles about imperial criminal law in practice has been its tense and fractured character. Originating in one environment, but applied (unlike civil law) without fundamental change to quite different environments, it has had from the first a dual nature, as an essential part of the mechanism of domination of non-British peoples and at the same time as a potential resource for those being dominated.[3] As the legal anthropologist John Comaroff has observed, colonial law in action was "dialectical." He explained its "bipolarity" as shaped by

> an ontological contradiction at the very core of nineteenth-century colonialism. On one hand, colonization was rationalized (in both senses of that term) by imperial Europe in the name of a humane, enlightened universalism that promised, under the sign of its civilizing mission, to usher "non-Europeans" into the "body of corporate nations," into citizenship of the modern world. On the other, it justified itself by sustaining the premodernity of "overseas subjects," whom it tribalized, ethnicized, and racialized, constantly deferring the erasure of precisely those differences that were held to make the difference between colonizer and colonized, white and black.[4]

Moreover, there was yet another fracture in colonial law—the way it could highlight and even stimulate conflict, not just between colonizers and colonized, but among the colonizers themselves—its role in what Fred Cooper and Ann Stoler have called the "tensions of empire."[5] Scholars have referred to this fracturing role but they have not yet explored it. In particular, criminal trials of Europeans for killing natives and of natives for killing Europeans brought some of these tensions to a head; they were in this case inevitably also political trials,[6] shaped by clashing interests and clashing ideologies of social order. A closer examination of such trials may advance our understanding of both the "tensions of empire" and the modern history of British criminal justice.

I

At two in the morning on November 7, 1889, four soldiers of the East Kent regiment stationed at Dum Dum, then a few miles outside Calcutta, restricted by regulations in their ability to buy liquor from nearby stores, set out in search of toddy, an Indian alcoholic drink. Breaking into a shop, they proceeded to drink up what they found and went on in search of more. Rousing a villager, who was sleeping on his veranda, they demanded toddy. They dragged him into a nearby ditch, and when he continued to insist that he had none, one of them shot him. The villager crawled back to his house, where he died that night.

This incident, by no means without precedent in British India, eventually led to a murder trial. So did a second, somewhat reversed, killing several years later in Assam, at the time part of the province of Bengal, in which seven Indian workers were charged with the murder of a British tea planter. Both cases produced convictions that were then reversed on appeal. Both cases caused trouble for the government, reaching as far as Parliament. They disrupted the smooth everyday operation of British rule, for they threw into public question the ideology that provided the strongest justification for British domination—the claim that Britain had brought to India the rule of law. One basic characteristic of such rule was held to be the principle that the law treated all British subjects equally. When this ideology collided in the courtroom with the actual inequality between "Europeans" and "natives," it created a problem for imperial rule. Such events put the administrators of law under great pressure, opened up fissures in the white ruling class, and thereby offer valuable illumination into the actual workings of law in the British Empire.

India was the heart of the British Empire, and Bengal was the heart of India—the first province to be conquered, the most populous, and the home of the viceroy. Thus, it was the most desirable posting, staffed with the most successful officials and judges. The central government of India, based in Calcutta, was guaranteed to pay attention to what happened in Bengal. These cases took place in 1890 and 1893, when that government was at the height of its power. The Mutiny of 1857 was safely in the past, and the stirrings of mass nationalism had yet to emerge. Here, even at the center of the Empire, even at the peak of its sway, these two legal cases demonstrated, in different ways, the *limits* on this power—limits vis-à-vis two different populations: the Europeans living in India, including members of its own forces, and the vastly larger population of native Indians.

That two of the four Dum Dum soldiers were arrested over a month later was somewhat surprising, since the day after the killing an Indian witness had been unable (or unwilling) to identify them in a regimental lineup, and the matter seemed closed. However, the widespread press reports were highly embarrassing, and it was observed in the Indian press that both the lieutenant governor of Bengal and the viceroy, Lord Lansdowne, "took a personal interest" in the case.[7] On orders from above, the local British magistrate continued to investigate. He identified the culprits and received authorization to offer pardons to two, who had not taken part in the killing, on condition they give full evidence in court. Armed with their statements, he committed the other two to the sessions of the Calcutta High Court.

They were tried in February 1890, one for the murder and the other for abetting. By law, Europeans were guaranteed a jury with a European majority, and such a jury—in this case indeed made up of eight European and one Indian gentlemen—acquitted the second but somewhat unexpectedly convicted the first, an Irishman, Thomas O'Hara, of murder, after the judge summed up strongly against him. Murder was a crime that in British India as in Britain itself then carried only one penalty, that of death.[8] The verdict created a public sensation among both Indians and the European community. The military authorities together with some friends of O'Hara got the opinion of the advocate-general of Bengal that the trial judge had committed some serious procedural errors. The most important objection was that he had allowed the jury to consider the evidence of a third soldier without establishing whether he was legally an accomplice. A rehearing was ordered before the full bench of the High Court, which found that indeed the judge should have declared the witness an accomplice, whose testimony should require further corroboration. It then quashed O'Hara's conviction. Indians demanded a new trial, but it was not called. Instead, a military court tried all four soldiers for breach of regimental law and imposed minor punishments.

Most of the Anglo-Indian press (that is, the press produced and read by the European residents in India) denounced the prisoners. The *Englishman*, the leading such paper in Bengal, went on to editorialize that "we realize that the Full Bench acted properly [in quashing O'Hara's conviction], but regret that a technical error by the trial judge should have allowed O'Hara to escape"; a correspondent even suggested that the men should at least still be tried for theft.[9] The paper, however, like others in the European community, passed over the possibility of a new murder trial. The Indian press expressed not regret but outrage. O'Hara, *Navavibhakar Sadharani* had noted after his conviction, had "shot down an innocent man like a dog." With the quashing of his conviction, "all natives, high and low," *Sahachar* declared, "have ceased to feel themselves safe in the presence of Europeans." *Al Punch* published a cartoon in which the sword of Justice and the serpent of unlawful murder with a soldier's hat on its head are weighed in a balance, and the serpent is found turning the scale. The female figure of Justice is pale and worn out.[10] Another Indian paper prophesied that "if the sympathies of the people of India are ever alienated from English rule, the alienation will be due to this very circumstance" of belief in judicial racial bias.[11]

Even the self-consciously moderate English-language *Hindoo Patriot* complained that Indians could hardly help but "be confirmed in the ignorant conviction that Europeans are above the law and British-born subjects may murder 'black bastards' with impunity." It resisted this conclusion: "We feel persuaded," it went on, "that Lord Lansdowne will not allow the case to rest where it does."[12] But he did. Complaints reached Britain, and censorious accounts published in the London press led to a question in the House of Commons. Even then, officials responded that no one could interfere with the normal course of the law.[13] However, when the issue resurfaced in Britain a few months later, leading to a threat to bring it up in the House of Lords, the viceroy's office ordered the victim's widow to be given a generous pension; there the matter ended.[14]

II

Three years later, on the night of April 11, 1893, the house of a tea planter near Balladhun, Assam, was broken into, some money was taken, and the planter and his watchman were murdered. Immediately there was an intense search for culprits—a reward was posted and pardons offered to participants who had not actually committed murder to come forward with information.[15] Nonetheless, the investigation went frustratingly slowly, while the Anglo-Indian press loudly complained. Finally, on June 27 a suspect who had gone into hiding, a coolie named Sajow, was arrested and after five days in police custody "confessed." In consequence, several other arrests occurred and another confession was obtained. Because of these, and almost nothing else, the district magistrate committed seven men for trial. A British sessions judge and a panel of assessors—no jury, as was the prescribed procedure for natives charged with felonies—tried them in September. Although the assessors unanimously acquitted all the men, the judge, not bound by their decision, found four guilty of murder and sentenced them to death, and three guilty of aiding and sentenced them to transportation to the Andaman Islands for life. An Indian barrister organized their appeal without charge, and an Anglo-Indian one argued their case strenuously in December in a weeklong hearing (attended by an inspector of police sent by the Assam government) before a panel of two judges of the Calcutta High Court (one an Indian Muslim). The High Court judges reversed the convictions, ordering all the men freed. In their ruling, they found a host of irregularities at every stage and called for an investigation into the behavior of police, magistrate, and sessions judge. They did not hide their belief that the Indian police, offered large rewards by the authorities, had coerced confessions, and the magistrate and judge had not only ignored those abuses but had acted more as prosecutors than as judicial officials.

This ruling created a double sensation, at the overturning of the convictions and at the judges' indictment of the administration of local justice. It would appear that one Indian newspaper put it accurately when it concluded that "to please the tea planters, the Assam authorities had ordered the police to find out the murderers, but failing to lay their hands on the real culprits... took steps to send four innocent men to the gallows and three innocent men to the Andamans for life."[16] Reports reached Britain, questions were asked in Parliament, and the India Office in response prodded the government of India to conduct the investigation called for by the High Court judges. On the basis of statements from the district police commissioner, the chief commissioner, the district magistrate, and the sessions judge, the government formally reprimanded the magistrate and judge for mistakes and "unwise" actions but defended them to the India Office as merely careless and inexperienced but not ill-intentioned. The defendants stayed free, the murders were never solved, the officials all kept their jobs, and the India Office dropped the matter.[17]

III

What do these two criminal justice stories signify about the rule of law in India under the British? I suggest that they underline the inadequacy of both of the two most familiar, apparently opposed, but in fact complementary, interpretive frameworks that have successively shaped the historiography of the Raj. First, that the law was a beneficial instrument whose use gradually empowered Indians, and second, a viewpoint increasingly dominant since the end of the Empire, that on the contrary the law was simply an instrument of British colonial-racial oppression. Rather, these events can best be understood through a third framework, that of the inner tensions generated by Empire, of the divergences, principled and practical, inherent and contingent, *within* British colonial rule and also within the supposed community of its Indian critics. This third narrative does not replace either of the first two (each of which has some truth) but adds a necessary further dimension to an otherwise overly simple dichotomy. This chapter is limited to bringing out some of the tensions on the side of the British rulers.

The single most important exemplar of the claimed beneficence of the British Empire was its system of laws. By the nineteenth century there was genuine and general pride in spreading the benefits of English law around the world. James Fitzjames Stephen evidenced this pride in the observations that open this chapter, as well as in innumerable less eloquent remarks by a multitude of British writers and speakers. Perhaps the best-known principle of that law was the equality of individuals—that all were equally subject to its strictures and that all could equally claim its protection. The Empire established this as early as 1774, when in the case of *Campbell v. Hall* Lord Mansfield declared that "an Englishman in Ireland, Minorca or the Plantations has no privilege distinct from the natives." Yet the most basic principle implicitly undergirding empire was *in*equality—a necessary inequality of power between the British conquerors and the subject populations they had conquered. As colonies of white settlement gained self-government, this distinction between conquerors and conquered gradually merged with that between white and colored races.

Thus, for nearly all the span of British rule in India (and elsewhere through the Empire), two modes of governing were in contestation: a rule of conquest and a rule of law, or, from another angle, a standard of national and racial hier-archy and one of individual rights and legal equality. Although in the end the latter gained the upper hand, it never, up until Independence, succeeded in vanquishing the former. Each had its moments of predominance. Together, they defined the special character of the Raj. This conflict of principle was enacted particularly clearly through the legal system, in the process serving to focus four forms of practical tensions with the Raj: first, between civil and military authorities; second, between officials and nonofficial Europeans (planters, businessmen, and others); third, between lower and higher officials; and fourth, between the executive and the judicial branches of officialdom. In this way, intense personal and institutional conflicts filled the more abstract clash of principles with human content.

British rule, as Stephen's statement implied, required both military and civilian modes of authority; however, these did not mesh very comfortably.[18] A substantial body of European troops was necessary to underpin the rule of law but was at the same time a permanent threat to it. For one thing, soldiers were a perennial source of disorder and, in particular, of uncontrolled violence directed at Indians. Out of the 199 cases of Europeans attacking natives officially reported in 1901, members of the army committed 146.[19] Here class and ethnic prejudice reinforced the concerns of civilian officials: European soldiers were drawn from the lower classes at home, and a disproportionate (if diminishing) number of them were Irish, like O'Hara.[20] Such men were not unlikely back in the United Kingdom to become criminal problems; in India, their behavior created political problems. Among soldiers, treated with little respect by their white superiors, the racism common to Europeans in India was present in an exaggerated form, enhanced by a sense of corporate solidarity, and not offset by the restraints of civilian or official life. These men, armed and frequently drunk (despite official efforts to restrict sales of liquor), were a continuing menace to public security and to political relations with the vast Indian population, without whose acquiescence British rule could hardly be sustained.[21]

Moreover, their superiors resisted their surrender to civilian authority. Except for felonies committed within 120 miles of a presidency town (Calcutta, Bombay, or Madras), the general practice was to try soldiers by courts-martial. Such military courts could be severe: In 1868, for instance, a corporal and a private were found guilty by court-martial of striking and wounding a Bengali from whom they stole nearly two thousand rupees. The corporal received five years' penal servitude; the private, four years'.[22] More frequently, however, out of concern for morale in the ranks, military authorities would overlook minor instances of abuse of Indians that had not become public issues.[23] Clashes with civilian authority over such cases were common: outside these towns, magistrates retained the right to take up any unfelonious case at their discretion, and sometimes did. In 1869 one Private Flynn knocked out a government *chaprassi* and was convicted of assault and fined by the justice of the peace at Landour, who ordered the recalcitrant commanding officer to imprison him unless the fine was paid. The commander-in-chief of Bengal appealed to the provincial government, asking that, whatever the strictly legal position was, magistrates be instructed to conform to the usual practice of regarding breaches of the peace committed by soldiers as prejudicial to military discipline and hence matters for commanding officers or courts-martial. While the government rejected this appeal, it was clear from the replies of senior officials that they believed punishment by commanding officers to be best, in part because of the lack of nonmilitary prisons suitable for Europeans.[24]

Even within the jurisdictional area of the presidency towns, the army tended to be as protective of its authority over its men as possible, usually seeking to deal with attacks on the local population through its own channels, unless subjected to pressure. After O'Hara's conviction, the military authorities at Dum Dum were active in pushing for a rehearing of the case, no doubt fearing the outrage in the ranks that the hanging of a soldier for killing a native would produce.

O'Hara's case was by no means an anomaly. For example, in February 1894 in Madras a lance corporal was tried for the ultimately fatal shooting of a villager who had interfered with his dealings with two native women. Upon complaint by the wounded villager, the commanding officer of the encampment had the 117 men in the regiment march past him, in single file, but he was (not surprisingly) unable to identify anyone. Further action, as with O'Hara, waited upon the matter becoming a public issue. A few days later, after the villager had died of his wounds, an Indian newspaper in Madras denounced the killing and the lack of official concern. Only then did the civil government intervene and, by offering immunity to soldiers who would come forward, identified a culprit and filed charges. As was more usual in such cases, a subscription raised money to hire a first-rate defense team, and (more typical than O'Hara's conviction) the trial ended in an acquittal, as the jury of five Europeans and four Indians accepted the dubious argument of self-defense. A radical member of Parliament, who called the matter "the Dum Dum/O'Hara case over again," asked a question in the House of Commons but the India Office replied (as it usually did to such questions) that the regular course of justice could not be interfered with.[25]

On occasion, soldiers went too far and did fall afoul of the law. In 1898 three soldiers from the cantonment at Barrackpore, sixteen miles from Calcutta, seized the carriage of a Dr. Suresh Chandri, a medical practitioner and a municipal commissioner of the town. He protested, and they responded by enthusiastically kicking him, from which he died. This time their victim was no humble villager; they were quickly arrested, convicted of causing grievous hurt (the next charge below murder), and sentenced each to seven years' "rigorous imprisonment"—an extremely severe sentence to pass on a European for an offense against a native. The military authorities made no effort in their favor, other than to see that they were adequately represented.[26]

Irregular violence of British soldiers against natives was of course an ongoing issue throughout the Empire, one that the ordinary institutions of criminal justice set up by British authorities were not able to deal with very well. In one of the best-known and politically portentous such incidents, the Dinshawai case in Egypt in 1906, such violence ended with military authorities seeing to it that a group of villagers were convicted of the murder of a British soldier. This outcome produced a public scandal back in Britain and a surge in Egyptian nationalism, leading to the establishment of the Egyptian National Congress four years later.[27] These incidents had similar consequences in India.

Yet military-civilian tension, although the most prominent, did not constitute the only important fault line within the Raj. A second ongoing tension was between civil servants and other Europeans in India, usually for business. Crucial to the self-image of civil servants was a view of themselves as acting without personal interest, seeking the larger interests of the Indian population.

Their low opinion of their fellow countrymen in India for commercial reasons, to trade, bank, or plant, was reinforced by the difference in their social origins: the civil servants came very disproportionately from clerical and other professional backgrounds and regarded businessmen as a social cut below themselves. The aristocratic viceroy Lord Mayo spoke for his subordinates generally when he remarked disdainfully but privately in 1870 that, unlike civil servants, these mere "birds of passage" had simply come to India "to get as much money out of the Blacks as they can, and ... go home as soon as possible."[28]

One form of European business was particularly likely to put official and nonofficial Anglo-Indians at odds—planting. Plantations of indigo or tea, expanding in the later nineteenth century to meet growing European demand, were located in the interior of Bengal, distant from the cities of Calcutta or Dacca. The men in charge of these plantations were generally either salaried managers or small capitalists dependent on borrowed money. It was not, from the vantage point of the metropole, either a secure or a high-status occupation. A 1904 letter from William Wickham to his uncle, Henry Gladstone, a partner in a Calcutta managing agency and one of the Victorian statesman's sons, brings that out well:

> I failed to get a scholarship at Winchester ... failed to get a scholarship at Oxford. Got a second in Mods and a third in Greats. Failed twice for the civil service and after being taken into business got kicked out. *It looks as though roughing it in Canada or that hope of the destitute and the failure tea planting, ought to be the last resort.* ... I don't feel much like going straight into politics as you suggest. Is Egypt any use or is that too full up?[29] (emphasis added)

These were often economically precarious enterprises, facing large obstacles ranging from uncertain property tenure to primitive transport facilities to a reluctant and often-hostile labor force, and they had a high failure rate.[30] As a result planters tended to bear down on their laborers as far as the market allowed, not only in terms of wages but also in terms of the control of the conditions of work. In their geographical isolation, insecure both economically and physically, planters felt pressed to maintain their authority over their workers. They saw themselves not as tyrannical individuals making their own law but as often-beleaguered private agents of the larger British authority, taking on the burden of acting where that authority was fragile if there at all, having often to ignore the unrealistic letter of the law to uphold its spirit. What civil servants saw as their problematic tendency to ignore or exceed the bounds of law, planters saw as their necessary efforts to preserve the order without which their enterprises could not be carried on and the ultimate universal benefits of developing the resources of the country realized. As one English sympathizer told his readers, "the planters have had but little recognition of the great work that they are performing for the State."[31] When, rather than recognition, they received from officials criticism, however justly by our lights, they felt genuinely aggrieved.

A third form of conflict within the Raj was particularly evident in plantation areas like Assam, but also elsewhere in India where indigo or tea was grown. With the passage of time, planters increasingly co-opted the local British magistrates and police superintendents, often the only other white men in the district, who came to share their sense of isolation amid the large native population. In such cases, the line of division would fall between these planters and local officials and the higher officials in the Bengal government or, indeed, the government of India, particularly the judicial officials, and helps explain the irregularities in the Balladhun case. As race underpinned the basic division between whites and natives, this division among whites was shored up by differences of social class: the growing numbers of police superintendents were on the whole drawn from a somewhat lower social level than members of the Indian Civil Service (ICS) or the High Court judges. With social backgrounds closer to planters and other nonofficials, these men tended to sympathize with the difficulties they encountered in dealing with Indians.[32] This difference between the lower and the higher levels of British administration was to defeat Henry Cotton in his reformist efforts between 1896 and 1902. An exceptionally capable civil servant of advanced liberal views, Cotton had risen to the chief commissionership of Assam in 1896 and immediately began to try to use his position to improve the situation of plantation-indentured laborers. This effort inevitably brought him into bitter contention with plantation managers and owners. In his efforts to concretely improve wages or working conditions, he was encouraged by frequent words of support from the new and assertive viceroy, Lord Curzon, but frustrated by resistance from below (coupled with lack of tangible support going beyond words from the viceroy). When in 1901 a planter was acquitted by a largely European jury of all charges in the killing of a laborer, Cotton outraged Anglo-Indians generally by officially criticizing the pro-planter bias in Assam trials and getting the case retried by the High Court of Calcutta, which convicted the planter of a lesser charge and sentenced him to a month's imprisonment. After this small achievement, however, Cotton was "thrown to the wolves," as he put it in his memoirs, by Curzon, who publicly rebuked him for his excessive zeal and privately suggested that his resignation would be welcome.[33]

However, Cotton's resignation did not prevent an increase in governmental regulation of abusive labor recruitment and management practices. Planters saw in this a pusillanimous concern for the rights of plantation coolies that was making it ever harder to run profitable enterprises.[34] When a planter was ordered to face a retrial for killing a coolie in 1903, planters and their friends filled outraged meetings and signed petitions of complaint, and Anglo-Indian newspapers sharply criticized the Bengal government.[35] A 1906 trial was very reminiscent of the previously described 1893 Balladhun case—the murder of a planter that spread alarm through white Assam, culminating in the acquittal of two coolies by the High Court for lack of evidence (similarly accompanied by strong judicial suspicion of police misconduct). Not surprisingly, the 1906 case produced a strong denunciation of the Court on the part of the Darjeeling Planters Association.[36]

The private violence of planters against natives was, like that of soldiers, Empire-wide, indeed more deeply rooted than the latter in the structures of everyday life. Plantations were important in most imperial possessions, from Assam to Africa to the Caribbean. Everywhere in the later nineteenth and early twentieth centuries, if in varying degrees, labor discipline shaded into a quasi-criminal violence that, particularly when local officials were co-opted by planter society, placed in question the legitimacy of the institutions of criminal justice and of British rule as a whole.[37]

The role of the Calcutta High Court in the case that ended Cotton's career points toward the fourth and final tension within the Raj. In the tension between judicial and executive officials (in the two cases we began with, between the High Court of Calcutta and the Bengal administration), the judges, looking back on British history since the seventeenth century, saw themselves as the chief check on the executive power and freely cited English precedents as authoritative. Executive officials, not surprisingly, for their part tended to resent being checked. They often became exasperated with judicial rhetoric that failed to appreciate that India was not England. From the executive point of view, the judges were all too prone to let serious criminals (usually Indian, of course) escape because of excessive concern with "legal technicalities." This concern, perhaps all very well back in Britain, was impractical in the subcontinent, where the welfare of hundreds of millions and the survival of British rule depended on the firm maintenance of authority. The distinctive character of criminal law in India added to this executive-judicial tension: the Indian Penal Code, shaped chiefly by Utilitarians from Thomas Macaulay to J. F. Stephen, was a rationalized version of England's. On the one hand, it facilitated prosecution of minor offenses by doing away with some burdensome procedural requirements inherited from earlier English times (which could include, for some jurisdictions, the requirement of jury trial). On the other, however, following nineteenth-century notions of culpability, it gave greater importance than hitherto to ascertaining intentions. This strengthened the armory of the defense in cases of serious offense. In England, the law assumed a homicide to be murder until established otherwise, whereas after 1862 India placed the burden of proving intention in homicide more clearly on the prosecution. In addition, while in England in the latter nineteenth century the scope of that degree of provocation that would reduce a homicide below murder was being restricted, there was no sign of this development in India.[38] As a result, this code would appear to have made it more difficult than previously, and more difficult than in England, to convict anyone of the capital offense of murder.[39] Thus, while at the lower levels of justice, the code facilitated the work of administrators, at the level of the High Courts it could frustrate them. As the code became a template for criminal law in many newer colonies, these effects were generalized, and conflicts between judges and other European colonials, official and nonofficial, in cases of serious violence became common.

Personal career rivalries exacerbated this clash of constitutional and criminal law principle, particularly in India. High Court judges in India were either barristers appointed by the Home government and sharing neither similar experiences nor an esprit de corps with executive officers of the ICS or members of that civil service who had taken the judicial route. That route, however, was of decidedly lower prestige than the executive route and tended to be avoided by the most ambitious and, probably, most skilled of the civilians. Thus, judicial members of the ICS labored under something of a stigma of inferiority, which they naturally resented. The result was to prevent the esprit de corps of the ICS from reaching very forcefully into the judicial branch and, rather, to reinforce what executive officials described as judicial touchiness about their powers and prerogatives. For their part, judges saw executive officials continually attempting to confine their role and circumvent their rulings. In January 1892, for example, the government of Bengal criticized the Calcutta High Court after it acquitted an Indian charged with attempted murder of a European by noting "the description of the facts given by the Commissioner of Police throws doubts on the propriety of the acquittal." In heated response, the Court formally complained to the viceroy's office, "In England, the efficiency of the Police is gauged by the results of their efforts in Court. In India, the efficiency of the Courts should not be judged by their agreement with, or dissent from, the Police."[40] In his unpublished memoirs, Justice Henry Prinsep of the Calcutta High Court (who had been one of the judges quashing the convictions and criticizing the Bengal officials in the Sajow case) recalled "constant friction" throughout his period of service between the Court and the government of Bengal. "As a Judicial Officer," he went on,

I may be regarded as biased, but I can confidently appeal to official records to show the provocation was always on the part of the Local Government prompted by an irresistible inclination to interfere with the undoubted prerogative of the High Court—the maintenance of the judicial independence of all Courts even of the lowest grade in all judicial matters. Since my early days as a Judge of the High Court, we have had a succession of Lieutenants-General of Bengal who with one exception have too openly shown their hostility to any judicial independence. What can be expected from such an example to their subordinate Executive officers who resented the power given by the law to correct them whenever they transgressed it? They held that the patriarchal system of Government in the early days of our rule should be maintained and restored, forgetting that by legislation, descending often into minute details, the Government had established the reign of law, that the past was dead beyond recall, and that they should unite with Judicial officers in working for the public weal, the loadstone of all modern Government.[41]

This conflict between executive and judiciary by no means made the latter a consistent champion of Indians against Europeans. Much depended on individuals. On the Calcutta High Court, for instance, in 1903 Justice Sale, a favorite of the Anglo-Indian community, strained accepted legal procedures to quash the conviction of a planter for causing grievous hurt in the death of one of his laborers. Then, a few months later, the same judge dealt with an appeal from other tea plantation laborers against a one-year prison sentence for assaulting their manager by *enhancing* their sentences to three years.[42] However, most members of the judiciary had less of an interest than executive officials in seeing proceedings against persons, whether Indians (as in the great majority of cases) or Europeans (in unusual circumstances), result in convictions. They consequently often became the target of the frustration felt by members of the executive when defendants went free. Since most criminal trials were of Indians, the independence of the courts tended to work in their favor, as in the two cases already cited. Judicial independence most notably made possible a large number of acquittals of nationalist agitators or terrorists in the succeeding years, but as the case of Private O'Hara demonstrates, it also could serve as a shield for Europeans whom the executive was seeking to convict for abusing natives.

IV

What lessons can we learn from the trials of O'Hara and Sajow, and others like them, in British India at the height of the Raj? Fundamentally, I argue, a lesson in complication. Even during its most secure years, the Raj was no government of platonic guardians, as its officials liked to think of themselves. Yet neither was it the "despotism of law" described by some anticolonialist scholars.[43] Nor, of course, a constitutional state like the United Kingdom. It was at one and the same time all of these seemingly incompatible things—a would-be benevolent despotism deeply distorted in its benevolence by racial prejudice on the one hand and hobbled in its despotism by constitutional principles on the other. Interestingly, equally powerful class prejudices and rivalries that were at times institutional and at times personal sometimes cancelled out these prejudices and reinforced these principles.

Such fault lines within British rule provided crevices that the agency of *either* Anglo-Indians or Indians could widen, the latter following the former in the late nineteenth century in organizing themselves for assertion and resistance. Following the example of the Anglo-Indian press, the rapidly developing Indian-owned newspaper press began to turn British legal rhetoric against the everyday realities of British rule. Repeatedly, this press urged England, as Madan Mohan, an editor of a weekly paper and later a president of the Indian National Congress, put it at the Congress's 1887 meeting, to "be true to her traditions, her instincts and herself and grant us our rights as free born British citizens."[44] Through such arguments, the principle of the rule of law in British India was kept alive and gradually realized down to Independence and after.

Notes

1. E. P. Thompson, *Whigs and Hunters: The Origin of the Black Act* (London: Allen Lane, 1975); David Garland, *Punishment and Welfare: A History of Penal Strategies* (Aldershot, UK: Gower, 1985); Martin J. Wiener, *Reconstructing the Criminal: Culture, Law and Policy in England, 1830–1900* (Cambridge: Cambridge Univ. Press, 1990), and *Men of Blood: Violence, Manliness and Criminal Justice in Victorian England* (Cambridge: Cambridge Univ. Press, 2004).

2. One set of connections between the two subjects now being formed can be seen in the important book edited by Douglas Hay and Paul Craven, *Masters, Servants and Magistrates in Britain and the Empire, 1562–1955* (Chapel Hill: Univ. of North Carolina Press, 2004).

3. See, e.g., Sally Engle Merry, "Law and Colonialism," *Law and Society Review* 25 (1991): 896.

4. John L. Comaroff, "Colonialism, Culture, and the Law: A Foreword," *Law and Social Inquiry* 26 (2001): 305–314.

5. Frederick Cooper and Ann Stoler, eds., *Tensions of Empire: Colonial Cultures in a Bourgeois World* (Berkeley: Univ. of California Press, 1997).

6. Indeed, Victoria Nourse has very persuasively argued that all criminal law is inevitably political, not only in the sense of resolving clashing interests but also clashing ideologies, or visions of political order. Victoria F. Nourse, "Reconceptualizing Criminal Law Defenses," *University of Pennsylvania Law Review* 151 (2003): 1691.

7. The *Hindoo Patriot*, English-language but Indian-owned and aimed at an educated Indian audience, doubted whether, without this interest, "the culprit would have been brought to justice." Feb. 24, 1890, p. 92. The lieutenant governor, Sir Steuart Bayley, had been appointed a few years before, when tensions were still high over the 1883–1884 Anglo-Indian revolt against the proposed Ilbert Bill, which would have made Europeans subject in certain criminal cases to being tried by Indian judges. Bayley had a strong interest in damping down the racial resentment that the successful revolt had aroused among educated Indians and had been seeking since his appointment to quietly increase the participation of Indians in low-level public affairs. P. C. Lyon, "Bayley, Sir Steuart Colvin (1836–1925)," rev. Katherine Prior, in *Oxford Dictionary of National Biography*, Oxford Univ. Press, 2004, http://www.oxforddnb.com/view/article/30647 (accessed Dec. 25, 2006).

8. Since the Mutiny of 1857, it appears that seven Europeans have been hanged for the murder of an Indian, four of them soldiers but only one later than 1867. See the chapter by Elizabeth Kolsky in this volume. See also John M. Compton, "British Government and Society in the Presidency of Bengal, c. 1858–c. 1880," D.Phil. thesis, Oxford, 1968.

9. *Englishman*, Mar. 13, 1890, p. 4 (editorial). It declared that "the original verdict had appeared most proper—an atrocious crime had been solved, its perpetrator brought to justice." "All the newspapers," observed the Hindi paper *Sahachar* on Mar. 19, "including even the *Pioneer* and the *Englishman* [two leading Anglo papers], are saying that a great wrong has been committed, and that the perpetrator of a brutal murder has gone unpunished." Quoted in British Library, Oriental and India Office Library (OIOL), L/R/5/15. *Report on Native Papers, Bengal, 1890.*

10. *Navavibhakar Sadharani*, Feb. 24, 1890; *Sahachar*, Mar. 19, 1890; *Al Punch*, Apr. 21, 1890. OIOL, L/R/5/15.

11. *Burdwan Sanjivan*, Mar. 18, 1890. OIOL, L/R/5/15.

12. *Hindoo Patriot*, Mar. 17, 1890, pp. 123–124 (editorial). It observed, "[T]he Hon. Gen. Chesney, the military member of the Supreme Council, also displayed great interest in the case and was present at the first day's Full Bench hearing. It is probably at the instance of the Hon. General that the four soldiers are now under military arrest awaiting trial for breach of regimental law. But the prevailing idea is that they will get off with a few 'cuts' and no retribution will follow poor Selim's violent death." Another Indian paper observed, "Europeans committing crimes in this country almost always escaped unscathed; and when they are convicted they live in a princely style in the Nainital or in the Jubbulpore Jail." In O'Hara's case, "the mountain has given birth to a mouse. The culprit is apprehended with much ado, he is brought to trial, and he is sentenced to be hanged." But in the end, he is given a mere slap on the wrist. "After the discharge of

O'Hara by the High Court, oppression by the soldiery is calculated to become simply intolerable." *Sakti*, Mar. 18, 1890.

13. OIOL, L/PJ/6/272, File 498. The *Morning Post*, a leading London newspaper, reported that O'Hara received an ovation from many Europeans at Allahabad as he returned to his regiment after discharge. Reported in *Sahachar*, Mar. 19, 1890.

14. OIOL, Cross Papers, Mss Eur/E243/30.

15. As Jenny Sharpe has noted, violence against Europeans by Indians was always potentially political and taken most seriously. "Since the legitimation of colonialism was premised on the presumed passivity of the colonized, the killing of even one European took on the exaggerated proportion of a massacre." *Allegories of Empire: The Figure of Woman in the Colonial Text* (Minneapolis: Univ. of Minnesota Press, 1993), p. 63.

16. *Dainik-o-Samachar Chandrika*, Dec. 14, 1893. OIOL, L/R/5/19. *Report on Native Papers, Bengal, 1893.*

17. *Papers Relating to the Baladhan Murder Case in Assam*, Parliamentary Papers 1894, House of Commons. 58:321 (C.7456); OIOL, L/PJ/6/374, Files 963, 1132. In her chapter in this volume, Elizabeth Kolsky gives further specifics of this case.

18. Stephen himself had been aware of the dangers, even within the civilian side, of abuse of authority. As he noted in his *A History of the Criminal Law of England*, "The smallness of the number of the European magistrates in India makes the police more important and relatively far more powerful in India than they are in England, and I was led by many circumstances to the opinion that no part of the institutions by which India is governed require more careful watching in order to prevent what is designed for the protection of the people from becoming a means of petty oppression. The Code of Criminal Procedure is full of provisions intended to guard against this and at the same time to make Indian police efficient for their purpose." *History*, vol. 3 (London: Macmillan, 1883), p. 331. However, cases like Sajow illustrate the limitations of procedural provisions alone to control official power.

19. E. M. Collingham, *Imperial Bodies: The Physical Experience of the Raj, c. 1800–1947* (Oxford: Polity, 2001), p. 143. Citing a report to the House of Commons ordered after a question had been raised there.

20. Edward M. Spiers has described the overrepresentation of Irish and Scots in the British army, though also how it was diminishing in the second half of the century: "Whereas Ireland and Scotland had provided over half the noncommissioned officers and men in the 1830's, their contributions had slumped with rural depopulation and the massive emigration from Ireland. By 1870 the Irish proportion of the army had fallen to 27.9%, and by 1898 to 13.2%." *The Late Victorian Army, 1868–1902* (Manchester, UK: Manchester Univ. Press, 1992), p. 131. Even then, however, it remained well above the Irish proportion of the total population of the United Kingdom.

21. See Spiers, ibid., on difficulties in recruiting and the low public opinion of soldiers; see also the thorough discussion in Compton, "British Government and Society."

22. Compton, "British Government and Society," p. 248.

23. A revealing example was given by Frank Richards in his memoirs of service as a private in India at the turn of the century. He recalled

a certain married sergeant of thirteen or fourteen years' service who, one day . . . went out for a gharri-ride and brought it to a sudden stop by shooting the gharri-driver dead with a revolver. The affair caused a mild sensation. The Sergeant always carried this revolver about with him, but had never threatened anyone with it or shown any murderous inclinations. He was a reserved man and respected by all ranks. Nor could anyone come forward, when the case was being inquired into, and give any evidence that the heat had been causing him to behave queerly of late. But the Commanding Officer allowed him the benefit of the doubt and had him confined in a small padded cell in hospital, where he was kept under observation. The gharri-wallah's widow came to the hospital to get justice done her. They explained to her there that the man who had shot her husband was a madman and that nothing could be done, except perhaps to give her compensation. They gave her ten rupees, which was a matter of thirteen shillings, and it is said that she went away well satisfied and smiling. We never discovered whether this compensation came out of the Sergeant's pocket or out of the Canteen funds. In any case, the excitement had completely died down a day or two later when the Sergeant officially recovered his reason, left the padded cell for the convalescent ward, and was soon afterwards invalided home to England with his wife and children. The truth never came out. . . . The general opinion was that the Sergeant's nerves were in a bad state after the heat of the summer and that the gharri-wallah must have demanded more money for the ride than what it was worth and given the Sergeant cheek when he refused; and that, with a revolver in his belt, the temptation to make a stern example of this cheeky gharri-wallah to warn all cheeky gharri-wallahs of the future proved too much for the Sergeant—he drew the revolver and ended the argument. So it was reckoned a good deed; for, as I have said, the Sergeant was not known as a bully or an unjust man, but was respected by all; and the gharri-drivers of Agra were certainly the limit. (*Old Soldier Sahib* [London: Faber & Faber, 1936], pp. 213–214.)

24. Compton, "British Government and Society," p. 69.
25. OIOL, L/PJ/6/369 Files 459, 464, 467, 468.
26. OIOL, L/PJ/6/480, File 945. However, after the case had faded from public attention, the men received early release.
27. See, among others, Roger Owen, *Lord Cromer: Victorian Imperialist, Edwardian Proconsul* (Oxford: Oxford Univ. Press, 2004), pp. 335–341, 345 347.
28. Mayo to Argyll, Nov. 9, 1870 (OIOL, Mayo Papers 41).
29. Mar. 30, 1904, quoted in Maria Misra, *Business, Race and Politics in British India c. 1850–1960* (Oxford: Clarendon Press, 1999), p. 49.
30. See Rajat Kanta Ray, *Social Conflict and Political Unrest in Bengal, 1875–1927* (Delhi: Oxford Univ. Press, 1984); Raymond K. Renford, *The Non-Official British in India to 1920* (Delhi: Oxford Univ. Press, 1987); Rana P. Behal and Prabhu P. Mohapatra, "Tea and Money versus Human Life: The Rise and Fall of the Indenture System in the Assam Tea Plantations, 1840–1908," *Journal of Peasant Studies* 19 (1992): 142–172.

31. George Barker, *A Tea Planter's Life in Assam* (Calcutta: Thacker, Spink, 1884), p. 230.

32. "[F]ormerly[,] local British officials had taken an interest in the people and tried to help and protect them," Sir Henry Cotton had written in 1885, "but now they were exiles sighing for home, who regarded their work in India as temporary and disagreeable." Quoted in Edwin Hirschmann, *"White Mutiny": The Ilbert Bill Crisis in India and Genesis of the Indian National Congress* (New Delhi: Heritage, 1980).

33. Henry Cotton, *Indian and Home Memories* (London: T. F. Unwin, 1911). Also see OIOL, L/R/5/27 (Reports on Native Papers, Bengal, 1901), for various Indian comments on this struggle.

34. See note 29.

35. OIOL, L/PJ/6/628, Files 418, 603, 609; L/PJ/5/29 (Reports on Native Papers, Bengal 1903), Part 1, pp. 219, 247, 791–792, 816–819, 840, 970–972; Part 2, pp. 337–338, 349–360, 361–362.

36. OIOL, L/R/5/32 (Report on Native Papers, Bengal 1906), Part 1, p. 741; Part 2, p. 347; Rajat Kanta Ray, *Social Conflict*, p. 140.

37. See David M. Anderson, "Master and Servant in Colonial Kenya, 1895–1939," *Journal of African History* 41 (2000): 459–485; Patrick Collinson, "The Cow Bells of Kitale," *London Review of Books*, June 5, 2003; Jock McCulloch, "Empire and Violence, 1900–1939," in *Gender and Empire*, Philippa Levine, ed. (Oxford: Oxford Univ. Press, 2004).

38. On this English development, see Wiener, *Men of Blood*. On the workings of the Indian Penal Code in cases of interracial homicide, see Jordanna Bailkin, "The Boot and the Spleen: When Was Murder Possible in British India?" *Comparative Studies in Society and History* 48 (2006): 463–494.

39. Until further study, we do not know just how much this difference in black-letter law helped Indian defendants; we do know it was of great aid to European ones. One may doubt whether it was as much help to Indian killers as to European ones, for an Indian paper, *Dacca Prakash*, recalled after the quashing of O'Hara's conviction that

> some time ago, one Suddabodha Bhattacharjya stood charged with the murder of his wife, and though there was no eye-witness of the murder, and though there were circumstances favouring the supposition that the deceased girl might have come by her death through other hands than those of her husband, yet Mr. Justice Norris [a member of the Calcutta High Court], who tried the case, refused to give the benefit of the doubt to the prisoner, and the prisoner was accordingly sentenced to death and hanged. No Full Bench sat for him, and the petition for his reprieve made by countrymen was rejected by the Government. (Mar. 23, 1890)

40. OIOL, Home Judicial Proceedings, no. 297, letter of Jan. 25, 1892.

41. Perhaps unsurprisingly, not long after public remarks along these lines, Prinsep was turned down for the position of judicial secretary in the India Office.

42. OIOL, L/PJ/5/29, part 1, p. 970; part 2, p. 338.

43. See Ranajit Guha, *Dominance without Hegemony: History and Power in Colonial India* (Cambridge, Mass.: Harvard Univ. Press, 1997) and Radhika Singha, *A Despotism of Law: Crime and Justice in Early Colonial India* (Delhi: Oxford Univ. Press, 1998).

44. Quoted in Harish Kaushik, *The Indian National Congress in England, 1885–1920* (Delhi: Research Publications in Social Science, 1973), p. 11.

ELEVEN

Crime and Punishment on the Tea Plantations of Colonial India

ELIZABETH KOLSKY

In imperial contexts, ideas about law, crime, and justice exist in tension. Empires past and present have defined their purpose as advancing civilization by spreading freedom, law, and order.[1] In practice, however, empires are built on asymmetrical relations of dominance, a fact that rubs up awkwardly against their promises of legal equality.

In colonial India, the law played a fundamental role in enabling territorial expansion, sustaining political dominion, and justifying British rule. The ideological role of law was particularly important for colonial legitimacy as justice was touted as the source and the benefit of British rule. As one British administrator wrote,

> The foundation of our empire in India rests on the principle of justice, and England retains its supremacy in India mainly by justice. Without justice we could not hold India for a moment, for it is that which inspires the people of India with a confidence in us and with a belief that in all our dealings with them we never act otherwise than fairly and justly, and which renders them on the whole satisfied and contented with our rule.[2]

The colonial rule of law not only held India by promising impartiality and equality to imperial subjects but also was seen as a disciplinary tool that would civilize Indians and prepare them for democracy and self-governance. The criminal law was particularly central to this project of ruling by reforming. Criminal legislation aimed at eradicating cultural differences and improving Indian society, such as the abolition of *sati* (widow immolation) in 1829, simultaneously produced and enabled colonial control.[3] The anti-*sati* legislation exemplified the liberal and reformist impulse of the civilizing mission while simultaneously establishing the state's power to intervene in Indian social life.

From the colonizers' perspective, the criminal law guaranteed order, power, and civilization; but from the anticolonial perspective it did the exact opposite. Critics of colonialism, such as Aimé Cesaire, challenged the legality of the colonial state and highlighted the inherent tension between law and empire by calling colonialism a crime against man.[4] Mahatma Gandhi, himself a trained lawyer, argued that the law perpetuated colonial power and that without it British rule in India would have no foundation. In *Hind Swaraj*, Gandhi wrote,

> [T]he lawyers have enslaved India ... and have confirmed English authority ... they have tightened the English grip. Do you think that it would be possible for the English to carry on their Government without law courts? It is wrong to consider that courts are established for the benefit of the people. Those who want to perpetuate their power do so through the courts. ... The chief thing, however, to be remembered is that without lawyers courts could not have been established or conducted and without the latter the English could not rule. ... If pleaders were to abandon and consider it just as degrading as prostitution, English rule would break up in a day.[5]

As Gandhi and others pointed out, the primary impediment to an impartial rule of law was the colonial state itself.

The central question posed by anticolonial critics of the law concerned the issue of legitimacy: if colonialism was an immoral and illegal political system, how could the colonial state define right from wrong or govern according to principles of justice? For the student of legal history, the relationship between law and empire poses other kinds of questions: was there something unique to the administration of colonial justice, and how does the history of colonial law tie in to the broader narratives of legal history? Could a legal system framed to serve the imperatives of imperial power also serve the principle of universal justice? Did the law provide a meaningful avenue to anticolonial emancipation or did engagement with colonial legal institutions always, as Gandhi argued, entrench colonial power? As Sally Engle Merry inquires more broadly, "What are the possibilities of resistance through law? Is law too complicitous in relations of power to constitute a site of resistance? Does resistance by means of law simply reinforce the power and legitimacy of the legal system itself?"[6]

In this chapter I will explore the meanings of crime, punishment, and power in colonial India by focusing on the history of European violence and Indian resistance in Assam, a province situated at the northeast margin of British India. During the colonial period, Assam was dominated by the

British tea industry and (until 1910) a system of indentured servitude that provided private penal powers to European planters to enforce labor contracts. The region of Assam provides an important example for the study of modern histories of crime and punishment as it sat on the geopolitical edge of Empire and possibly beyond the pale of justice. Within an imperial framework that distinguished the center from the periphery, metropole from colony, a frontier zone such as Assam occupied a marginal space that one English writer called "a wild—almost unknown—tract of jungle."[7]

Viewed through the prism of the colonial plantation, the political foundations, cultural conditions, and legitimizing functions that structure law and legal practice appear in bold relief. Although British law was ideologically staged as the guarantor of liberty and the agent of progress, in letter and in practice, the law of the plantations was designed to secure capitalist control over labor. As a result, the law tended to obstruct rather than deliver justice. When traditional concepts in the study of criminal jurisprudence, such as liability, responsibility, and punishment, are examined from a transnational perspective that brings the colonial experience back into the history of modernity, the conventional narrative of legal progress is fractured and disrupted.

1. The Balladhun Murder Case

Around 11 p.m. on April 11, 1893, a British tea planter named Cockburn heard two dogs barking loudly outside his bungalow at the Balladhun Tea Garden.[8] When Cockburn stepped out onto the veranda to investigate the commotion, he saw the dead body of his *chowkidar* (watchman) lying on the ground surrounded by a group of men. Cockburn quickly attempted to retreat into his bedroom but fell over the threshold of the door where he was "hacked to death." The next morning, Cockburn's butler discovered his corpse lying in blood pooled in the entranceway to the bedroom. The *chowkidar*'s body lay several feet away covered by a blanket. Sadi, Cockburn's Indian paramour and the only eyewitness to his murder, was found alive but seriously wounded and naked in the woods near the bungalow.

Although physical violence against European planters was not terribly rare, murder was quite unusual and, given the powerful influence that the European planting community exerted over the colonial state, such cases were always attended to with great vigilance. After Cockburn's death, as often happened following incidents of extreme violence on the tea gardens, all of the laborers fled the Balladhun plantation. Sadi died within days of being discovered, and with no one to question, the police summoned a Bengali police inspector named Joy Chunder Bhadra, a man who presumably knew how to deal with what the government of India later called the special difficulties on the "remote and irascible" northeast border. When Inspector Chunder arrived in the area, he indiscriminately began to arrest men, women, and children, confining, tutoring, and torturing them to procure confessions. Several witnesses claimed that Chunder and his men had threatened many of the local women and their daughters with "dishonor" if they refused to turn over Cockburn's murderers. On August 8, 1893, upon the uncorroborated statements of two men who turned state's evidence, seven people were charged with murder committed in the course of committing *dacoity* (a colonial form of armed robbery).

Judge John Clark and a panel of three Indian assessors initially tried the accused men at the Cachar sessions court. The case for the prosecution rested entirely on the evidence of two *approvers* (an Indian legal term for a witness who turns state's evidence), Mohan and Mukhta Singh, who testified in court that the murders were premeditated. Mukhta Singh stated that Cockburn

> troubled us much; he made his coolies break down work we had done, and made us do it over again two or three times, and said that he would not pay us until we did it. Most of us left Manipur because we had no food, and we could not get food for our work here. Therefore we are all very angry with the Sahib. Some of us said we would like to bury our teeth in his throat. . . . We had come to fight; those whose fate it was to die would have died.

The prosecution held that the seven defendants were former employees of Cockburn's who came to the bungalow that night to kill him over the thirteen and a half rupees they were owed in back pay. They further contended that Cockburn had a volatile relationship with his own employees and the local people in the surrounding area. In this regard, Cockburn's dogs were symbolically important for they guarded the borders of the plantation and prevented villagers from passing through to the local marketplace. Like many plantations in Assam, the Balladhun Tea Garden was built on land that previously contained local access roads used by people in the area.[9]

In a devastating blow to the defense, Judge Clark excluded Sadi's dying deposition from the admissible evidence because it had not been taken under oath or in the presence of the accused. Even so, the testimony of the seven defendants provided damaging evidence to the prosecution in the horrifically consistent details about police torture. Sagal Samba Sajow, the alleged ringleader of the group, testified that he was arrested, tortured, and pressured into a making a confession. He claimed that for two or three nights the police physically brutalized and threatened to hang him, "[T]hey beat me very much and ill-used me in other ways." He finally agreed to say "yes yes" before the *bara sahib* ("big man," Assistant Magistrate Lees) in exchange for his freedom. After he confessed, however, Sagal Samba Sajow was thrown into *hazat* (a form of solitary confinement). The six other defendants were also tortured by the police into confessing and were later confined in *hazat* where they were not given access to lawyers or to anyone else.

At the conclusion of the sessions court trial, the three Indian assessors acquitted all seven men because they believed that the two approvers had been tutored and tampered with "in view of the large reward offered [2,500 rupees] for bringing home the guilt to anybody." Judge Clark, however, dismissed their acquittal, accepting the prosecution's argument that the prisoners had gone to the bungalow that night to murder Cockburn out of revenge for the money they were owed. Clark sentenced four of the men to death and three to transportation for life. According to standard sentencing procedure, the case was referred to the Calcutta High Court for confirmation of the death sentences.

By the time the Balladhun murder case reached the High Court, the larger issues and grievances that it evoked overshadowed the specificities of the trial. Both the British and the Indian press closely followed the six days of proceedings in Calcutta. On December 11, 1893, when Judges Ameer Ali and H. T. Prinsep acquitted all of the prisoners on account of the many "irregularities" and "illegalities" conducted in the course of the police investigation and the sessions court trial, the press erupted. The proplanter newspaper the *Englishman* lamented the vulnerable position of the lonely Englishman on the lawless northern frontier. Condemning the government's failure to "safeguard the lives and property of the men who have made the wealth and prosperity of Assam," the editors wrote,

> The conditions obtaining in remote and lonely tea districts, where solitary Englishmen are practically at the mercy of the predatory hordes of the frontier should make a more imperative demand for protection from Government than any other circumstances under which our fellow countrymen live and work in India. Instead of granting it a *laissez faire* policy as has been largely adopted, the planter has been left to the protection, visibly growing weaker, of his own prestige as an Englishman.[10]

The Indian press was also critical of what the *Amrita Bazar Patrika* called the "atrocious manner in which criminal justice is often administered in this country.... We do not know how to begin with this case, what comments to offer upon it, and how to end it."[11] The *Hindoo Patriot* noted, "There was absolutely not a scintilla of evidence against any of the accused men, but when a European is murdered, British prestige and British revenge require the shedding of some blood—sometimes even of innocent men. 'Life for life' is the procedure usually observed in such cases, and sometimes for one European murdered, two, three, or four natives are hanged."[12]

Under pressure from Parliament, the government of India subsequently launched an inquiry into the allegations of police and judicial misconduct. Most officials from Assam, including the chief commissioner, reported back that they believed they had arrested the right men. Furthermore, they found that no hard evidence of torture had turned up and that the police had behaved precisely as they must in the "wilder parts of the country"[13] where the people were "notorious for their clannish habits, and their indisposition to assist the authorities in making enquiries among them."[14] As the deputy commissioner of Cachar put it, the confessions confirmed what local officials already knew about the "treacherous and unscrupulous" Manipuris, who

> lived under no law till lately, except that of their village custom. Their conduct in the Manipur rebellion in 1891 brought into the strongest light their savage disposition and their lawless conduct in this district have necessitated the quartering of a small punitive police upon their villages near Baladhan [*sic*] and in the South Cachar, where Sagal Samba was hidden away for many weeks.[15]

According to this logic of frontier lawlessness and the exceptional measures it demanded, the colonial administration determined that nothing untoward, illegal, or irregular had occurred in Balladhun. In fact, rather than constituting evidence of police misconduct and torture, the forced confessions were interpreted as proof of perjury and indicative of "the corrupt nature of the class of persons with whom this enquiry had to deal, the low class Manipuris." In its final report to London, the government of India concluded, "There is no reason for regarding this case as anything very special."[16]

The Balladhun murder case raised a number of significant questions regarding the administration of criminal justice in colonial India and the politics of violence on the tea gardens of Assam. It was, as the *Amrita Bazar Patrika* pointed out, highly unusual that a European was murdered and no one was punished for it. Given the violence and oppression that accompanied the enforcement of labor on the Assam tea plantations, it was rather rare for a European to be murdered at all. We will use this unusual case as a jumping-off point to explore colonial notions about criminal responsibility and justice, the politics of law and violence, and the possibilities for law as a "weapon of the weak" in an imperial setting.[17]

2. Law and Labor in Colonial Assam

In 1826, when the East India Company annexed the region of Assam, British planters had already begun to experiment with the cultivation of tea. While the colonial government provided very favorable conditions to attract European planters, labor shortages and the high cost of local workers posed major obstacles to the growth of the industry. In 1865, the government passed the first of a series of special laws designed to secure the recruitment, transportation, and employment of laborers on the tea gardens. Under the new indenture system, most tea workers were recruited from outside Assam and were bound by a penal contract that gave employers the right to arrest any laborer in the district who was alleged to have absconded from a garden. In 1882, a new law loosened restrictions on labor recruitment and strengthened the private penal powers of the planters by permitting them to arrest deserters without a warrant or the assistance of the police.

The stated rationale for the exceptional labor legislation in Assam was that, in return for secure pay and working conditions (and to protect the planter's economic investment), the laborer should be bound to the estate for a certain number of years. In defense of the penal contract, Assam Chief Commissioner C. A. Elliot wrote, "As to the tea-coolie, the protection he gets, the excellent cottage he lives in, the good water-supply, the fairly cheap food, and the fairly reasonable wage he gets are a *quid pro quo* granted in return for the penal clauses which compel him to carry out his part of the contract."[18] Like the captain of a vessel at sea or the officer in an army, the planter was characterized as an authority figure who required special disciplinary powers: "[D]iscipline must be maintained upon tea gardens and that for its maintenance we must depend upon the authority of the Manager not upon that of the Magistrate."[19] While one could argue that planter and police power were mutually contradictory, Eugene Genovese has described the somewhat similar system of U.S. slave law as a "system of complementary law" in that the authority of the planter to enforce work operated in tandem with the police power of the state.[20]

The rosy picture painted by Commissioner Elliott did not square up with the reality on the gardens nor did it acknowledge the underlying economic logic of the penal contract. Whereas labor contracts are generally adjudicated by civil means (such as a civil suit), the colonial state recognized that one could not sue a person who owned no property. Rather than alleviating the roots of poverty and landlessness that drew laborers into the indenture system, desertion was criminalized to bind workers to the tea plantations.[21]

While the exceptional legislation did increase the labor supply to Assam—by 1883, 95 percent of the labor force on the tea plantations came from outside Assam[22]—it certainly did not protect the workers. If anything, the special laws can be directly linked to widespread criminal fraud, abduction, and abuse of labor. Contemporary critics likened the indenture system and the penal contract to semislavery and consistently used the conditions on the U.S. slave plantations and the specious moral arguments of Southern slaveholders as scurrilous points of comparison.[23] In response to the planters' demand for more "freedom" to define and defend their industry, Reverend Charles Dowding, a longtime chaplain and social activist in Assam, replied, "The 'fight for freedom' is a noble thing: but it is a whimsical suggestion in this connection, and somehow reminds one of the Confederate States of America, who fought for freedom to hold slaves and liberty to 'whop their niggers.'"[24]

3. The Politics of Violence in Colonial Assam

Although controlling Indian crime was critical to the maintenance of imperial order, the colonial state accepted the fact that a certain amount of European crime was necessary to keep the plantations going. The devolution of authority from the magistrate to the garden manager reflected the state's interest in allowing the industry to police itself. Criminal behavior, including physical violence, confinement, and abduction, which would ordinarily have been punishable by the state, was effectively decriminalized and legitimated under provisions of the penal contract.[25] Nonetheless, the farming out of disciplinary powers presented its own problems in terms of political legitimacy and social control: having authorized the private use of force, could the state set limits on the extent of planter violence, thereby extending the protection of law over the body of the laborer? When the planters legitimately took the law into their own hands in incidents that resulted in "flogging a wretched man to death," were they transgressing or enforcing law and social order?[26] Orlando Patterson has described slavery as a form of social death caused by, among other factors, the power of the master to commit violence against the slave.[27] In thinking analogously about indentured servitude as a form of legal death, one wonders, just as you cannot sue a person with no property, could you kill a person with no legal status? Was killing a "coolie" really murder?[28]

The government of Assam spent significant administrative energy monitoring labor recruitment, employment, and social relations on the tea plantations. The relations between tea planters and their employees formed what one Assam official called "a source of constant anxiety" and the government maintained a watchful if tolerant attitude toward the frequency of criminal complaints and the outcome of trials involving interracial crime.[29] The annual reports on labor immigration into Assam provide a chilling insight into the brutal and deadly conditions on the tea plantations and indicate the state's intimate awareness about the inhumanity of the system. Despite the appalling conditions documented by these reports, colonial officials consistently remarked that "the coolie is better off in Assam than he would be probably anywhere else."[30] But as members of the London-based Humanitarian League rhetorically asked in 1906, if the conditions on the plantations were so good, why was it so difficult to recruit labor?[31]

One of the interesting facts about reported crime in colonial Assam is that, as the number of gardens in the area began to grow, the number of trials of European British subjects declined. In contrast, the number of trials involving Indian defendants increased along with the size of the Indian population. Some officials explained this decline by the logic of capitalism, arguing that it was in the financial interests of employers to maintain good labor relations. Others surmised that the negative publicity surrounding violent crimes had improved the planters' treatment of laborers. In 1900, the deputy commissioner of Darrang wrote, "The publicity attaching to cases of systematic ill-treatment, and the consequences entailed, are sufficient in most cases to deter any who may not be alive to the necessity for treating the coolie well."[32] It is unlikely that either of these explanations is true as there is no evidence that colonial justice became more just over time. If anything, the increasingly close social and political ties between the nonofficial and official European populations forged in the face of a growing nationalist movement provide a more likely explanation for the decline in European trials and convictions.[33]

Official claims about good relations between capital and labor were strongly contradicted by the public perception of the "planters' *zulum*" (oppression).[34] The expansion of the tea industry closely coincided with the rise of Indian nationalism, and the Indian press and other nationalist organizations increasingly monitored incidents of criminal violence and contractual oppression in Assam. Tyrannical, Kurtz-like characters like Cockburn were relentlessly exposed and condemned by journalists such as Dwarkanath Ganguli, who published a series of celebrated articles on the mistreatment of Assam tea laborers.[35] To many Indians, the official partiality shown to the planters clearly demonstrated that "[t]he primary object of British rule in India is to benefit the European capitalist and merchant, even, if necessary, at the sacrifice of justice and humanity."[36]

Jordanna Bailkin has argued that the colonial investment in the rule of law rested on "[i]llusions of peaceableness [that] depended on rendering certain forms of violence acceptable or invisible."[37] The notion that most planters were generally "just and considerate" and that a certain number of crimes were to be expected amid such a large population was one of these illusions that is widely belied by the government's own figures and by the consistent reports of abuse in the press.[38] As Indian critics exposed the state's failure to balance the scales of justice, the cruel behavior of the planters raised larger questions about the culture of state terror and the criminality of colonialism itself.

Colonial administrators had always been cautious about the presence of European planters and capitalists in India. Many were concerned about the damage that the "adventuring class" posed to British prestige and to the "basis of our rule in India, which is to secure justice between man and man."[39] The early colonial state feared that the presence of the "lower orders" of British society would threaten political stability by undermining the British image of superiority and respectability.[40] In 1793, Henry Dundas warned that "indiscriminate and unrestrained colonization" could destroy the "respect or rather eradicate that feeling [on which] the preservation of our empire depends."[41] Until 1813, most colonial officials agreed that: "Europeans should be discouraged and prevented as much as possible from colonizing and settling in our possessions of India."[42] Even after the abolition of the East India Company's trade monopoly in 1813, there were always fears about British capitalists in India following the example of the American Revolutionaries.[43] Reverend Dowding sought to win official support for closer monitoring and control of the Assam planters by calling them "openly seditious" and warning that "a non-civilian European community in a province is a dangerous element, unless the administration is strong enough to keep them in their place, and make them understand that they must obey the law as instantly as their native neighbors."[44]

Having shared disciplinary authority with the very cohort it felt threatened by (but also needed), the colonial state was ambivalent about subjecting the planter class to forms of state sovereignty and punishment. In the late nineteenth century, members of the Indian public, local Christian missionaries, and parliamentary British reformers increasingly called on the colonial regime to bring offending planters to justice. However, the punitive practices found on the tea plantations, including caning, flogging, and confinement in subterranean lockups, eerily resembled the legal forms of punishment regularly meted out in colonial prisons.[45] How was the behavior of the "wild European tribes on the frontier"[46] qualitatively different from the state's own exercise of "pain-related power?"[47] This uncomfortable question troubled many colonial administrators who in a Cockburn or a Joy Chunder Bhadra undoubtedly saw an ugly and frightful reflection of themselves.

4. "One Scale of Justice for the Planter and Another for the Coolie": European Violence in Colonial Assam

On April 28, 1893, shortly after the Balladhun murders, the proplanter Indian Tea Association met to determine an appropriate course of action. "We must appeal unto Caesar," they decided, "the sooner it is done the better. . . . Think of the number of Europeans in Cachar who consider, and rightly consider, their lives and the lives of their families to be in jeopardy." In response to this familiar invocation of black peril, Reverend Dowding replied, "Does an appeal unto Caesar only lie when Europeans—or natives, at least wealthy ones—are concerned?" In a series of critical articles, Reverend Dowding contrasted the stir caused by the Balladhun murder case with "the indifference shown as to the death of thousands of coolies." As Dowding ironically noted, one European manager had condemned Cockburn's death even though the mortality rate on his own estate had reached 30 percent![48]

Like many missionaries in nineteenth-century India, Reverend Charles Dowding was tireless in his efforts to expose British tyranny and oppression on the plantations. Dowding was an ardent moral critic of the physical, economic, and social abuses on the tea gardens and the irresponsible behavior of the government toward the planting industry. In Dowding's view, if the tea gardens could not function in an ethically responsible fashion, they should not be permitted to function at all:

> If you cannot open out Assam without this frightful waste of life, you had better leave it unopened. It is not to be borne that the defense-less coolie is to be pushed hither and thither in the interest of the idle capital of England with absolute indifference (coolies being cheap) whether he lives or dies. A coolie is not a pawn but a living man with wife and children depending on him. He is not to be classed with livestock.[49]

Dowding's was one dissident voice amid a much larger chorus of European planters who exerted tremendous influence over the colonial bureaucracy. The formal and informal legal and political privileges of the planters are the keys to understanding the administration of justice in Assam. Unlike the tea workers, who were poor, disenfranchised, and lived only temporarily in the area, the planter class was extremely powerful, organized, and well connected. They worked through various lobbying groups, such as the Indian Tea Association, exerting formal and informal pressure on the governments in India and England.[50] The intimate links between official and nonofficial Europeans in Assam were evident in subtle forms of social interaction, as when they dined, hunted, or played polo together. These informal social relations also translated into partial legal and police practices. As Dowding pointed out, "in spite of enactments meant to protect the coolie, local officers of the highest rank consider themselves entitled to put them aside or soften their action if they seem likely to embarrass those who are engaged in 'opening up the Province'."[51] Owing to these racial affinities, differential criminal charges and punishments along with prejudiced legal and medico-legal practices tilted the scale of justice in Assam in favor of the planter. As India's Viceroy Lord Curzon himself put it, there was "one scale of justice for the planter and another for the coolie."[52]

The tea plantations were generally located a great distance away from the nearest magistrate, and the planters acted as mediators and judges for workers residing in their gardens. As George Barker writes in his memoir, *A Tea Planter's Life in Assam*, "The sahib acts as judge and jury, and often sits in judgment, listening to the evidence brought forward... it is impossible to believe one word that a native utters in an affair of this kind."[53] The tea planters (like all Europeans in India) also possessed other forms of cultural capital that placed them at a great legal advantage: they spoke the court language of record (English); they understood English courtroom rituals; they typically had legal representation in court; and family members often used their contacts and knowledge of the system to advocate their causes by sending personal petitions, letters of good character, and other persuasive documents to colonial authorities. In contrast, most laborers arrived on the gardens without the basic language skills to communicate their grievances either to the planters or to the authorities. They were often unfamiliar with the written provisions of the law and generally appeared in court without legal counsel.[54]

One of the primary functions of planter violence was the enforcement of work. Public and private floggings, as well as confinement, cuffing, kicking, and other forms of physical assault, were routine elements of daily life on the tea gardens. Violence was used to create a culture of fear designed to enforce the labor regime and to prevent workers from deserting the plantation. As the Secretary of State noted in 1903, the planters expected the government to support their right of abuse: "The function of the Viceroy in their judgment is to prevent them from being punished when they whack their niggers; and they have talked themselves into a belief that if he does not so shield them the foundations of British rule are endangered."[55]

In 1878, a number of laborers from the Balipara Tea Plantation set out for the subdivisional station to lay their grievances before the magistrate. The European assistant manager in charge of the garden pursued them and attempted to force the group to return to the garden. During the ensuing confrontation, the European struck one of the laborers over the head with his heavy walking staff, and a few days later the laborer died. The assistant manager was subsequently tried in Calcutta, where he was convicted and sentenced to fifteen months of rigorous imprisonment.[56] The Balipara case is a good example of the overt methods used by the planters to subvert justice—physically preventing laborers from lodging criminal complaints—as well as the exceedingly light sentences passed on Europeans convicted of serious crimes.[57] (Incidentally, it also reveals a prevalent cause of Indian violence, which was the inability of a laborer with a grievance to leave the estate and lodge a formal complaint.[58])

Racially differential sentences flew in the face of colonial claims to impartial and impersonal justice. As Viceroy Curzon described it, the "reign of unjust and partial sentences" ensured "light measure for the white manager, cruel measure for the coolie."[59] In 1903, Mr. Bain, the assistant manager of the Kumbirgram Tea Estate, was tried in connection with the death of one of his workers.[60] Three laborers from Bain's garden—Lalsu, his wife, and his niece—had attempted to flee but were caught by the estate guards and brought back. Lalsu was tied up and beaten by Bain with a stirrup leather until he fell unconscious and shortly afterward died. Bain was tried at the Silchar sessions court before a jury of fellow planters and others connected with the tea industry for culpable homicide and causing grievous hurt. A medical doctor who was also a social acquaintance of Bain's testified in court that the marks discovered the following morning all over Lalsu's back, shoulders, buttocks, heels, and legs were caused by cadaverous lividity. The European doctor also claimed that although Lalsu appeared well outwardly, he was actually in "weak health," and suffered from heart and lung disease. The jury of Bain's peers acquitted him of both charges, passing down a conviction of simple hurt for which he was sentenced to six months of simple imprisonment. As the editors of the *Surodaya Prakasika* noted, the same punishment (in addition to a fine of thirty rupees) had recently been inflicted on an Indian clerk whose only offense was that a deficit of just over one rupee had been found in the accounts.[61]

The problem of light sentences for Europeans was directly connected to the light charges lodged against them. As Curzon noted, often times "what is called 'grievous hurt' in India bears the more uncompromising title of 'murder' at home."[62] In 1890, the European manager of a garden in north Lakhimpur was tried for voluntarily causing grievous hurt to a laborer who later died. The examining doctor testified in court that "the body of deceased was in many parts a pulp. There were four medical men present and none had ever before come across such a case." Not only did the initial charge of grievous hurt not square up to the facts of the man's death but the defendant was ultimately convicted of only simple assault, for which he was fined fifty rupees.[63] "In England, we should speak of these things as murder or manslaughter," Hypatia Bradlaugh Bonner observed, "in India they manage these things differently."[64]

Compounding the linked problem of light charges and light sentences was what Assam Chief Commissioner Henry Cotton called "the difficulty, if not impossibility, of bringing an offending planter to justice."[65] Owing to the great physical distance separating most gardens from local police stations, the social ties that bound the planter class to the colonial bureaucracy, the physical restrictions placed on the laborers' movement, and the planters' legal possession of disciplinary authority, the cases that did make it to court undoubtedly represent a small fraction of the actual incidents of criminal violence. Even within this subset of cases, the racial affinities that bound the white community in Assam had an important effect on trial outcomes. As suggested by several of the trials previously discussed, this was most clearly evident in the expert testimony provided by medical doctors that frequently excused European defendants from criminal culpability.

Medical testimony played an unusually important role in all sorts of criminal trials in colonial India because of prevalent notions about the wily and untrustworthy native and the unreliability of oral evidence. As Dr. Isidore Lyon explained, expert medical testimony, which had become "an essential part of the medical course of every university and licensing body in the United Kingdom ... is especially so in the East, where it is often the only trustworthy evidence on which hangs the liberty or life of a human being."[66] In the second half of the nineteenth century, "Indian medical jurisprudence," a distinctly colonial branch of medico-legal knowledge, developed to serve the social and political needs of the colonial state.[67]

The diseased spleen defense was an especially important example of the political embeddedness of the practice of colonial medical jurisprudence. Planters were frequently exonerated by the testimony of medical experts (often social acquaintances) who claimed that weak Indian insides belied apparently healthy Indian bodies, which appeared capable of withstanding "one or two slight blows."[68] In a case from Namdang where a laborer died after a severe beating by his manager, the court decided that the manager did not know about the enlarged spleen of his victim, and he was therefore convicted of voluntarily causing hurt for which he was fined two hundred and fifty rupees.[69] In another notorious case from Mysore, a coffee planter named De Winton had given his cook a "box in the ear" and a few kicks. The cook died several weeks later and De Winton was tried for culpable homicide not amounting to murder. The court ultimately convicted De Winton of simple hurt and sentenced him to one month's imprisonment. The verdict infuriated members of the local European community, including the "indignant" editors of *Madras Mail* who reminded their readers that the frail and childlike constitutions of Indian bodies required paternalistic restraint:

> Englishmen ought to refrain from striking natives much on the same principle that would restrain them from aiming a blow at a cripple. Added to this the knowledge that the average constitution of natives does not fit them for rough treatment, which among English boys at school, and even among adults in certain classes, is taken as a matter of course, should make Europeans scrupulous beyond measure in their treatment of natives.[70]

European planters were often absolved of guilt by medical evidence that disconnected the cause of death from an incident of violence without providing an alternative explanation for Indian mortality. In 1899, Mr. Cumming, the manager of the Ranglíting Estate, seriously flogged a boy who died three days later. The civil surgeon testified in court that the flogging had nothing to do with the boy's death, and Cumming was given a nominal fine for causing hurt.[71] A year later, the superintendent of the Rajmai Tea Estate, Mr. Greig, heard that one of his workers was stealing firewood. Greig summoned the man to his bungalow and struck him on the head with a stick, causing the man to die on the spot. Greig was tried before the sessions court for causing the man's death but was unanimously acquitted by the jury.[72]

One of the first Indian cartoons to make a major political impact appeared in 1870 in the Bengali newspaper *Sulabh Samachar*.[73] The cartoon depicted a European doctor conducting a perfunctory postmortem examination of a plantation worker. In the background, the accused European stands nonchalantly smoking a cigar. This cartoon expressed widespread Indian frustration about miscarriages of justice and the racialized nature of colonial legal and medico-legal practice.

The notion of law as an abstract system of principles designed to govern relationships between equals—a notion introduced into India by the British themselves—was quite obviously undermined by the overt partiality shown to Europeans in both legal letter and practice. Medical claims about weak Indian insides were part of the much larger system that tended to protect the planter class from criminal liability, responsibility, and punishment. In a collection of documents sent by a group of Indian reformers to the British Parliament, searing questions were posed about the record of European violence:

Who will make a catalogue of all the cases in which natives of India have been killed by Europeans, from "mistakes" and "unfortunate circumstances" of various kinds? One has his spleen ruptured, another is mistaken for a boar, another for a pigeon, and a fourth for an elephant—as if India were a hospital of moribund patients ready to die at the slightest touch, or a jungle of beasts fit only to be killed.[74]

If colonial plantation law looked at the laborer as an economic object, a "moribund patient," or a subhuman beast, how did the laborer look at the law?

5. Law, Violence, and Collective Resistance on the Tea Gardens

European tea-garden managers worked on the geographical margins of colonial India, and their aggressiveness was a reflection of both their virtually unrestrained powers to control the lives and movement of laborers and their fear of collective resistance. In the section of George Barker's tea memoir titled "Fanaticism," he advises newcomers about environmental and other dangers in the area, "If well in the jungle or near the Naga territory, it is advisable to sleep with a loaded revolver either under the pillow or near at hand for use against tigers or panthers.... Again there is the fear of a vindictive coolie, who perchance may think it a happy deliverance, so far as he is personally interest[ed] in your demise to brain you."[75] The fear and vulnerability that shaped the brutality and violence of European planters in Assam were common characteristics of racially stratified plantation societies in other world regions.[76]

Although official reports of European crime in Assam were routinely and deliberately underestimated, reports of Indian riots, assaults, and acts of intimidation offer an alternative method of recuperating both histories of planter violence and strategies of subaltern resistance. Individual and collective violence on the plantation generally occurred in response to European assaults, and read this way each reported incident of Indian crime has dual implications. As the chief commissioner of Assam acknowledged in the annual labor report of 1902–1903, official punishment of the tea workers had to be balanced by proper monitoring of the planters: "Discipline must be maintained on tea gardens, and unruliness which may lead to rioting must be strictly checked. But the occurrence of cases of this description throws upon the State some responsibility for preventing any such injustice as would give the coolies a substantial grievance."[77]

Multiple incidents of Indian resistance are found in every annual labor report, although the political basis of these acts was generally denied until the early twentieth century, when local peasant movements were drawn into the larger nationalist challenge. Whereas European violence was seen as a rational and necessary mode of labor control, peasant attacks were usually described as acts of insubordination, fanaticism, or insanity rather than politically grounded acts involving "determined and premeditated resistance."[78] George Barker tells the story of a European planter in Assam who awoke to find an employee standing over him with a knife in his hand. At his trial, the worker stated, "he had a dream, wherein, at the peril of offending his deities, he was ordered to kill the sahib. . . . When asked in court to give some explanation for his dastardly behavior, and whether the sahib was cruel, he candidly confessed that the sahib was an exceptionally good master, treated all the coolies well, and they had no grounds for complaint in any way."[79]

Contrary to Barker's description of the politically unconscious and irrational "coolie," accounts of peasant violence almost always reflected premeditation, organization, determination, and rational motivation. The attacks on European planters usually involved one of four elements: a manager with an abusive reputation and record (the clichéd brutal planter); refusal to work (often on a Sunday, a holiday, or after the expiration of a labor contract); retaliation for having been struck first or having seen a fellow worker struck; and physical and sexual assaults on women workers.

Laborers tended to act collectively and often used the "instruments of their industry," such as hoes and pickaxes, to attack and threaten their superiors, strategically turning the oppressive plantation environment on its head.[80] As J. H. Williams recalls in his memoir, *Tea Estates and Their Management*, "It is quite startling to be surrounded by a gang of 100-odd pruners armed with their pruning knives."[81] The bungalow itself was often used a symbolic target, and it was not uncommon for workers to either burn the bungalow—"mischief by fire"[82] was a common strategy of resistance—or use it to imprison the planters. In 1884, the manager of the Bowalia Tea Garden was seriously assaulted and confined in his home for several hours after he publicly caned a boy in the presence of assembled laborers.[83] Twelve tea workers were sentenced to rigorous imprisonment for terms ranging from three days to one year; and the manager was fined fifty rupees.

Collective attacks on European planters were coordinated group efforts that usually evinced advance planning. On February 6, 1892, the manager of the Barhalla Tea Estate ordered his laborers to remove a man named Harilas who was causing a disturbance as pay was being distributed. Harilas called out to his coworkers to "seize Mr. Smith," and a large group threw broken bricks and dry clay at Smith and his assistant.[84] In 1883, at the Baramchal Tea Garden, a large group of workers attacked the manager and his assistant on payday and fled with the cash. After resisting arrest, fourteen of the ringleaders were tried and sentenced to long terms of rigorous imprisonment. As the chief commissioner of Assam wrote in his annual report, "Examples have to be made in cases of this description on tea-gardens, as insubordination is contagious."[85]

Refusal to work was another common tactic of collective resistance that often led to violent confrontations. In 1891, ten workers from the Borjuli Tea Garden refused to turn out and work. According to the manager, Mr. Creagh, they had been up the night before celebrating *karma puja*, and some were "sulky and obstinate and refused to speak" to him as he made his way through the lines. At one point Creagh turned on his heel and found a worker with his stick raised above his head poised to strike him. Creagh knocked the man down and was attacked by the others on the line who chased him as he ran toward his bungalow.[86] The following year on the Tiphuk Tea Estate, thirty Ganjamese laborers struck work and left the garden. The guard who was sent after the group was beat up, and the armed workers returned to attack the European manager.[87]

Violent confrontations between capital and labor frequently involved the sexual exploitation and physical abuse of women. In 1893, the Assam chief commissioner directed "all Magistrates distinctly to recognize the principle that any employer who flogs a coolie woman or causes her to be flogged should be sentenced to a substantial term of imprisonment."[88] As Diana Paton demonstrates in the context of Jamaica, colonial concern with appropriately gendered punishment reflected the widely held nineteenth-century view that a civilization could be measured by its treatment of women.[89] In Assam, planters and officials were keenly aware of the incendiary use of women as signs by which positions of power and powerlessness were communicated between men. European managers often flaunted their despotic authority by laying their hands on Indian women workers. Owing to cross-culturally held notions about women as property and specifically South Asian ideas about male honor (*izzat*), European sexual advances and physical assaults on Indian women provoked serious resistance.

In 1893, the manager and assistant manager of the Kellyden Tea Estate tried to force their laborers to return to work after a three-day *Holi* holiday. When the laborers refused to obey, the assistant manager took a woman by the hand to force her to work at which point a "number of coolies attacked him and the manager with sticks, while one made a dangerous assault on the manager with a hoe. The labor force was in a dangerously excited state for two or three days, the police, who were called up, being at first not strong enough to restore order." The ringleaders in the incident were sentenced to up to two years of rigorous imprisonment.[90] In 1890, at the Silghat Tea Garden, the manager H. L. Smith, who had gone outside to inspect the work, was "set upon and somewhat severely handled by about forty coolies, who at the trial alleged that the manager had assaulted a coolie woman for disobedience [to] orders and that this led to their attack upon him." Fourteen men were sentenced to nine months of rigorous imprisonment.[91]

When the physical laying of hands on Indians involved sexual assaults, the results were even more inflammatory. In 1899, Mr. Bellwood, the manager of the Nadua Tea Estate, was seriously assaulted with sticks by six of his workers, who claimed that they were enraged by charges that Bellwood raped a girl on the garden. Bellwood remained in critical condition for many weeks and the men who attacked him were each sentenced to two years of rigorous imprisonment.[92] In another case, C. O. Walling, manager of the Maduri Tea Estate, allegedly summoned a fifteen-year-old girl who was plastering the walls in his bathroom to come into his bedroom and fan him. Walling had previously made "indecent overtures" to the girl, and when she refused to enter the bedroom, he hit her over the shoulders with a cane and detained her for the rest of the day in the bathroom. Although the girl and her mother made a complaint at the police station, three months later Walling again began to harass the girl, grabbing her arm in the garden and trying to force her back to his bungalow. Walling was ultimately convicted of wrongful restraint and sentenced to one week of rigorous imprisonment.[93]

Though it is difficult, given the sources, to reconstruct peasant consciousness, it is clear that the police and the courts were viewed as unstable allies and frequent foes. Laborers not only acted collectively when resisting the planters' authority they also brought the power of numbers before the law. During the trial of eleven laborers who had attacked the manager of the Bojran Tea Estate, three hundred workers from the garden sat outside the *kutcherry* on strike.[94] In 1892, the deputy commissioner of Sibsagar wrote to his superior, "One special device [that] has been resorted to by coolies of a few gardens in the Sadr subdivision deserves special mention. It is that of coming into the headquarters in a body to the number of one hundred to two hundred on the pretext of making some complaint."[95] In 1910, after attacking the manager of Kurma Tea Estate, the laborers gave a "formidable show of resistance to the Subdivisional Officer and the police which necessitated the despatch of armed police to the garden."[96] These types of actions remind us that, although the legal system clearly favored the planters, the law did not simply act on oppressed peoples.

Official responses to Indian violence starkly contrasted the leniency shown toward accused Europeans. This was partly due to proplanter lobbying groups and press outlets such as the *Englishman* that produced an unrelenting environment of hysteria in cases where their countrymen were assaulted or murdered. In 1907, in regard to the murder of an English planter named Bloomfield, the editors of the *Englishman* urged the government in no uncertain terms to take "the promptest of action. . . . Once the impression is allowed to get out that a European may be assaulted and even murdered without any risk there will be an end to the British prestige in India."[97] European planters who killed their laborers were generally punished with minimal fines, whereas Indians were seriously punished for much lesser crimes. In 1900, the European manager of the Eraligul Tea Estate was fined one hundred and fifty rupees for wrongfully confining and severely assaulting the wife and daughter of his *chaukidar* (guard). That same year, a group of laborers at the Alinagar Tea Estate who attacked an assistant manager for trying to "take their *izzat*" (a phrase that referred to sexual assault) were sentenced to between three months and five years of rigorous imprisonment.[98]

The racially differential treatment of British and Indian defendants reflected the hierarchical legal relationship that formed the fundamental structure of British rule. Unlike Chief Commissioner Henry Cotton, who was horrified by the "innumerable abuses"[99] and cases where "justice has not been always well and duly administered between man and man,"[100] most colonial administrators were less troubled by the way the system functioned. After all, how could the law deliver equal justice to those who were legally and politically unequal? In 1900, Deputy Commissioner Meltius (Darrang district) reported an incident involving a European manager named Wilcox who had struck a laborer with a cane. In response to the public beating, thirty of the man's coworkers threatened to assault Wilcox with their hoes but refrained. Wilcox reported the threat to the police and six of the laborers were sentenced to six months of rigorous imprisonment. In his comments on the case, Deputy Commissioner Meltius remarked, "As between man and man, I should consider this sentence excessive, but as between the Manager of a garden and his coolies, I am not prepared to say it is excessive."[101] If the relationship between planter and laborer was not between man and man, then how *could* killing a coolie be considered murder?

Conclusion

Issues of crime, punishment, and justice defined politics in colonial Assam. In spite of David Cannadine's claim that the British imperialists were motivated by class and not race, it is clear that Europeans in India collaborated across hierarchies of class to tip the scale of justice in favor of their countrymen.[102] As Harald Fischer-Tiné argues, even the lowliest European could cash in on the "racial dividends" of whiteness.[103] This is evident in the preferential treatment given to European prisoners and the racial differentiation in criminal charges, sentences, and punishments in Assam and elsewhere in India.[104]

What does the legal treatment of murder and violence in Assam tell us more broadly about the meanings of crime, punishment, and power in colonial India? How did colonial notions of criminal responsibility and justice fit in with the larger project of governing India? Was the law simply, as Ranajit Guha argues, the "state's emissary,"[105] or did local people find ways to negotiate law and legal institutions on their own terms?

As various chapters in this volume demonstrate, criminal law in all historical contexts is linked to modes of governance and social control. This is especially evident in colonial Assam where the law, in both letter and practice, clearly bore the mark of the dominant socioeconomic class. Not only did European planters in Assam possess private powers of punishment that effectively sanctioned acts of criminal violence but the strength of racial feeling in the region produced startlingly biased standards of criminal liability and responsibility. Criminal trials in colonial Assam reveal social and cultural ideas about Indian difference—the "treacherous and unscrupulous" Manipuris, weak Indian insides, the diseased spleen defense—as well as the power of the privileged to monopolize spaces of legal protection.

The daily acts of disobedience, dissent, and violence on the tea gardens mark the tension between law and labor. It was, after all, the law that bound the worker to the oppressive plantation environment, and it is therefore not surprising that labor confrontations frequently involved collective violence rather than formal legal redress. On the other hand, it is clear that laborers devised clever strategies of resistance by means of law that did not simply reinforce the power of the legal system. For example, mass strikes during criminal trials of coworkers simultaneously demonstrated the demand for justice and public accountability as well as a formal transgression of law.

It is evident that those who had the least access to it did not see the law in starkly oppositional terms. For the bonded laborers of Assam, and for the Indian activists who made their legal disenfranchisement a nationalist issue, the colonial promise of justice could be a potent language of resistance. The failure of law to deliver equal justice was an important catalyst for organized Indian nationalism, and concern about the mistreatment of laborers in Assam was part of a rising tide of complaints about European violence and unjust verdicts across the subcontinent.[106] Indian newspapers consistently reported on racial tyranny and the many cases where Europeans charged with murder, assault, wrongful confinement, and other forms of violence were acquitted with impunity. In 1895, the editors of the *Bengalee* expressed "the firm conviction that no justice is to be had in our courts where Europeans are charged with acts of violence done to the natives of India. It is not a baseless conviction. A long series of cases support it."[107] The searing critiques framed by Indian nationalists were carried into the halls of Parliament by British reformers and members of Parliament such as William Caine, who made the charge that "the Administration of Criminal Justice in India is such as to bring it into contempt and render it a terror to Law-abiding people."[108]

The final point we should note is that the legal history of crime in colonial Assam was not made in a geographical vacuum or a wild jungle isolated from wider trends and developments. In fact, the transnational nature of legal moves and debates in Assam—the links to global capitalism, the references to U.S. slavery, and the centrality of India (the jewel in the crown) to the far-flung British Empire—entreats us to think more seriously about the place of colonial crime and punishment within the broader narrative of modern legal history.

Notes

1. For the most recent manifestation of this tension between the law, violence, and empire, see Amnesty International's May 2005 report, "Guantánamo and Beyond: The Continuing Pursuit of Unchecked Executive Power," http://web.amnesty.org/library/ Index/ ENGAMR510632005.

2. Sir Robert Fulton, quoted in J. T. Sunderland, *India in Bondage: Her Right to Freedom* (Delhi, 1929), p. 105.

3. There is a rich body of scholarship on crime and social control in colonial India. See Sandra Frietag, "Crime in the Social Order of Colonial North India," *Modern Asian Studies* 25 (1991): 227–261; Lata Mani, "Contentious Traditions: The Debate on *Sati* in Colonial India," in *Recasting Women: Essays in Colonial History*, Kumkum Sangari and Sudesh Vaid, eds. (New Delhi: Kali for Women, 1989); Veena Talwar Oldenburg, *Dowry Murder: The Imperial Origins of a Cultural Crime* (Oxford: Oxford Univ. Press, 2002); Sanjay Nigam, "Disciplining and Policing the 'Criminals by Birth': The Making of a Colonial Stereotype," *Indian Economic and Social History Review* 27 (1990): 257–287; Radhika Singha, "The Privilege of Taking Life: Some 'Anomalies' in the Law of Homicide in the Bengal Presidency," *Indian Economic and Social History Review* 30 (1993): 181–215; Radhika Singha, "'Providential Circumstances': The Thuggee Campaign of the 1830s and Legal Innovation," *Modern Asian Studies*, 27 (1993): 83–146; Anand A. Yang, ed., *Crime and Criminality in British India* (Tucson: Univ. of Arizona Press, 1985).

4. Aimé Cesaire, *Discourse on Colonialism*, Joan Pinkham trans. (New York: Monthly Review Press, 1972) (originally published in 1955).

5. See M. K. Gandhi, *Hind Swaraj*, "The Condition of India (Continued): Lawyers," chap. 11, http://www.mkgandhi.org/swarajya/coverpage.htm.

6. Sally Engle Merry, "Resistance and the Cultural Power of Law," *Law and Society Review* 29 (1995): 11–27, 15.

7. *Indian Planters' Gazette and Sporting News*, July 7, 1885.

8. See the following India Office records pertaining to the Balladhun murder case: L/PJ/6/365, File 44; L/PJ/6/366, Files 143 and 169; L/PJ/6/369, Files 459, 467, and 468; L/PJ/6/374, Files 961, 962, and 963; L/PJ/6/376, Files 1132, 1133, and 1134; L/PJ/6/377, File 1287.

9. Sanjib Baruah, *India against Itself: Assam and the Politics of Nationality* (Oxford: Oxford Univ. Press 1999), pp. 48–49.

10. "The Tragedy of Balladhun," *Englishman*, Dec. 13, 1893.

11. *Amrita Bazar Patrika*, Dec. 13, 1893. Also see *Bengalee*, Dec. 16, 1893.

12. *Hindoo Patriot*, Dec. 14, 1893.

13. Government of India's "Minute" to the secretary of State, June 5, 1894, India Office Records (IOR), L/PJ/6/376, Files 1132 and 1133.

14. Police Department Proceedings, June 4, 1894, L/PJ/6/376, Files 1132 and 1133.

15. Herald's Report, Feb. 28, 1894, in IOR, L/PJ/6/376, Files 1132 and 1133.

16. Government of India's "Minute" to the secretary of State, June 5, 1894, IOR, L/PJ/6/376, Files 1132 and 1133.

17. James C. Scott, *Weapons of the Weak: Everyday Forms of Peasant Resistance* (New Haven: Yale Univ. Press, 1985).

18. "Conditions of Tea Laborers on the Tea Plantations in Assam" IOR, L/PJ/6/233, File 1431.

19. Letter from the chief commissioner of Assam, Feb. 13, 1903, IOR, L/PJ/6/767, File 1982, and James Buckingham's pamphlet, *Tea-Garden Coolies in Assam: Replying to a Communication on the Subject which appeared in the "Indian Churchman"; Reprinted with an Introduction and an Answer by The Rev. Charles Dowding* (Calcutta: n.p., 1894).

20. Eugene Genovese, *Roll, Jordan, Roll: The World the Slaves Made* (New York: Pantheon, 1974), p. 47.

21. Buckingham, *Tea-Garden Coolies in Assam*.

22. Rajani Kanta Das, *Plantation Labor in India* (Calcutta: R. Chatterjee, 1931), p. 27.

23. See, for example, Henry Cotton's private papers including his dispute with the tea planters from 1901 to 1904 in IOR, Mss Eur/D1202/3; Reverend Charles Dowding's pamphlet, "Coolie Notes" (Dibrugarh, India: Radhanath Press, 1895); Emma Williams' letters regarding the Assam tea laborers, IOR, L/PJ/6/749, File 632; and the countless appeals by the Indian Association and critical articles in the Indian press.

24. See Charles Dowding, "Assam Coolie Recruiting," in Buckingham's *Tea-Garden Coolies in Assam*.

25. Andrew Fede, "Legitimized Violent Slave Abuse in the American South, 1619–1865: A Case Study of Law and Social Change in Six Southern States," *American Journal of Legal History* 29 (1985): 93–150.

26. See letter no. 66, Oct. 2, 1901, from the Secretary of State to Viceroy Lord Curzon in Curzon's private papers, IOR, Mss Eur/F111/160 (1901).

27. Orlando Patterson, *Slavery and Social Death: A Comparative Study* (Cambridge, Mass.: Harvard Univ. Press, 1982).

28. On the legal treatment of the murder and abuse of U.S. slaves, see Thomas D. Morris, *Southern Slavery and the Law, 1619–1860* (Chapel Hill: Univ. of North Carolina Press, 1996), pp. 161–208. Also see Jordanna Bailkin, "The Boot and the Spleen: When Was Murder Possible in British India?" *Comparative Studies in Society and History* 48 (2006): 463–494.

29. "Report on Labour Immigration into the Province of Assam for the Year 1899," IOR, V/24/1223, Chief Commissioner Henry Cotton's remarks.

30. "Labour Immigration, 1877," IOR, V/24/1222.

31. "The Labour System of Assam," a pamphlet reissued by the Humanitarian League in 1906, IOR, L/PJ/6/765, File 1731.

32. "Labour Immigration, 1900," IOR, V/24/1223.

33. The term *nonofficial* refers to Europeans in India who did not work for the government in an official capacity.

34. *Beharee*, "The Planter and the Ryot," Sep. 11, 1912.

35. The articles were reprinted in book form. Dwarkanath Ganguli, *Slavery in British Dominion* (Calcutta: Jijnasa, 1972).

36. *Bengalee*, Mar., 10, 1901.

37. Bailkin, "Boot and the Spleen."

38. "Labour Immigration, 1893," IOR, V/24/1222.

39. See letter no. 55, from the Secretary of State to Lord Curzon, Aug. 15, 1901, in Curzon's private papers, IOR, Mss Eur/F111/160 (1901).

40. See the letter from John Bebb and James Pattison to George Canning, dated Feb. 27, 1818, IOR, *Papers Relating to the Settlement of Europeans in India* (1854); and Thomas Macaulay, *Speeches and Poems with the Report and Notes on the Indian Penal Code* (New York: Hurd & Houghton, 1867).

41. *Parliamentary Papers*, Apr. 23, 1893, 7:106–114. Charles Grant worried that under a liberal immigration policy "low and licentious" Europeans would "vex, harass and perplex the weak natives." As Harald Fischer-Tiné argues, there are obviously class prejudices writ large over these fears about "discharged or dismissed European soldiers . . . wandering about in the country." Grant quoted in Ainslie Embree, *Charles Grant and British Rule in India* (New York: Columbia Univ. Press, 1962), p. 169. See also Waltraud Ernst, "Idioms of Madness and Colonial Boundaries," *Comparative Studies in Society and History* 39 (1997): 153–181; and Harald Fischer-Tiné, "Low and Licentious Europeans": White Subalterns in Colonial India, ca. 1784–1914" (manuscript in progress).

42. See the letter from Governor General Cornwallis to Henry Dundas, dated Nov. 7, 1794, IOR, *Papers Relating to the Settlement of Europeans in India* (1854).

43. See the debates on colonization in *Parliamentary Papers*, 1831–1832, 8:339–467.

44. See the letter from Reverend Charles Dowding, Feb. 25, 1902, IOR, L/PJ/6/595, File 403.

45. See Radhika Singha, *A Despotism of Law: Crime and Justice in Early Colonial India* (Oxford: Oxford Univ. Press, 1998); Jörg Fisch, *Cheap Lives and Dear Limbs: The British Transformation of the Bengal Criminal Law, 1769–1817* (Wiesbaden: Franz Steiner Verlag,

1983); Satadru Sen, *Disciplining Punishment: Colonialism and Convict Society in the Andaman Islands* (Oxford: Oxford Univ. Press, 2000).

46. *Indian Planters' Gazette and Sporting News*, July 7, 1885. Also see Anupama Rao, "Problems of Violence, States of Terror: Torture in Colonial India," in a special issue of *Interventions: Journal of Postcolonial Studies* titled "Discipline and the Other Body," 3 (2001): 186–205.

47. Diana Paton, *No Bond but the Law: Punishment, Race, Gender and Jamaican State Formation, 1780–1870* (Durham, N.C.: Duke Univ. Press, 2004), p. 12.

48. See Dowding's introduction in the pamphlet by James Buckingham, *Tea-Garden Coolies in Assam*.

49. See the letter from Dowding to the Secretary of State dated Sep. 23, 1896, IOR, L/PJ/6/417, File 575. Dowding's position was shared by the Indian nationalist press. Compare his view to the position voiced by the editors of the Bengali-language *Sanjivani* that "the tea trade should be ruined and Assam should become the abode of wild beasts [rather] than that this fearful custom of selling coolies as slaves should be kept up." Cited in Bipan Chandra, *The Rise and Growth of Economic Nationalism in India* (New Delhi: People's Publishing House, 1966), p. 370.

50. On planters' organizations, see Raymond K. Renford, *The Non-Official British in India to 1920* (Oxford: Oxford Univ. Press, 1987).

51. See the letter from Dowding to the Secretary of State dated Sep. 23, 1896, IOR, L/PJ/6/417, File 575.

52. See Lord Curzon's letter to the Secretary of State, Letter No. 62, Sep. 11, 1901, in Curzon's private papers, IOR Mss Eur/F111/160.

53. See George Barker, *A Tea Planter's Life in Assam* (Calcutta: Thacker, Spink, 1884), p. 174.

54. See Emma Williams' letter regarding Assam tea laborers, Mar. 24, 1906, IOR, L/PJ/6/749, File 632, and Ganguli, *Slavery in British Dominion*, p. 4.

55. See the letter to Curzon in Curzon's private papers IOR, Mss Eur/F111/162 (1903).

56. "Labour Immigration, 1878," IOR, V/24/1222.

57. In colonial Calcutta, Richard Hula found, Indian prisoners faced jail sentences that were on average ten times as long as those of their Europeans in the same prisons. See Richard Hula, "Calcutta: The Politics of Crime and Conflict, 1800 to the 1970s," in *The Politics of Crime and Conflict: A Comparative History of Four Cities*, Ted Robert Gurr, Peter N. Grabosky, and Richard C. Hula, eds. (London: Sage, 1977), pp. 467–616.

58. "Assam Labor Enquiry and Committee's Report and Amendment of Labor and Emigration (Assam) Act 1901," IOR, L/PJ/6/753, File 954.

59. See Curzon's letter to Cotton, July 22, 1901, in Cotton's private papers, IOR, Mss Eur/D1202/2.

60. See the case file at National Archives of India Home/Public (A), Apr. 1903, pp. 261–271.

61. Excerpt from *Surodaya Prakasika*, Mar. 11, 1901, in IOR, RNNM L/R/5/111.

62. See Lord Curzon's Letter No. 59 to the Secretary of State, Aug. 28, 1901, IOR, Mss Eur/F111/160.

63. See "Labour Immigration, 1890," IOR, V/24/1222.

64. Humanitarian League, "Labour System of Assam."

65. See Cotton's clippings on his confrontation with the Assam planters, 1901–1904, in IOR, Mss Eur/D1202/3 and the reports on labor immigration, 1899 and 1900, IOR, V/24/1223.

66. Isidore Lyon, *A Textbook of Medical Jurisprudence for India* (Calcutta: Thacker, Spink, 1888).

67. See chap. 5 of my unpublished dissertation, "'The Body Evidencing the Crime': Gender, Law and Medicine in Colonial India" (New York: Columbia Univ., 2002).

68. This comment was made by the editors of the *Madras Mail* in reference to the North-West Province High Court trial of Mr. Fox, who struck and killed his *punkhawallah*. The medical evidence concluded that the *punkhawallah* had an enlarged spleen and that he would not have died had he been healthy. Fox was charged with one month's rigorous imprisonment and a fine of two hundred rupees. *Madras Mail*, Feb. 14, 1882.

69. See "Labour Immigration, 1904–05," IOR, V/24/1223.

70. *Madras Mail*, Feb. 14, 1882.

71. See "Labour Immigration, 1899," IOR, V/24/1223.

72. See "Labour Immigration, 1900," IOR, V/24/1223.

73. Partha Mitter, "Cartoons of the Raj," *History Today* 47, no. 9 (Sep. 1997): 16.

74. "Justice Murdered in India," republished in Ganguli, *Slavery in British Dominion*, pp. 64–65.

75. Barker, *Tea Planter's Life in Assam*, pp. 112–113.

76. See Ann Stoler, *Capitalism and Confrontation in Sumatra's Plantation Belt, 1870–1979* (New Haven, Conn.: Yale Univ. Press, 1985).

77. "Labour Immigration, 1902–1903," IOR, V/24/1223.

78. See "Labour Immigration, 1884," IOR, V/24/1222.

79. Barker, *Tea Planter's Life in Assam*, pp. 112–113.

80. See "Labour Immigration, 1899," IOR, V/24/1223.

81. IOR, Mss Eur/235/1. George Barker describes how the hoe "has a blade about eight inches wide, with a long handle, and in the hands of an irate coolie forms a very awkward weapon." Barker, *Tea Planter's Life in Assam*, p. 130.

82. See "Labour Immigration, 1888," IOR, V/24/1222.

83. "Labour Immigration, 1890," IOR, V/24/1223, and "Labour Immigration, 1884," IOR, V/24/1222.

84. "Labour Immigration, 1892," IOR, V/24/1222.

85. "Labour Immigration, 1883," IOR, V/24/1222.

86. "Labour Immigration, 1891," IOR, V/24/1223.

87. "Labour Immigration, 1892," IOR, V/24/1223.

88. "Labour Immigration, 1893," IOR, V/24/1223.

89. "In Jamaica, the flogging of women by their owners was banned in 1834. Paton, *No Bond but the Law*, p. 7.

90. "Labour Immigration, 1893," IOR, V/24/1223.

91. "Labour Immigration, 1890," IOR, V/24/1222.

92. "Labour Immigration, 1899," IOR, V/24/1223.

93. "Labour Immigration, 1892," IOR V/24/1223.

94. "Labour Immigration, 1896," IOR, V/24/1223.

95. "Labour Immigration, 1892," IOR V/24/1223.

96. See "Report on Immigrant Labour in the Assam Districts of Eastern Bengal and Assam for the Year ending June 30, 1911," IOR, V/24/1224.

97. See the *Englishman*, July 21, 1907, and IOR, L/PJ/6/802, File 846. In the Bloomfield case, the entire village seems to have participated in the attack.

98. "Labour Immigration, 1900," IOR V/24/1223.

99. See Cotton's letter to Curzon dated Sep. 17, 1901, in Cotton's private papers IOR, Mss Eur/D1202/2.

100. See "Labour Immigration, 1900," IOR, V/24/1223.

101. "Labour Immigration, 1900," IOR, V/24/1223.

102. David Cannadine, *Ornamentalism: How the British Saw Their Empire* (Oxford: Oxford Univ. Press 2002).

103. Fischer-Tiné, "Low and Licentious Europeans."

104. For evidence of racially differential justice in colonial Calcutta, see Hula, "Calcutta."

105. Ranajit Guha, *Dominance without Hegemony: History and Power in Colonial India* (Cambridge, Mass.: Harvard Univ. Press, 1997).

106. The various regional versions of *Report on Native Newspapers* contain scores of articles on this issue.

107. These kinds of reports were cited by the colonial government in 1878 when it passed the Vernacular Press Act, aimed at repressing seditious propaganda in the vernacular newspapers. See Ram Gopal Sanyal, *Record of Criminal Cases between Europeans and Indians* (Calcutta: India Daily News Press, 1893).

108. OR, L/PJ/6/369, Files 459, 467, and 468. On many occasions during this period, different members in the House of Commons pressed the Secretary of State on the issue of European brutality. On Apr. 17, 1890, member of Parliament Mr. Bradlaugh requested the full proceedings of the Thomas O'Hara murder trial and a return showing the number of murders committed in India over the past five years, distinguishing cases where Indians had been murdered by Europeans and where such murders had remained undetected, as well as convictions, acquittals, and punishments in such cases. IOR, L/PJ/6/275, File 672. On Nov. 9, 1893, member Mr. Webb asked whether the Secretary of State had made inquiry into the case of private John Rigby, who had kicked a punkhawallah to death and been fined one hundred rupees, as well as the case of a judge who, while trying a white man accused of raping a Rajput woman, admitted charging the jury with a strong bias in favor of the accused. IOR, L/PJ/6/360, File 2170. On May 5, 1898, member William Wedderburn asked the Secretary of State for more information about the murder of an Indian doctor who was attacked in his carriage and murdered near the railway station in Barrackpore. IOR, L/PJ/6/480, File 945.

TWELVE

"Enfeebling the Arm of Justice"
Perjury and Prevarication in British India

WENDIE ELLEN SCHNEIDER

In 1858 the governor-general of India, Charles Canning, passed on a remarkable petition to the Court of Directors of the East India Company (EIC) in London. The petition was from Ishri Pershad, described by Canning as a "native of respectability" in the city of Allahabad.[1] Writing in the aftermath of the Mutiny-Rebellion of 1857–1858, which had sorely challenged British rule, Pershad had a simple message for the British government of the North-Western Provinces in India: I told you so. Pershad reminded the government that in 1856, before the outbreak of the Mutiny-Rebellion, he had proposed a scheme of governance. If only they had listened to him, Pershad wrote, "the mutinies of some 40 or 50 regiments would never have occurred."[2] Pershad's scheme was a curious one: he advised that sweepers, the so-called untouchables who could pollute higher-caste Hindus through even slight contact, be specially attached to each criminal court. These sweepers would be employed to spit into the mouths of natives convicted of perjury, thereby defiling them. Those convicted of perjury and defiled could then be converted to Christianity and employed as a regiment to defend Allahabad.

The British never seriously considered Pershad's suggestions; Canning forwarded his petition to London merely as evidence of popular belief among inhabitants of the North-Western Provinces that the British sought widespread conversions. The Court of Directors, for its part, noted that Pershad "wish[ed] to recommend himself to the authorities and to obtain preferment for himself and his brother," and the directors urged the government in India to "strictly abstain from all measures" that might support the belief that the British wished to force Indians to become Christians.[3] But Pershad's letter is evocative nonetheless. His linkage of effective control of perjury to colonial governance uncovers the complicated consequences of an ideology of colonialism based on the rule of law.

Pershad did not hit on perjury by accident. Perjury loomed large in the colonial imagination because of the British conviction of its prevalence. British administrators in India tended to see most, if not all, witnesses as likely perjurers. Pershad appears to have known this; certainly, he seems to have thought that the British would accept his assumption that the ranks of perjurers were numerous enough to provide a credible defense for a large city like Allahabad. In part because of their unshakable belief that perjury was rampant in India, British administrators returned repeatedly to the question of identifying, regulating, and punishing liars. Pershad might be forgiven for thinking that his suggestion would simply have been the latest in a long series of related legal innovations.

Nor, for that matter, was Pershad's solution as far out of line as it initially seems. In proposing a quasi-religious sanction—defiling contact with a sweeper—Pershad's proposal combined two other themes that characterized British attempts to combat perjury under the EIC's rule. First, Pershad's suggestion employed shame as a crucial tool of governance. During the company's control of the legal system, the British sought a sanction or form of oath that would mobilize community sentiment against perjury. They identified lack of ignominy as a key reason why their efforts against perjury appeared to fail and tried to develop ways of cultivating the revulsion they felt was missing. Pershad would have been familiar with other British attempts to inculcate shame, such as branding on the forehead or forcing an offender to blacken his face and ride backward on an ass; in this context, his suggestion looks rather less bizarre. Second, Pershad's framing of his punishment within a religious context—in this case Hinduism—is consonant with the British history of placing their criminal law in India within indigenous religious traditions. The British radically transformed the Islamic law of perjury—ostensibly the law that they administered—while maintaining at least the facade of continuity with Islamic tradition. Pershad's linkage of a criminal offense with military defense suggests that forensic deceit was a question of order as much as it was of law.

This chapter will explore the process by which the British redefined perjury in response to the perceived exigencies of colonial rule. British legislative efforts in India stand in stark contrast to the history of law reform in England, where little redefinition of the substantive law took place in the same period. British legislative creativity in the subcontinent was driven by anxiety about the ability of British administrators to uncover the truth in disputes before them. Perjury justified colonial rule by separating rulers from ruled—with the British convinced that they were honest and Indians inherently mendacious—but it also complicated it by suggesting that colonial administrators were constantly at risk of being duped. Perjury's contradictions crossed the boundaries between substantive and procedural law, challenging both the definition of the crime itself and the legitimacy of the judicial system in British India. The tension between these contradictory aspects of the ideology of the rule of law forced administrators to revisit the question of perjury constantly, searching for a solution to a dilemma created, in large part, by the very nature of colonialism. British interest in redefining perjury took multiple forms. They were not only concerned with the evidentiary requirements of the crime and its punishment but also sought to develop an analogous offense—prevarication— that would strengthen their control over the colonial legal process without extensive investigation into underlying facts or the intent of the accused.

Perjury had a special role to play in maintaining the legitimacy of the legal system. Belief in widespread perjury challenged administrators' and spectators' confidence in the validity of judicial decisions; combating perjury, therefore, was crucial to maintaining colonial rule. The rule of law has long been advanced as one of the central rationales for colonial rule by many imperialists themselves.[4] As Peter Fitzpatrick writes, "[L]aw was a prime justification and instrument of imperialism."[5] With specific reference to India, Thomas Metcalf similarly argues, "[I]n place of a religious faith shared with its subject, the British colonial state . . . found its legitimacy in a moralization of 'law.'"[6] Examining the struggle over perjury in the British administration of India highlights profound anxieties and contradictions in the use of the rule of law as a sustaining ideology of colonial rule. It can therefore contribute to the growing interest in looking at contradictions and conflicts within the colonial project.[7] Scholars such as Martin Chanock, for example, have pointed to the tensions caused by embedding the universality promised in the rhetoric of the rule of law within a framework of colonial difference.[8] But these tensions should not be seen as limited to the colonial setting: the rhetoric of legal equality in the metropole was both undergirded and in some ways contradicted by a notion of police power that drew on profound distinctions between the ruler and the ruled, between the head of the family writ large and the subordinate members of his household.[9]

British notions of the prevalence of perjury in India paradoxically served both to destabilize and to sustain faith in rule of law as colonial justification. For those closest to the administration of law in India—the magistrates and judges working for the EIC—belief in the ubiquity of perjury caused them to doubt the practical benefits of the vaunted rule of law. Unsure of the veracity of much of the evidence that they relied on in their decisions, magistrates and judges questioned the justice of their judgments. A. Tufton, magistrate in Bahar, complained along these lines in 1801:

In short, to speak my mind without reserve, this crime is so common and audacious, that it has excited in me the most complete scepticism with respect to all evidence which is offered, and I seldom pass a judgment, without having cause to doubt if I have not been imposed upon.[10]

For the lawgivers, the rule of law was a hopeful pretense, covering up the awkward reality of justice based on guesswork. In John Comaroff's apt description, the search for truth in British Indian courtrooms was one of the "disarticulated, semicoherent, inefficient strivings for modes of rule that might work in unfamiliar, intermittently hostile places a long way from home."[11]

Yet at the same time, British ideas about perjury helped deflect criticism of the practical workings of the colonial state. Native perjury could explain why the rule of law seemed to bring little in the way of actual progress in its wake.[12] In Metcalf's summary, "[I]f Indians were people without moral principles, then inevitably they lied in court, pocketed bribes, and willfully rejected the benefits of British justice."[13] As James Mill argued, Indian vices "enfeebled the arm of justice" in British India.[14] The British, as they saw it, brought the horse to water, but the Indians, habituated to perjury by centuries of despotic government, refused to drink. Perjury and prevarication, in the form of prosecutions and discourse regarding their prevalence, also sustained colonial ideology by providing a concrete location for and confirmation of beliefs about native mendacity.[15] Metcalf has pointed out that British ideology depended on the construction of polarities, among them *honesty* and *deceit*, with the British as paragons of the former and Indians as embodiments of the latter.[16] Perjury prosecutions and discussion of the prevalence of perjury and prevarication ceaselessly created and re-created this polarity, giving it the imprimatur of juridical truth. This differentiation echoed the treatment of slaves in the U.S.: there, testimony by enslaved persons was strictly limited, and degrading punishments for perjury, such as public whipping or pillorying, were adopted to combat what was seen as their inherent mendacity and irreligion.[17] In both cases, the distinction between ruler and ruled justified methods of control within the procedural structure of the courts that were directed at entire populations.

Perjury, moreover, speaks to the recent interest in understanding colonialism as a system of production and control of knowledge. As Nicholas Dirks writes, "[C]olonialism was made possible, and then sustained and strengthened, as much by cultural technologies of rule as it was by the more obvious and brutal modes of conquest that first established power on foreign shores."[18] Bernard Cohn has identified one of the most important of these "cultural technologies": British colonialism's assumption that society could be represented as a series of facts and that administrative power stemmed from efficient use of those facts. The British therefore needed to collect the facts, through what Cohn calls "investigative modalities." These modalities took a variety of forms, from historiography and museology, surveys and the census, to sciences such as economics and ethnology.[19] Subsequent historians have pointed out that British production of knowledge took place on different levels of generality, from the broad-ranging ideological constructions of James Mill or William Jones, to what C. A. Bayly calls "the level of practical, *ad hoc*, 'satisficing' administration."[20]

Perjury was a problem at the level of "satisficing" administration and, like other problems on this level, has received little attention. When British administration depended on native informants, there was almost inevitably fear of deceit. This fear has been explored in the context of native informers in *dacoity* and *thuggee* cases,[21] as well as suspicion of political informers[22] and revenue officials.[23] I argue here that the anxiety about perjury and prevarication in courtroom testimony should be set alongside the other "knowledge panics" that periodically marked the interaction between British attempts to develop systematic knowledge and their dependence on the opaque native informant.

I

The British not only saw perjury everywhere but also had an unprecedented level of agreement among themselves as to its ubiquity. Britons of all political orientations and statuses in India saw perjury as a significant threat to colonial administration. Joachim Hayward Stocqueler, author of popular guidebooks on India,[24] warned newcomers that the "prevalence of perjury among all classes of native witnesses" constituted one of the greatest obstacles to the administration of justice.[25] Phrase books also inculcated the expectation that Indians would lie. George Hadley's *A Compendious Grammar of the Current Corrupt Dialect of the Jargon of Hindostan* taught its reader to declaim, "[A] liar you are!" and "[F]alse news do not bring!" for the edification of servants and sepoys.[26]

The idea that perjury was common because there was no community sanction against it had its roots in missionary attempts to discredit Hinduism. While missionaries were not allowed to proselytize in British India until 1813, evangelical critiques of Indian religions dated back to the late eighteenth century, with Charles Grant's condemnation of Hinduism. Missionaries were eager to dispute the conservatives' support for native beliefs by demonstrating that lying was a vice encouraged among Indians by religious ideas and community sentiment. As the missionary J. Statham wrote in 1832, "Lying is not considered a vice with them; but on the contrary, the man who can dissimulate most successfully is most applauded; and the greatest lies, so far from being considered as worthy of censure, are extolled."[27] Another missionary tied this affection for rule breakers to the example set by Hindu gods, noting, "[A]s most of these gods are thieves or liars, the practice of theft and falsehood among men, cannot be looked on, in a very serious light."[28] But the idea spread beyond missionary circles to become one of the most common British analyses of perjury: legislators, as we will explore later, sought repeatedly to create community revulsion against perjury through manipulation of either the religious oath guaranteeing testimony or the punishment awarded to perjurers.

Those Britons who sought to maintain local traditions in India, meanwhile, turned the missionary analysis on its head. In their view, British education and institutions did not bring progress but instead had a demoralizing effect. The longer the British controlled Indian territory, they argued, the more prevalent perjury became. In the 1840s William Sleeman,[29] commissioner for Thuggee and Dacoity, devoted an entire chapter of his memoirs to the question of Indian mendacity.[30] He argued that honesty was universal in India among the wildest hill tribes, because members of small communities depended on the veracity of others, but that experience with British rule quickly convinced Indians that the British judges and magistrates were incapable of detecting falsehood.[31]

As Metcalf notes, "[T]he British saw deception and deceit everywhere in India."[32] He links this fear to colonial anxiety, a British sense of their own "inability to know and control their colonial subjects."[33] Because the anxiety stemmed from an inescapable condition of colonial rule, no amount of legislative reform or vigorous enforcement of the law could quiet it. Nonetheless, the British sought to do precisely that—to invent new laws and ways of enforcing them that would finally put to rest their own anxieties about perjury. The following sections trace the remarkable creativity with which they pursued this largely futile quest.

II

The British decided early on that they would govern India through local law.[34] As a result, they had to discover that law or be entirely dependent on their native law officers, the Hindu *pandits* and Islamic *maulavi*, *kazis*, and *muftis*. Bernard Cohn and J. D. M. Derrett record how the British attempted to cement their power by imposing a rigid structure, particularly on Hindu law. This endeavor stemmed from their belief that the law could be made stable by locating and identifying the oldest exposition as the most authoritative. In short, the British sought to locate India's "ancient constitution."[35]

As the British assumed control of the criminal justice system in Bengal in 1790, they confronted a law in which even the categories were alien to them. Crimes, they discovered, were divided in Islamic law by types of punishment: *qisas*, or retaliation; *diyut*, or blood money; *hadd*, or fixed punishment; and *tazir* or *siyasa*, or discretionary or exemplary, punishment.[36] In some cases, moreover, control of prosecution remained in the hands of the victim's family members. The crimes for which the punishment was fixed—such as illicit intercourse, wine drinking, and robbery—were limited in number.[37] Perjury was not among them. It was considered punishable by *tazir*, a category of discretionary punishments that could include imprisonment, exile, corporal punishment, reprimand, or humiliating treatment. The British saw Mughal administration of Islamic law, however, as at once too harsh and too lenient. Corporal punishments such as mutilation seemed too severe; by contrast, the actual punishments normally inflicted in cases of perjury struck British observers as too lenient.[38] In the last years of Mughal criminal administration, British commentators observed, prisoners convicted of perjury had received "inadequate" sentences: they were released without any punishment at all.[39] The British, therefore, sought to work within the flexibility provided by the amorphous category of *tazir* to ensure that perjury received consistent and stringent punishment. Among the possible forms of *tazir* applicable to perjury was *tashhir*, or exemplary punishment. The history of *tashhir* in Mughal India combined both Islamic and Hindu precedents.[40] It was to become, as we will see later, one of the favored British responses to the never-ending problem of perjury.

The first English treatise on Islamic law, Charles Hamilton's *Hedaya*, published in 1791, provided the basic outlines of perjury's position in Islamic law. The *Hedaya* declared, "A false witness must be stigmatized."[41] According to the Hanifite authorities relied on in the *Hedaya*, perjury should be punished with shaming, or *tashhir*. What exactly constituted shaming, however, was a matter of dispute. Public shaming, scourging, and imprisonment all had some form of precedential authority according to the *Hedaya*.[42] The authorities cited in the *Hedaya* were silent on a number of other questions, including the definition of perjury and the standard of proof to be applied.

Hindu law proved even more elusive for British officials. In part because the Mughal government had enforced Islamic criminal law, the British found it difficult to determine the parameters of Hindu law on perjury. The earliest attempt to translate Hindu law was Nathaniel Halhed's *A Code of Gentoo Laws* published in 1776.[43] Halhed's work was an English translation of a Persian translation of the work of a committee of eleven pandits, assembled by Hastings to compile a digest of Hindu law on various topics.[44] In the words of one modern commentator, "The Hindu criminal law as presented in the 'Gentoo Code' is full of impracticable and absurd direction which cannot represent any systematic practice."[45] Halhed's section on the punishments for false evidence must have deeply puzzled English lawyers. "The crime of false witness," he translated,

> is the same as if a man had murdered a Brahmin, or had deprived a woman of life, or had assassinated his friend; or of one, who, in return for good, gives evil; or who, having learned a science or profession, gives his tutor no reward; or of a woman, who, having neither son, nor grandson, nor grandson's son, after her husband's death, celebrates not the seradeh [feast in honor of the dead] to his memory.[46]

But from there, Halhed's translation went on to detail how moral culpability changed in relation to the nature of the dispute. For example, false witnessing in a matter concerning a horse resulted in guilt "as great as the guilt of murdering one hundred persons" while that in a matter concerning gold resulted in guilt equivalent to that "incurred in murdering all the men who have been born, who shall be born in the world."[47] Despite these extravagant declarations of culpability, Halhed's text was strangely silent (to legal ears) about what, if any, punishment might be imposed in these cases.

These scholarly pursuits were, however, a matter of pressing concern to British administrators as they sought to establish control over their new subjects. It seems likely that perjury under the Raj was an everyday form of resistance, defined by scholars as a "form[] of struggle present in the behaviors and cultural practices of subordinated people at times other than overt revolt."[48] It would be surprising if there were not some elements of everyday resistance in the perjury cases that plagued British officials in India. Similar anticolonial resistance has been described by John Rogers in colonial Sri Lanka, where popular support for the illegal activity of gambling led to what he calls "resistance within the law" marked by false accusations and misleading testimony. "Faced with the necessity of dealing with an alien but effective form of power," Rogers observes, "Sri Lankans treated the colonial courts as morally neutral, and manipulated them to their own advantage. They regarded testimony not as true or false, but as effective or ineffective."[49]

Anecdotal evidence from perjury cases appealed to the Sadar (literally, "High") Courts suggests that, at the very least, Indian witnesses were likely to put loyalty to family members, friends, or perhaps employers above legality. There are a surprising number of impersonation cases, in which relatives pretended to be unrelated witnesses.[50] The Bengal Sadar Court opted for mercy in the case of an ailing seventy-year-old man who had pretended to be unrelated to his son, citing his age.[51] Nor were the personators just relatives. Mahommed Alee, for example, impersonated the son of a local official, the *chuprassee*.[52] Unrelated impersonators[53] or friends[54] also figure in the cases. Still other cases present circumstances suggesting that British fears of paid, professional witnesses were not unfounded. One convicted perjurer, for example, gave evidence twice in the space of a month, each time under a different name.[55] While it is difficult to discern precise motives from the terse accounts of reported cases, the number of impersonation cases suggests that giving false testimony on something as basic as one's own identity was comparatively common.

III

Throughout the period covered in this chapter, there were two court systems in EIC-ruled territory. The first, the supreme courts within the presidency towns themselves, operated as English courts, staffed by common law judges and possessing jurisdiction over suits involving British citizens and employees of the EIC.[56] The second, the *adalat* or *mofussil* system, administered justice in the *mofussil*, or countryside outside the presidency towns. It was staffed by a combination of company civil servants and native officials and applied local law. While the EIC had initially been content to assume a merely supervisory role, leaving the previous Mughal system of government largely unchanged, successive administrations toward the end of the eighteenth century dramatically expanded their control. This process culminated during the governor-generalship of Lord Cornwallis, from 1786 to 1793.[57]

Under the criminal justice system instituted by Cornwallis in 1790, the Indian official previously in charge of the criminal side of the judiciary was divested of that power, and the governor-general and council served as the Sadar Court.[58] At the apex of the *mofussil* system were the Sadar Courts: the Sadar Nizamat Adalat on the criminal side, and the Sadar Diwani Adalat on the civil side.[59] The 1790 system also reorganized the lower criminal courts. Bengal was divided into four divisions, or circuits, which in turn comprised several districts. The Court of Circuit, which consisted of two EIC civil servants assisted by native law officers, was to hear all criminal cases.[60] The role of the native law officers, or *kazis* and *muftis*, was to decide the law applicable to the case and issue a *fatwa*, or statement of that law. When the judges disagreed with their law officers, the dispute was referred to the Nizamat Adalat.[61] The magistrate, also a company civil servant, was the principal officer in each district and was responsible for investigation of cases. The magistrate, however, had authority only to try offenders and inflict punishment in petty cases; all serious cases had to be committed for trial before the circuit court.[62] After 1790, therefore, the company had assumed direct control over the administration of criminal justice, ousting Indians with the exception of the native law officers.[63]

The process of lawmaking in India under the company proceeded through a variety of means. While Islamic law formed the basis of the criminal law in Bengal and Madras, and for many of the residents of Bombay, it could be and was modified through legislation. Before the Charter Act of 1833, each presidency separately passed legislation and new laws were referred to as regulations; after 1833 lawmaking was consolidated for all of British India and new laws were referred to as acts. Below the level of legislative enactment, however, the picture of lawmaking becomes rather murkier. The Sadar Courts of Bengal did not adopt the principle of stare decisis,[64] so that, while selected case decisions were published, they provided an erratic guide to the nature of the law. In addition to case law, the Sadar Courts of each presidency also issued two types of general letters, known as circular orders and constructions, distributed to all inferior judges. These letters reflected the Sadar Court's bureaucratic role in supervising the lower courts and responding to queries and problems raised in monthly reports from the judges. Constructions, in theory, provided just that: the authoritative construction placed by the Sadar Court on regulations.[65]

In this hybrid legal system, perjury presented an immediate problem. While the British sought to retain Islamic criminal law in Bengal, they found it impossible to maintain Islamic law regarding perjury. After 1790, when the British first fully assumed direct control over the administration of criminal justice in Bengal, selected aspects of Islamic law were changed because the British found them unworkable, most notably, the law of evidence; certain punishments, such as mutilation; and the law of murder,[66] which had left prosecution largely within the discretion of the victim's relations. These changes have been ably studied by Jörg Fisch;[67] what is less well known is that the British quickly discovered that redefinition of the substantive law of perjury and its punishments was also crucial to their assumption of judicial control. In this context, the demands of colonial governance drove change in both the procedural and substantive laws.

BENGAL: INSCRIBING THE SENTENCE

In 1797 the government of Bengal moved to amend the law of perjury, one of the first changes made to the substantive criminal law outside of the law of murder.[68] As mentioned previously, British judges feared that the discretionary punishment administered to perjurers was too mild. While the British were, in theory, administering Islamic law, the impetus for this change clearly came from the British judges themselves, not their Islamic law officers. In October 1797 the third judge of the circuit court, Dacca Division, reported to the register of the Nizamat Adalat on the state of affairs he had observed while on circuit in Chittagong. He complained that "[perjury] is prevalent to a most gross and notorious degree in this district. Hardly a trial occurred before me, in which I did not find reason to impeach the veracity of the witnesses on one side or the other."[69] The third judge had a solution that he believed other British judges would concur with: harsher penalties than those possible under Islamic law. Specifically, the third judge recommended that a convicted perjurer be branded, both to create the stigma of infamy and to alert subsequent judges to the unreliability of his or her testimony.[70]

The Nizamat Adalat was inclined to agree with the third judge, but felt that his suggestion should first be circulated to and approved by their Islamic law officers.[71] They suggested use of a form of permanent tattooing, called *godna*, that was commonly used by women for decoration.[72] A month later, the judges of the Nizamat Adalat obtained a representation from the law officers that the proposed punishment was not forbidden under Islamic law.[73] The law officers pointed out that discretionary punishments for perjury already included blackening an offender's face and public exposure on an ass. New discretionary punishments, such as the branding proposed by the third judge, were permissible by analogy. Moreover, they interpreted the Koran's prohibition on *wusheer* (tattooing) as designed to stop women from ornamenting themselves. As to the question of what text to brand on the face of the unfortunate perjurer, the law officers recommended "der gowahe duroogh go asteen" (this person is a perjured witness), which, they assured the Nizamat Adalat, could be read in both verse and prose.[74]

Satisfied by this, the Nizamat Adalat submitted a draft regulation allowing a judge to impose a "mark of ignominy" in addition to the usual punishment of exposure.[75] Adopted as Regulation XVII of 1797, it noticed "the prevalence of perjury" in the courts. Under it, judges who determined that the prisoner would not be sufficiently punished by the "usual mode of public exposure" could direct "the words 'derogh go,' or such other words as, in the most current local language, may concisely express the nature of the crime, to be marked on the forehead of the prisoner, by the process commonly denominated 'godena.' "[76] The regulation cautioned judges that it should be used with "utmost deliberation and caution" to ensure that only offenders truly deserving of the lifelong stigma of branding be selected.[77] Finally, in passing, it defined the crime of perjury, declaring it to be "the willful delivery of false evidence on oath, or under solemn obligation esteemed equivalent to an oath, in some judicial proceeding; and in a matter material to the issue thereof."[78]

The use of *godna* as punishment was innovative on a number of levels. As Radhika Singha points out, it "was probably the Company's peculiar contribution to punishments of infamy."[79] *Godna* had begun as a form of feminine decoration and had previously been used by British authorities to reduce the danger of escapes by convicts sentenced to life terms. By extending it to perjury, the company administrators responded to specifically colonial anxieties by attempting to make the lie visible. They attempted a (literally) Kafkaesque unification of the criminal and the identity of his crime, immediately and indelibly legible to all who might survey it. This emphasis on legibility was both an attempt to create public infamy and a practical tool for colonial magistrates, who could prohibit convicted perjurers from any subsequent testimony in court.[80]

Ironically, despite the role of the judges in suggesting the new punishment, they proved extremely hesitant to employ it. In 1801 in response to a survey of the company's district officers magistrates from eight districts (one quarter of the respondents) said that they had not used the punishment of *godna* even once over the past four years.[81] Another five respondents said they had seldom used *godna*.[82] Nor were these respondents from quiet districts in which perjury cases were unheard of: in Patna, a district in which few usages of *godna* were reported, there had been thirty-two convictions for perjury over the same four years.[83] Similarly, Nuddea, where *godna* had never been used, saw twenty-nine trials of forty-five individuals, yielding twenty-six convictions.[84] The judges, it would seem, were squeamish about their new powers. Curiously, this did not stop some of them from suggesting that what was needed were still stronger sanctions. The magistrates of Chittagong, Jelalpore, Shahabad, and Juanpore, for example, recommended extending the punishment for perjury to include transportation as well,[85] while the magistrate at Dinagepore wanted to add the pillory to the repertoire of discretionary punishments.[86] The magistrate at Bahar wanted to go still further and called for the power to confiscate all property, permanent disqualification from testifying, prohibition on inheriting property in the future, and transportation in cases where the perjury could have led to the imposition of the death penalty.[87]

At almost the same time as the 1801 survey, the Nizamat Adalat received another suggestion from a local judge that resulted in a new amendment in the law of perjury. The report of the Third judge of the Moorshedabad Court of Circuit prompted the Nizamat Adalat to propose another regulation altering the law of perjury.[88] The Third judge complained, and the Nizamat Adalat agreed, that a

> practice has become very prevalent in different parts of the Company's provinces, for parties in civil suits to prefer unfounded charges of perjury against the witnesses of their opponents, and against their own witnesses, where their evidence does not establish every point which they may have been brought to prove, and similar charges of subornation of perjury against the adverse parties in such suits.[89]

Not only did perjury tend to multiply exponentially under these circumstances, with perjured evidence brought in to support charges of perjury, but this practice also compounded the difficulties of getting witnesses to testify in the company courts, as any potential witness feared prosecution, either from his own side or from the opposing party.[90] Accordingly, the Nizamat Adalat proposed a regulation that, as adopted, prohibited magistrates from receiving charges of perjury proffered by parties in civil suits against their own witnesses or those of the other party and held all witnesses, plaintiffs, and defendants in civil suit not liable to be prosecuted for perjury unless they were committed by the *zillah* (local) judge.[91]

The new regulation diminished the power of the Indian legal profession, which was then in its infancy, having only begun to be regulated by law in 1793.[92] This innovation also placed the problem of perjury in India on substantially different footing than in England. In England, the absence of a system of public prosecution until late in the nineteenth century meant that the responsibility for detecting and prosecuting perjury fell almost entirely on the opposing party's counsel. Detection of perjury in England relied on cross-examination by the opposing party's barrister. In India, by contrast, the judge was expected both to detect perjury and initiate prosecutions. The regulation prohibiting party-initiated perjury prosecutions explicitly countenanced cross-examination by the judge: "[L]eave it in the discretion of the Judge to determine when any witnesses brought before him are guilty of perjury, which he may always be able to do by cross-examining them minutely, and by confronting them, when necessary, with the witnesses of the adverse party."[93] By severely restricting the power of citizens to initiate perjury cases, the colonial government confirmed its primary responsibility for policing the populace.

312 CHAPTER TWELVE

Administrators remained uncomfortable about leaving so much power—both in evidentiary determination and in sentencing—in the hands of the native law officers who sat alongside British judges. The Bengal government went so far as to propose vesting the circuit judges with the power to determine guilt or innocence, but the Nizamat Adalat rejected the suggestion.[94] Instead, the court proposed a regulation specifically tailored to meet complaints about the administration of Islamic law. It gave judges the power to overrule native law officers' *fatwas*.[95] The regulation of 1807 had already provided for submission to the Nizamat Adalat when the law officers and the company judges disagreed about the punishment;[96] the new regulation of 1817 went further, authorizing the judge, on his own initiative, to alter sentences. At the same time, the limitation banning party-initiated perjury prosecutions in civil cases was extended to criminal cases.[97]

The changes of 1817 demonstrate just how far the British had strayed from Islamic law. The convoluted treatment of perjury in Regulation XVII of 1817 reflects Fisch's thesis that, by this time, the British version of Islamic law was largely, but not entirely, superficial. In Fisch's description, "with Regulation 17, 1817 the foundation of the British system of criminal justice was laid. It was the last regulation concentrating on basic issues between the European and the Islamic conception of justice."[98] Overall, the Sadar Court opted not to abolish the structure of Islamic law but arrogated to themselves the power to control entirely the decisions of the law officers interpreting that law. Similarly, the Bengal Sadar Court subsequently continued to refer to Islamic legal authorities in determining perjury cases while enforcing a law of perjury almost entirely derived from statutory enactments.

At the same time British authorities were restricting the ability of Indians to initiate perjury suits, they also legislated to expand the domains of potential perjury. In Bengal this process began almost as soon as the British assumed control of the criminal justice system. In 1793 *putwarries*, or local revenue-collecting officials, were made liable to the penalties of perjury for any falsification in their accounts.[99] Statements before land assessors were also made subject to the penalties of perjury,[100] as were statements before collectors regarding land assessments.[101] Other presidencies followed Bengal's lead.[102] The result of this expansion was to bring much of Indian interaction with the colonial government under possible perjury penalties. Not only did British administrators see perjury everywhere, they also gave themselves power to prosecute for perjury in almost any interaction.

Given the attention paid to making prosecution for perjury easier, what were the consequences of these reforms? In the late 1820s, Henry Strachey, a retired judge who was a member of a prominent family of Indian civil servants and whose work James Mill praised in the *History of British India*, compiled figures on perjury in Bengal.[103] Strachey was no advocate of ideas of character or innate Indian mendacity; he took violent exception to Mill's assertion of a distinctive Indian national character, for example, noting the difficulty of forming "a correct judgment on such a subject."[104] Nevertheless, his figures reveal frequent prosecutions for perjury among Bengalis: according to his numbers, convictions for perjury in Bengal alone outstripped those for all of England and Wales. For 1826 and 1827, for example, there were 219 convictions in both the Lower and Western provinces of Bengal. In England, meanwhile, there were approximately twenty perjury cases yearly, resulting in around 10 convictions.[105] While direct comparisons are difficult to make, because of not only differences in population but also access to the judicial system, Strachey's figures suggest that—despite the complaints of magistrates about the difficulty of prosecuting perjury cases in India—many more cases were being brought in India, and many led to convictions.

Overall, however, while the British in Bengal had ensured that they remained in control of judicial decisions, redefined the law of perjury to correspond with the common law, specified the standard of proof, and searched for shame sanctions meaningful to Bengalis, they nonetheless remained attached to the idea that they were administering Islamic law. Their native law officers were frequently called on to render opinions. In other presidencies, however, this level of solicitude for at least the facade of Islamic law was noticeably lacking.

MADRAS: THE INVENTION OF PREVARICATION

After 1817 the innovation in the law of perjury came from the south, in the presidency of Madras. Under the governorship of Edward Clive in 1802, a judiciary was established in Madras largely in imitation of that in Bengal.[106] The company's highest criminal court, however, was called the Foujdari (as opposed to *Nizamat*) Adalat in Madras. The law of perjury in Madras was, initially, borrowed from Bengal, albeit in piecemeal fashion. One of the first regulations establishing the criminal justice system in 1802 provided for punishment by *godna* in cases of perjury[107] and echoed the definition of perjury adopted in Bengal.[108] Prosecution of cases by parties in civil suits was prohibited in 1810;[109] this was reenacted in 1816 after the reorganization of the lower courts,[110] extended to criminal cases in 1822,[111] and extended to all tribunals in 1829.[112] Meanwhile, concern that sentencing discretion was allowing the law to be applied too leniently led to a tightening of the law of perjury in 1811. Under Regulation VI of that year, imprisonment was to be between four and seven years only, banishment was provided for, a reward was offered, and bail was not available for the offense except under special circumstances.[113]

The Foujdari Adalat offered its own contributions to the law of perjury during this period, through circular orders. In 1814 the court instructed lower tribunals on procedure in perjury cases.[114] The court noted that prosecutions for perjury against Indians were frequent, but "generally unsuccessful."[115] Warning, "[I]t is scarcely to be expected that an uneducated native should, of himself, state facts and circumstances with the precision here required,"[116] the court placed the responsibility for developing a complete record on the criminal judge. A proper charge should contain the words spoken by the accused, the place and time, the judicial proceeding in which they were relevant, and the falsehood of the accused's statement. In particular, the court reminded judges, "No person should be made the object of a prosecution for perjury, who has not been cautioned against committing himself on his oath, and has, subsequently, persisted in maintaining falsehood for truth."[117] Seven years later, the court intervened again to clear up confusion as to the standard of proof required for conviction in perjury cases.[118]

In 1822 the law of perjury in Madras began to depart significantly from that of Bengal. Prodded by the discontent of local judges, Madras innovated, first, through the invention of a crime of prevarication and, second, by legislating against false accusations. As in Bengal, local judges took the lead. But in Madras their suggestions met resistance from the Sadar Court. The Foujdari Adalat was at best a reluctant partner in legislation. Thomas Warden, the Second judge on Circuit, Western Division, wrote the court angrily in 1822, annoyed that it had focused on the question of materiality in responding to his complaints about perjury. Instead, Warden wrote, "it is where contradictory evidence by the same witness is given on points material to the issue that I wish to engage the consideration of the Court."[119] Warden protested that the requirement of some evidence demonstrating the falsehood of the alleged perjury prevented prosecution of cases of contradiction apparent on the face of the depositions. He suggested instead the creation of an intermediate crime, between perjury and contempt of court, if the law of perjury itself could not be altered.

The Foujdari Adalat, however, was not immediately swayed by Warden's plea. They responded by dismissing the two scenarios Warden had posed: first, a witness testifying successively to a murder happening by "torchlight" and by "daylight" and, second, an actual case where witnesses had testified that death resulted from different causes, despite the alleged deceased's relatives seeming unconvinced that he was, in fact, deceased.[120] The first, they argued, was merely speculative, while the second called for more diligent investigation by the police and magistrates, not a change in the law. Nonetheless, they were willing to consider penalties for prevarication that would be less than those for perjury but more severe than those for contempt of court.[121] Accordingly, a draft regulation was prepared to create a new crime of prevarication that would respond to administrative concerns about the limited investigative abilities of colonial officials. R. Clarke, secretary to the Regulation Board, explained,

> The difference between [perjury and prevarication] consists in this, that perjury is a distinct assertion of that which can be proved not to be, or a denial of that which can be proved to be; whereas prevarication is the giving of contradictory or inconsistent evidence, which affects the credibility of the evidence, though neither the extent of the witness's falsehood, nor the precise points in which he has departed from the truth be capable of ascertainment.[122]

Under the proposed regulation, prevarication would be punishable by a fine of one hundred rupees, six months' imprisonment, or up to a year's imprisonment if a convict could not pay the fine.[123] Despite approval from the Foujdari Adalat, the regulation was not enacted.

Insight into why the question of conflicting depositions appeared so critical to Madras judges can be found in George Campbell's description of criminal process in British India.[124] Campbell describes a process that repeatedly created depositions. Beginning with the original complaint, each police station was required to keep a diary of daily events, including statements from witnesses, which was forwarded to the local magistrate for his review each morning. The magistrate would then take depositions in the course of investigating the cases forwarded to him. If the case was committed for trial, all the witnesses would appear for a third time before the judge, generating a second set of depositions.[125] All of this took place prior to the trial itself, generating a dossier of statements and depositions for review by the trial judge. As Archibald Galloway,[126] a military officer and chairman of the Court of Directors of the EIC, observed, the problem of mendacity in India resulted in increased reliance on written evidence: "The necessity of written documents is therefore greater in India than in our own country; and any expedient suggested with the view of multiplying them ought of all things to be encouraged."[127] Making perjury discoverable merely through contradictory depositions, therefore, responded to the largely written nature of judicial proceedings under the company. While the use of *godna* united the convicted perjurer with his sentence, the invention of prevarication reduced the complexity of testimony and credibility assessment to a simple dossier. Both made the crime legible to officials who feared its obscurity.

The following year, the process of criminalizing prevarication began anew. This time C. M. Lushington, the Second judge on Circuit, Western Division, initiated the process with a report claiming that "the most common case of perjury as it appears in our Courts, is totally unprovided for,"[128] namely, swearing to opposing facts before the magistrate and circuit judge respectively. Unlike three years previously, the Foujdari Adalat was extremely resistant to the suggestion of change. He declared peevishly, "It seems extraordinary to the Court that explanation to the extent to which it has already been required and seems still called for, should be necessary to the understanding of so clear a point as that the willful falsehood of a witness's false assertion must mainly be established by proving the fact he has denied." The Foujdari Adalat then concluded that it "will here dismiss the subject."[129]

Despite this attempt to close the door on the topic of prevarication, the matter was soon forced back into the Court's purview. The presidency government took the unusual step of referring the question to the advocate-general, a solicitor employed by the EIC to manage the company's legal affairs with respect to English law, asking him if an individual swearing to two contradictory depositions in England would be liable to the punishment for perjury.[130] The advocate-general responded that there was some precedent for taking two contradictory depositions as evidence of perjury;[131] the government responded by forwarding his letter to the Foujdari Adalat, along with a pointed hint that "Governor in Council is satisfied of the expediency and propriety of admitting the same kind of proof to establish perjury in the Company's Courts," and suggested that the Foujdari should effect this object, either by issuing a circular order or by drafting a new regulation.[132] The Foujdari Adalat balked, respectfully taking issue with the advocate-general's interpretation of English case law.[133] The court also noticed the problem of possible reprosecution for perjury, with the accused tried twice, first on the basis of a contradiction and subsequently on the falsity of one or another of his statements. After further prodding from the government,[134] the court agreed that the law could be changed, but insisted on a new regulation rather than making the change through a circular order.[135]

At the suggestion of the Foujdari Adalat, the law as eventually enacted[136] contained a number of protections for potential defendants. First, the court urged that prosecution be used "exclusively for cases where the contradiction is direct and positive" and where a distinct corrupt motive could be discerned.[137] Second, the regulation expressly prohibited subsequent trial for perjury by the usual way of proving the falsehood of one of the two statements.[138] Finally, the regulation required evidence that the defendant was duly sworn and that, before affixing his signature to the contradictory depositions, their contents were distinctly read to him.[139] Shortly after passage of this regulation, the Foujdari Adalat issued a circular order clarifying the new requirements for composing indictments.[140] Contradiction had been made a crime, albeit one amalgamated into the definition of perjury. This, however, did not appear to be enough for the judges of Madras. Six years later, they supported another bill to create a separate offense of prevarication, this time punishable by one month's imprisonment or a fine of fifty rupees.[141] While the court had stressed determination of a corrupt motive in the earlier regulation, later commentators concluded that motive could be inferred from the depositions themselves, relieving the courts of any additional factual inquiry into intent.[142]

Perhaps chastened by this unusually contentious process, the Foujdari Adalat actively consulted the local judges before embarking on its next initiative. In February 1827 the court sent out a request for input from the judges on a new regulation that would make preferring false accusations a crime.[143] As with the earlier prohibition against accusations of perjury by opposing parties, the effect would be to further concentrate the power of policing in colonial hands. The response to the suggestion was overwhelming. Judges from throughout the presidency wrote in to complain of the problem in their district.[144] W. Lavie, the assistant criminal judge at Combaconum saw the practice as spanning social classes: "[T]he better class of native are for the most part rich, and are in consequence enabled to purchase evidence, and . . . the lower orders are so very depraved that a person possessing the means may at any time procure as many witnesses as he pleases."[145] J. Monro of Tinnevelly attached a multiple-page accounting of some of the false accusations brought over the past four years.[146] A. Sinclair estimated that the average number of false complaints seen yearly was "around 76."[147] S. Nicholls, criminal judge at Madura, attributed most false accusations to a desire for revenge.[148]

The judges differed among themselves as to the best means of deterring false accusations: fines,[149] degrading punishment,[150] imprisonment and fines,[151] or lashings.[152] E. Smalley, magistrate of Nellore, wanted to discriminate among classes in punishment: men of property, he wrote, should be fined up to three hundred rupees; "persons without property but above the lower orders" should be confined for two months with hard labor; and members of the lower orders should be flogged.[153] Still others thought that the best way to prevent false accusations was to create a more stringent form of oath, such as requiring an accuser to swear "in the village Pagoda."[154] After reviewing all of these suggestions, the Foujdari Adalat recommended a graded approach, based on severity of the accused offense. The police were authorized to administer a solemn declaration to the complainant in all offense cases for which bail was not available, along with a warning about the penalties for perjury. For offenses for which bail was available, a criminal court could punish the complainant by a fine of up to two hundred rupees or imprisonment with or without hard labor up to one year. For offenses for which bail was not available, the offender would be committed for trial before the Court of Circuit and liable to punishment of up to seven years' imprisonment with hard labor and lashing with cat-o-nine-tails.[155] This structure was subsequently modified to abandon the distinction between offenses for which bail was or was not available. Instead, all false charges could be punished by imprisonment for up to six months, although the regulation noted that judges could consider "the apparent motives and tendency" of the charge in sentencing.[156]

Taken together, the two innovations in Madras worked to extend the purview of perjury and to greatly ease detection of the offense. They responded to fears about the duplicitous native informant, either as witness or accuser, with new penalties and new technologies for detection.

BENGAL SEQUEL: MAKING INNOVATIONS ISLAMIC

While the original outlines of the law of perjury had been settled in Bengal, the innovations in Madras left judges in Bengal with a dilemma: should they join their southern colleagues in expanding the definition of perjury? In an early decision, the Nizamat Adalat had rejected the argument that perjury could be proved simply through contradictory depositions; instead, they demanded that, in conformity with English practice, one of the depositions had to be proved false.[157] The Madras law, however, revived the question. In 1841 the Nizamat Adalat changed course and adopted the Madras rule.[158] Henceforth, "the mere fact of a witness having willfully given two statements directly at variance with each other, on a point material to the issue of the case in which he gives the testimony, must be held to be perjury."[159] Evidence that prisoners in Bengal were already being convicted of perjury because of contradictory depositions prompted this decision. In the monthly report of H. Nisbet, session judge of Sarum, five individuals were listed as convicted for perjury on the basis of contradictory depositions, including one in which two years had elapsed between the original statement before a magistrate and the testimony given at trial.[160]

However, the judges of the Nizamat did not justify their volte-face by reference to the Madras law; instead, they argued that it was merely a recognition of Islamic law. In their circular order, they referred to a ten-year-old construction, containing an extended opinion by the Islamic law officers of the Calcutta Sadar Court.[161] The opinion responded to a query asking what evidence was sufficient to convict in cases of perjury. Among the circumstances considered by the law officers was the delivery of contradictory evidence by the same witness before different courts. According to the law officers, if a witness claimed to have witnessed a crime and then dropped his accusation, it then became the responsibility of the judge to assess his motives. If "the retraction be made under a proper sense of repentance and contrition," the witness was not liable to *tazir* (discretionary punishment); but "if with contempt and boldness," then he was liable.[162] Subsequently remembering details initially forgotten, however, did not make a witness liable to *tazir*.[163] At the same time, the law officers went further than the Madras law by declaring that a witness making a statement that "is highly improbable, and bordering close upon impossibility" was also liable to *tazir*.[164]

Bengal judges sought also to soften the impact of the innovation. In a circular order of 1850, they cautioned sessions judges against indiscriminately using their power to commit parties for perjury based on contradictory depositions. The court warned,

> By an indiscriminate or injudicious use of the power vested in the sessions judge, witnesses would be forced to adhere to any perjury, which they may have committed before the magistrate, whereas by abstaining from punishment of those witnesses who may appear to correct at the sessions the falsehood of their first evidence, and limiting the order of committal to those who manifestly make a false deposition before the sessions judge, the ends of justice would be more satisfactorily attained.[165]

Like the earlier opinion by the Sadar Court law officers, and unlike their counterparts in Madras, the circular order sought to discriminate between motives for inconsistency and thereby temper the new law. Interestingly, however, they did not once again invoke Islamic or Hindu precedent to justify this qualification, although both types of precedent could be found. While consistency with Islamic law seems to have been a powerful trope in Bengal jurisprudence, the Sadar Court in grounding their opinions did not always employ it.

The eventual adoption of the Indian Penal Code in 1860 brought this period of innovation in the law of perjury and prevarication to a close. By the time Pershad wrote his curious letter, British administrators' attempts to confront what they saw as widespread mendacity in India, and what Indians may well have seen as justifiable resistance to an imposed judicial system, amounted to little more than an enduring obsession. Justice in many cases had become a quixotic attempt to discern which of the parties was honest, not who had the better case. Disturbingly, judges confronted with the same case could come to radically different assessments of the credibility of witnesses. More than half a century of attempts to control perjury through legal innovations had led, not to more efficient application of the law, but to the creation of a cadre of judges ruling on the basis of the perceived mendacity of witnesses. The imperatives of policing the courtroom had come to overshadow the touted gift of impartial justice according to law.

Notes

1. India Political Department, Foreign Letter, May 25, 1858, No. 9 of 1858, Oriental and India Office Collections, British Library, India Office Records (IOR), F/4/2723.
2. Ibid.
3. Perjury, suggestion to defile natives accused of, Aug. 30, 1858, draft no. 53 of 1858, IOR, E/4/854.
4. Diane Kirkby and Catherine Coleborne, "Introduction," in *Law, History, Colonialism: The Reach of Empire*, Diane Kirkby and Catherine Coleborne, eds. (Manchester, UK: Manchester Univ. Press, 2001), pp. 1, 3.
5. Peter Fitzpatrick, *Mythology of Modern Law* (London: Routledge, 1992), p. 107.
6. Thomas R. Metcalf, *Ideologies of the Raj* (Cambridge: Cambridge Univ. Press, 1995), p. 39.
7. See, for example, John L. Comaroff, "Images of Empire, Contests of Conscience," in *Tensions of Empire: Colonial Cultures in a Bourgeois World*, Frederick Cooper and Ann Laura Stoler, eds. (Berkeley: Univ. of California Press, 1997), pp. 163, 165.
8. Martin Chanock, "Criminological Science and the Criminal Law on the Colonial Periphery," *Law and Social Inquiry* 20 (1995): 911, 938.
9. Markus Dirk Dubber, *The Police Power: Patriarchy and the Foundations of Government* (New York: Columbia Univ. Press, 2005), p. 91.
10. *Answers of the Judges of Circuit to Interrogatories*, Parliamentary Papers 1812–1813, 10:250.
11. John L. Comaroff, "Colonialism, Culture, and the Law: A Foreword," *Law and Social Inquiry* 26 (2001): 305, 311.
12. Ibid., p. 307.
13. Metcalf, *Ideologies of the Raj*, p. 24.
14. James Mill, *The History of British India* (Chicago: Univ. of Chicago, 1975), p. 564 (originally published in 1820).
15. On ideas about native chicanery, see Ranajit Guha, *An Indian Historiography of India* (Calcutta: K. P. Bagchi, 1984), p. 10.
16. Metcalf, *Ideologies of the Raj*, p. 12.
17. Thomas D. Morris, *Southern Slavery and the Law, 1619–1860* (Chapel Hill: Univ. of North Carolina Press, 1996), p. 233.

18. Nicholas Dirks, "Foreword," in *Colonialism and Its Forms of Knowledge: The British in India*, Bernard S. Cohn, ed. (Princeton, N.J.: Princeton Univ. Press, 1996), p. ix.

19. Cohn, *Colonialism and Its Forms of Knowledge*, p. 4.

20. C. A. Bayly, *Empire and Information: Intelligence Gathering and Social Communication in India, 1780–1870* (Cambridge: Cambridge Univ. Press, 1996), pp. 167–168.

21. Radhika Singha, "'Providential Circumstances': The Thuggee Campaign of the 1830s and Legal Innovation," *Modern Asian Studies* 27 (1993): 83.

22. Ibid., pp. 143–149; C. A. Bayly, "Knowing the Country: Empire and Information in India," *Modern Asian Studies* 27 (1993): 3, 38.

23. Bayly, *Empire and Information*, p. 151–154.

24. Joachim Hayward Stocqueler (1800–1885) was a journalist in Calcutta from 1821–1841. He was also the author of handbooks on India. Charles Buckland, *Dictionary of Indian Biography* (Detroit: Gale Research Co., 1968), pp. 405–406.

25. Joachim Hayward Stocqueler, *The Hand-Book of India, A Guide to the Stranger and the Traveller, and a Companion to the Resident*, 2d ed. (London: W. H. Allen, 1845), p. 142.

26. Bayly, "Knowing the Country," p. 288 (quoting George Hadley, *A Compendious Grammar of the Current Corrupt Dialect of the Jargon of Hindostan, (Commonly called the Moors)* [London: J. Sewell, 1796], p. 130).

27. J. Statham, *Indian Recollections* (London: S. Bagster, 1832).

28. William Buyers, *Recollections of Northern India* (London: J. Snow, 1848), p. 505.

29. Sir William Henry Sleeman (1788–1856). Joined Bengal Army in 1809. Assistant to the governor-general for Sagar and Nerbudda territories from 1820, in charge of thugee suppression from 1835 and dacoity as well from 1839. Resident at Gwalior, 1843–1849, and Lucknow, 1849–1856. Survived assassination attempt in 1851. Author of a thugee vocabulary. Buckland, *Dictionary of Indian Biography*, p. 392.

30. W. H. Sleeman, *Rambles and Recollections of an Indian Official*, vol. 2 (London: J. Hatchard, 1844), pp. 109–145.

31. Ibid., pp. 109–112.

32. Metcalf, *Ideologies of the Raj*, p. 41.

33. Ibid.

34. Lata Mani, *Contentious Traditions: The Debate on* Sati *in Colonial India* (Berkeley: Univ. of California Press, 1998), p. 16.

35. Cohn, *Colonialism and Its Forms of Knowledge*, p. 66; J. Duncan and M. Derrett, *Religion, Law and the State in India* (London: Fabar, 1968).

36. Tapas Kumar Banerjee, *Background to Indian Criminal Law* (Bombay: Orient Longmans, 1963), p. 40; George Claus Rankin, *Background to Indian Law* (Cambridge: Cambridge Univ. Press 1946), p. 164.

37. Rankin, *Background to Indian Law*, p. 165.

38. Jörg Fisch, *Cheap Lives and Dear Limbs: The British Transformation of the Bengal Criminal Law* (Wiesbaden: F. Steiner, 1983).

39. N. Majumdar, *Justice and Police in Bengal, 1756–1793: A Study of the Nizamat in Decline* (Calcutta: K. L. Mukhopadhyay, 1960), p. 326 (app. F).

322 CHAPTER TWELVE

40. Satya Prakash Sangar, *Crime and Punishment in Mughal India* (New Delhi: Reliance, 1967), pp. 37–38.

41. Charles Hamilton, *The Hedaya or Guide, A Commentary on the Mussulman Laws* (Delhi: Islamic Book Trust, 1982), p. 372 (originally published in 1791).

42. Ibid.

43. Nathaniel Brassey Halhed, *A Code of Gentoo Laws; or, Ordinations of the Pundits, From a Persian Translation, Made from the Original, written in the Shanscrit Language* (London: n.p., 1776).

44. Derrett, *Religion, Law and the State in India*, pp. 239–241.

45. Rankin, *Background to Indian Law*, p. 190.

46. Halhed, *Code of Gentoo Laws*, p. 127.

47. Ibid., p. 128.

48. Douglas Haynes and Gyan Prakash, "Introduction: The Entanglement of Power and Resistance," in *Contesting Power: Resistance and Everyday Social Relations in South Asia*, Douglas Haynes and Gyan Prakash, eds. (Oxford: Oxford Univ. Press, 1991), pp. 1, 2. On resistance and the study of colonial legal institutions, see also Sally Engle Merry, "Resistance and the Cultural Power of Law," *Law and Society Review* 29 (1995): 11.

49. John D. Rogers, "Cultural and Social Resistance: Gambling in Colonial Sri Lanka," in *Contesting Power*, Haynes and Prakash, eds., pp. 175, 194.

50. *Government v. Degumbur Gowallah and Others, Nizamut Adawlut Reports* 4 (Feb. 4, 1831), p. 10; *Government v. Haro Mochee, Nizamut Adawlut Reports* 4 (Dec. 19, 1831), p. 99; *Government v. Sumbhoo*, Aged 23, *Nizamut Adawlut Reports* 4 (Oct. 5, 1835), p. 259; Case of Sopannah bin Kalljee, *Reports of Cases in the Court of Sudder Foujdaree Adawlut* 1 (Sept. 15, 1841), p. 144.

51. *Government v. Soomut Rajpoot, Nizamut Adawlut Reports* 2 (Jan. 16, 1824), p. 313.

52. *Government v. Mahommed Alee, Nizamut Adawlut Reports* 2 (Sept. 17, 1822), p. 204.

53. *Government v. Ramsoondur Bhagul, Nizamut Adawlut Reports* 2 (Feb. 21, 1825), p. 363.

54. Case of Luxiah bin Budiah Bheel, *Reports of cases in the Court of Sudder Foujdaree Adawlut* 1 (Jul. 31, 1837), p. 116.

55. *Government v. Sheeboo Doss Byragee, Nizamut Adawlut Reports* 5 (Oct. 12, 1839), p. 144.

56. Mahabir Prashad Jain, *Outlines of Indian Legal History* (Bombay: N. M. Tripathi, 1952), pp. 70–130.

57. Ibid., pp. 143–199.

58. Ibid., p. 154.

59. Orby Mootham, *The East India Company's Sadar Courts, 1801–1834* (1983).

60. Jain, *Outlines of Indian Legal History*, pp. 154–156.

61. Ibid., p. 157.

62. Ibid., p. 158.

63. Ibid., p. 197.

64. Mootham, *East India Company's Sadar Courts*, p. 23.

65. Ibid., p. 47.

66. Jain, *Outlines of Indian Legal History*.

67. Fisch, *Cheap Lives and Dear Limbs*.

68. Ibid., pp. 49–56.

69. Letter from the Third judge, Circuit Court, Dacca Division, to the register of the Nizamut Adawlut, Oct. 10, 1797, in Bengal Proceedings, Nov. 24, 1797, no. 24, IOR, P/128/34.

70. Ibid.

71. Resolution of the Court, Nizamut Adawlut, in Bengal Proceedings, Nov. 24, 1797, no. 24, IOR, P/128/34.

72. Clare Anderson, *Legible Bodies: Race, Criminality and Colonialism in South Asia* (New York: Berg, 2004), p. 16.

73. Extract from the proceedings of the Nizamut Adawlut, Nov. 8, 1797, in Bengal Proceedings, Nov. 24, 1797, no. 24, IOR, P/128/34.

74. Ibid.

75. Letter from the deputy register of the Nizamut Adawlut to G. H. Burlow, secretary to government, Bengal, Nov. 22, 1797, in Bengal Proceedings, Nov. 24, 1797, no. 18, IOR, P/128/34.

76. Regulation XVII. 1797. § 3.

77. Regulation XVII. 1797. § 3.

78. Regulation XVII. 1797. § 2.

79. Radhika Singha, *A Despotism of Law: Crime and Justice in Early Colonial India* (Delhi: Oxford Univ. Press, 1998), p. 245.

80. Anderson, *Legible Bodies*, p. 19.

81. Parliamentary Papers 1812–1813; Jessore, p. 16; Juanpore, p. 33; Hooghly, p. 45; Nuddea, p. 55; Burdwan, pp. 67, 24; Pergunnas, p. 74; Sylhet, p. 131; Sarun, p. 240.

82. Ibid. Backergunge, p. 117; Tipperah, p. 124; Moorshedabad, p. 179; Patna, p. 232; Benares, p. 276.

83. Ibid., pp. 226–227.

84. Ibid., pp. 56–57.

85. Ibid., pp. 149, 164, 257, and 287.

86. Ibid., p. 196.

87. Ibid., p. 251.

88. Letter from J. Lumsden, register of the Nizamut Adawlut, to Henry St. George Tucker, secretary to government in the Revenue and Judicial Departments, Bengal, in Bengal Proceedings, Mar. 19, 1801, IOR, P/128/54. My thanks to Ray Cocks for directing me to this source.

89. Regulation III. 1801. § 1.

90. F. L. Beaufort, *A Digest of the Criminal Law of the Presidency of Fort William* (Calcutta: Le Page, 1850), pp. 655–656.

91. Regulation III. 1801. § 2.

92. Jain, *Outlines of Indian Legal History*, pp. 185–187, Regulation VII. 1793; Samuel Schmitthener, "A Sketch of the Development of the Legal Profession in India," *Law and Society Review* 3 (1968–1969): 337, 349–355.

93. Regulation III. 1801. § 1.
94. Letter from W. B. Bayley, secretary to government, to register of Nizamut Adawlut, Feb. 16, 1817, in Bengal Criminal Consultation, Feb. 16, 1817, IOR, P/132/64.
95. Regulation XVII. 1817. § IV.
96. Regulation II. 1807. § II. Cl. 2.
97. Regulation XVII. 1817. § XIV. Cl. 4.
98. Fisch, *Cheap Lives and Dear Limbs*, p. 84.
99. Regulation VIII. 1793. § LXII.
100. Regulation II. 1819. § XIX. Cl. 2.
101. Regulation VII. 1822. § XIX. Cl. 2.
102. See, for example, Bombay Regulations. II. 1812. § VIII (subjecting village accountants, or tullaties, to penalties of perjury); IV. 1819. § XIII (penalties of perjury for complaints offered before commissioners against collectors, commercial residents); X. 1827. § IX (witnesses examined before boundary commissions subject to perjury).
103. Henry Strachey Papers, Folder 190, in Strachey Papers, IOR, Mss Eur/F 128.
104. Henry Strachey, "On the moral character of the Hindoos as described in Mill's British India, with some general reflexions on the evidence of national character," Henry Strachey Papers, Folder 218, in Strachey Papers, IOR, MSS Eur/F 128.
105. *Criminal Offenders (Committals Statistics)*, Parliamentary Papers 1835, 45:21. In 1830 there were nine convictions out of eighteen committals.
106. Rankin, *Background to Indian Law*, p. 183.
107. Regulation VII. 1802. § XL. Cl. 2.
108. Ibid. Cl. 1.
109. Regulation I. 1810. See also "Extract from the Proceedings of the Foujdaree Adawlut," Mar. 14, 1809, in Madras Proceedings, Mar. 27, 1810, IOR, P/322/45.
110. Regulation IX. 1816.
111. Regulation II. 1822.
112. Regulation VIII. 1829.
113. Regulation VI. 1811. See also Judicial Consultation, Madras, Apr. 23, 1811, IOR, P/322/56.
114. Circular Order Jan. 31, 1814, in Circular Orders of the Court of Foujdaree Udalut, from 1803 to June 30, 1834, at pp. 3–6 (Madras, 1835). IOR, V/27/144/48.
115. Ibid., p. 4.
116. Ibid., p. 3.
117. Ibid., p. 5.
118. Circular Order May 3, 1821, in Circular Orders of the Court of Foujdaree Udalut, from 1803 to June 30, 1834, at pp. 47–48 (Madras, 1835). IOR, V/27/144/48.
119. Letter from Thomas Warden, Esq., Second judge on Circuit, Western Division, to the register of the Foujdarry Adawlut, Nov. 20, 1822, in Board Collections, Judicial Letter, Dec. 31, 1823, no. 22906, IOR, F/4/867.
120. "Extract from the Proceedings of the Foujdarry Adawlut," Dec. 30, 1822, in Board Collections, Judicial Letter, Dec. 31, 1823, no. 22906, IOR, F/4/867.

121. Ibid.; Letter from D. Hill, secretary to government, to Board for Preparing Regulation, Apr. 18, 1823, in Board Collections, Judicial Letter, Dec. 31, 1823, no. 22906, IOR, F/4/867; Letter from W. Oliver, register of the Foujdarry Adawlut, to D. Hill, secretary to government, July 9, 1823, in Board Collections, Judicial Letter, Dec. 31, 1823, no. 22906, IOR, F/4/867.

122. Letter from R. Clarke, secretary to Regulation Board, to D. Hill, secretary to government, Dec. 18, 1823, in Board Collections, Judicial Letter, Dec. 31, 1823, no. 22906, IOR, F/4/867.

123. Letter from W. Hudleston, register of the Foujdarry Adawlut, to D. Hill, secretary to government, Jan. 30, in Board Collections, Judicial Letter, Dec. 31, 1823, no. 22906, IOR, F/4/867.

124. Note that this is a description of procedure in Bengal; Madras was somewhat different, in that more of the local-level policing remained in the hands of traditional officials.

125. George Campbell, *Modern India: A Sketch of the System of Civil Government: To which is Prefixed Some Account of the Natives and Native Institutions* (London: J. Murray, 1852), p. 459.

126. Sir Archibald Galloway (1780?–1850). Joined the Bengal infantry in 1800, nominated Companion of the Order of the Bath in 1838 and Knight Commander in 1848, chairman of the Court of Directors of the EIC in 1849. Buckland, *Dictionary of Indian Biography*, p. 158.

127. Lt. Col. Archibald Galloway, *Observations on the Law and Constitution, and Present Government of India*, 2d ed. (London: Parbury, Allen, 1832), p. 349. See also Judicial Letter to Madras, Apr. 29, 1814, in *Selections of Papers from the Records at the East-India House, Relating to the Revenue, Police, and Civil and Criminal Justice, Under the Company's Government in India* (London, 1820), p. 240.

128. Letter from C. M. Lushington, Second judge of Circuit, Southern Division, to W. Hudleston, register of the Foujdarry Adawlut, Aug. 17, 1825, in Judicial Letter, Jan. 23, 1827, Board Collection no. 28516, IOR, F/4/1035.

129. Proceedings of the Foujdarry Adawlut, Dec. 16, 1825, in Judicial Letter, Jan. 23, 1827, Board Collection no. 28516, IOR, F/4/1035.

130. Letter from J. M. McLeod, secretary to government, to Herbert Compton, advocate-general, Feb. 24, 1826, in Judicial Letter, Jan. 23, 1827, Board Collection no. 28516, IOR, F/4/1035.

131. Letter from Herbert Compton, advocate-general, to D. Mill, chief secretary to government, Mar. 6, 1826, in Judicial Letter, Jan. 23, 1827, Board Collection no. 28516, IOR, F/4/1035.

132. Letter from J. M. McLeod, secretary to government, Judicial Department, to W. Hudleston, register of the Foujdarry Adawlut, Mar. 17, 1826, in Judicial Letter, Jan. 23, 1827, Board Collection no. 28516, IOR, F/4/1035.

133. Proceedings of the Foujdarry Adawlut, June 21, 1826, in Judicial Letter, Jan. 23, 1827, Board Collection no. 28516, IOR, F/4/1035.

326 CHAPTER TWELVE

134. Letter from J. M. McLeod, secretary to government, Judicial Department, to G. J. Casamajor, register of the Foujdarry Adawlut, July 18, 1826, in Judicial Letter, Jan. 23, 1827, Board Collection no. 28516, IOR, F/4/1035.

135. Letter from G. J. Casamajor, register of the Foujdarry Adawlut, to J. M. McLeod, secretary to government, Judicial Department, Aug. 28, 1826, in Judicial Letter, Jan. 23, 1827, Board Collection no. 28516, IOR, F/4/1035.

136. Regulation III. 1826.

137. Letter from G. J. Casamajor, register of the Foujdarry Adawlut, to J. M. McLeod, secretary to government, Judicial Department, Aug. 28, 1826, in Judicial Letter, Jan. 23, 1827, Board Collection no. 28516, IOR, F/4/1035.

138. Regulation III. 1826. § 3.

139. Ibid. § 2. Cl. 2.

140. Circular Order Nov. 23, 1826, in Circular Orders of the Court of Foujdaree Udalut, from 1803 to June 30, 1834, at pp. 141–142 (Madras, 1835). IOR, V/27/144/48.

141. Regulation XIII. 1832.

142. Indian Law Commissioners, *Second Report on the Indian Penal Code* (Calcutta: W. Ridsdale, 1847), p. 60.

143. Letter from G. J. Casamajor, register of the Foujdarry Adawlut, to the acting secretary to government, Feb. 27, 1827, in Judicial Letter, Mar. 20, 1833, Board's Collection no. 52893, IOR, F/4/1336.

144. But see Minute of the Second judge, C. M. Lushington, Second judge, Trichinopoly, Mar. 22, 1827, in Judicial Letter, Mar. 20, 1833, Board's Collection no. 52893, IOR, F/4/1336. Lushington questioned whether false accusations were genuinely so numerous as to call for new legislation.

145. Letter from W. Lavie, assistant criminal judge, Combaconum, to the register of the Provincial Court of Circuit, Southern District, Feb. 22, 1827, in Judicial Letter, Mar. 20, 1833, Board's Collection no. 52893, IOR, F/4/1336.

146. Letter from J. Monro, magistrate of Tinnevelly, to register of Court of Circuit, Southern Division, Feb. 21, 1827, in Judicial Letter, Mar. 20, 1833, Board's Collection no. 52893, IOR, F/4/1336.

147. Letter from A. Sinclair, acting magistrate, Tanjore, to register of the Court of Circuit, Southern Division, Feb. 21, 1827, in Judicial Letter, Mar. 20, 1833, Board's Collection no. 52893, IOR, F/4/1336.

148. Letter from S. Nicholls, criminal judge of Madura, to register of Court of Circuit, Southern Division, Feb. 21, 1827, in Judicial Letter, Mar. 20, 1833, Board's Collection no. 52893, IOR, F/4/1336.

149. Letter from W. Lavie, assistant criminal judge, Combaconum, to the register of the Provincial Court of Circuit, Southern District, Feb. 22, 1827, in Judicial Letter, Mar. 20, 1833, Board's Collection no. 52893, IOR, F/4/1336.

150. Minute of James Taylor, First judge, Trichinopoly, Mar. 17, 1827, in Judicial Letter, Mar. 20, 1833, Board's Collection no. 52893, IOR, F/4/1336.

151. Minute of John Bird, Third judge, Trichinopoly, Mar. 12, 1827, in Judicial Letter, Mar. 20, 1833, Board's Collection no. 52893, IOR, F/4/1336.

152. Letter from H. Dickinson, Magistrate, Trichinopoly, to the register of the Court of Circuit, Southern Division, Mar. 2, 1827, in Judicial Letter, Mar. 20, 1833, Board's Collection no. 52893, IOR, F/4/1336; Letter from J. Sullivan, magistrate, Coimbatore, to the register of the Court of Circuit, Southern Division, Feb. 22, 1827, in ibid.

153. Letter from E. Smalley, magistrate, Nellore, to register of the Court of Circuit, Northern Division, Feb. 22, 1827, in Judicial Letter, Mar. 20, 1833, Board's Collection no. 52893, IOR, F/4/1336.

154. Letter from R. Bayard, magistrate, Ganjam, to the register of the Court of Circuit, Northern Division, Mar. 8, 1827, in Judicial Letter, Mar. 20, 1833, Board's Collection no. 52893, IOR, F/4/1336.

155. Draft regulation for better prosecution and punishment of false and willfully malicious accusations of heinous crimes, in Judicial Letter, Mar. 20, 1833, Board's Collection no. 52893, IOR, F/4/1336.

156. Regulation IX. 1832. § II.

157. *Bhola Pandeh v. Sumbhoo Rajpoot, Nizamut Adawlut Reports* 1 (Aug. 16, 1813), pp. 282, 284. See also *Government v. Mussummaut Kukha, Nizamut Adawlut Reports* 1 (Sept. 27, 1815), p. 314 ("to constitute the offence of perjury punishable by the Regulations, it is requisite that one of the two contradictory statements be satisfactorily established").

158. Circular Order no. 126, July 18, 1841, in The Circular Orders Passed by the Nizamut Adawlut for the Lower and Western Provinces and Communicated to the Criminal Authorities in the Bengal and Agra Provinces by the Registers of those Courts, from 1796 to 1844 (Calcutta: n.p., 1846), p. 374.

159. Ibid., p. 375.

160. Letter from J. Hawkins, register, Nizamut Adawlut, to T. J. Halliday, secretary to the government of Bengal, Judicial Department, July 22, 1842, in Legislative Letter, Mar. 17, 1843, Board Collection no. 90255, IOR, F/4/2016.

161. Construction no. 656, Sept. 2, 1831, in 2 Constructions by the Courts of the Sudder Dewanny and Nizamut Adawlut of the Regulations and Laws, for the Civil Government of the Whole of the Territories under the Presidency of Fort William in Bengal 21 (Calcutta: F. Carbury, 1833).

162. Ibid., pp. 21–22.

163. Ibid., p. 22.

164. Ibid., pp. 22–23.

165. Circuit order no. 34, Mar. 4, 1850, in J. Carrau, The Circular Orders of the Court of Nizamut Adawlut, Communicated to the Criminal Authorities. From 1796 to 1853 inclusive (Calcutta: Thacker, Spink, 1855), p. 439.

Index

actus reus, 6, 8, 81
Adams, Herbert Baxter, 128
Albion's Fatal Tree (Hay et al.), 1
Al Punch, 255
Alverstone, Chief Justice, 54, 56
American Revolution: criminal law and, 115–17
Amrita Bazar Patrika, 276–77
Anglo-American criminal law, 6
antipositivists, 190–91
Assam, colonial: Balipara Tea Plantation case, 283–84; collective resistance in, 289; Dowding and, 279; Elliot and, 278; European crime in, 282–88; Indian nationalism and, 280; labor immigration and, 280; labor violence in, 288–90; law and labor in, 278–79; police in, 175; politics of violence in, 279–81
associationism, 74
Aurelius, Marcus, 119
Austin, John, 200
Autobiography of Thomas Jefferson, The, 129, 132–33
autonomy, 9–10, 21, 44, 54, 58, 117, 124, 127

Bailkin, Jonathan, 280–81
Balipara Tea Plantation case, 283–84
Balladhum murder case, 274–78
Barker, George, 283, 287
Bayles, Michael, 28
Beccaria, Cesare, 116, 134
Bendix, Ludwig, 187
"Bill for Proportioning Crimes and Punishments in Cases Heretofore Capital" (Jefferson), 117, 127

biopower, 2
Bishop, Joel Prentiss, 200, 203
Blackstone, William, 20, 133
Blandy, Mary, 49
Bloody Code, 1, 45–46
Bowers v. Hardwick, 240–44
Boyett, 209–10
Bracton, Henri de, 69
British colonialism, India: criminal law and, 252–54; rule of law and, 257–58
Bucknill, J. C., 82
B v. D.P.P., 27

Calcutta High Court, 263, 265, 276
Campbell v. Hall, 258
Cannadine, David, 291–92
capacity-based criminal responsibility, 23, 28; in English criminal law, 35
capital punishment, 45, 115; Jefferson on, 139; proportionality and, 139
careless conduct: criminal responsibility for, 106; manslaughter and, 104
Carr, Elizabeth: trial of, 77–78
Castel, Robert, 225
causation, 91; killing and, 89–90; medical testimony about, 93
Cesaire, Aimé, 273
Chanock, Martin, 301
character, 55; criminal law norms and, 28–30
Charter Act of 1833, 308
Chauncey, George, 232
Chetwynd, William: trial of, 96
child neglect: homicide resulting from, 105
circumstantial evidence, 52, 58
Clive, Edward, 313

329

Cock, H. G., 230–31
Code of Gentoo Laws, A (Halhed), 305–6
"Codes, and the Arrangement of the Law" (Holmes), 200
Cohn, Bernard, 302, 304
Coke, Lord Edward: Jefferson and, 133–34
College of William and Mary, 128
colonial state: impartial rule of law and, 273; policing, prosecution in, 33; state-sanctioned violence in, 5–6
Colquhoun, Patrick, 158–59
Comaroff, John, 253, 302
Commentaries on Criminal Law (Bishop), 203
Commentaries on the Laws of England (Blackstone), 20, 133
common law: culpability and, 76, 81; killing and, 92; mental state and, 72; murder cases and, 96; religious influence in, 92
Common Law, The (Holmes), 198–207, 214–18
Communist Party of Germany (KPD), 178
Compendious Grammar of the Current Corrupt Dialect of the Jargon of Hindostan, A (Hadley), 303
conflict of laws, 244–46
Cotton, Henry, 262–63, 285
Cottu, Charles, 151
Courtie case, 239–40
crime and punishment: general theories of, 7; Jefferson on, 127–40; utilitarianism on, 189
Crimes and Punishments, On (Beccaria), 116, 134
Criminal Code of Canada (1892): sodomy and, 232
criminal conduct: mental state *vs.*, 93; pathology of, 74; scientific view of, 17
Criminal Evidence Act of 1898 (England), 22, 53
criminal justice, 18; in colonial India, 277; crime, law enforcement and, 3; in eighteenth-, early nineteenth-century England, 1–2; legitimacy of, 45; scholarship in, 3–4; symbolism in, 45–48
criminal law: American Revolution and, 115–17; Anglo-American, 6, 89–90; autonomy-based conception of, 9;
causation in, 91; Christian police and, 124–27; in colonial India, 252–54, 257–58; *The Common Law*'s account of, 201–3; comparative history of, 5, 7; criminal process and, 17; early American, 115–17; governance, social control and, 292; Jefferson and, 131–33, 137, 140; mental element in, 42–43; modernity and, 6, 9; norms, character principles and, 29–30; political uses of, 9; postcolonial theory, 3, 5; prevention theory of, 205–7, 211, 215, 218–19; social justice, state power and, 2; state-sanctioned violence and, 5–6
Criminal Law Amendment Act of 1885 (England), 53, 231
Criminal Law Commissioners' Reports (England), 21
criminal law reform: after American Revolution, 116–17; Christian influence in, 124–26; Jefferson's attempt at, 127
criminal liability: ignorance of law and, 211; standards of, 198, 212–14, 216, 219
Criminal Lunatics Act of 1800 (England), 69–73, 76, 80
criminal process: in colonial India, 315; responsibility attribution and, 30–35
criminal psychology: texts on, 53
criminal responsibility, 7; agency and, 14–15, 69; capacity theory of, 14–15, 23; for careless conduct, 106; emergence in English law of, 21; H. L. A. Hart's theory of, 18–19; in modern English Law, 17–18; opportunity *vs.* outcome based, 23; socially grounded jurisprudential analysis of, 24; treatises on, 18
criminal trials: Carr, Elizabeth, 77–78; Chetwynd, William, 96; communicative process of, 47; Criminal Evidence Act of 1898 (England) impact on, 53–54; Crippen, Hawley Harvey, 48–50, 55; Eden Dance Palace, 176–82; evidence and, 3; Ferrers, Earl, 70–71; formalization of, 52–53; Hadfield, James, 71–72; lawyers' role in, 51; legalization of, 48; legitimacy of, 186; length of, 48–49; Maclean, Roderick, 80; Masters, Thomas, 95–96; McNaughtan, Daniel, 75; as melodramas, 57; of

mentally deranged, 67; modern, 58; Oxford, Edward, 74–75, 77; Proctor, Sarah, 66–68, 79; witnesses' impact on, 49
Crippen, Hawley Harvey: murder trial of, 48–50, 55
cross-examination, 56–58
culpability: common law and, 76, 81

Darjeeling Planters Association, 263
Darwin, Charles, 202
Darwinism, 198–200, 202, 206–7
Davis, John Birt, 77
Defense of Marriage acts (U.S.A), 227, 245
delusion: medical diagnosis of, 75–76
Derrett, J. D. M., 304–5
deterrence, 82–83, 116, 138–39, 204, 209, 213; prevention *vs.*, 204–5
Director of Public Prosecutions (D.P.P.), 151
Dirks, Nicholas, 302
discipline, 2, 34, 118–24, 259, 263, 297
Discipline and Punish (Foucault), 2
Dowding, Charles, 279
D.P.P. *See* Director of Public Prosecutions
Drummond, Edward, 75
Dundas, Henry, 281

East India Company (EIC), 281, 299; court systems and, 307
Eden Dance Palace trial, 176–82
EIC. *See* East India Company
Elliot, C. A., 278
Ellis, Havelock, 236–37
English criminal law: Bill of Rights (1689), 116; capacity responsibility, 21, 35; Criminal Law Amendment Act, 231; criminal procedure, 151; criminal responsibility, 17–18; eighteenth-, early nineteenth-century theft prosecutions, 154–59; noncriminalization of lesbian sex in, 235; perjury detection and, 311; private prosecution of, 152–53; seventeenth- and eighteenth-century homicide law in, 88; victims' role in, 151–53
Englishman, 255, 276, 291
Erskine, Thomas, 71–72
Eskridge, William, 232, 233
evidence: of character, 55; circumstantial *vs.* factual, 52, 58; counsel, judge and, 54; Criminal Evidence Act of 1898 (England), 22; criminal trials and, 3; forensic, 50–51; of intention, 56–57, 97; interpretation of, 52–57; legal presumptions *vs.*, 52; psychiatric, 68
expert witnesses, 51
extreme indifference murder, 104

fatal falls: manslaughter and, 103–4
felony murder, 54, 100, 214
Felseneck trial, 176, 183–88; Litten and, 183–88; prosecution conspiracy in, 184
Ferrers, Earl: trial of, 70–71
Fischer-Tiné, Harald, 292
Fish, Jörg, 308
Fletcher, George, 89–91
Ford, Gerald, 80
forensic evidence, 50–51; psychiatric, 68
Forster, E. M., 236
Foucault, Michel, 2, 247
Foujdari Adalat, 313–17; local judges and, 317
Fuchs, Ernst, 191
Fürst, Max, 189, 193

Galloway, Archibald, 315
Gandhi, Mahatma, 273
Gardner, John, 28
Gaskill, Malcolm, 91
General View of the Criminal Law of England, A (Stephen), 204
Genet, Jean, 247
Genovese, Eugene, 278
Georget, Etienne-Jean, 74
godna, 309–10; as punishment, 309–10
Goebbels, Joseph, 178–80, 184
governance: conquest *vs.* rule of law and, 258; criminal law and, 292; household management and, 119–21; punishment and, 128
guilt: political *vs.* criminal *vs.* moral, 184; proof of, 57–58

Hadfield, James: trial of, 71–72
Hadley, George, 303
Hale, Matthew, 70, 91
Halhed, Nathaniel, 305–6
Hamilton, Charles, 305
Hansard's Parliamentary Debates, 81
Hardwick, Michael, 241–42
Hart, H. L. A., 18

Hartley, David, 74
hate crimes: homosexuality and, 246–47
Hay, Douglas, 1, 154
Hedaya (Hamilton), 305
Henning, Otto, 187
Hindoo Patriot, 256, 277
Hind Swaraj (Gandhi), 273
History of British India (Mill), 313
History of the Criminal Law of England (Stephens), 204, 208
History of the Pleas of the Crown (Hale), 70
Hitler, Adolf: Eden Dance Palace trial and, 176–82
Holmes, Oliver Wendell, 9–10, 198–207, 214–18; in 1870s, 200–203; American law and, 198; critics of, 211–12; on logic, 217; positivism impact on, 200–201; prevention principle and, 205–19; universal theory of law and, 216
homicide: causation and, 89–90; from child neglect, 105; Old Bailey cases, cross-section, 93–107; as result offense, 88; seventeenth- and eighteenth-century England law and, 88. *See also* manslaughter
homosexuality: *Bowers v. Hardwick*, 240–41; Colorado ballot action and, 243; in English statute law, 239; Foucaultian account of, 240; hate crimes and, 246–47; *Romer v. Evans*, 244; U.S. Supreme Court and, 240–44; voters' rights cases and, 243–44. *See also* sodomy
Honoré, Tony, 30
household management: governance and, 119–21
human agency, 83; criminal responsibility and, 69; medical testimony and, 82
Humanitarian League, 280

ICS. *See* Indian Civil Service
ignorance of law, 210; exceptions to, 211; Holmes and, 208
Ihering, Rudolf von, 190
incapacitation, 138, 156
indecency: criminal statutes targeting, 232–33
India, colonial, 252–54, 257–58; anti-sati legislation, 272; Assam and, 280; Balladun murder case, 274–78; Charter Act of 1833 and, 308; civil servants in, 260–61; constitutional *vs.* criminal law principles in, 264; criminal justice administration in, 277; criminal law, religious traditions and, 300; criminal process in, 315; EIC in, 281, 299, 307; equality of justice in, 291; *godna* as punishment in, 309–10; ideological role of law and, 272; Islamic law in, 300, 305, 307–8, 311; local law and, 304; medical testimony in, 285–86; Mutiny Rebellion in, 299; O'Hara murder verdict, 255; perjury in, 300–5, 308, 311–14, 318–20; prevarication in, 303, 313–18; religious traditions and, 300; rule of law in, 257–58; Sadar courts, 307–8
Indian Civil Service (ICS), 262, 264
Indian Penal Code, 263; perjury, prevarication and, 319
Indian Tea Association, 282
insanity defense: England's political class and, 83; intellectual derangement and, 73–74; medical basis for, 73–74; medicine's role in, 82; political assassinations and, 80; Victorian, 66
intention, 73–75, 104, 215, 264; evidence of, 56–57, 97; exercise of choice and, 68–69, 73; J. W. C. Turner on, 42–44; malice and, 101
intentional battery: manslaughter and, 102–3
Islamic law: in colonial India, 307–8; perjury and, 300, 305, 308, 311

Jefferson, Thomas, 9, 117, 127–32; on capital punishment, 139; Coke's impact on, 133–34; College of William and Mary and, 128; on crime and punishment, 127–40; criminal law interest of, 131–33; criminal law reform by, 127; on repression of crime, 138; on republican punishment, 137, 140; on role of government, 136
Jones, William, 303
Justinian's Digest, 69

Kelsen, Hans, 190
killing, 88; causation and, 89–90; common law and, 92; in course of felony, 100; malice and, 91–93, 106–7
Klemke, Fritz, 183
Kornhauser, Lewis, 26

KPD. *See* Communist Party of Germany
Krafft-Ebing, Richard von, 237

labor violence: in colonial Assam, 288–90
Lane, Christopher, 236
Langbein, John, 21
larceny, 90, 135, 156, 162, 209, 216. *See also* theft
Larenz, Karl, 192
law: constitutive effects of, 226; as instrument of oppression, 257; as science, 199–200
Lawrence v. Texas, 245–46
Lee, Thomas Lightfoot, 129
legitimacy, 175, 194, 203; of criminal justice, 45; of criminal trials, 186; perjury and, 301
lesion of the will, 75
liability: in Anglo-American criminal law, 89–90; cultural meanings and, 90
Lieberman, David, 164
Liszt, Franz von, 189
Litten, Hans, 176–82, 192–93; on art history and theory, 192; Eden Dance Palace trial and, 176–82; Felseneck trial and, 183–88
London's lower criminal courts: criminal law in, 159; jurisdiction of, 162; late eighteenth- and early nineteenth-century summary proceedings, 162–64
Lushington, C. M., 316
Lyon, Isidore, 285

Machiavelli, Niccolo, 119
Maclean, Roderick: trial of, 80
Madras: Foujdari Adalat in, 313–17; perjury treatment in, 313–18
Madras Mail, 286
Maine, Henry, 200
malice, 21, 43, 88–93, 94–107, 123, 204, 213, 214–15; aforethought, 54, 88–90, 94–107; indifference to human life and, 98–99; intention and, 101; killing and, 91–93, 106–7; manifest, 90; mental states and, 89; in murder cases, 95–101
manslaughter: carelessly inflicted injuries and, 104; categories of, 94, 101; evidence of provocation and, 103; fatal falls and, 103–4; intentional batteries and, 102–3; medical malpractice and,

105; mitigation of, 101–6; provocation and, 103; self-defense claims and, 102; unarmed assaults and, 103; unintended shootings and, 105; vehicular accidents and, 106
Mason, George, 129
Masters, Thomas: murder trial, conviction of, 95–96
Mayes v. People, 104
McNaughtan, Daniel, 67; trial of, 75
McNaughtan *(M'Naghten)* Rules, 67, 76, 80, 83
medical testimony, 50–51, 73–76, 78–80; about causation, 93; in colonial India, 285–86; human agency *vs.*, 82
Meditations (Aurelius), 119
mens rea, 6, 8, 18, 24, 27, 43, 69, 81; culpability without, 81; defenses and, 30–33
mental state, 42–43, 67; common law and, 72; conduct *vs.*, 93; criminal behavior *vs.*, 93; cultural notions about, 69; evidence, evaluation of, 54; unconsciousness and, 77
Merrion, Edward, 77
Merry, Sally Engle, 273
Metropolitan Police Act of 1839 (England), 162
Mill, James, 302–3, 313
modernity, 6, 176, 194, 274
modern society: exercise of power in, 2
mofussil (adalat) system, 307
Moran, Leslie, 229, 240, 247
murder, 21, 24, 31, 45, 48, 50, 54–55, 58, 69, 74–75, 88, 92–107, 129, 135, 179, 213–14, 217, 225, 254–57, 260, 263–64, 267, 269, 274–93, 306–9, 314; felony, 54, 100, 214. *See also* homicide
Mutiny-Rebellion (1857-1858), 299

National Socialist German Workers' Party (NSDAP), 178, 180
Nazi Roll Commandos, 178–79
Nizamat Adalat. *See* Foujdari Adalat
Notes on Locke (Jefferson), 136
Notes on the State of Virginia (Jefferson), 136
NSDAP. *See* National Socialist German Workers' Party

OBSP. *See Old Bailey Sessions Papers*
O'Hara, Thomas, 255

334 INDEX

Old Bailey Sessions Papers (OBSP), 67, 93–94; contents of, 94
outcome-based criminal responsibility, 23, 30
Oxford, Edward: trial of, 77, 82

"Path of the Law, The" (Holmes), 215
patriarchy, 115, 121–24, 127, 130, 265
Patterson, Orlando, 279
Peel, Robert, 75
Pendleton, Edmund, 129
perjury: in colonial India, 300–5, 308, 311–14, 318–20; Hindu law and, 305; Indian Penal Code and, 319; Islamic law and, 300, 305, 308, 311; legitimacy and, 301; rule of law and, 302. *See also* prevarication
Philadelphia Society for Alleviating the Misery of Public Prisons, 116, 125
Pinel, Philippe, 73
police: Adam Smith on, 143; board of, 209; Christian, 124–27; in colonial Assam, 175; concept of, 130–31; crime and, 175; custody, 256; efficiency, 264; forces, 152; Indian, 256, 275; law and, 117–27, 139, 175; magistrates, 159–63; Metropolitan Police Act of 1839, 162; misconduct, 263, 276–77; model, 135–36; offenses, 135; officers, 152, 157, 160, 184, 230; offices (London), 159–63; power, 7, 8, 23, 36, 130, 278, 301; prosecution and, 33; punishment and, 117–24; regulations, 131; surveillance, 232; Thames Police Office, 161, 164; torture, 276
Police Gazette, 160–61
politics: insanity defense and, 80; law and, 9, 176–77; punishment and, 139; of violence, 279–81
positivism: Holmes and, 200–201
possession, 7, 9, 153–66
postcolonial theory, 3, 5
pre-trial practices, 33
prevarication: in colonial India, 303, 313–18; Indian Penal Code and, 319. *See also* perjury
prevention, 205–19; deterrence *vs.,* 204–5
Prince, The (Machiavelli), 119
Prisoner's Counsel Act of 1836 (England), 47, 54
prisons, early American: Christian benevolence in, 166

Proceedings of the Old Bailey. See Old Bailey Sessions Papers
Proctor, Sarah: trial of, 66–68, 79
proof of guilt, 57–58
"Property, Authority and the Criminal Law" (Hay), 1
proportionate punishment, 122–23, 138–39; capital punishment *vs.,* 139; Jefferson on, 127–40
Protestantism: American intellectual life and, 199–200
provocation: manslaughter and, 103
punishment, 116; as good governance, 128; of infamy, 309–10; patriarchal underpinnings of, 121; police and, 117–24; as political problem, 139; power and, 117–18; proportionate, 122–23, 128–31, 138–39; public, 45; republican, 137, 140; sentencing and, 34–35; state power, 5, 117, 123. *See also* capital punishment; crime and punishment; proportionate punishment

Radbruch, Gustav, 189
rape, 28, 32, 55, 100, 214, 217, 228, 235, 239, 290
reconstructive trial: in late nineteenth century, 45–52
Regina v. Dudley and Stephens, 206
rehabilitation, 138, 206
responsibility attribution, 26–30; criminal process and, 30–35
Rethinking Criminal Law (Fletcher), 89
retribution, 206, 211
Richardson, Edward, 96, 98
Romer v. Evans, 244–45
Rose, Nikolas, 225
Royal Society of Prisons, France, 151
rule of law: in colonial India, 257–58; colonial state and, 273; perjury and, 302
R. v. Lad, 100
R. v. Morgan, 27

Sadar courts, 312; in colonial India, 307–8
Sadar Nizamat Adalat, 307, 309
Scalia, Antonin: on *Bowers v. Hardwick,* 244
Schmitt, Carl, 190, 192
Schwartz, Ernst, 183
science: law as, 199–200
self-defense, 25, 29, 81, 89, 90, 101–2, 180, 260; manslaughter and, 102

sentencing and punishment, 34–35
sexology, 236–38; German criminal code and, 238
Sexual Offenses Act of 1967 (England), 239
Sexual Offenses Act of 2003 (England), 27
Skeggs, Bev, 247
Sleeman, William, 304
Smith, Adam, 118, 143
Snyder, Francis, 154
social order: law and, 2, 4, 292
sodomy: Criminal Code of Canada (1892) and, 232; eighteenth-century prosecutions, 224; in English legal history, 228; orientalist construction of, 236; prosecution of, 230, 232; in U.S., 230, 232–34, 241, 243–46
Spilsbury, Bernard, 50
state: criminal law and, 2; power of, 119, 128
state punishment, 117, 123; normative justification of, 5
state-sanctioned violence: in colonial governance, 5–6; criminal law and, 5–6
Stennes, Walter, 178
Stephen, James Fitzjames, 20, 88–89, 164, 200, 203–4, 208, 258
Stief and Others. *See* Eden Dance Palace trial
Stocqueler, Joachim Hayward, 303
Strachey, Henry, 312–13
Sulabh Samachar, 286
Symonds, John Addington, 236

Tadros, Victor, 28, 32
Tea Estates and Their Management (Williams), 288
Tea Planter's Life in Assam, A (Barker), 283
theft, 7, 9, 24, 90, 100, 101, 153–66. *See also* larceny
"Theory of Torts, The" (Holmes), 202

treason, 71, 80, 129–30, 135, 137, 154, 234
Trial of Lunatics Act of 1883 (England), 67, 83
Turner, J. W. C.: on intention, 42–44

Ulrichs, Carl Heinrich, 236
unarmed assaults: manslaughter and, 103
unconsciousness: mental states and, 77
unintended shootings: manslaughter and, 105
United States (U.S.): sodomy in, 230, 232–34, 241, 243–46
U.S. Supreme Court: homosexuality and, 240–44
U.S. v. Holmes, 207

vehicular accidents: manslaughter and, 106
Veyne, Paul, 225
Virginia Committee for the Revision of the Laws, 128–31
voluntariness, 72, 74, 76, 79–80, 83

Warden, Thomas, 314
weapons: intentional blow *vs.* reckless handling, 104
Weimar Germany: antipositivist legal thinking in, 190–91; judicial legitimacy, 175; law and politics in, 176–77; legal positivism in, 190; prisoner treatment in, 181
Wetzel, Ernst, 178
Whale, Charlotte, 66
Wilde, Oscar, 231, 247
willfulness, 6, 32, 79, 94, 106, 310, 316, 318
Williams, Bernard, 16
Williams, Glanville, 20, 162, 165–66
Williams, J. H., 288
witnesses: criminal trial impact by, 49; expert, 51; medical, 50–51; trial length and, 49
Wolfenden Committee, 235, 238–40
Wythe, George, 128, 129